INNOVATION, TECHNOLOGY AND THE ECONOMY
VOLUME I

ECONOMISTS OF THE TWENTIETH CENTURY

General Editors: Mark Perlman, *University Professor of Economics, Emeritus, University of Pittsburgh* and Mark Blaug, *Professor Emeritus, University of London, Professor Emeritus, University of Buckingham and Visiting Professor, University of Exeter*

This innovative series comprises specially invited collections of articles and papers by economists whose work has made an important contribution to economics in the late twentieth century.

The proliferation of new journals and the ever-increasing number of new articles make it difficult for even the most assiduous economist to keep track of all the important recent advances. By focusing on those economists whose work is generally recognized to be at the forefront of the discipline, the series will be an essential reference point for the different specialisms included.

A list of published and future titles in this series is printed at the end of this volume.

Innovation, Technology and the Economy

The Selected Essays of Edwin Mansfield
Volume I

Edwin Mansfield

Director, Center for Economics and Technology and
Professor of Economics, University of Pennsylvania

ECONOMISTS OF THE TWENTIETH CENTURY

Edward Elgar
Aldershot, UK • Brookfield, US

Published by
Edward Elgar Publishing Limited
Gower House
Croft Road
Aldershot
Hants GU11 3HR
UK

Edward Elgar Publishing Company
Old Post Road
Brookfield
Vermont 05036
US

British Library Cataloguing in Publication Data
Mansfield, Edwin
    Innovation, Technology and the Economy:
    Selected Essays of Edwin Mansfield. –
    (Economists of the Twentieth Century
    Series)
    I. Title   II. Series
    338.927

Library of Congress Cataloguing in Publication Data
Mansfield, Edwin.
JL   Innovation, technology and the economy : the selected essays of
    Edwin Mansfield / Edwin Mansfield.
        v. cm. — (Economists of the twentieth century)
        Includes bibliographical references and index.
        1. Technological innovations—Economic aspects. 2. Research,
    Industrial. 3. Technology—Forecasting. I. Title. II. Series.
    HC79.T4M348 1995
    338′.064—dc20   95–5533
                                                               CIP

ISBN 1 85898 035 6 (2 volume set)

Printed and bound in Great Britain by
Hartnolls Limited, Bodmin, Cornwall

Contents

Acknowledgements

The publishers wish to thank the following who have kindly given permission for the use of copyright material.

American Association for the Advancement of Science for articles: 'Contribution of R & D to Economic Growth in the United States', *Science*, **175**, 4 February 1972, pp. 487–94; 'Research and Development, Productivity, and Inflation, *Science*, **209**, 5 September 1980, pp. 1091–3.

American Economic Association for articles: 'Entry, Gibrat's Law, Innovation, and the Growth of Firms', *American Economic Review*, **52**, December 1962, pp. 1023–51; 'Basic Research and Productivity Increase in Manufacturing', *American Economic Review*, **70**(5), December 1980, pp. 863–73; 'Rates of Return from Industrial Research and Development', *American Economic Review*, LV(2), May 1965, pp. 310–22; 'Industrial Research and Development: Characteristics, Costs, and Diffusion of Results', *American Economic Review*, May 1969, pp. 65–71; 'Industrial R&D in Japan and the United States: A Comparative Study', *American Economic Review*, **78**(2), May 1988, pp. 223–8; 'Long Waves and Technological Innovation', *American Economic Review*, **73**(2), May 1983, pp. 141–5; 'Technological Change and Market Structure: An Empirical Study', *American Economic Review*, **73**(2), May 1983, pp. 205–9.

Elsevier Science Publishers for article: 'Flexible Manufacturing Systems: Economic Effects in Japan, United States, and Western Europe', *Japan and the World Economy*, **4**, 1992, pp. 1–16.

Institute for Defense Analysis for article: 'Overruns and Errors in Estimating Development Cost, Time, and Outcome' (with Jerome Schnee and Samuel Wagner), *IDA Economic Papers*, September 1971, pp. 1–3, 5–25, 27–39, 41–5, 47–50.

Institute of Management Sciences for articles: 'The Costs of Industrial Product Innovations' (with John Rapoport), *Management Science*, **21**(12), August 1975, pp. 1380–86; 'The Speed and Cost of Industrial Innovation in Japan and the United States: External vs. Internal Technology', *Management Science*, **34**(10), October 1988, pp. 1157–68; 'Firms' Forecasts of Engineering Employment' (with Peter Brach), *Management Science*, **28**(2), February 1982, pp. 156–60; Price Indexes for R and D Inputs, 1969–1983', *Management Science*, **33**(1), January 1987, pp. 124–9.

John Wiley & Sons Ltd for article: 'Technological Change in Robotics: Japan and the United States', *Managerial and Decision Economics*, Special Issue, 1989, pp. 19–25.

The Macmillan Press Ltd for article: 'Technological Forecasting' in T.S. Khachaturov (ed.), *Methods of Long-term Planning and Forecasting*, The Macmillan Press Ltd, 1976, pp. 334–49.

MIT Press for article: 'Social and Private Rates of Return from Industrial Innovations' (with John Rapoport, Anthony Romeo, Samuel Wagner and George Beardsley), *Quarterly Journal of Economics*, **91**, May 1977, pp. 221–40.

The Review of Economics and Statistics for article: 'Composition of R and D Expenditures: Relationship to Size of Firm, Concentration, and Innovative Output', **LXIII**(4), November 1981, pp. 610–15.

University of Chicago Press for articles: 'The Allocation, Characteristics and Outcome of the Firm's Research and Development Portfolio: A Case Study' (with Richard Brandenburg), *The Journal of Business*, **XXXIX**(4), October 1966, pp. 447–64; 'Organizational and Strategic Factors Associated with Probabilities of Success in Industrial R & D' (with Samuel Wagner), *The Journal of Business*, **48**(2), April 1975, pp. 179–98; 'A Note on the Accuracy of Industrial Forecasts of the Profitability of New Products and Processes' (with George Beardsley), *Journal of Business*, **51**(1), 1978, pp. 127–35; 'Size of Firm, Market Structure, and Innovation', *Journal of Political Economy*, **71**, December 1963, pp. 556–76.

Introduction

In early 1957, while a 26-year-old faculty member at the Graduate School of Industrial Administration at Carnegie Institute of Technology (now Carnegie Mellon University), I began a series of studies in the economics of technological change that has continued for almost 40 years (and is still going on). This field, which has burgeoned, really did not exist then, except for the writings of Joseph Schumpeter and a relatively few scholars who were influenced by him. Since technology tended to be considered outside the province of economists, it was not surprising that empirical studies of technology by economists were few and far between. It was an exciting time to begin such work, which I have continued at a variety of universities and research institutions in the United States and elsewhere.

These two volumes contain selected papers of mine on this topic.[1] All are in their original form which means, of course, that subsequent developments are not included. In general, my approach has been to try to get a reasonably solid empirical footing before attempting to model complex phenomena about which very little is known; to keep the theoretical apparatus as simple, transparent and robust as possible; to collect data directly from firms (and other economic units) carefully tailored to shed light on the problem at hand (rather than try to adapt readily available general-purpose data, which often is hazardous), and to check the results as thoroughly as possible with technologists, executives, government officials and others who are close to whatever phenomenon is being studied. It was a privilege and a great pleasure to have contributed to the formation and growth of this young field, which now is a major and vibrant sector of economics; and when Edward Elgar asked to reprint two volumes of my selected works, I was glad to provide this introductory essay.

Industrial innovation

Schumpeter impressed upon economists the importance of innovation – the first commercial introduction of a new product or process – but very little was known even in the 1970s about the innovation process. From the point of view of public policy, one of the most notable gaps was the absence of information concerning social and private returns from investments in industrial innovations. The opening paper, 'Social and Private Rates of Return from Industrial Innovations' (1977), undertaken with four of my former students at the University of Pennsylvania's Wharton School (where I became professor of economics in 1964) – George Beardsley, John Rapoport, Anthony Romeo and Samuel Wagner – was the first study of this topic, although related work had been carried out in agriculture.[2] It indicated that the social returns were very high, over double the private returns. The National Science Foundation[3] commissioned two replications of our study; their findings were in accord with ours. Almost 20 years later, this article (together with the replications) remains the only broad-based investigation of this topic, which is at the core of discussions of (and controversies over) technology policy in the US and elsewhere.

Innovation influences the growth of firms and the dynamic behaviour of industries. Since very little was known in the 1960s about the quantitative effects of successful innovation on these phenomena, it seemed worthwhile to explore this topic. Influenced by the work of my Carnegie colleague, Herbert Simon, I imbedded this study in an investigation of the usefulness of Gibrat's Law in representing the growth of firms. The resulting paper, 'Entry, Gibrat's Law, Innovation, and the Growth of Firms' (1962), which was written while I was visiting professor at Yale University, indicated that, in terms of short-term growth, the rewards for successful innovation were substantial, particularly for smaller firms. As for Gibrat's Law, some versions of it passed muster; others did not.

Another topic about which surprisingly little was known was the cost of innovation. In 'The Costs of Industrial Product Innovations' (1975), John Rapoport and I obtained cost data regarding a sample of chemical innovations. On the average, R & D accounted for less than half of total innovation costs, which was of interest because economists had often tended to neglect non-R & D costs. (Indeed, they sometimes assumed them away entirely.) Another noteworthy finding was that 'learning by doing' seemed to be important in R & D, just as it was known to be in production.

In more recent years, these topics assumed particular significance in connection with the intense technological rivalry that has developed between Japan and the US. Some prominent observers asserted that the Japanese had a great advantage over the US in terms of the speed and cost of innovation. Chapter 4, 'The Speed and Cost of Industrial Innovation in Japan and the United States' (1988), provided what seemed to be the first comprehensive investigation of how these two countries compared in this regard. This work helped to launch the Center for Economics and Technology at the University of Pennsylvania, established to provide a focus for my work with students and others in this and related areas.

Whereas the Japanese are shown in this paper to have substantial advantages in some industries (notably machinery), they do not seem to have a substantial advantage in others (notably chemicals). Whereas they have great advantages in carrying out innovations based on external technology, they do not seem to have any in effecting innovations based on internal technology. Japanese firms allocate their resources quite differently than do American firms, a bigger percentage of total innovation cost being devoted to tooling and manufacturing equipment and facilities, and a smaller percentage to marketing startup. A large part of America's problem in this regard seems to have stemmed from its apparent inability to match Japan as a quick and effective user of external technology.

Chapter 5 on 'Technological Change in Robotics: Japan and the United States' (1989) is a comparison of the two countries in the important area of robotics. The Japanese advantage seemed to increase as one moved from R & D towards the market. Whereas the Japanese seemed to be quicker and more efficient innovators, they did not appear to be more effective at R & D. If, as many observers claimed, American industry failed to utilize robots as fully as it should, the principal fault did not seem to lie with American R & D. Instead, the case of robotics seemed to illustrate the contention that, if the US was falling behind, it was not so much in R & D or inventiveness, but in the commercial application of scientific discoveries and technological advances. These points were developed more fully in lectures I gave in Sweden in 1987.

The final paper in this section – 'Flexible Manufacturing Systems' (1992) – dealt with another of the most important manufacturing innovations in recent decades. It presented and analysed data obtained from over 200 firms in Japan, the US and Europe concerning the economic effects of flexible manufacturing systems, and then compared the effectiveness and profitability of these systems in various countries. The estimated rate of return from relevant investment seemed to have been substantially lower in the US than in Japan. In comparison with Japan and Germany, US firms continued to spend more time and money to develop and install a system and to produce fewer parts (and higher annual volumes per part). In comparison with Japan, US firms continued to introduce fewer new parts, to have a smaller percentage of untended systems and to have lower utilization rates. This appears to be an area where the US still faces a serious challenge.

Industrial research and development

Industrial research and development is a key part of the innovation process, consisting of basic research and applied R & D. Chapter 7, 'Basic Research and Productivity Increase in Manufacturing' (1980), attempted to determine how significant a contribution basic research, as contrasted to applied R & D, has made to productivity change in manufacturing. Previous work by Zvi Griliches, Jora Minasian, Nestor Terleckyj and myself (see the paper described in the next paragraph) had shown that R & D as a whole influenced productivity growth, but nothing was known about the separate influences of basic research and applied R & D. The results indicated that, when expenditures on applied R & D are held constant, there was a statistically significant and direct relationship between the amount of basic research carried out by an industry or firm and its rate of increase of total factor productivity. Indeed, the regression coefficient of basic research in the relevant equation was much higher than that of applied R & D. These results (and those of subsequent studies confirming this finding) have been used frequently in discussions of science policy in the US and elsewhere.

Decision makers in industry and government must continually be concerned with judging the effectiveness of R & D. Chapter 8 was the first attempt to use econometric techniques to estimate rates of return from industrial R & D. Based on its findings (which stemmed from work carried out while I was visiting professor at Harvard University), the rate of return tended to be high. But as stressed in the paper, these estimates should be viewed with considerable caution. While I continue to believe that econometric estimates of this sort (which are now reasonably abundant, based on models not very different from that used here) are interesting and useful, as a result of consulting and other experience, I have become convinced that the more micro project-by-project analysis undertaken in other papers in these volumes is often more trustworthy.

One of the problems facing economists during the 1950s and 1960s was that so little was known about the activities included under the rubric of R & D. Benefiting from experience I obtained as a consultant to the RAND Corporation (where Burton Klein and his colleagues were involved in a number of detailed case studies of military R & D), my students and I, funded by a generous grant from the Ford Foundation, examined the nitty-gritty of hundreds of industrial R & D projects. The picture that emerged was quite different from that previously assumed by many economists. For example, models supposing that the technical risks were large seemed to be misconceived; for the bulk of industrial R & D, the commercial risks seemed to outweigh the technical risks. In other words, it was quite likely that a firm could solve the technical problems involved in developing a particular new or improved product or process, but much less likely that it would be economically worthwhile to do so (in the sense that the result would be a commercial success). This and other findings are summarized in Chapter 9, 'Industrial Research and Development: Characteristics, Costs, and Diffusion of Results' (1969).

In a further attempt to understand how industrial R & D laboratories function, Richard Brandenburg and I made a very intensive study of the R & D portfolio of the central research laboratory of one of the nation's largest firms, a prominent electrical and electronic equipment and appliance manufacturer. The resulting paper, 'The Allocation, Characteristics, and Outcome of the Firm's Research and Development Portfolio: A Case Study' (1966), indicated that the assumption of profit maximization was of use in explaining the allocation of funds among applied R & D projects, but that a variety of other factors, such as intrafirm politics, were also important. Further, based on this firm's experience, estimates of the probability of a project's technical success have some predictive value, but not much.

By the mid-1970s, an enormous amount had been written concerning the management of industrial research and development, but much of this literature was so vague and qualitative that it was hard either to verify or to apply. In 'Organizational and Strategic Factors Associated with Probabilities of Success in Industrial R & D' (1975), Samuel Wagner and I presented the results of some econometric and statistical studies carried out to test a number of the suggested hypotheses. Our findings indicated that the probabilities of success were increased by an early investigation of the profit potential of projects, by proper integration of R & D and marketing, and by the reduction of intrafirm barriers to the utilization of R & D results. A number of firms and consulting groups made use of these findings and extended them to meet their own needs and problems.

In the 1980s and 1990s, policy makers in the US were impressed by, and concerned about, the efficiency of Japanese industrial R & D. Chapter 12, 'Industrial R&D in Japan and the United States: A Comparative Study' (1988), presented evidence indicating that the Japanese advantage had been confined largely to applied R & D (particularly that concerned with the adaptation and improvement of existing technology), not basic research. Related to this advantage was a striking difference between Japanese and American firms in their allocation of R & D resources between projects aimed at improved *product* technology and those aimed at improved *process* technology. Whereas American firms devoted about two-thirds of their R & D expenditures to improving product technology, the Japanese devoted only about one-third for this purpose. This finding received considerable attention, in both government agencies and firms in the US, Japan and elsewhere.

Technological forecasting

Technological forecasting is a necessary part of the decision-making process in firms and government agencies. Just as there is no way to avoid forecasting the economic future – explicitly or implicitly – so there is no way to avoid forecasting the technological future. In the 1960s, just as economic forecasting began to be taken more seriously, so technological forecasting began to attract attention in industry and government. Chapter 13 on 'Technological Forecasting' (1976), presented in Moscow at the meetings of the International Economic Association, argued that most of the techniques commonly used for exploratory forecasting seem crude, even by the standards of the social and management sciences. Technological forecasting, if done correctly, involves much more than science and engineering. One cannot estimate the probability that a particular technology will come into being on the basis of technological considerations alone; economic, social and political factors often play an equally important role. Many of these points were elaborated in the lectures I gave in the People's Republic of China in 1979.

In determining whether or not to invest in the development and introduction of a new product or process, firms must forecast how profitable such an investment will be. In 'A Note on the Accuracy of Industrial Forecasts of the Profitability of New Products and Processes' (1978), George Beardsley and I presented detailed empirical evidence concerning all of the major innovations developed by one of the largest firms in the US in the early 1960s. Because these data had been systematically and carefully updated by the firm, they provided a relatively unique opportunity to study how quickly forecasts of this sort converge on their true value. The findings indicate that, because of inherent uncertainties, forecasts of this sort are frail reeds on which to base decisions. Indeed, a remarkable fact was that it took four or five years after the development of a new product or process before this firm could estimate reasonably accurately the discounted profits achieved. My impression is that forecasting of this sort is not appreciably better today.

To help make decisions regarding which proposed R & D projects to accept, firms generally make forecasts of their respective development cost and time. In 'Overruns and Errors in Estimating Development Cost, Time and Outcome' (1971), Jerome Schnee, Samuel Wagner and I studied the accuracy of such forecasts. (Some of this work occurred while I was visiting professor at California Institute of Technology.) Based on detailed data obtained from a variety of firms, the errors in these forecasts tended to be large. When attempts were made to develop distinctly new products, the cost overruns began to approximate those in weapons development, which were notoriously large. We found that practically all laboratories in our sample made use of such forecasts, and that laboratory administrators tended to be unduly optimistic concerning their accuracy. We argued that project selection techniques should recognize and take account of the significant errors evident in such forecasts.

Policy makers in government, universities and business must make decisions based, explicitly or implicitly, on forecasts of how many engineers will be employed in various sectors of the economy at various times. Although these are sometimes based on a collection of forecasts made by firms of their own engineering employment, very little was known in the early 1980s concerning the accuracy of such firms' forecasts. Peter Brach (a graduate student at Penn) and I carried out a study – 'Firms' Forecasts of Engineering Employment' (1982) – to shed light on this topic. Forecasting errors turn out to be substantial, particularly in the aerospace industry. Suggestions are made in this chapter concerning ways to reduce these errors.

Technological change, economic growth and inflation

The pioneering studies by Robert Solow, Moses Abramowitz and Solomon Fabricant in the 1950s indicated that technological change plays a key role in the process of economic growth. This conclusion was of major importance, causing some consternation among economists who previously had focused much more attention on factors underlying the amount of capital utilized per worker than on those underlying the rate of technological change. In 1970, the National Science Foundation commissioned a conference paper aimed at suggesting directions for research to promote further understanding of the relationships between technological change and economic growth. Chapter 17, 'Contribution of R & D to Economic Growth in the United States' (1972), was used by Congress, the executive branch and other groups to help establish research priorities in this area.

Some economists, following Schumpeter, believe that long waves are part of the process of economic growth. In the late 1970s and early 1980s, proponents of long waves argued that the rate of technological innovation had been falling in recent decades. In 1982, Walt Rostow requested a paper to be given at the meetings of the American Economic Association reviewing the available evidence on this subject. Chapter 18, 'Long Waves and Technological Innovation' (1983), did not turn up persuasive evidence that the number of major technological innovations conforms to long waves. The hypothesis that severe depressions trigger and accelerate innovations is also questionable. As for a slackening of the rate of innovation, there was evidence that this had occurred in some industries, but not in others.

A nation's macroeconomic climate plays a significant role in determining its rate of technological change. In 1980, when inflation was at double-digit levels in the US, the American Association for the Advancement of Science asked for a speech entitled 'Research and Development, Productivity, and Inflation' (1980), which they subsequently published. This pointed out that high rates of inflation damage the workings of the price system and impair the efficiency of practically all economic activities, including R & D. Serious inflation tends to discourage investment, including investment in long-term R & D, because it increases uncertainties concerning relative prices in the future. Also, serious inflation can stimulate an anti-inflationary fiscal policy that affects the size and type of government R & D programmes.

Further, inflation can distort the basic R & D statistics on which policy makers depend. In making basic estimates of real R & D expenditures in the US, government agencies use the GNP (now GDP) deflator to deflate R & D expenditures. Many observers have questioned this procedure and have emphasized that inaccurate price indexes can result in substantial analytical and policy errors. Chapter 20 on 'Price Indexes for R & D Inputs, 1969–1983' (1987), presented the first R & D price indexes based largely on actual prices and expenditures reported by firms. The results, which reflect the experience of a carefully designed sample of about 100 firms, show that the GNP deflator tended to underestimate the rate of inflation in R & D. These indexes have found widespread use and were updated by the National Science Foundation in 1993.[4]

Market structure, size of firm and technological change

Economists have long been interested in the relationship between market structure and size of firm on the one hand, and technological change on the other hand. For example, Richard Nelson and F.M. Scherer have made influential investigations in this area. Schumpeter argued that innovations are carried out primarily by very large firms. In 'Size of Firm, Market Structure, and Innovation' (1963), data of more than a fragmentary nature were collected for the first time from a small number of important industries to test this hypothesis. The results vary from one industry to another. In petroleum refining, bituminous coal and railroads, the largest four firms accounted for a larger share of the innovations than they did of the market; but in steel, they accounted for less. However, in most of these industries, the largest few firms carried out no more innovations, relative to their size, than did somewhat (sometimes, considerably) smaller firms.

Whereas a variety of studies had been carried out of the relationship between size of firm and concentration on the one hand, and the extent of R & D expenditures on the other,[5] little or nothing was known in the early 1980s about the relationship between these factors and the composition of industrial R & D expenditures. Chapter 22, 'Composition of R and D Expenditures: Relationship to Size of Firm, Concentration, and Innovative Output' (1981), was an attempt to fill this gap. While the largest firms seemed to carry out a disproportionately large share of basic research (and perhaps of long-term R & D) in most industries, they generally seemed to undertake a disproportionately small share of the R & D aimed at entirely new products and processes. Nor was there any evidence to suggest that very concentrated industries tended to devote a relatively large share of their R & D to basic research or to long-term, ambitious or risky projects.

Few would deny that technological change is one of the major forces influencing an industry's market structure. Karl Marx stressed this fact over a century ago. Some models advanced in recent years suggest that a relatively rapid rate of technological change in a particular industry is likely to result in a relatively high level of concentration. The last chapter in Volume I, 'Technological Change and Market Structure: An Empirical Study' (1983), obtained data regarding innovations in the chemical, drugs, petroleum and steel industries. These data did not support this proposition. For example, there was essentially no correlation in those industries between the rate of productivity growth and the per cent of product innovations that were concentration-increasing (or the per cent of process innovations that were scale-increasing). Based on these data, the conclusion was (and is) that, unless we understand the nature and sources of new technology, any prediction of the effects of technological change on concentration is hazardous indeed.

The diffusion of industrial innovations
The original studies I undertook at Carnegie in the late 1950s involved the diffusion of innovations. Chapter 1 of Volume II on 'Technical Change and the Rate of Imitation' (1961) presented and tested a model to explain the rate of diffusion of an industrial innovation. My first inclination was to use a stochastic process to fit the data; this worked effectively, as shown in the paper. But a simpler, deterministic version also did well, and this deterministic version has generally been used in subsequent work. This version predicts that the growth of the number of adopters of an innovation will conform to the logistic function; moreover, the diffusion rate

will be linearly related to the profitability of the innovation. It thus helps to explain why the diffusion process often conforms to the familiar S-shaped growth curve of the sort found by Zvi Griliches (for hybrid corn) and others.[6] This model has been applied very often in the past few decades.

The article on 'The Speed of Response of Firms to New Techniques' (1963) was concerned with the factors determining how rapidly a particular firm would begin to use a process innovation. Detailed data were obtained regarding 14 innovations in a variety of industries. The results indicated that the length of time a firm waits before using a new technique tends to be inversely related to its size and the profitability of its investment in the innovation. (However, for reasons given in the paper, this does not mean that large firms were necessarily more progressive than small ones.) When the size of the firm and the profitability of the investment in the innovation were held constant, there was no significant tendency for the length of time a firm waited to be inversely related to its profitability, its growth rate and its liquidity, or directly related to the age of its president or its profit trend. Moreover, technical leadership of this kind was not very highly concentrated in most of the industries for which I obtained data.

To understand how rapidly a new technique displaces an old one, we must consider both the rate of imitation and the intrafirm rate of diffusion – the rate at which a particular firm proceeds to substitute its use of a new technique for older methods. Together, the rate of imitation and the intrafirm rates of diffusion determine how rapidly productivity rises in response to the new technique. Chapter 3 on 'Intrafirm Rates of Diffusion of an Innovation' (1963) reports the results of an intensive study of the diesel locomotive, one of the most important innovations of the 20th century. Although the model was obviously highly simplified, it has been of help in explaining the substantial differences which exist among the intrafirm rates of diffusion of this innovation and others.

As pointed out above, many observers in recent years have asserted that Japanese firms accept new technology more quickly than American firms. 'The Diffusion of Industrial Robots in Japan and the United States' (1989) indicated that industrial robots have spread relatively slowly in the US, both in comparison with other innovations and with robotic diffusion in Japan. This seemed to be due in part to the comparatively low profitability of robots in the US and to Japan's late start. Also, the fact that American firms seemed to be slower to use robots in large numbers appeared in part to reflect their insistence on higher minimum rates of return than in Japan.

Another important recent innovation is the flexible manufacturing system, described in detail in the sixth chapter in Volume I of these essays. Chapter 5 on 'The Diffusion of Flexible Manufacturing Systems in Japan, Europe and the United States' (1993) analysed diffusion rates in each of these areas, a major purpose being to determine whether, as is often claimed, US firms have been relatively slow to use this innovation and, if so, why. One conclusion is that intrafirm rates of diffusion do seem to have been lower in the US than in Japan or Europe. This may have been due to the innovation's actual rate of return being lower in the US than elsewhere and to the minimum required rate of return being higher in the US than elsewhere. (Note the similarity between these findings and those of the robot study in the previous paragraph.)

International technology transfer

During the 1970s, economists became much more interested in international technology transfer, due partly to developments in the theory of international trade and the emergence of various related policy issues. In this period, my students and I explored a variety of aspects of this general topic, some of this work being done while I was a Fellow at the Center for Advanced Study in the Behavioral Sciences at Stanford. The article on 'International Technology Transfer: Forms, Resource Requirements, and Policies' (1975) describes briefly various forms of technology transfer, discusses the problems and costs involved in the transfer process, and comments on some aspects of technology transfer between the US and the former Soviet Union. (These comments reflected in part the work done while I was US chairman of the US–USSR Working Party on the Economics of Science and Technology.) One important finding was that the costs of transferring technology were often substantial, a point denied at that time by some leading economists.

In 1973, the National Science Foundation convened a conference of economists that considered the following question: What effects do international trade, foreign direct investment and foreign licensing have on US technological innovation? It concluded that, 'in spite of the importance of this question, there seems to be a complete void in our knowledge'.[7] In 'Foreign Trade and U.S. Research and Development' (1979), Anthony Romeo, Samuel Wagner and I presented some findings aimed at helping to fill this gap, and also at exploring the ways in which American firms transfer their technology abroad. A finding that received considerable attention was that foreign subsidiaries had become the principal channel of international technology transfer during the first five years after commercialization. This contrasted with the traditional view, according to which the first channel of international technology transfer tended to be exports.

In the United States, some groups felt that the apparent narrowing of the American technological lead was due to the transfer of technology by US-based multinational firms, and argued that such firms should be subjected to various new kinds of regulations. On the other hand, in the countries where the subsidiaries were located, there was sometimes the feeling that the terms on which the transfers occurred were inequitable, and that there were dangers in becoming too dependent on outside technology. Despite the enormous amount of attention devoted to this topic, very little was actually known about the nature of the technology that was being transferred overseas in this way, the extent to which it leaked out to non-US competitors, the size of the benefits it conferred on the host (and other non-US) countries, and the sorts of non-US firms that received the largest relevant benefits. Chapter 8 on 'Technology Transfer to Overseas Subsidiaries by U.S.-Based Firms' (1980), authored with Anthony Romeo, presented findings on each of these topics. My Anderson Lectures at the University of Brussels in 1979 also touched on many of them.

The overseas R & D activities of US-based firms also became the focus of controversy. Some observers viewed such activities with suspicion, regarding them as a device to 'export' R & D jobs or as a channel through which American technology might be transmitted to actual or potential foreign competitors. Others, particularly the governments of many developing (and some developed) countries, viewed them as highly desirable activities that would help to stimulate indigenous R & D. Although the amount of controversy might suggest that the nature of existing overseas R & D activities of US-based firms had been studied quite thoroughly, this was far from the case. In 'Overseas Research and Development by U.S.-Based Firms', David Teece, Anthony Romeo and I summarized the results of a study designed to help provide basic information on this issue.

In 'Reverse Transfer of Technology from Overseas Subsidiaries to American Firms' (1984), Anthony Romeo and I explored the 'reverse' flows of technology from overseas R & D labs to the US and found these to be substantial. The article showed that the rate of productivity increase in US-based firms depended on overseas as well as domestic R & D. Pointing out that technology was becoming increasingly internationalized, we stressed the importance of including international technology flows in economic models of productivity change. While such flows are still not included in econometric models of this sort, Coe and Helpman have begun to carry out explorations along these lines.[8] In my view, such work is badly needed.

In 1985, the Royal Commission on the Economic Union and Development Prospects for Canada requested a paper on the international diffusion of technology and on technology policy. Chapter 11, 'Technological Change and the International Diffusion of Technology' (1986), reached several conclusions: (1) that technology policy in many countries is prone to over-emphasize R & D; (2) that governments sometimes tend to compartmentalize problems and assume that a nation's techno-logical capabilities should be influenced by various forms of technology policy, rather than by economic, trade or other policies; (3) that, from many points of view, diffusion or imitation may be much more important than innovation; and (4) that governments seem most successful in stimulating civilian technology when they emphasize broad policies rather than attempt to make detailed decisions concerning which specific designs and types of commercial products should be developed and at what pace.

Academic research

In the late 1980s and early 1990s, economists began to devote more attention to academic research, which previously had attracted little analysis. Chapter 12 on 'Academic Research and Industrial Innovation' (1991) estimated the extent to which technological innovation in various industries has been based on recent academic reseearch, and also the time lags between the investment in recent academic research projects and the industrial utilization of their findings. In addition, a rough estimate was made for the first time of the social rate of return from academic research. This estimate, while subject to a variety of limitations stressed in the paper, received a great deal of attention and was used by George Bush's administration to justify the federal government's investment in academic research.

In making such an estimate, one very difficult question is how to allocate the social returns between academic and industrial research. While no full or complete solution is proposed for this problem, my data suggest that, if previous estimates of the typical time form of social benefits and costs from industrial innovation are reasonably reliable, the social rate of return from academic research is over 20 per cent. This pertains even if seemingly generous assumptions are made concerning the social rate of return from industrial R & D, plant and equipment, and startup costs. For details, see Chapter 13, 'Academic Research and Industrial Innovation: A Further Note' (1992).[9]

Public policy towards civilian technology

Because of the gap between social and private returns from industrial innovations (examined in the first essay in Volume I) and for other reasons, economists have often suggested that there may be underinvestment in civilian technology. In 1982, the American Assembly commissioned a paper discussing, first, the role that science and technology would play in determining the state of the American economy in the year 2000 and, second, the major issues regarding US technology policies that were likely to arise prior to the end of this century. The resulting paper, 'Science and Technology' (1983), drew on my work as an adviser to President Jimmy Carter's Domestic Policy Review of Industrial Innovation, and reflected many of the views expressed in my earlier report to the Joint Economic Committee of Congress.[10]

One of the principal innovations in technology policy introduced by President Ronald Reagan was the R & D tax credit, enacted in 1981. To obtain information concerning its effects on firms' R & D expenditures, an analysis was carried out of over 100 firms, which included about 30 per cent of all company-financed R & D in the United States. According to the results, the tax credit seemed to have increased R & D expenditures by about 1 (or at most 2) per cent; the ratio of the tax-incentive-induced increase in R & D spending to the revenue lost by the government was about 0.3. Moreover, there was evidence that the tax cut had resulted in a considerable redefinition of activities as R & D. The findings, summarized in 'Public Policy Toward Industrial Innovation: An International Study of Direct Tax Incentives for Research and Development' (1985) and presented at the 75th anniversary of the Harvard Business School, played a role in Congressional discussions of the tax credit and in changes therein.

As part of this project, a study was also made of the effects of Canada's R & D tax credit, which has been in existence for about 20 years. In 'The Effects of R & D Tax Credits and Allowances in Canada' (1985), Lorne Switzer (a former graduate student at Penn) and I summarized the findings. The survey results, the econometric results and some simple calculations based on rough measures of the price elasticity of demand for R & D all suggested that the special research allowance increased R & D expenditures by about 1 per cent and that the investment tax credit increased them by about 2 per cent. These increases seemed to be appreciably less than the revenue losses to the government. As in the US, there was considerable evidence of a redefinition of activities as R & D.

For decades, policy makers in both the public and private sectors have been concerned with the following question: What is the impact of changes in federal R & D support on company-financed R & D expenditures? In 'Effects of Federal Support on Company-Financed R and D: The Case of Energy' (Chapter 17), Lorne Switzer and I carried out one of the first empirical studies at a micro level of this topic. The findings, which pertained to energy R & D, indicated a complementarity between government-financed and company-financed R & D on the average, although there was a considerable amount of interfirm variation in this regard. In about a third of the projects studied, federally-financed R & D projects stimulated some further R & D into which the firm invested its own funds. The results of a logit analysis suggested that whether or not a government-financed R & D project results in such a spinoff depends on the extent to which the performing firm contributed to the original formulation of the project's goals and strategies.

Intellectual property rights

The patent system is an old and prominent element of public policy relating to technology. While imitation costs (which patents are meant to increase) had long played a major role in economic models of innovation and technological change, systematic empirical investigations into the size and determinants of imitation costs were completely lacking until the early 1980s. In 'Imitation Costs and Patents: An Empirical Study' (1981), Mark Schwartz (a graduate student at Penn), Samuel Wagner and I carried out a detailed study of the chemical, drug, electronics and machinery industries. On average, imitation cost and time were found to be about 70 per cent of innovation cost and time. Patents seemed to increase imitation costs, particularly in the drug industry; in every other industry, however, patent protection did not seem essential for the development and introduction of at least three-quarters of the patented innovations studied.

No systematic empirical studies existed either of the speed at which various kinds of technological information leak out to rival firms. To help fill this gap, data were obtained from 100 American firms. According to the results, published in 'How Rapidly Does New Industrial Technology Leak Out?' (1985), information concerning development decisions is generally in the hands of rivals within about 12 to 18 months on average, while that concerning the detailed nature and operation of a new product or process generally leaks out within about a year. As pointed out in Chapter 19, these findings have important implications both for incentives for innovation and for public policies aimed at stemming the outflow of technology. Some of these implications were discussed in a series of lectures I gave in Sweden in 1983.

Despite the long history of the patent system, remarkably little is known about its effects. Chapter 20 on 'Patents and Innovation: An Empirical Study' (1986) investigated this topic. According to detailed data obtained from a random sample of 100 firms from 12 manufacturing industries, in only two – drugs and chemicals – was patent protection judged to be essential for the development or introduction of one-third or more of inventions. But this does not mean that firms patent only a small percentage of their inventions. On the contrary, for reasons given in the paper, they seemed to patent about 50–80 per cent of them. Moreover, despite the frequent assertions that firms were making less use of the patent system than in the past, the evidence did not bear this out.

During the early 1990s, intellectual property rights assumed enormous importance, both to policy makers and to economic analysts and theorists. Financed by the Research Committee of the World Bank, a study was conducted into the relationship between a country's strength of intellectual property rights protection and the transfer of technology to it, particularly through foreign direct investment. The countries in the sample perceived to have the weakest protection were India, Thailand, Brazil and Nigeria. Some industries – notably the chemical (including drugs) industry – regard intellectual property rights protection as much more important than others –

including the food and transportation equipment industries. In the former, intellectual property rights protection seems to have a major influence on whether US firms make direct investments in, or transfer technology to, a particular country. These findings are contained in Chapter 24, 'Unauthorized Use of Intellectual Property: Effects on Investment, Technology Transfer, and Innovation' (1993),[11] which was presented at the National Academy of Sciences.

Final remarks

Finally, it seems appropriate to comment on the economics of technological change, which has grown enormously in the past 40 years. It is now a well-developed field, stocked with theorists, empiricists, historians, policy analysts, consultants, and a variety of other types of experts. Many talented people have been attracted to this area of economics, which has benefited accordingly. Schools of business, law, engineering, and public policy, as well as economics departments, have contributed significantly to knowledge in this field; business executives and government officials, as well as academicians, have also helped substantially.

But regardless of its growth, the economics of technological change has altered very little in many respects. Specifically, it remains an area where there is a particular need for people who are comfortable working in, and drawing on, a variety of disciplines. Very few problems of any consequence can be solved within the confines of a single discipline. It continues to require persons who have a lively interest in both basic and applied work, and who are able to use each to enrich the other. It is still an area needing people who like to work on ill-defined problems where little is known and nothing is tidy, but where the rewards for even a partial solution are very high. Those with such attributes should be encouraged to enter this field because the opportunities continue to be enormous. While a lot more is known now than 40 years ago, the truth is that economists have only scratched the surface.

Notes

1. Besides these and other papers, I have published the following five books on this topic: *Industrial Research and Technological Innovation*, New York: W.W. Norton, 1968; *The Economics of Technological Change*, New York: W.W. Norton, 1968; *Research and Innovation in the Modern Corporation* (with J. Rapoport, J. Schnee, S. Wagner and M. Hamburger), New York: W.W. Norton, 1971; *The Production and Application of New Industrial Technology* (with J. Rapoport, A. Romeo, E. Villani, S. Wagner and F. Husic), New York: W.W. Norton, 1977; and *Technology Transfer, Productivity, and Economic Policy* (with A. Romeo, M. Schwartz, D. Teece and S. Wagner), New York: W.W. Norton, 1981.
2. Zvi Griliches had published his excellent and influential study of hybrid corn, but since it was a case study of a single innovation (known to be successful) in agriculture, it could shed no light on the social returns from a wide range of (both successful and unsuccessful) innovations in industry. Nor was it concerned with comparisons of social and private rates of return. Other early agricultural studies were carried out by Robert Evenson and Willis Peterson.
3. From the very beginning of my work, the National Science Foundation has provided generous financial support without interruption. I (and my students) are very grateful for this support, which now has continued for almost 40 years.
4. J. Jankowski (1993), 'Do We Need a Price Index for Industrial R and D?', *Research Policy*, **22**, pp. 195–205.
5. For a summary, see M. Kamien and N. Schwartz (1982), *Market Structure and Innovation*, Cambridge: Cambridge University Press.
6. Their work did not attempt to explain why the logistic function fit so well; they simply used it to summarize their data conveniently.

7. National Science Foundation (1974), *The Effects of International Technology Transfers on U.S. Economy*, Washington, D.C.: Government Printing Office, p. 5.

8. D. Coe and E. Helpman (1993), 'International R and D Spillovers', National Bureau of Economic Research, Working Paper No. 4444, August.

9. More recently, research has been carried out to determine the characteristics of the universities and academic researchers that seem to have contributed most to industrial innovation, and their sources of finance. See E. Mansfield, 'Academic Research Underlying Industrial Innovations: Sources, Characteristics, and Financing', *Review of Economics and Statistics*, forthcoming. Also, we have studied the factors influencing industrial support of academic research. See J. Lee and E. Mansfield (1994), 'Industrial Support of Industrial Innovation', Center for Economics and Technology, University of Pennsylvania.

10. E. Mansfield (1976), 'Federal Support of R and D Activities in the Private Sector', *Priorities and Efficiency in Federal Research and Development*, Joint Economic Committee of Congress, October 29.

11. For more recent findings, see E. Mansfield (1994), *Intellectual Property Protection, Foreign Direct Investment, and Technology Transfer*, Washington, D.C.: International Finance Corporation; E. Mansfield (1995), 'Intellectual Property Protection, Direct Investment, and Technology Transfer: Japan, Germany and U.S.', Center for Economics and Technology, University of Pennsylvania; and J. Lee and E. Mansfield, 'Intellectual Property Protection and U.S. Foreign Direct Investment', *Review of Economics and Statistics*, forthcoming.

PART I

INDUSTRIAL INNOVATION

[1]

SOCIAL AND PRIVATE RATES OF RETURN
FROM INDUSTRIAL INNOVATIONS*

EDWIN MANSFIELD
JOHN RAPOPORT
ANTHONY ROMEO
SAMUEL WAGNER
GEORGE BEARDSLEY

I. INTRODUCTION

For many years, economic analysts and policy-makers have been interested in developing and obtaining better and more complete data concerning social and private rates of return from industrial innovations. It has long been recognized that information of this sort is essential if public policy concerning civilian technology is to be formulated rationally. Yet despite the work of Denison, Fellner, Griliches, Mansfield, Minasian, Peterson, Terleckyj, and others, existing knowledge in this area is far too weak to provide a reasonably adequate foundation for analysis and policy.[1] The purpose of this paper is to report the results of seventeen case studies, each of which estimates the social and private rate of return from the investment in a particular industrial innovation. The results of this paper, although subject to obvious limitations and shortcomings, should provide us with a somewhat better understanding of this topic. The studies described

* The work on which this paper is based was supported by a grant to Mansfield from the Office of National R and D Assessment of the National Science Foundation. The bulk of the basic data on which this study is based was collected by Beardsley, Rapoport, Romeo, and Wagner. A preliminary version of this paper was presented by Mansfield at the meetings of the Eastern Economic Association on October 26, 1974; at the National Bureau of Standards; in a paper at the 1975 meetings of the American Economic Association; and in a paper at the First U.S.–U.S.S.R. Symposium; at M.I.T.; at the RAND Corporation; and at the National Science Foundation. Also, he presented some of this material in his Schmookler Memorial Lecture at the University of Minnesota in 1975 on the Economics of Information.

1. For a summary of existing knowledge in this area, see E. Mansfield, "Contribution of R and D to Economic Growth in the United States," *Science*, CLXXV (Feb. 4, 1972), 477–86.

here seem to be the first attempts to make direct measurements of this sort in the industrial sector.

II. THE SAMPLE OF INNOVATIONS

Our first step in carrying out this investigation was to contact a number of business firms in the Northeast and to try to persuade them to provide us with data bearing on the social and private returns from innovations that they had carried out. As would be expected, a substantial percentage of those who were contacted refused to cooperate because, despite our assurance that the data would be held in strictest confidence, they felt that such data were too sensitive to show outsiders. Those firms that were willing to cooperate were asked to pick one or more of their recent innovations more or less at random. Then many manweeks were spent gathering data concerning each innovation and its effects from the innovating firm, from firms using the innovation (if it was used by firms), and from other sources. These innovations occurred in a wide variety of industries (described below), and in firms of quite different sizes. Most of them are of average or routine importance, not major breakthroughs. Although the sample cannot be regarded as randomly selected, there is no obvious indication that it is biased toward very profitable innovations (socially or privately) or relatively unprofitable ones. The sample is described in Table I.

III. ESTIMATION OF SOCIAL BENEFITS: PRODUCT INNOVATIONS USED BY FIRMS

As is evident from Table I, the innovations in our sample can be divided into three classes: product innovations used by firms, product innovations used by households, and process innovations. Based on an intensive study of each of the innovations in each of these classes, it appears that the same general kind of model is applicable to all of the innovations in our sample in a particular class. In this and the following sections we describe the model that is used to measure the social benefits in a particular period from product innovations used by firms.

In each case these new products resulted in a potential saving to users. For example, the product innovation in the primary metals industry resulted in a potential saving to makers of household appliances. Thus, each of these innovations could shift downward the supply curve of the industry using the innovation. How far downward

TABLE I

CHARACTERISTICS OF SAMPLE OF SEVENTEEN INNOVATIONS

Industry producing the innovation	Type of innovation	Nature of innovation	Type of user	Approximate date of innovation
1. Primary metals	New product	New type of metal that reduced cost of appliances	Firms	Late 1950's
2. Machine tools	New product	New computer controls	Firms	Early 1970's
3. Control systems	New product	New type of component	Firms	Late 1960's
4. Construction	New product	New material that cut cost of building	Firms	Mid 1950's
5. Drilling	New product	Reduced cost of drilling wells	Firms	Mid 1960's
6. Industrial equipment	New process	New type of drafting	Firms	Early 1960's
7. Paper	New product	New paper product that cut costs of users	Firms	Mid 1960's
8. Thread	New product	New type of thread that cut costs of garment makers	Firms	Early 1960's
9. Industrial controls	New product	New mechanism for doors	Firms	Early 1970's
10. Electronics	New product	New device that reduced costs of certain video tape operations	Firms	Early 1970's
11. Chemicals[a]	New product	New product that reduced costs of users	Firms	Late 1960's
12. Chemicals[a]	New process	Reduced costs of production	Firms	Mid 1960's
13. Chemicals[a]	New process	Reduced cost of certain aromatic chemicals	Firms	Late 1960's
14. Chemicals[a]	New process	Major process improvement	Firms	Early 1960's
15. Household cleaners	New product	New product that reduced cost of cleaning floors	Households	Early 1960's
16. Stain removers	New product	New stain remover	Households	Mid 1960's
17. Dishwashing liquids	New product	New product that cut costs of operating dishwashers	Households	Early 1960's

a. Chemicals are defined to include petroleum refining.

this supply curve will shift depends, of course, on the pricing policy of the innovator. If the innovator charges a relatively high price for the new product, the supply curve may shift only slightly. Indeed, if the innovator charges a high enough price, the supply curve will not shift downward at all.

Suppose that the innovator decides to set a price for its new product that yields a profit[2] to the innovator equivalent to r dollars per unit of output of the industry using the innovation (for example, r dollars per appliance in the case of the new type of metal). Also, suppose that the industry using the innovation is competitive and that its supply curve is horizontal in the relevant range. In particular, assume that, before the advent of the innovation, this supply curve was S_1 in Figure I, and the price charged by the industry using the innovation was P_1. After the advent of the innovation, this supply curve is S_2, and the price is P_2.

Under these circumstances, the social benefits from the innovation can be measured by the sum of the two shaded areas in Figure I. The top shaded area is the consumers' surplus due to the lower price (P_2 rather than P_1) resulting from the use of the innovation.[3] In addition, there is a resource saving, and a corresponding increase in output elsewhere in the economy, due to the fact that the resource

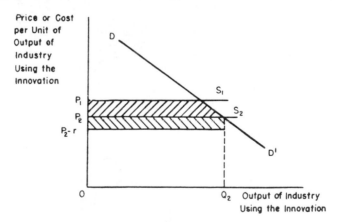

FIGURE I
Social Benefit from Product Innovation That Reduces the Costs of the Industry
Using It

2. Profit here is defined to be gross of any depreciation on the investment in the innovation. Basically, it is a cash flow concept.
3. Of course, one problem in any model of this sort is that the concept of consumers' surplus is a controversial one. But as so many writers have pointed out, it is hard to do applied work in this area without adopting some such concept. See, for example, J. Currie, J. Murphy, and A. Schmitz, "The Concept of Economic Surplus and Its Use in Economic Analysis," *Economic Journal*, LXXXI (Dec. 1971), 741–99.

costs of producing the good using the innovation—including the resource costs of producing the innovation—are less than P_2Q_2. Instead,
they are P_2Q_2 minus the profits of the innovator from the innovation,
the latter being merely a transfer from the producers of the good using
the innovation to the innovator. Thus, besides the consumers' surplus
arising from the price reduction, there is a resource saving amounting
to the profits of the innovator.[4]

However, two adjustments must frequently be made in this estimate corresponding to the lower shaded area in Figure I. First, if the
innovation replaces another product, the resource saving cited in the
previous paragraph does not equal the profits of the innovator (from
the innovation), but these profits less those that would have been
made (by the innovator or other firms) if the innovation had not occurred and the displaced product had been used instead. This is the
correct measure of the resource saving. Second, if other firms imitate
the innovator and begin selling the innovation to the industry that
uses it, their profits from the sale of the innovation must be added to
those of the innovator to get a full measure of the extent of the resource saving due to the innovation.

Based on this model, an estimate was made of the social benefit
in each period from the investment in each of these innovations. For
each innovation, the top shaded area in Figure I equals

$$(1) \qquad (P_1 - P_2)Q_2 (1 - 1/2\,Kn),$$

where $K = (P_1 - P_2)/P_2$, and n is the price elasticity of demand (in
absolute value) of the product of the industry using the innovation.
To estimate $P_1 - P_2$, we obtained as much information as we could
concerning the size of the unit cost reduction due to the innovation
in the industry using the innovation. Based on interviews with executives of the innovating firm, executives of a sample of firms using
the innovation, and reports and studies made by these firms for internal purposes, it was possible to obtain reasonably reliable estimates
of $(P_1 - P_2)$.[5] And once we had an estimate of $(P_1 - P_2)$, it was simple

4. To put matters somewhat differently, the sum of the two shaded areas in Figure
I can easily be shown to equal the social value of the extra output of the product (as
measured by the area under the demand curve) plus the value of the resources
saved.

5. We assume that the cost reduction experienced by the industry using the innovation is passed on to consumers. In view of the market structures of the industries
in question, this seems to be a reasonable assumption. Also, the available evidence seems
to support this assumption. But it is important to note that, if the cost reduction were
kept by the industry using the innovation, the social benefit would equal this industry's
cost saving due to the innovation plus the innovator's (adjusted) profits. Since the
industry's cost saving must be greater than our measure of the upper shaded area in
Figure I, our measure of social benefit would be conservative.

to compute K. Also Q_2 was generally available from published records. Rough estimates of n were obtained from published studies and from the firms. Since K is generally very small, the results are not sensitive to errors in n. Indeed, the expression in equation (1) can be approximated quite well in most cases by $(P_1 - P_2)Q_2$, which is the total savings to consumers due to the lower price, if they buy Q_2 units of the product of the industry using the innovation.

To estimate the additional resource saving from the innovation, which equals the bottom shaded area in Figure I (if the adjustments described in the paragraph before the last are unnecessary), the innovator's profit from the new product was obtained from detailed discussions with the firm's executives, as well as study of relevant financial records. For each year, the costs of marketing and producing the innovation, as well as the costs of carrying out the innovation (R and D, plant and equipment, manufacturing start-up, and marketing start-up),[6] were deducted from the innovator's revenues from the innovation. Note that the R and D costs were adjusted to allow for the fact that the innovator invested R and D resources in uncommercialized R and D projects. To make this adjustment, we obtained estimates from each of the innovating firms of the average number of dollars spent on uncommercialized R and D projects per dollar spent on a commercialized R and D project during the relevant period. Then we multiplied the innovator's R and D outlays (in each year) on the innovation by this number in order to get an estimate of the total R and D investment, including a prorated allowance for uncommercialized projects. In cases where the adjustments described in the paragraph before the last were necessary, estimates of the foregone profits from displaced products were deducted, and the profits of imitators were added, to the innovator's profits. These estimates were obtained from the relevant firms.

IV. PARALLEL INNOVATIVE EFFORTS, TIME HORIZON, AND RATES OF RETURN

In calculating the social rate of return, we must recognize that, besides the innovator, other firms or research organizations in the United States[7] may have invested resources (prior to the introduction

6. For discussions of the cost categories involved, see E. Mansfield and J. Rapoport, "The Costs of Industrial Product Innovations," *Management Science*, XXI (Aug. 1975), 1380–86; and E. Mansfield, J. Rapoport, J. Schnee, S. Wagner, and M. Hamburger, *Research and Innovation in the Modern Corporation* (New York: Norton, 1971).
7. We are concerned here only with the costs and benefits arising within the United States. Thus, we ignore the fact that some of these innovations resulted in significant

of the innovation in question) in R and D and related innovative activities aimed at innovations of essentially the same kind as this one. Clearly, it is not easy to obtain data on the extent of such investments, but fortunately the difficulties seem to be less than they might appear, for two reasons. First, only a limited number of organizations could reasonably have been expected to be doing R and D in the relevant area, and if they had been devoting any substantial amount of resources to such work in the relevant time frame, it is inconceivable that the current executives of these organizations (and all their competitors) would have been unaware of it. Second, since these innovations occurred some time ago, firms generally are quite willing to discuss whether they were carrying out work of the relevant kind at that time. Moreover, and this is particularly fortunate, our results are quite insensitive to errors in the estimated investment in R and D carried out by others. Even if the true social research expenditures were ten times our estimate, and the true social development expenditures were double our estimate, the results change remarkably little.

Based on interviews with executives of the innovating firm, as well as with other firms that could reasonably be expected to do (and be aware of) R and D of the relevant kind, it appears that, in most of the cases in our sample, no other firm or research organization was doing work aimed at roughly the same kind of innovation. Thus, in these cases, the private investment seems to be a good approximation to the social investment. In the remaining cases, other firms or individuals were engaged in R and D aimed at the same kind of innovation. In the cases where this R and D was *unsuccessful,* we obtained as accurate an estimate as possible of the cost of this unsuccessful R and D, and added this figure to the R and D costs described in the previous section to get an estimate of the total social cost of the relevant R and D carried out by the innovator and others.[8]

---

social benefits in other countries, and we do not attempt to include whatever costs may have been incurred in other countries in an attempt to produce innovations of roughly the same kind. Also, each rate of return estimated here is on the investment in the innovation in question, given that previous investments in basic science, education, and so forth had already occurred. Clearly, the rates of return on the investments considered here were dependent on these previous investments.

8. Of course, some of the unsuccessful R and D directed at one innovation may be part of the uncommercialized R and D carried out by the innovator in the case of another innovation. Really, the social cost of an innovation should include a prorated share of the cost of uncommercialized R and D carried out by the innovator, excluding the cost of its uncommercialized R and D aimed at innovations where other firms beat it to the punch. But there is no way to estimate the latter cost, and our procedure clearly biases the social rates of return downward.

In the one case (among product innovations used by firms) where other firms or individuals were engaged (prior to the introduction of the innovation in question[9]) in R and D aimed at roughly the same kind of innovation, and where this R and D was *successful,* we must recognize that the innovator's investment resulted only in the innovation's availability at an earlier point in time, not in all of the social benefits from the innovation date up to the relevant time horizon. In other words, the proper comparison is between what would have occurred if the innovator had not carried out the innovation (but other firms were free to do so) and what in fact occurred. In this case, we obtained as accurate an appraisal as we could of the date when the innovation would have appeared if the innovator had not carried out the innovation, and we calculated the social benefits only during the period between the date when the innovation occurred and the date when it would have appeared if the innovator had done nothing.[10] Of course, it frequently is very difficult to estimate when the innovation would have occurred if the innovator had not carried it out. But in this particular case a realistic (if perhaps somewhat conservative) estimate is that the second firm to produce the innovation would have come up with it when in fact it did so, regardless of whether the innovator preceded it or not.

For most innovations these calculations were carried out for each year from the beginning of work on the innovation until 1973. Thus, our estimates of the social benefits are conservative, since all benefits after 1973 are ignored. But in some cases, this would introduce a serious distortion, since the innovation is relatively new. In these cases, forecasts were made of the consumers' surplus and the innovator's profits (adjusted for imitators' profits and for profits on older products) in each year up to 1980. These forecasts are based on firms' expectations concerning $(P_1 - P_2)$, Q_2, and the relevant profits in the next few years. They are intentionally very conservative, so whatever bias there is in the resulting rates of return should be downward.

Finally, having made the calculations described in this and the previous section for each year, we have an estimate of the net social benefits from the innovation for each year. Then we can compute the

9. Work of this sort that occurs after the innovation takes place is of a different kind. It is directed at *imitating* or *improving on* the innovation, and is not properly regarded as part of the work *producing* the innovation.

10. Note that this procedure assumes that, once the innovator is joined by another firm producing the innovation, they adopt a pricing policy that is just the same as the other firm would have adopted if it were the sole producer of the innovation. Needless to say, this may not be true, since there may be advantages stemming from competition between the two firms. However, we adopt this assumption because it results in a conservative estimate of the social rate of return and because any other assumption would have to be based largely on speculation.

internal social rate of return, the interest rate that makes the present value of the net social benefits equal to zero. In other words, it is the interest rate i that results in the following equality:

$$(2) \qquad B(t) + \frac{B(t+1)}{1+i} + \frac{B(t+2)}{(1+i)^2} + \cdots + \frac{B(t+n)}{(1+i)^n} = 0,$$

where $B(t)$ is the net social benefit year in t, t is the first year in which the net social benefit is nonzero, and $(t+n)$ is the last year in which the net social benefit is nonzero.

Finally, we also compute the private rate of return from the innovator's investment in each innovation. To do so, we calculate the cash flow to the innovator from the innovation during each year. This calculation involves the subtraction of all costs incurred by the innovator to carry out, produce, and sell the innovation (including the allowance described in the previous section for R and D on uncommercialized projects) from the innovator's revenues from the innovation. Also, profits that the innovator would have earned on products displaced by the innovation must be subtracted as well.[11] The time period over which these computations were made was generally up to 1973, but in some cases (as in the case of the social rate of return) it extended to 1980. Again, the forecasts in the latter cases are decidedly conservative. The net private benefits in each year, like the B's in equation (2), were deflated. The Consumer Price Index, which generally was used, is not ideal, but it seems very unlikely that the results will be affected in an important way by this choice of a deflator.

V. PRODUCT INNOVATIONS USED BY HOUSEHOLDS

In this section we turn to the model used to calculate the social benefits for product innovations used by households. Since all of the innovations of this type in our sample are meant to reduce the cost of some particular household activity, basically the same model will apply. Suppose that the demand curve for this activity is DD' in Figure II and that the innovation reduced the price of performing this activity from P_1 to P_2. Suppose too that the innovator makes a profit

---

11. In all but one case, it is assumed that the profits from the displaced product would have continued (up to the time horizon indicated below) at their previous level if the innovation had not occurred. This seems reasonable, based on the facts. But in the one remaining case, there is reason to believe that, if the innovation had not occurred, another innovation superior to this one would have occurred at a particular point in time afterward. Thus, we assume that the innovator would have earned nothing on the displaced product after this point in time. Of course, it also earned nothing on the innovation after this point.

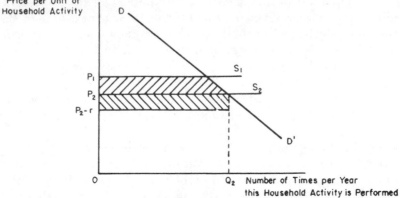

FIGURE II
Social Benefit from Product Innovation That Reduces the Price of a Household
Activity

of r dollars every time this activity is performed using the product innovation. Then the social benefits from the innovation can be measured by the sum of the two shaded areas in Figure II. These two areas are exactly analogous to those in Figure I, and the methods used to estimate them are similar to those described above, except that no interviews were carried out with users. Instead, the results are based entirely on the estimates and findings of the firms. As in the previous sections, it is necessary to correct the R and D costs for uncommercialized projects, to estimate R and D costs incurred by firms and organizations other than the innovator, to deduct the profit from displaced products from the innovator's profit, and to include the profits of imitators.

However, not everything is the same as in previous sections. For one thing, one of these innovations, the stain remover, resulted in some environmental costs, since it increased the amount of a certain chemical that is put into our water supplies. As a rough measure of these costs, we used an estimate (obtained from an official of the Environmental Protection Agency) of the cost of removing a unit of this chemical from water, given that it occurs in a particular concentration. Then we multiplied this cost times the number of units of the chemical that is deposited in the water, given that consumers use the innovation to perform the relevant household activity Q_2 times per year. Finally, this estimate was deducted from the social benefit to correct, at least roughly, for the environmental costs. Note that this was the only innovation in our entire sample that resulted in any substantial environmental costs, so far as we could determine.[12]

In all but one of these cases, there is no reason to believe that, if the innovator had not introduced the new product, any other firm would have done so in the relevant time frame. But in the remaining case, a competitor introduced a similar new product only a short while after the innovator introduced its new product. In this case, we obtained estimates from the relevant firms concerning the quantity of its new product that the competitor would have sold each year if the innovator had not developed and introduced its new product. Then we deducted this amount from the actual combined sales of both new products to get the extra amount that was used each year because the new product was introduced earlier than it otherwise would have been, due to the innovator's actions. Then we calculated the consumers' surplus based on this extra amount. Also, we calculated the innovator's profit less the profit that would have been earned by the competitor on the share of the innovator's sales that the competitor would have gotten if the innovator had not introduced its product (and less the profit on products displaced in the remainder of cases). Based on these calculations, we computed the social rate of return.

Finally, as in the case of product innovations used by firms, we computed private as well as social rates of return. The calculations are entirely analogous to those described in the previous section. In all cases the calculations end with 1973.

VI. PROCESS INNOVATIONS

Next, let us turn to the model underlying our calculation of the social benefits from process innovations. In the case of three of the four process innovations included in our sample, there was no apparent effect on product prices. By lowering the costs of the innovators, these process innovations increased the innovator's profits. Also, since they were imitated (or used at nominal cost) by other firms, they soon increased the profits of other firms as well. The total decrease in costs (which equals the increase in profits) of all of the relevant firms is a measure of the social benefit of each of these innovations in a particular period. It equals the social saving in resources due to the innovation. For each of these innovations, we estimated the total reduction in costs on the basis of interviews with the relevant firms

---

12. Note that some of these innovations had positive environmental effects. However, since these benefits are hard to measure, we ignore them. Of course, whatever bias this introduces results in our estimates of the social rate of return being conservative.

and of studies and reports concerning the cost reductions due to the innovations and the extent of their utilization.

In the case of the fourth process innovation (the innovation in industrial heating equipment), the situation was different. In this case, the innovator shared the gains with its customers. As shown in Figure III, it reduced the price of its product from P_1 to P_2. Thus, the social

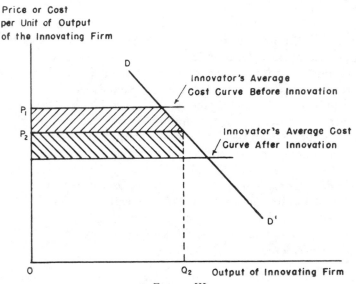

FIGURE III
Social Benefit from Process Innovation That Results in Price Reduction by Innovator

benefit equals the sum of the two shaded areas, the top shaded area being the consumers' surplus resulting from the price reduction, and the bottom shaded area being the profits to the innovator from the innovation. The situation is almost exactly the same as in Figures I and II.

For one of the process innovations, it was necessary to estimate the length of time that the innovator hastened the appearance and introduction of the new process. (In the other cases, there is no reason to believe that if the innovator had not introduced the innovation in the relevant time period, any other firm would have done so.) In this case other firms were doing R and D along somewhat similar lines, and there was some feeling among knowledgeable engineers and managers that the new process might have been developed and introduced about four years later than in fact occurred if the innovator had not done so. In this case we assume that the diffusion of the new process would have begun four years later (but that it would have proceeded at the same rate) if the innovator had not developed and introduced it. Then the social and private savings are computed by comparing the actual extent of use of the innovation with what it would have been under this assumption. In addition, the social rate of return based on the entire industry's investment in this sort of innovation is estimated, this estimate having the advantage that it is free of any such assumption about how quickly competitors of the innovator would have developed and introduced the innovation.[13] (The latter estimate, which is the lower of the two, is shown in Table II.)

TABLE II

SOCIAL AND PRIVATE RATES OF RETURN FROM INVESTMENT IN
SEVENTEEN INNOVATIONS

Innovation	Rate of return (percent)	
	Social	Private
Primary metals innovation	17	18
Machine tool innovation	83	35
Component for control system	29	7
Construction material	96	9
Drilling material	54	16
Drafting innovation	92	47
Paper innovation	82	42
Thread innovation	307	27
Door control innovation	27	37
New electronic device	Negative	Negative
Chemical product innovation	71	9
Chemical process innovation	32	25
Chemical process innovation	13	4
Major chemical process innovation	56[a]	31
Household cleaning device	209	214
Stain remover	116	4
Dishwashing liquid	45	46
Median	56	25

a. Based on investment of entire industry. See Section VI.

VII. SOCIAL AND PRIVATE RATES OF RETURN

The results, shown in Table II, seem to have at least three implications. First, they indicate that the social rate of return from the

---

13. For two of the processes the calculations end with 1972 or 1973; for the other two, forecasts are used up to 1980 (and in one case, beyond).

investments in these seventeen innovations has been very high. The median estimated social rate of return is about 56 percent. Moreover, for a variety of reasons, these estimates are likely to be conservative lower bounds.[14] To put these results in perspective, recall that Griliches found that the internal social rate of return from hybrid corn—a very successful innovation—was 37 percent.[15] Clearly, the investments that have been made in industrial innovations have, on the average, yielded handsome social returns, if these innovations are at all typical.

Second, the results indicate that the private rates of return from the investments in these innovations have been much lower than the social rates of return.[16] The median private rate of return (before taxes) was about 25 percent. In interpreting this number, it is important to recognize the riskiness of this kind of investment (and the fact that these are pretax figures). This riskiness is evidenced by the enormous variation in the private rates of return in Table II. In the case of six innovations the private rate of return (before taxes) was less than 10 percent, while for five innovations, it was more than 40 percent.

14. For example, in many cases, we ignore all post-1973 benefits from the innovations. Throughout this study, we have tried to use estimates and procedures that, if biased at all, would be biased in this direction.

15. See his "Research Costs and Social Returns: Hybrid Corn and Related Innovations," *Journal of Political Economy*, LXVI (Oct. 1958), 419–31. The models used in Sections III and IV are in the same spirit as the one applied by Griliches. The principal differences are that we have extended the analysis to include the pricing policies of the innovator, the effect on displaced products, and the costs of uncommercialized R and D and of R and D done outside the innovating organization. Another noteworthy study of this kind is W. Peterson, "Returns to Poultry Research in the United States," *Journal of Farm Economics*, XLIX (Aug. 1967), 656–69. This study concludes that the average rate of return from the investment in poultry research was 18 percent.

16. Note that there is nothing in our procedures that makes it inevitable that an innovation's social rate of return exceeds its private rate of return. For a variety of reasons (such as investments in R and D by organizations other than the innovator, and the transfer of profits from the producers of displaced products to the innovator), the social rate of return can be less than the private rate of return—and in fact this turns out to be the case for four of the innovations in our sample. For a study of some of the factors associated with a firm's probabilities of success in R and D, see E. Mansfield and S. Wagner, "Organizational and Strategic Factors Associated with Probabilities of Success in Industrial R and D," *Journal of Business*, XLVIII (April 1975), 179–98.

One of the innovations was developed by a nonprofit organization. In this case the private rate of return is defined to be the rate of return to this organization and the licensees that produced and marketed the innovation.

When we compute a confidence interval for the proportions of innovations where the social rate of return exceeds the private rate of return, we find that the probability is 0.90 that this percentage lies between 60 percent and 92 percent. Thus, if we could treat our sample as randomly chosen, we could be quite confident that the social rate of return exceeds the private rate of return in the majority of cases. Also, a t-test indicates that the mean difference between social and private rates of return, which is 47 percent, differs significantly from zero at the 0.01 level. And so does a sign test, which does not assume normality.

Third, the results indicate that, in about 30 percent of the cases, the private rate of return was so low that no firm, with the advantage of hindsight, would have invested in the innovation, but the social rate of return from the innovation was so high that, from society's point of view, the investment was well worthwhile. We would also like to estimate the extent to which innovations with favorable social rates of return have anticipated rates of return that are so low that they are not carried out. Unfortunately, Table II cannot provide much information on this score for the obvious reason that all of these innovations were carried out. Also, expected and actual private rates of return may differ considerably.[17]

VIII. FACTORS ASSOCIATED WITH THE GAP BETWEEN SOCIAL AND PRIVATE RATES OF RETURN

Economists have long been interested in the sorts of innovative activity where the gap between social and private rates of return, if it exists, is particularly large. There has been considerable speculation on this score, but it seems fair to say that the current state of knowledge in this regard is extremely limited. Economic theorists have generally singled out three factors as being of considerable importance in determining the extent of the gap between the social and private rates of return from an innovation. The first of these factors is the market structure of the innovator's industry. If the innovator is faced with a highly competitive environment, it is less likely that it will be able to appropriate a large proportion of the social benefits than if it has a secure monopoly position or if it is part of a tight oligopoly. Of course, the extent to which the innovator is subjected to competition, and how rapidly, may depend on whether the innovation is patented. Moreover, another consideration of at least equal importance is how expensive it is for potential competitors to "invent around" the innovator's patents, if they exist, and to obtain the equipment needed to begin producing the new product (or using the new process). In some cases, like DuPont's nylon, it would have been extremely diffi-

---

17. However, a limited amount of evidence can be given on this score. We could obtain data for nine of the innovations concerning the approximate private rate of return expected from the innovation by the innovator when it began the project. In five of the nine cases, the expected private rate of return was less than 15 percent, indicating that these five projects were quite marginal; yet the average social rate of return of these five projects was over 100 percent! Unless there is a marked discontinuity of some sort, it would appear from this that there may be many projects where the expected private rate of return was a bit lower (with the result that they were not carried out), but where the social rate of return would have been quite high. (The rank correlation between the expected private rate of return and the social rate of return does not differ significantly from zero in this sample.) However, the very small sample and the crudeness of the analysis should be borne in mind.

cult to imitate the innovation (legally). In other cases, a potential competitor could obtain and begin producing a "me too" product (or using a "me too" process) at relatively little cost.

A second factor that economists have emphasized as a determinant of the size of the gap between social and private rates of return is whether the innovation is major or minor. (A reasonable measure of an innovation's importance (at least in our sample) might be the annual net social benefits derived from it.) According to R. C. O. Matthews, the "degree of appropriability is likely to be less . . . in major innovations than in minor ones. . . ," [18] since major innovations are more likely, in his view, to be imitated quickly. Similarly, on the basis of a model stressing the indivisibility of information, Kenneth Arrow concludes that "the inventor obtains the entire realized social benefit of moderately cost reducing inventions but not of more radical inventions." [19]

A third factor that is sometimes cited is whether the innovation is a new product or process. Thus, Matthews thinks that the degree of appropriability may be less for process innovations than for product innovations. On the other hand, Nelson, Peck, and Kalachek stress that new processes can often be kept secret and that it frequently is difficult for one firm to find out what processes another firm is using.[20] This, of course, suggests that the gap between social and private rates of return might be greater for products than for processes. Neither Matthews nor Nelson, Peck, and Kalachek present any evidence on this score.

Although most of these hypotheses seem quite plausible, the truth is that none of them have been subjected to any sort of systematic empirical tests. Based on the results presented in the previous section, it is possible for the first time to attempt some empirical tests of these hypotheses. These tests are made in two steps. First, we divide the sample into two groups, processes and products, to see whether the average difference between the social and private rates of return is different in one group than in the other. Second, looking at products alone (since there are too few processes to support such an analysis),

18. R. C. O. Matthews, "The Contribution of Science and Technology to Economic Development," in B. Williams, ed., *Science and Technology in Economic Growth* (London: Macmillan, 1973), p. 14.

19. K. Arrow, "Economic Welfare and the Allocation of Resources for Invention," in National Bureau of Economic Research, *The Rate and Direction of Inventive Activity* (Princeton: Princeton University Press, 1962), p. 622. Arrow's model bears a resemblance to ours in Section III, but he was interested in a somewhat different set of questions, and no attempt was made to use it as a basis for empirical work.

20. R. Nelson, M. Peck, and E. Kalachek, *Technology, Economic Growth, and Public Policy* (Washington: Brookings Institution, 1967), p. 161.

we assume that

(3) $$D_i = \alpha_0 + \alpha_1 S_i + \alpha_2 P_i + \alpha_3 I_i + z_i,$$

where D_i is the difference between the social and private rates of return for the ith innovation, S_i is the annual net social benefit (in thousands of dollars) from the ith innovation three years after its initial introduction (a crude, but reasonable, measure of the innovation's importance), P_i is a dummy variable that equals 1 if the innovation is patented and 0 otherwise, I_i is an estimate of the minimum amount of money (in thousands of dollars) it would have cost any of the innovator's competitors to imitate legally and introduce the ith innovation, and z_i is a random error term. According to the hypotheses stated above, one would expect α_1 to be positive and α_2 and α_3 to be negative. Ordinary regression techniques were used to determine whether this was the case.

The results suggest that the difference between the social and private rates of return tended to be higher for products than for processes. (The average value of D_i was about 57 percent for products and about 21 percent for processes.) But this difference is not statistically significant. Turning to the estimation of the α's, we obtained data concerning I_i for each innovation.[21] Then, combining these data with the information concerning D_i, P_i, and S_i (which stems from the work in previous sections), we used least squares to estimate the α's, the resulting equation being

(4) $$D_i = 12.4 \;\; + 0.0313 S_i - 0.0509 I_i, \; (R^2 = 0.67),$$
          (0.46)   (4.34)   (1.87)

where the t-statistic of each of the regression coefficients is shown in parentheses, and P_i is excluded because its regression coefficient is not even close to being statistically significant. Despite the relatively small sample size, the estimate of α_1 is highly significant, and the estimate of α_3 is significant at the 0.05 level. Both have the expected signs.

Thus, the results seem to support the hypothesis that the gap between social and private rates of return tends to be greater for more important innovations and for innovations that can be imitated relatively cheaply by competitors. Apparently, when the cost of imitating

---

21. These estimates were obtained from the innovating firms. In each case executives of the innovating firm were asked to estimate the minimum amount that it would have cost a competitor to imitate the innovation (legally). In some cases the estimate of I_i was as high as $2 million; in other cases, it was as low as $3,000. Although these estimates are rough, the executives seemed to think that they were not very wide of the mark.

the innovation is held constant, it makes little or no difference whether the innovation is patented—which seems reasonable because whether or not a patent exists is of relevance largely (perhaps only) because of its effects on the costs of imitation. It is important to note that S_i and I_i can explain about two-thirds of the observed variation in this gap among the product innovations in our sample.[22] However, at the same time, it is important to bear in mind the smallness of the sample and its nonrandom character.

IX. UNEMPLOYMENT, REPERCUSSIONS ON OTHER MARKETS, AND FUTURE CHANGES IN TECHNOLOGY

Before concluding, we must take up several additional factors that have not been mentioned explicitly in previous sections. First, new technology can, of course, result in prolonged and serious unemployment of particular kinds of labor. Recognizing this fact, we tried to determine whether there was any substantial unemployment (or change in job content) resulting from each innovation described in Section II. In no case could we find any evidence of an appreciable change of this sort: although labor requirements sometimes were reduced by the innovation, growth in output offset these reductions. Thus, in this sample at least, this factor does not seem of substantial importance. Obviously, however, it can be of importance in other cases; and in situations where it is of importance, one must adjust the social benefits, as calculated in previous sections, for the fact that (for a certain period of time) some of the resources saved by the innovation do not find employment elsewhere.[23]

Second, new technology can, of course, have an effect on other industries and markets besides the ones directly involved. For example, by reducing the cost and price of the product using an innovation, the innovation affects the outputs of goods that are substitutes or complements of this product. However, so long as the prices of these and other goods (other than the product using the innovation) are not materially affected, the effects of these output changes are already included in the measures specified above.[24] In our sample there is no

22. One innovation had to be excluded from the regression (and the t-test in note 16) because its private rate of return was incalculable, since the private net benefit in each year was negative. Note too that the ratio of I_i to the innovator's cost in carrying out the ith innovation was tried as an additional explanatory variable in equation (4), but it was not close to being significant. Apparently, the absolute, not relative, cost is what matters most.

23. See A. Schmitz and D. Seckler, "Mechanized Agriculture and Social Welfare: The Case of the Tomato Harvester," *American Journal of Agricultural Economics*, LII (Nov. 1970), 569–77.

24. See E. Mishan, *Economics for Social Decisions* (New York: Praeger, 1972), Ch. 6.

evidence that any of these innovations had any appreciable impact on any price other than that of the good using the innovation (in Section IV) or of the household activity in question (in Section V) or of the good based on the one relevant process (in Section VI). Also, one must assume that inputs that were displaced from industries producing goods competing with the product using the innovation readily found employment elsewhere. There is no evidence that this was not the case.

Third, new technology can, of course, play an important role in suggesting and prompting further innovations. Without question, practically all of the innovations in our sample had this effect. Thus, since each of these innovations is instrumental in bringing about future innovations, each results in social benefits above and beyond what we have measured. However, each of these innovations may have been suggested, prompted, or aided by previous innovations, and there is no feasible way to estimate the extent to which there is a net understatement of benefits.

X. CONCLUSION

As everyone who writes on this subject is quick to point out, very little is known about the social and private returns from industrial research and technological innovation. The need for measurement in this area is acute and widely recognized. For example, the Council of Economic Advisers, in its 1972 Annual Report, stressed the need for further analysis "to show the benefits, costs, and processes associated with R and D." [25] Our purpose in this study has been to measure, as best we can, the social and private rates of return from a sample of innovations.[26] We believe that our results go far beyond anything heretofore attempted in this area. (Also, to check and extend our results, we obtained very rich and detailed data concerning the returns from the innovative activities from 1960 to 1972 of one of the nation's largest firms. The results bear out our present findings.[27])

25. Economic Report of the President, 1972, pp. 127–28.

26. Griliches, Mansfield, Minasian, and Terleckyj have estimated rates of return from nonagricultural R and D based on econometric studies where R and D is inserted into production functions. Where the results of these studies can be compared with this one, the results are quite similar. For example, see N. Terleckyj, *Effects of R and D on the Productivity Growth of Industries: An Exploratory Study* (Washington: National Planning Association, 1974).

27. For each year, this firm has made a careful inventory of the technological innovations arising from its R and D and related activities, and it has made detailed estimates of the effect of each of these innovations on its profit stream. We computed the average rate of return from this firm's total investment in innovative activities during 1960–1972, the result being 19 percent, which is not too different from the

Of course, proper caution should be exercised in interpreting our results. For a host of reasons, they can tell us little about the extent to which there is an underinvestment (or whether an underinvestment exists) in innovative activities of various kinds.[28] Our sample of innovations is not a random sample, the data sometimes are rough, and for a few of the innovations they are based partly on forecasts. Further, the models that we use are simplified in many respects.[29] For these and other reasons, our results should be treated with considerable caution. The measurement of social and private rates of return from investments in new technology is an extremely difficult business, which is one good reason why so few such measurements have been attempted. Nonetheless, it is important that we make the best estimates we can.

UNIVERSITY OF PENNSYLVANIA
MOUNT HOLYOKE COLLEGE
UNIVERSITY OF CONNECTICUT
TEMPLE UNIVERSITY
CALIFORNIA POLYTECHNIC STATE UNIVERSITY

---

median private rate of return in Table II. Also, we computed lower bounds for the social rate of return from the firm's investment, and found that they were about double its private rates of return. For further discussion of this study, see G. Beardsley's Ph.D. thesis, University of Pennsylvania; E. Mansfield, J. Rapoport, A. Romeo, E. Villani, S. Wagner, and F. Husic, *The Production and Application of New Industrial Technology* (New York: W. W. Norton, 1977); and E. Mansfield, "Comments on Returns to R and D Expenditures in the Private Sector," Conference on Research in Income and Wealth, November 1975.

28. See E. Mansfield, "Federal Support of R and D in the Private Sector," *Priorities and Efficiency in Federal Research and Development,* Joint Economic Committee of Congress, October 29, 1976; his testimony before the House Committee on Science and Technology, published in *Federal Research and Development Expenditures and the National Economy* (Washington: Government Printing Office, 1976); and G. Eads, "U. S. Government Support for Civilian Technology: Economic Theory vs. Political Practice," *Research Policy* (1974).

29. An important point to bear in mind is that the models used here cannot cope with innovations whose effects cannot be regarded as a form of cost reduction. This limitation is likely to be much more important for very major innovations than for lesser ones.

[2]

ENTRY, GIBRAT'S LAW, INNOVATION, AND THE GROWTH OF FIRMS

By EDWIN MANSFIELD*

Because there have been so few econometric studies of the birth, growth and death of firms, we lack even crude answers to the following basic questions regarding the dynamic processes governing an industry's structure. What are the quantitative effects of various factors on the rates of entry and exit? How well can the growth of firms be represented by Gibrat's law of proportionate effect? What have been the effects of successful innovations on a firm's growth rate? What determines the amount of mobility within an industry's size structure?[1]

This paper provides some tentative answers to these questions. First, it constructs some simple models to estimate the effects of an industry's capital requirements, profitability, and other such factors on its entry and exit rates. Second, it investigates how well Gibrat's law of proportionate effect can represent the growth of firms in each of the industries for which we have appropriate data. Although this law has played a prominent role in models designed to explain the size distribution of firms, it has been tested only a few times against data for very large firms. Third, we estimate the difference in growth rate between firms that carried out significant innovations and other firms of comparable initial size. The results help to measure the importance of successful innovation as a cause of interfirm differences in growth rates, and they shed new light on the rewards for such innovations. Fourth, the paper presents and tests a simple model to explain interindustry and

* The author is associate professor of economics at Carnegie Institute of Technology. This paper, a preliminary version of which was read at the August 1961 meetings of the Econometric Society, will be reprinted as a Cowles Foundation Paper. The work on which it is based is part of a larger project on technical change and economic growth, supported by the Office of Economic and Statistical Studies of the National Science Foundation, by a Ford Foundation Faculty Research Fellowship, and by the Cowles Foundation for Research in Economics at Yale University. The paper has benefited from discussions with D. Fink, J. Muth, and N. Seeber. My thanks also go to G. Haines and D. Remington for their assistance and to various companies for data.

[1] With regard to the effects of various factors on the rates of entry and exit, there has been considerable theorizing [4] [14] [21] [30] and a few relevant empirical studies [4] [7], but there has been no systematic attempt to estimate the quantitative effect of various factors. With regard to the growth of firms, there have been several studies of Gibrat's law [11] [13] [15] [27] based only on the largest firms (one of which dealt in part with the determinants of the amount of mobility) and an analysis [8] of the size structure of the largest firms in the economy. There are no previous studies (as far as I know) of the effects of innovation on a firm's growth rate.

temporal differences in the extent to which firms change relative positions in the size distribution.

I. *Determinants of Rates of Entry and Exit*

A. *Entry, Profitability, and Capital Requirements*

Entry can be defined as the net change in the number of firms in an industry. Alternatively, it can be defined as the extent to which new owners of productive facilities become established in an industry either through the construction of new plants or the purchase of existing firms. Each concept has its own set of uses. The first concept is useful in analyzing problems regarding market structure and industrial concentration, since the number of firms in an industry is a significant factor in such problems. The second concept is useful in measuring the ease with which new entrepreneurs can become established in an industry and the extent to which they do so. For this purpose, it would be misleading to ignore those that entered by purchasing existing concerns.[2]

The second of these concepts is employed in the present subsection; the first will be employed in the next one. Regardless of which concept is used, perhaps the most obvious measure of the amount of entry into the ith industry during the tth period is E_{it}'—the number of firms that entered during the period as a proportion of the number of firms in the industry at the beginning of the period. But the available data force us to use E_{it}—the number of firms that entered during the period and survived until the end as a proportion of the original number of firms. Since E_{it}' and E_{it} should be highly correlated, this discrepancy is probably not too important for our purposes.[3]

Letting C_{it} be the investment required to establish a firm of minimum

---

[2] Of course, the second concept of entry is somewhat slippery, since it is sometimes difficult to define and detect a significant change in the ownership of a firm. This is particularly true in the case of large companies. In practice, we generally use changes in company names as indicators of changes in ownership (see the Appendix), but this is very crude. This problem also occurs in the next subsection and in Sections II and III.

A third definition of entry would be useful for some purposes. This would measure the number of firms that entered with new plant, regardless of the number of firms that scrapped their plant during the period. That is, it would be a gross measure of entry. Bain's discussion [4, p. 4ff.] generally runs in these terms. The available data do not permit us to measure this gross concept of entry. See the Appendix.

[3] Other measures might be used: e.g., the absolute number of entrants. But the establishment of two new firms would seem to mean one thing if there previously were two firms and something else if there previously were 100. Moreover, one would expect that ease of entry would be directly related to the number of firms in the industry [23]. Although it is somewhat arbitrary, it seems sensible to follow the Department of Commerce's procedure [7] and to normalize in this way for the original number of firms.

The size of the entrants—as well as their number—might be very important for some problems. Although we ignore this aspect of the problem, it could be included fairly easily. Note too that, in comparisons of the values of E_{it}, differences in length of the period might be important. Although we tried to obtain periods of equal length, this was not always feasible. However, when introduced into equations (3), (7), and (16), this factor has no significant effect on E_{it}, R_{it}, or P_{it}. See Section IV A.

MANSFIELD: THE GROWTH OF FIRMS

efficient size in the ith industry during the tth period and letting Π_{it} be the average ratio of the rate of return in the ith industry to that in all manufacturing during this period, we assume that

$$(1) \qquad E_{it} = f(\Pi_{it}, C_{it}, \cdots).$$

Increases in Π_{it}—because of their presumed effect on profit expectations—make entry more attractive, and increases in C_{it} make it more difficult. Thus, E_{it} should be directly related to Π_{it} and inversely related to C_{it}.[4]

More specifically, since the effects of these variables are likely to be multiplicative, we assume that

$$(2) \qquad E_{it} = \alpha_0 \Pi_{it}^{\alpha_1} C_{it}^{-\alpha_2} Z_{it},$$

where Z_{it} is a random error term and the α's are presumed to be positive. To estimate the α's, data are needed on E_{it}, Π_{it}, and C_{it}. Table 1 shows the values of E_{it} during various periods in the history of the steel, petroleum refining, rubber tire, and automobile industries. It also contains corresponding estimates of Π_{it} and C_{it}, the latter being based on Bain's figures [4] and the assumption that the ratio of the minimum efficient size to the average size of firm remained constant over time in each industry. Although these data are very rough they should be useful first approximations.[5]

Having only the transition matrices in the Appendix, we had no choice but to use E_{it}. So long as the survival rate for new firms is relatively independent of E_{it}' or positively correlated with it, E_{it} should be a reasonably good surrogate. Moreover, if one believes that we should only be concerned with entrants that survive for some specified length of time, E_{it} may be closer to what we want then E_{it}'. Finally, E_{it} has the advantage that it equals $D_{it}+R_{it}$. See Section I B.

[4] As a first approximation, it may not be too unreasonable to assume that the profit expectation of potential entrants during the period is a function of Π_{it}. But many other factors are obviously of importance—the variability of the industry's profits during the period, the absolute level of profits, the probability that new processes or related new products will be developed, the outlook with regard to factor prices, etc. Note too that C_{it} may vary, depending on whether the entrant is an existing firm in a related industry or an entirely new enterprise; that C_{it} should be measured in real terms; and that the effect of C_{it} will depend on the ease with which a given amount of capital can be obtained.

Equation (2) should be much more effective in explaining changes in the number of new firms with new plant than changes in the numbers of firms that are bought. For example, if Π_{it} is relatively high, relatively few firms may be sold. But, since new firms with new plant are a large percentage of the total number of entrants included in E_{it} (about two-thirds of the total in recent years, according to [7]), equation (2) is a reasonable first approximation. (However, one might argue from this that the error term is additive.) Unfortunately, the data are such that one cannot treat the entrants with new plant separately from those that bought existing plant.

[5] The Appendix describes the data on entry for each industry and explains how the data regarding C_{it} and Π_{it} were derived. It also points out the difficulties in these measures. I suspect that the true values of C_{it} (and $\tilde{S}_{it}/\bar{S}_{it}$) for petroleum in 1921-27 and 1927-37 were substantially lower than those shown in Table I and that the true values of C_{it} (and $\tilde{S}_{it}\backslash\bar{S}_{it}$) for steel in 1916-26 and 1926-35 were somewhat higher than those shown in Table I. Errors of this sort, assuming they are randomly distributed, are taken into account in the analysis below.

Taking logarithms of both sides of equation (2) and using these data to obtain least-squares estimates of the α's, we find that

(3) $\ln E_{it} = .49 + 1.15 \ln \Pi_{it} - .27 \ln C_{it}$

                        $(.43)$ $(.14)$

where the quantities in parentheses are standard errors and $\ln Z_{it}$ is omitted. As one would expect, there is considerable variation about equation (3), the coefficient of correlation (corrected for degrees of freedom) being about .70 (Figure 1). The residuals reflect the effects of dif-

TABLE 1—VALUES OF EXOGENOUS AND ENDOGENOUS VARIABLES IN EQUATIONS (3), (7), AND (16), STEEL, PETROLEUM, RUBBER TIRE, AND AUTOMOBILE INDUSTRIES, SELECTED PERIODS[a]

Industry and Time Period	E_{it}	Π_{it}	C_{it}	R_{it}	V_{it}^2	$\bar{S}_{it}/\hat{S}_{it}$	P_{it}	A_{it}	n_{it}
Steel:									
1916–26	.57	1.38	228	.20	18	1.15	.20	271	90
1926–35	.08	.38	214	.46	20	1.15	.17	281	122
1935–45	.20	.73	423	.16	12	1.15	.17	290	76
1945–54	.17	.77	465	.15	9	1.15	.26	300	81
Petroleum:									
1921–27	.66	.84	93	.59	11	.17	.36	62	314
1927–37	.46	.60	138	.65	13	.17	.42	68	335
1937–47	.78	.82	231	.42	15	.17	.35	78	269
1947–57	.25	1.01	238	.71	21	.17	.26	88	366
Tires:									
1937–45	.45	.84	11	.31	8	1.18	.30	41	49
1945–52	.68	.88	22	.46	10	1.18	.26	49	57
Autos:									
1939–49	.20	.94[b]	316	.20	3	1.00	—	—	—
1949–59	.10	.36[b]	575	.50	4	1.00	—	—	—

[a] Symbols: E_{it} is the number of firms that entered the ith industry during the tth period (and survived until the end of the period) as a proportion of the number in the industry at the beginning of the period; Π_{it} is the average ratio of the rate of return in the ith industry during the tth period to that in all manufacturing; C_{it} is the investment (in millions of dollars) required to establish a firm of minimum efficient size in the ith industry during the tth period; R_{it} is the proportion of the firms in the ith industry at the beginning of the tth period that left during the period; V_{it} is the coefficient of variation of the firm sizes in the ith industry at the beginning of the tth period; $\bar{S}_{it}/\hat{S}_{it}$ is the ratio of the average size of firm to the minimum efficient size of firm in the ith industry at the beginning of the tth period; P_{it} is the probability that a randomly drawn firm in the ith industry will be smaller at the end of the tth period than another firm drawn randomly from those 60–70 per cent of its size at the beginning of the tth period; A_{it} is the age of the ith industry (in years) at the beginning of the tth period; and n_{it} is the number of firms in the ith industry at the beginning of the tth period. For a discussion of some of the difficulties in these measures, see the Appendix and notes 3, 26 and 27.

[b] See the Appendix, paragraph 7, for some discussion of these figures.

Source: See the Appendix.

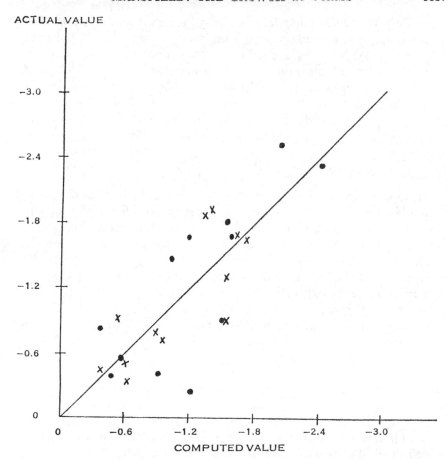

FIGURE 1. PLOT OF ACTUAL VALUES OF ln E_{it} AND ln R_{it} AGAINST THOSE COMPUTED FROM
EQUATIONS (3) AND (7), STEEL, PETROLEUM, RUBBER TIRE, AND
AUTOMOBILE INDUSTRIES, SELECTED PERIODS.[a]

[a] The dots represent ln E_{it} and the X's represent ln R_{it}. E_{it} is the number of firms that entered the ith industry during the tth period (and survived until the end of the period) as a proportion of the number in the industry at the beginning of the period. R_{it} is the proportion of the firms in the ith industry at the beginning of the tth period that left during the period.

Source: Table 1 and equations (3) and (7). The line is a 45° line through the origin.

ferences in the capacity of a firm of minimum efficient size as a per cent of the total market, availability of raw materials, and other important factors that are omitted.[6]

The estimates of α_1 and α_2 have the expected signs and are both statistically significant (.05 level). Because of the small number of ob-

[6] For an elementary account of some of the factors omitted here, see [24]. For a discussion of the automobile industry, see [31]. Of course, the influence of the Second World War (with controls of various sorts) should not be overlooked either.

servations, they have fairly large standard errors, and because of errors in the exogenous variables and the probable effects of ln E_{it} on ln Π_{it} (cf. Section IV A), they are probably biased somewhat toward zero. But despite these limitations, they shed new light on the effects of Π_{it} and C_{it} on E_{it}. For example, if the bias is in the expected direction, one can be reasonably sure that the average value of E_{it} would increase by at least 60 per cent if Π_{it} doubled and that it would decrease at least 7 per cent if C_{it} doubled. Lower bounds of this sort are obviously useful.[7]

B. *Exit Rates and Changes in the Number of Firms*

This subsection estimates the effects of several factors on the rate at which firms leave an industry, and it takes up the effects of these, and related, variables on the amount of entry defined in terms of changes in the number of firms—the first of the two concepts of entry defined at the beginning of this section. We use R_{it}—the proportion of firms in the ith industry at the beginning of the tth period that had left by the end— as a measure of the exit rate. Both firms that scrapped their plant and those that sold out are counted as departures.

Letting $R_{it}(S)$ be the proportion of firms of size S (at the beginning of the period) that left during the period, we assume that

$$(4) \qquad R_{it}(S) = g(S/\hat{S}_{it}, \Pi_{it}, \cdots),$$

where $\hat{S}_{it}$ is the minimum efficient size of firm at the beginning of the period. As a firm becomes smaller relative to the minimum efficient size, its chance of survival decreases; and as the industry becomes less profitable relative to others, firms become more likely to leave. Thus, $R_{it}(S)$ should be inversely related to both $S/\hat{S}_{it}$ and Π_{it}.[8]

Since their effects are likely to be multiplicative, we assume that

$$(5) \qquad R_{it}(S) = \nu_0 (S/\hat{S}_{it})^{-\gamma_1} \Pi_{it}^{-\gamma_2} Z'_{it}$$

[7] The tests described above are one-tailed tests—which are appropriate here. Our primary purpose is to estimate the effects of Π_{it} and C_{it} on E_{it}, rather than to see if they have any effect. They almost certainly do have an effect but research to date provides little or no clue regarding its magnitude.

For a discussion of the biases due to measurement errors and least-squares, see Section IV A and note 31 in particular. If there were no bias, the likelihood that the lower bounds in the test would be exceeded would equal .85. Given the probable bias, it should be much higher.

The percentage change in the average value of E_{it}, given a doubling of Π_{it}, is $2^{\alpha_1} - 1$. The effect of doubling C_{it} is given by substituting $-\alpha_2$ for α_1. Of course, one could get lower bounds for the effects of a 10, 20, $\cdots$ per cent change in Π_{it} and C_{it} in exactly the same way.

[8] Of course, the sale of a firm need not mean that it was a failure. Equation (4) is likely to represent the scrappage or abandonment rate better than the rate at which firms are sold. But the former is likely to be a large part of the total and hence equation (4) is likely to represent R_{it} fairly well. The data are such that firms which scrapped their plant cannot be separated from those that sold out. See the Appendix.

where Z'_{it} is a random error term and the ν's are presumed to be positive. Letting $\rho_{it}(S)$ be the probability that a firm in the ith industry at the beginning of the period is of size S and assuming that the distribution of firms by size is log-normal,[9] we have

$$(6) \quad R_{it} = \int_0^\infty R_{it}(S)\rho_{it}(S)dS = \nu_0 \left[\int_0^\infty (S/\hat{S}_{it})^{-\nu_1}\rho_{it}(S)dS \right] \Pi_{it}^{-\nu_2} Z'_{it},$$

$$R_{it} = \nu_0 [\overline{S}_{it}/\hat{S}_{it}]^{-\nu_1} (1 + V_{it}^2)^{\nu_1(\nu_1+1)/2} \Pi_{it}^{-\nu_2} Z'_{it}$$

where $\overline{S}_{it}$ is the mean and V_{it} is the coefficient of variation of the distribution of firm sizes.

Table 1 contains rough estimates of R_{it}, $\overline{S}_{it}/\hat{S}_{it}$, and V_i^2.[10] Taking logarithms of both sides of equation (6), we can use these data to obtain least-squares estimates of the ν's. The results are

$$(7) \quad \ln R_{it} = -1.68 - .41 \ln (\overline{S}_{it}/\hat{S}_{it}) + .10 \ln (1 + V_{it}^2) - .60 \ln \Pi_{it},$$
$$(.14) \qquad\qquad (.25) \qquad\qquad (.33)$$

where the quantities in parentheses are standard errors and $\ln Z'_{it}$ is omitted. For simplicity, the coefficient of $\ln (1+V_i^2)$ was not constrained to equal $\hat{\nu}_1 (\hat{\nu}_1+1)/2$—although this constraint would have resulted in somewhat better estimates of the ν's. Figure 1 shows that there is considerable variation about equation (7), the coefficient of correlation (corrected for degrees of freedom) being .70.[11]

The estimates of ν_1 and ν_2 have the correct signs and are statistically significant. Although they contain fairly large sampling errors and are probably biased somewhat toward zero (because of errors in the exogenous variables and the probable effects of $\ln R_{it}$ on $\ln \Pi_{it}$), they provide useful information regarding the effects of $\overline{S}_{it}/\hat{S}_{it}$ and Π_{it} on R_{it}. For example, if the bias is in the expected direction, one can be reasonably sure that the average value of R_{it} would decrease by at least 15 per cent

[9] The log-normal distribution seems to provide a reasonably good (but by no means perfect) fit to the distribution of firms by size. See [13]. Note that we assume only that it is a serviceable approximation from an empirical point of view. Some other distribution (e.g., the Yule distribution) may be more appropriate, but, if it can be approximated by a log-normal, this is good enough for present purposes. The Appendix gives the units in which a firm's size is measured.

[10] The sources and limitations of the data regarding R_{it}, $\overline{S}_{it}/\hat{S}_{it}$, and V_i^2 are discussed in the Appendix.

[11] The residuals reflect the effects of various important variables that are omitted—the extent to which the plants in the industry can be adapted for other uses, the adaptability and mobility of the management and the work force, the liquidity of the firms, the durability of their equipment, the rate at which costs rise when firms are less than minimum efficient size, etc.

if Π_{it} or $\overline{S}_{it}/\hat{S}_{it}$ doubled. Lower bounds of this sort can easily be computed for the effects of other percentage increases in Π_{it} or $\overline{S}_{it}/\hat{S}_{it}$.[12]

We are now in a position to consider the first, and probably for most purposes the more important, definition of entry. A reasonable measure in this case is D_{it}—the change in the number of firms during the period as a proportion of the number at the beginning. Since the number of firms bought during the period must equal the number sold,

$$(8) \qquad\qquad D_{it} = E_{it} - R_{it}.$$

Taking antilogs of both sides of equations (3) and (7), multiplying the resulting right-hand-side of each equation by $e^{\sigma^2/2}$ (where σ^2 is the variance of Z_{it} or Z'_{it}) to obtain an unbiased estimate of E_{it} or R_{it}, and inserting the results into equation (8), we can estimate the change in the number of firms, given that the values of Π_{it}, C_{it}, $\overline{S}_{it}/\hat{S}_{it}$, and V_{it}^2 are given.

Of course, such estimates are likely to be rough because of the crudeness of the estimates of the α's and ν's and the likelihood that there will be considerable variation about the expected value of D_{it}. (In the 12 cases for which we have data, the correlation between the actual and computed values of D_{it} is .60.) Nonetheless, they may be of use as first approximations in estimating D_{it} and in estimating the effects of changes in Π_{it}, C_{it}, $\overline{S}_{it}/\hat{S}_{it}$ and V_{it}^2 on the average value of D_{it}.

Two further points should be noted. First, it would be preferable to combine equations (2) and (6), obtain D_{it} as a function of Π_{it}, C_{it}, etc., and estimate the α's and ν's all at once. But the difference between equations (2) and (6) is awkward to work with. [Perhaps future work will show that some other form of equations (2) and (6) that is more convenient in this respect will fit as well.] Second, the empirical results in this section, like those in Section III, pertain to periods of 7–10 years. They should not be applied to periods much longer or shorter than this.

II. *The Process of Firm Growth*

A. *Gibrat's Law and the Growth of Firms*

Gibrat's law is a proposition regarding the process of firm growth. According to this law, the probability of a given proportionate change in

---

[12] The procedure used to obtain these figures is just like that described in note 7. Again, our primary purpose is to estimate the effects of the exogenous variables, not to test whether they have any effect. Almost certainly, they have some effect on R_{it}.

This model also suggests a technique for estimating the minimum efficient size of firm in an industry. Suppose that $\hat{S}_{it}$, rather than R_{it}, were regarded as the "dependent" variable. If data regarding R_{it}, $\overline{S}_{it}$, Π_{it} and V_{it}^2 were obtained for some new industry or time period, they could then be used to estimate $\hat{S}_{it}$. This technique is likely to be rough, but some work might be carried out to see how accurate it is and to sharpen it. Of course, this presumes that the size during a specified period is the same for all firms in a given industry—regardless of their size at the beginning of the period. For example, a firm with sales of $100 million is as likely to double in size during a given period as a firm with sales of $100 thousand. Put differently, Gibrat's law states that:

$$(9) \qquad\qquad S_{ij}^{t+\Delta} = U_{ij}(t, \Delta)S_{ij}^{t},$$

where S_{ij}^{t} is the size of the jth firm in the ith industry at time t, $S_{ij}^{t+\Delta}$ is its size at time $t+\Delta$, and $U_{ij}(t, \Delta)$ is a random variable distributed independently of S_{ij}^{t}.

Since this law is a basic ingredient in many mathematical models designed to explain the shape of the size distribution of firms and since this law has interesting implications regarding the determinants of the amount of concentration in an industry, some importance attaches to whether or not it holds. This section provides tests based on data for practically all firms—large and small—in three individual industries: the steel, petroleum, and rubber tire industries. The automobile industry is omitted because, with only a handful of firms, it is unlikely to provide much evidence regarding a proposition of this sort.[13]

A simple way to test Gibrat's law is to classify firms by their initial size (S_{ij}^{t}), compute the frequency distribution of $S_{ij}^{t+\Delta}/S_{ij}^{t}$ within each of these classes, and use a χ^2 test to determine whether the frequency distributions are the same in each class. We rely heavily on this test, but supplement it with others. The basic data used in these tests are described and presented in the Appendix.

Gibrat's law can be formulated in at least three ways, depending on the treatment of the death of firms and the comprehensiveness claimed for the law. First, one can postulate that it holds for all firms—including those that leave the industry during the period. If we regard the size (at the end of the period) of each of these departing firms as zero (or approximately zero), this version can easily be tested. The results—shown in Table 2—indicate that it generally fails to hold. In seven of the ten cases, the observed value of χ^2 exceeds the critical limit corresponding to the .05 significance level.[14]

Why does this version of the law fail to hold? Even a quick inspection of the transition matrices in the Appendix shows one principal reason. The probability that a firm will die is certainly not independent of its

---

long-run average cost curve is J-shaped and consequently that a minimum efficient size of firm exists in the new industry. For another technique that is somewhat similar in spirit, see Stigler [29].

[13] For a discussion of the use of Gibrat's law in explaining the size distribution of firms, see [12] [13] [27]. For previous tests, see also [11] [15]. In connection with [27], see note 17.

[14] The size classes and the cut-off points for $S_{ij}^{t+\Delta}/S_{ij}^{t}$ used in these tests are described in the Appendix.

TABLE 2—OBSERVED VALUE OF χ^2 CRITERION, ESTIMATED SLOPE OF REGRESSION OF ln $S_{ij}^{t+\Delta}$
ON ln S_{ij}^t, AND RATIO OF VARIANCES OF GROWTH RATES OF LARGE AND SMALL FIRMS,
STEEL, PETROLEUM, AND RUBBER TIRE INDUSTRIES, SELECTED PERIODS.[a]

Item	Steel				Petroleum				Tires	
	1916–1926	1926–1935	1935–1945	1945–1954	1921–1927	1927–1937	1937–1947	1947–1957	1937–1945	1945–1952
χ^2 criterion:										
Including deaths	9.0	17.0[b]	22.5[b]	7.8	29.2[b]	44.9[b]	25.6[b]	42.7[b]	9.3	22.9[b]
Excluding deaths	7.1	3.3	9.5[b]	3.4	2.8	22.1[b]	17.7[b]	8.9	6.3	6.6[b]
Degrees of freedom (χ^2 tests):										
Including deaths	6	6	6	6	6	6	6	6	6	4
Excluding deaths	4	4	4	4	4	4	4	4	4	2
Estimated slope:[c]										
Excluding deaths	.88[b]	.99	.92[b]	1.00	.94	.88[b]	.99	.94	.97	.97
Large firms only	.94	.96	1.00	.98	.99	.98	.93	1.10	1.07	.89
Standard error of slope:										
Excluding deaths	.05	.04	.03	.04	.05	.04	.03	.04	.05	.04
Large firms only	.16	.16	.07	.06	.24	.14	.07	.07	.10	.05
Number of firms:										
Excluding deaths	72	66	64	69	128	116	156	106	34	31
Large firms only	7	9	11	12	7	11	16	17	11	12
Ratio of variances of growth rates of large and small firms:[d]										
Excluding deaths	8.96[b]	.80	37.40[b]	5.06[b]	43.27[b]	19.25[b]	63.56[b]	147.1[b]	16.16[b]	.31
Large firms only	.63	161.00[b]	.90	8.50[b]	3.50	7.75[b]	4.00[b]	3.6[b]	39.25[b]	8.67

[a] Symbols: S_{ij}^t is the size of the jth firm in the ith industry at time t, and $S_{ij}^{t+\Delta}$ is its size at time $t+\Delta$. For the classification of firms by size and the classification of $S_{ij}^{t+\Delta}/S_{ij}^t$ used in each industry in the χ^2 tests, see the Appendix. The number of degrees of freedom equals $(a-1)(b-1)$ where a is the number of size classes and b is the number of classes of $S_{ij}^{t+\Delta}/S_{ij}^t$ in the contingency table.

[b] For χ^2 criteria and ratios of variances, this means that the probability is less than .05 that a value would be this large (or larger) if Gibrat's law held. For estimated slopes, this means that they differ significantly from unity (.05 significance level).

[c] The number of firms in each regression is shown under "Number of firms."

[d] The firms regarded as "small" and "large" in the first row are as follows: In steel, small firms have 4,000–16,000 and large firms have 256,000–4,096,000 tons of capacity. In petroleum, small firms have 500–999 and large firms have 32,000–511,999 barrels of capacity. In tires, small firms have 80–159 and large firms have 640–5,119 employees. The firms regarded as "small" and "large" in the second row are described in note 18.

Source: See the Appendix.

size. In every industry and time interval, the smaller firms were more likely than the larger ones to leave the industry. For this reason (and others indicated below), this version of the law seems to be incorrect.[15]

Second, one can postulate that the law holds for all firms other than those that leave the industry. Hart and Prais [13] seem to adopt this version. Omitting such firms, we ran another series of χ^2 tests, the results of which are shown in Table 2. In four of the ten cases, the evidence seems to contradict the hypothesis, the observed value of χ^2 exceeding the limit corresponding to the .05 significance level.

To see why this version must be rejected, note that equation (9) implies that

(10) $\ln S_{ij}^{t+\Delta} = V_i(t, \Delta) + \ln S_{ij}^t + W_{ij}(t, \Delta)$,

[15] The way mergers are handled here (see the Appendix) may help to produce an inverse relationship between a firm's size and its probability of death. But this alone cannot account for this result. Such a relationship has often been noted before. E.g., see [1] [23].

where $V_i(t, \Delta)$ is the mean of ln $U_{ij}(t, \Delta)$ and $W_{ij}(t, \Delta)$ is a homoscedastic random variable with zero mean. Thus, if ln $S_{ij}^{t+\Delta}$ is plotted against ln S_{ij}^t, the data should be scattered with constant variance about a line with slope of one. Table 2 contains the least-squares estimate of the slope of each of these lines. In half of the cases where the law was rejected the slope is significantly less than one.

In addition, the variance of $S_{ij}^{t+\Delta}/S_{ij}^t$ tends to be inversely related to S_{ij}^t. Taking in each case a group of small firms and dividing the variance of their values of $S_{ij}^{t+\Delta}/S_{ij}^t$ by the variance among a group of large firms, we obtain the results shown in Table 2. In eight of the ten cases the variances differed significantly. Thus, contrary to this version of the law smaller firms often tend to have higher and more variable growth rates than larger firms.[16]

Third, one can postulate that the law holds only for firms exceeding the minimum efficient size in the industry—the size (assuming the long-run average cost curve is J-shaped) below which unit costs rise sharply and above which they vary only slightly. This is the version put forth by Simon and Bonini [27], although it seems to be a stronger assumption than they require.[17] One is faced once again with the problem of whether or not to include firms that die. We excluded them, but the major results would almost certainly have been the same if they had been included.

This version was tested in two ways. First, we estimated the slope of the regression of ln $S_{ij}^{t+\Delta}$ on ln S_{ij}^t, but included only those firms that were larger than Bain's [4] estimate of the minimum efficient size. The results are quite consistent with Gibrat's law (the slopes never differing significantly from one). Second, we used F tests to determine whether the variance of $S_{ij}^{t+\Delta}/S_{ij}^t$ was constant among these firms. Contrary to

---

[16] These results differ in part from those of [13] [27] [11] [15]. The latter conclude that there was no tendency for the smaller firms to grow more rapidly than the large ones. But this was due to the fact that they included only very large firms. With regard to the larger variation in growth rates among smaller firms, our findings agree with those in [11] [15], but differ from those in [27]. There is no treatment of this in [13].

All firms that survived during the period are included in these regressions. Note that all crude capacity—domestic and foreign—is included for each firm in the petroleum industry. The data on foreign capacity had to be obtained from the individual firms.

In one case in steel, the slope is significantly less than one but this does not show up in the χ^2 test—largely because of the incomplete coverage in the latter. See the Appendix. One-tailed F tests are used to determine whether the variances differ. In several cases, the variances differ significantly, but it does not show up in the χ^2 tests.

[17] Herbert Simon informs me that the version of Gibrat's law they used in [27] is not required to obtain the Yule distribution and that their proof will hold if the expected value of $S_{ij}^{t+\Delta}/S_{ij}^t$ does not vary with S_{ij}^t regardless of whether or not the variance of $S_{ij}^{t+\Delta}/S_{ij}^t$ depends on S_{ij}^t. Our results do not contradict these weaker assumptions for firms above the minimum efficient size and consequently they do not contradict their findings based on them. But they do contradict the version of Gibrat's law in [27].

Gibrat's law, the variance of $S_{ij}^{t+\Delta}/S_{ij}^{t}$ tends to be inversely related to S_{ij}^{t} in six of the ten cases.[18]

Thus, regardless of which version one chooses, Gibrat's law fails to. hold in more than one-half of these cases. What sort of mechanism produced the observed departures from this law? The reasons for the inverse relationships between a firm's chance of death and its initial size seem fairly obvious, but why should the data for the survivors show that the smaller firms tend to have higher and more variable growth rates than the larger ones?[19]

One very simple model that might help to account for this is as follows. Consider the distribution of growth rates of firms of size S_{ij}^{t} that would have resulted if none had left the industry. It is not unreasonable to suppose that above some minimum value of S_{ij}^{t} the average of this distribution would have been about the same in each size class and that it would have exceeded the average growth rate that would have been experienced by firms that left the industry. For simplicity, we assume that the difference between these averages was the same in each size class. Moreover, because each large firm can be viewed as a collection of somewhat independent smaller firms, the variance of this distribution would be expected to be inversely related to S_{ij}^{t}.[20]

Then, under the fairly reasonable assumption that the actual growth rate of each survivor is proportional to what it would have been if all

---

[18] The χ^2 tests had to be abandoned here because of the small number of firms. Firms with more than 64,000 barrels of capacity (petroleum), 1,000,000 net tons of capacity (steel), or .8 per cent of total employment (tires) were included in the regression. The number included in each case is shown in Table 2. The fact that none of the slopes differs significantly from one indicates that there is no evidence that among these firms the average growth rate depended on a firm's initial size.

In the variance ratio tests we divided these firms into two size (S_{ij}^{t}) groups, the dividing line being 150,000 barrels of capacity (petroleum), 3,000,000 tons of capacity (steel), and 30,000 employment (tires). Then F tests were used to determine whether the variances of $S_{ij}^{t+\Delta}/S_{ij}^{t}$ differed. This test is not too robust with regard to departures from normality, but it should perform reasonably well here.

Note that in petroleum and tires we include firms that are more than one-half of the minimum efficient sizes given in the Appendix. According to Bain [4], the cost curve is quite flat back to one-half of those sizes. Thus, it seemed acceptable to include the additional firms and to increase the power of the tests in this way.

[19] Note that the inverse relationship between S_{ij}^{t} and the average growth rate shows up only when all firms are included. There is no evidence of this among firms exceeding the minimum efficient size. (The inverse relationship between S_{ij}^{t} and the variability of growth rates shows up in both cases.)

[20] The growth rate of a large firm can be viewed as the mean of the growth rates of its smaller "components" (e.g. plants). This point has also been made in [15]. Note that, if the growth rates of the components (plants or otherwise) were independent, the standard deviation would be inversely proportional to the square-root of a firm's size. But, since they tend to be located in the same region and have other similarities, one would expect the growth rate of such components to be positively correlated. Thus, the standard deviation would not be expected to decrease as rapidly with increases in size as the square-root formula suggests. In fact, this expectation turns out to be true.

firms had survived, one can show that

$$\sigma_S^2(S) = \mu^2 \left\{ \sigma_t^2(S) - \frac{P(S)K^2}{[1 - P(S)]^2} \right\},$$

where $\sigma_S^2(S)$ is the variance of the growth rates of the survivors (originally of sizes $S_{ij}{}^t$), $\sigma_t^2(S)$ is the variance of the growth rates of all firms (originally of size $S_{ij}{}^t$) that would have resulted if all had survived, K is the difference between the average growth rate of all firms (if none had left) and the average growth rate that would have been experienced by those leaving the industry, $P(S)$ is the probability of death for firms initially of size $S_{ij}{}^t$ and μ is the ratio of a survivor's actual growth rate to what it would have been if all had survived. (This assumes that if they had not left, the firms originally of size $S_{ij}{}^t$ that left the industry would have had growth rates with a variance of $\sigma_t^2(S)$.)

In addition, one can show that the average growth rate of the survivors originally of size $S_{ij}{}^t$ equals

$$\overline{S}(S) = \mu \left\{ \bar{\imath} + \frac{P(S)K}{1 - P(S)} \right\},$$

where $\bar{\imath}$ is the average growth rate for all firms of size $S_{ij}{}^t$ if none had left the industry. Note that we, in the same spirit as [27], are stipulating only that $\bar{\imath}$ will be constant above some minimum size.

Thus, if $\sigma_t^2(S)$ is inversely related to $S_{ij}{}^t$ (for the reason discussed in note 20) and if $P(S)$ is inversely related to S (which certainly is true), it follows that $\sigma_S^2(S)$ will be inversely related to $S_{ij}{}^t$ so long as $P(S) > 1/3$ or $d\sigma_t^2(S)/dS_{ij}{}^t$ is large in absolute terms relative to $dP(S)/dS_{ij}{}^t$. Moreover, it follows that $\overline{S}(S)$ will be inversely related to $S_{ij}{}^t$.

Thus, if this highly simplified model should be at all reliable, one would often expect to observe departures from Gibrat's law of the sort found in Table 2. Research should be carried out to develop and study more sophisticated models of the growth process. Although Gibrat's law is very convenient from an analytical point of view, it does not seem to hold up very well empirically. It seems to be a rather unreliable base on which to rest theories of the size distribution of firms.

B. *Successful Innovation and the Growth of Firms*

How much of an impact does a successful innovation have on a firm's growth rate? In another study [17], I presented a list of the firms that were first to introduce the significant new processes and products that emerged since the First World War in the steel and petroleum refining industries. (See the Appendix for a brief description of this list.) A comparison of their growth rates—during the period in which the innovation occurred—with those of other comparable firms should help to indicate how great the pay-off is (in terms of growth) for a successful innovation.

For each period for which we have data, Table 3 estimates the average annual growth rate of (1) firms that carried out significant innovations during the period, and (2) other firms that were equal in size to the successful innovators at the beginning of the period. There is a marked difference between the two groups. In every time interval and in both industries, the successful innovators grew more rapidly than the others; and in some cases, their average rate of growth was more than twice that of the others.[21]

Taking each innovator separately, the difference between its growth rate and the average growth rate of other comparable firms seems to have been inversely related to its size. As one would expect, a successful innovation had a much greater impact on a small firm's growth rate than on a large firm's. The fact that fewer of the successful innovators in more recent periods were small firms probably accounts in part for the decrease over time in the average difference (in Table 3) between the two groups.[22]

Each growth rate in Table 3 pertains to the entire period indicated in the caption—whereas the innovations occurred sometime within the period. Consider the period from time t to time $t+\Delta$. Suppose that the jth successful innovator in this period introduced its innovation at time t_j, that its average annual growth rate from time t to time t_j exceeded that of other comparable firms by e_j, and that its average annual growth rate from time t_j to time $t+\Delta$ exceeded that of other comparable firms by e_j+d_j. What were the average values of e_j and d_j? If the innovators grew more rapidly than other firms because of certain characteristics associated with the innovation, but not because of the innovation itself, and if these characteristics had approximately the same effect throughout the period, the average value of d_j would be expected to be zero.

[21] Note: (1) We are not comparing innovators with noninnovators, since some of the "other firms" may have been unsuccessful innovators. Because we can only include successful innovators (the data being what they are), it is not surprising that they have higher growth rates, and we are much more interested in the size of the difference than in its existence. (2) Some of the innovators introduced more than one innovation during the period. Thus, the difference in growth rates is not due entirely to a single innovation. But in the subsequent analysis (involving $\bar{d}$) only cases involving a single innovation are included. (3) It would be interesting to see how an innovation's effects depended on its character, but we have too little data to attempt this. (4) The way in which the average annual growth rate of the "other firms" in Table 3 was computed is described in the Appendix.

[22] If the innovators in steel are divided into two groups—those above 1,000,000 tons and those less than (or equal to) 1,000,000 tons at the beginning of the period—the average difference between their growth rates and the growth rates of other comparable firms differs considerably between the groups. Among the larger firms, the average difference is generally about .5 points whereas it is 3–10 points among the smaller ones. Similarly, if the innovators in petroleum are divided into two groups—those above 32,000 barrels and those less than (or equal to) 32,000 barrels at the beginning of the period—the average difference is practically zero among the larger firms but 6–24 points among the smaller ones.

MANSFIELD: THE GROWTH OF FIRMS 1037

TABLE 3—AVERAGE ANNUAL GROWTH RATES OF SUCCESSFUL INNOVATORS AND OTHER FIRMS
(OF COMPARABLE INITIAL SIZE), COMPUTED VALUES OF $\bar{e}$ AND $\bar{d}$, AND REGRESSIONS
(EXCLUDING INNOVATORS) OF $\ln S_{ij}{}^{t+\Delta}$ ON $\ln S_{ij}{}^{t}$, STEEL AND
PETROLEUM REFINING INDUSTRIES, SELECTED PERIODS.[a]

Item	Steel				Petroleum			
	1916–1926	1926–1935	1935–1945	1945–1954	1921–1927	1927–1937	1937–1947	1947–1957
Average annual growth rate (per cent):								
Innovators	13.7	6.5	3.4	3.2	13.1	7.9	3.6	6.7
Other Firms	3.7	3.3	2.0	2.4	6.6	4.1	3.6	4.2
Computed value of:[b]								
$\bar{e}$ (per cent)	—	0.7	0.7	—	—	4.2	−2.5	−2.8
$\bar{d}$ (per cent)	—	3.9	5.2	—	—	5.7	3.6	13.4
Regression (excluding innovators) of $\ln S_{ij}{}^{t+\Delta}$ on $\ln S_{ij}{}^{t}$:								
Intercept (a_i)	1.68	.55	1.34	.18	1.10	1.68	.41	1.27
Slope (b_i)	.88	.97	.90	1.01	.93	.84	.98	.90

[a] Symbols: $S_{ij}{}^{t}$ is the size of the jth firm in the ith industry at time t; $S_{ij}{}^{t+\Delta}$ is its size at time $t+\Delta$; $\bar{e}$ is the average value of e_j, where e_j is the difference between the average annual growth rate of the jth innovator during the period from time t to time t_j and that of "other firms" of equivalent size (at time t) during the same period; and $\bar{d}$ is the average value of d_j, where $e_j + d_j$ is the difference between the average annual growth rate of the jth innovator during the period from time t_j to time $t+\Delta$ and that of "other firms" of equivalent size (at time t) during the same period. See the Appendix for the way in which the regressions described here are used to estimate the figures in the second row of this table.

[b] No figures are computed in cases where there were only a few innovators. See note 23 and the Appendix for a discussion of the derivation of these figures.

Source: See the Appendix and Mansfield [17].

Letting $S_j^{t+\Delta}$ be the size (i.e., capacity) at time $t+\Delta$ of the jth innovator and $Q_j^{t+\Delta}$ be the average logarithm of the sizes at time $t+\Delta$ of the other firms that were equal in size to the jth innovator at time t, one can show that

(11) $$(\ln S_j^{t+\Delta} - Q_j^{t+\Delta})/\Delta = e_j + [1 - (t_j - t)/\Delta]d_j.$$

To see this, consider the kth "other firm" of the same size as the jth innovator at time t. If r_{1k} is its average rate of growth between time t and time $t+j$, r_{2k} is its average rate of growth between time t_j and time $t+\Delta$, and $S_{jk}^{t+\Delta}$ is its size at time $t+\Delta$,

$$\ln S_{jk}^{t+\Delta} = \ln S_j^{t} + r_{1k}(t_j - t) + r_{2k}(t + \Delta - t_j).$$

Thus, if r_1 is the average value of r_{1k} and r_2 is the average value of r_{2k},

$$Q_j^{t+\Delta} = \ln S_j^t + r_1(t_j - t) + r_2(t + \Delta - t_j).$$

But by the definitions of e_j and d_j,

$$\ln S_j^{t+\Delta} = \ln S_j^t + (r_1 + e_j)(t_j - t) + (r_2 + e_j + d_j)(t + \Delta - t_j).$$

Thus,

$$\ln S_j^{t+\Delta} - Q_j^{t+\Delta} = e_j\Delta + d_j(t + \Delta - t_j),$$

and equation (11) follows.

Letting $\bar{e}$ and $\bar{d}$ be the average values of e_j and d_j and assuming that $(e_j - \bar{e})$ and $(d_j - \bar{d})$ are statistically independent of $(t_j - t)/\Delta$, we have

(12) $(\ln S_j^{t+\Delta} - Q_j^{t+\Delta})/\Delta = \bar{e} + [1 - (t_j - t)/\Delta]\bar{d} + W_j,$

where W_j can be treated as a random error term. Using equation (12) we can apply least-squares to obtain $\bar{e}$ and $\bar{d}$.[23]

The results (in Table 3) indicate that $\bar{d}$ was always positive, but that the sign of $\bar{e}$ varied. This means two things. First, in the period immediately before they introduced the innovations, there was no persistent tendency for the successful innovators to grow more rapidly than other comparable firms. In some cases they grew more rapidly, but in others they did not. Thus, their higher growth rate cannot be attributed to their preinnovation behavior. Second, in the period after they introduced the innovations their mean growth rate consistently exceeded that of other comparable firms by more than it had before their introduction—which is what one would expect.

If one makes the crude assumption that the pre-innovation difference in average growth rate between successful innovators and other firms would have been maintained from time t to time $t+\Delta$ if the innovations had not been introduced, $\bar{d}$ measures the average effect of these successful innovations on a firm's growth rate during the relevant period. Based on this assumption, their average effect was to raise a firm's growth rate by 4–13 percentage points, depending on the particular time interval and industry. In view of the widespread interest in measures of the pay-

[23] To estimate $Q_j^{t+\Delta}$, we use the procedure described in the Appendix. In computing $\bar{e}$ and $\bar{d}$, innovators that introduced more than one innovation had to be excluded (except in a few cases where the innovations were all introduced at the same time). These relatively few omissions are ignored, and we act as if we had the entire population of innovators in the analysis.

Of course, the assumption that $(e_j - \bar{e})$ and $(d_j - \bar{d})$ are statistically independent of $(t_j - t)/\Delta$ is rather bold. Some bias may result if d_j is higher immediately after the introduction of an innovation. If so $(d_j - \bar{d})$ and $1 - (t_j - t)/\Delta$ may be negatively correlated, and we would probably overestimate $\bar{e}$ and underestimate $\bar{d}$.

Where there were only a few innovators, this assumption (and the one in the previous paragraph) seemed particularly risky and we did not compute values of $\bar{e}$ and $\bar{d}$. But some preliminary work suggested that, had we done so, the results would have been much the same.

off from successful innovation, these estimates, despite their crudeness, should be useful. Of course, estimates of the effects of successful innovation on a firm's profits would be even more useful, but they lie outside the scope of this paper.[24]

III. *Mobility within an Industry's Size Structure*

In recent years, economists have become quite interested in the amount of mobility in an industry—i.e., the extent to which firms change their relative positions in the size distribution. The importance of this characteristic of an industry has been pointed out by Adelman [1], Hart and Prais [13], Simon and Bonini [27], and others [22] [28]. This section measures the amount of mobility in several industries and constructs a simple model to help explain its observed variation. The results shed additional light on the process of firm growth, since the amount of mobility is obviously related to the amount of interfirm variation in growth rates.[25]

To measure the amount of mobility in the ith industry during the tth period, suppose that we have a list of all firms that were in existence at both the beginning and end of the period. Suppose that a firm is chosen at random from this list. Then suppose that another firm is chosen at random from those that were 60–70 per cent as large as the first firm at the beginning of the period. The probability that the second (initially smaller) firm will be bigger than the first (initially larger) firm at the end of the period is a rough measure of the amount of mobility. Let this probability be P_{it}.[26]

[21] Note that the successful innovators tend to be the large spenders on research. (For evidence on this score and discussions of the imitation process, see [16] [18] [19] [20].)

If we had complete, year-by-year data on each firm's size, we could compute $\bar{e}$ and $\bar{d}$ without making the assumption discussed in note 23. The differences in growth rates shown in Table 3 are averages over periods of 1–10 years after an innovation was introduced. Obviously, the effects of an innovation decrease as time goes on.

Finally, for the reason cited in note 23, the estimates of $\bar{d}$ may be biased downward. On the other hand, in the petroleum industry in 1947–57, $\bar{d}$ may be unduly affected by one firm and is probably too high. Note, too, that the observed differences in growth rate may still be due in part to other factors that are associated with a firm's willingness to innovate and the timing of the innovation.

[25] If Gibrat's law held and if $W_{ij}(t, \Delta)$ were normally distributed, the amount of mobility would be solely a function of the latter's variance. For this reason, its variance has sometimes been suggested as a measure of the amount of mobility. But, since Gibrat's law generally does not hold and then normal distribution is only an approximation, the measure discussed below seems preferable.

[26] The choice of 60–70 per cent is arbitrary. We could have experimented with alternative ranges, but the amount of clerical work involved would have been prohibitive. Note that this measure is based on all firms; if one were interested in the amount of mobility among the larger firms only, the measure could easily be modified to that end.

This measure is based solely on firms that survived until the end of the period. If we included all firms—regardless of whether or not they survived—the results would depend heavily on the death rate. Because the latter was already taken up in Section I, it seemed preferable to use

Table 1 contains estimates of P_{it} for various periods in the history of the steel, petroleum refining, and rubber tire industries. Because of the small number of firms, it was impossible to obtain meaningful estimates for the automobile industry. To help explain the considerable variation in P_{it}, we assume that

(13) $$P_{it}(S) = h(S/(n_{it}\bar{S}_{it}), A_{it}, S_{it}^*/\tilde{S}_{it}, n_{it}, \cdots),$$

where $P_{it}(S)$ is the probability that a firm of size S at the beginning of the period will be smaller at the end of the period than a firm originally of size $.6S-.7S$, n_{it} is the number of firms in the industry at the beginning of the period, $\bar{S}_{it}$ is their mean size, $\tilde{S}_{it}$ is their median size, S_{it}^* is the size of firm such that firms exceeding it accounted for one-half of the market, and A_{it} is the age of the industry.

What are the effects of these variables? First, the smaller firm's chance of overtaking the larger one will be inversely related to the initial difference between their market shares—which is proportional to $S/(n_{it}\bar{S}_{it})$. Second, as an industry grows older, stronger ties are established between firms and their customers, the technology becomes more settled, and the industry's structure tends to become more rigid. Thus, A_{it}—which is a proxy variable for these factors—is likely to be important.[27] Third, $P_{it}(S)$ is likely to be inversely related to the amount of concentration in the industry. Thus, n_{it} and $S_{it}^*/\tilde{S}_{it}$ (a convenient measure of the amount of inequality among firm sizes) are included.[28]

---

this measure. If one is interested in results that include deaths, it is relatively easy to combine the findings in this Section with those in Section I.

Let $P_{it}'(S)$ be the probability that a firm initially of size S will be smaller at the end of the period than—or as small as—a firm that initially was 60–70 per cent of its size. If a firm dies, let its size be zero. Then

$$P_{it}'(S) = R_{it}(S) + [1 - R_{it}(S)][1 - R_{it}(S')]P_{it}(S),$$

where $R_{it}(S')$ is the probability that a firm of initial size, $.6S-.7S$, will die during the period. Since Section I B takes up $R_{it}(S)$—and $R_{it}(S')$—and this section analyzes $P_{it}(S)$, together they provide information regarding $P_{it}'(S)$.

[27] The age of an industry is a somewhat slippery concept. In 1896, Goodyear made the first U.S. tires for commercial vehicles. In 1859, oil production began in the United States. The production of iron began here in 1645. Using these years as estimates of the dates of birth of the industries, A_{it} was derived by subtracting them from the initial year of the tth period. Although the results seem reasonable, their crudeness should be obvious.

[28] Since we assume that the distribution of firms by size is log-normal, the obvious measure of their inequality is the variance of the logarithms of the firm sizes. It can be shown that the latter is equal to ln $(S_{it}^*/\tilde{S}_{it})$. Thus, our measure—which is convenient because it allows some terms in equation (15) to be collected—is a monotonic increasing function of the variance.

The chief reason for using a measure of inequality of firm sizes plus the number of firms as a measure of concentration is convenience. For some disadvantages in the use of such measures, see [2]. For some evidence that increases in concentration are associated with decreases in mobility, see [15]. Of course, one would expect this variable to be important because where markets are highly concentrated it is more likely that discipline can and will be maintained to see to it that firms remain in about the same relative positions. E.g., there may be explicit or tacit agreements to share markets, each firm maintaining a certain per cent of the total.

Since the effects of these variables are likely to be multiplicative, we assume that

(14) $$P_{it}(S) = \beta_0[S/(n_{it}\bar{S}_{it})]^{-\beta_1} A_{it}^{-\beta_2}(S_{it}^*/\tilde{S}_{it})^{-\beta_3} n_{it}^{\beta_4} Z_{it}''$$

where Z_{it}'' is a random error term and the β's are presumed to be positive. Assuming again that the distribution of firms by size is log-normal, we have:

$$P_{it} = \int_0^\infty P_{it}(S)\rho_{it}(S)dS$$

$$= \beta_0 \left[\int_0^\infty S^{-\beta_1}\rho_{it}(S)dS \right] \bar{S}_{it}^{\beta_1} A_{it}^{-\beta_2} (S_{it}^*/\tilde{S}_{it})^{-\beta_3} n_{it}^{\beta_4+\beta_1} Z_{it}''$$

(15) $$P_{it} = \beta_0(1 + V_{it}^2)^{\beta_1(1+\beta_1)/2-\beta_3} A_{it}^{-\beta_2} n_{it}^{\beta_4+\beta_1} Z_{it}''.$$

To see how well this model can represent the data, we take logarithms of both sides of equation (15), and using the data in Table 1, we obtain least-squares estimates of the coefficients. The results are:

(16) $$\ln P_{it} = -.55 - .57 \ln (1 + V_{it}^2) - .15 \ln A_{it} + .29 \ln n_{it},$$
$$\qquad\qquad\quad (.20) \qquad\qquad\quad (.07) \qquad\quad (.08)$$

where the quantities in parentheses are standard errors and $\ln Z_{it}''$ is omitted. Figure 2 shows that equation (16) can explain much of the variation in $\ln P_{it}$, the coefficient of correlation (corrected for degrees of freedom) being about .90. All of the regression coefficients have the expected signs and are statistically significant at the .05 level. Thus, what evidence we have seems to be quite consistent with the model. Indeed, it fits the data surprisingly well.[29]

IV. Concluding Remarks

A. Limitations

Some of the limitations of this study are the following: First, the empirical results in Sections I and III are based on relatively few ob-

---

[29] The expression in equation (15) is not a very obvious one. E.g., it is not obvious (at least to me) that $\ln P_{it}$ should be a linear function of $\ln (1+V_{it}^2)$. Consequently, it is all the more satisfying that this function turns out to be such a good representation of the data.

There is some evidence that the variability of firm growth rates increases with the industry's over-all rate of growth [15]. Of course, A_{it} and the industry's growth rate are liable to be related in general. But in the cases used here, there is no correlation between the two variables. Consequently, the observed effects of A_{it} are not mere reflections of the effects of the industry's growth rate.

Another factor that may be important is the extent to which the smaller firms tend to be the innovators. In addition, Hart and Prais [13] provide some evidence that there is more mobility during depressions, but this may be due to the differences among industries in the extent to which sales fall during a recession. Our data—which do not lump all industries together—do not show any obvious signs of such a tendency.

In deriving equation (15), we presume that $P_{it}(S)$ exists for all S. But in some cases there are no firms 60-70 per cent as large as another firm. Thus, strictly speaking, we should use the size distribution of firms where it exists.

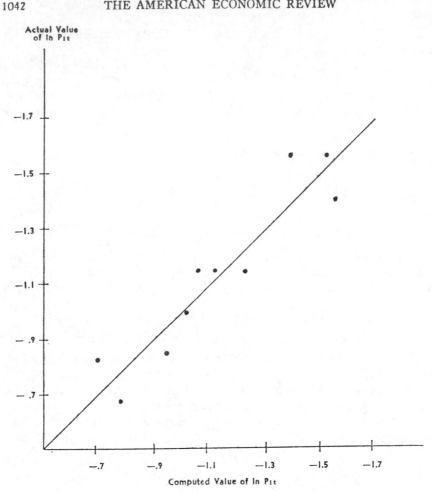

FIGURE 2. PLOT OF ACTUAL VALUES OF P_{it} AGAINST THOSE COMPUTED FROM EQUATION
(16), STEEL, PETROLEUM, AND RUBBER TIRE INDUSTRIES, SELECTED PERIODS.

Source: Table 1 and equation (16). P_{it} is the probability that a randomly drawn firm in the
ith industry will be smaller at the end of the tth period than another firm drawn randomly from
those 60–70 per cent of its size at the beginning of the tth period.

servations. Considerable work was required to obtain even this small
number because each observation is based on a large amount of relatively inaccessible data. But regardless of the reasons, the small number
of industries and time periods results in fairly substantial sampling
errors and obvious dangers of bias.

Second, the basic data in Table 1 are often very rough. The estimates
of E_{it}, R_{it}, C_{it}, Π_{it}, A_{it}, and $\overline{S}_{it}/S_{it}$ are based on the rather crude assumptions described in the Appendix. Unfortunately, no better data
could be found. To the extent that they are distributed randomly, the

errors of measurement in the exogenous variables tend to bias the estimates of the coefficients in equations (3), (7), and (16) toward zero.

Third, the models in Sections I and III are obviously oversimplified. The small number of observations, as well as measurement problems and lack of data, limited the number of explanatory variables that could be included. One other explanatory variable—the length of the time period—was used initially in equations (3), (7), and (16), and its effect turned out to be nonsignificant.[30] Note too that the residuals in these equations may not be entirely independent because of the effects of factors that persist in a given industry or time period.

Fourth, the estimating procedures are sometimes rough. In Section II, the computed values of $\bar{e}$ and $\bar{d}$ are based on a rather bold assumption. In Section I, there is probably some least-squares bias toward zero in the estimates of the α's and ν's because Π_{it} is inversely related to E_{it} and directly related to R_{it}. But in the case of α_2 and ν_2, this bias should not be very large, and considering the quality of the basic data, it did not seem worthwhile to use more complicated estimating procedures.[31]

B. *Summary and Conclusions*

Despite their limitations, the results contribute in at least four ways to a better understanding of the processes of firm formation, growth, and decline. First, they help to gauge the effects of an industry's profitability, capital requirements, and minimum efficient size of firm on its rates of entry and exit. For example, they suggest that the entry rate would increase by at least 60 per cent if an industry's profitability doubled and that it would decrease by at least 7 per cent if its capital requirements doubled. Similarly, they suggest that the exit rate would decrease by at least 15 per cent if an industry's profitability doubled or if the ratio of the average size of firm to the minimum efficient size of firm doubled.

[30] Of course, the exclusion of important factors can create biases of various sorts. E.g., it is possible that C_{it} is correlated with other barriers to entry and that consequently its effects on E_{it} are overstated.

[31] For an elementary discussion of least-squares bias of this sort, see [5]. To evaluate the bias, we first formed a complete system of equations by adding to equations (3) and (7) a third equation in which $\ln \Pi_{it}$ is represented as a linear function of $\ln E_{it}$, $\ln R_{it}$, $\ln \Pi_{i(t-1)}$, an unspecified exogenous variable, and an error term. As noted in the text, the coefficient of $\ln E_{it}$ in the third equation is assumed to be negative and the coefficient of $\ln R_{it}$ is assumed to be positive. What we have in mind is that the rate of change of Π_{it} (i.e., $\Pi_{it}/\Pi_{i(t-1)}$) is an increasing function of R_{it}, a decreasing function of E_{it}, and a function of some other (unspecified) exogenous variable. Next, we assumed that the residuals in the equations were uncorrelated (which is consistent with the data we have), and we assumed for simplicity that the covariances of the exogenous variables were all zero.

Under these conditions we found that the asymptotic bias in the estimates of the α's and ν's was always towards zero and that it was likely to be a small percentage of the estimates of α_2 and ν_2. But this only holds in the limit and our assumptions are obviously rough.

Second, the tests of several variants of Gibrat's law of proportionate effect reveal that, contrary to the law, smaller firms have relatively high death rates and those that survive tend to have higher and more variable growth rates than larger firms. Moreover, a simple theory is presented which may help to account for these deviations from the law of proportionate effect.

Third, evidence as to the effects of successful innovations on a firm's rate of growth indicate that on the average the successful innovators in these industries grew about twice as rapidly as other comparable firms during the relevant period.[32] In terms of short-term growth, the rewards for successful innovation seem to have been substantial, particularly for smaller firms.

Fourth, a simple model is presented to help explain variation among industries and over time in the extent to which firms change their relative positions in the size distribution of an industry. Our tentative findings indicate that the amount of mobility in an industry depends significantly on its age and its market structure, the model fitting data for several industries surprisingly well.

In recent years, economists have begun to study in a systematic way the changes over time in an industry's composition and structure, but because so little econometric work has been carried out, they have had relatively little to go on in constructing models to represent the relevant dynamic processes. For this reason and others, they have not proceeded far beyond the simplest sorts of stochastic models, e.g., Markov processes with constant transition probabilities based on Gibrat's law.[33] By providing some of the necessary econometric results, this paper should contribute to the development of a richer theory of the dynamic aspects of industrial structure.

APPENDIX: DATA AND METHODS

First, this Appendix presents the basic data regarding the birth, growth, and death of firms in the steel, petroleum refining, and rubber tire industries. (The data for the automobile industry pertain to only a small number of firms and are readily available in the annual statistical issues of *Automobile Industries*.) These data can be summarized most easily in the form of transition matrices—shown in Tables A, B, and C. If all firms are classified into n size classes, the ijth element of the transition matrix for a particular period $(i, j = 1, \cdots, n)$ is the number of firms in the ith class at the beginning of the period that were in the jth class at the end. Despite the pioneering work of Hart and Prais [13] and Adelman [1], few such transition matrices have been constructed.

[32] The average growth rate in the first row of Table 3 is approximately double the average growth rate in the second row.

[33] Judging by our results and the transition matrices in the Appendix, the assumption—sometimes made—that the transition probabilities are constant over time is likely to be a poor one; e.g., the extent of "mixing" [27] seems to decrease with time.

Table A contains transition matrices for the steel industry for 1916–26, 1926–35, 1935–45, and 1945–54; Table B, for petroleum refining for 1921–27, 1927–37, 1937–47, and 1947–57; Table C, for the rubber tire industry for 1937–45 and 1945–52. Some of these periods were dictated by the availability of data; others were chosen rather arbitrarily. A firm's size is measured in terms of gross tons of ingot capacity (steel), daily crude capacity (petroleum), or employment (tires). In steel and petroleum, all firms with ingot capacity or crude capacity are included. In rubber tires, all firms cited in the *Rubber Red Book* as manufacturers of rubber tires are included.

The basic data were derived from the *Directory of the American Iron and Steel Institute* [3] Bureau of Mines bulletins [6], the *Petroleum Refiner*, the *Rubber Red Book*, *Moody's Industrials*, and correspondence with particular firms. To construct each matrix, we obtained from these sources complete lists of the firms in the industry at the beginning and end of the period and

TABLE A—TRANSITION MATRICES FOR THE STEEL INDUSTRY, 1916–26, 1926–35, 1935–45, AND 1945–54[a]

Capacity (Tons) at Beginning of the Period	Ingot Capacity (Tons) at End of the Period								
	Total	Disap- pearances	Under 4,000	4,000- 15,999	16,000- 63,999	64,000- 255,999	256,000- 1,023,999	1,024,000- 4,095,999	Over 4,095,999
	[Number of firms] 1916–26								
Entrants	51	—	10	10	15	12	4	0	0
Under 4,000	10	2	4	3	1	0	0	0	0
4,000–15,999	17	5	1	6	4	1	0	0	0
16,000–63,999	14	1	0	1	11	1	0	0	0
64,000–255,999	31	6	0	0	0	16	8	1	0
256,000–1,023,999	10	2	0	0	0	0	7	1	0
1,024,000–4,095,999	7	2	0	0	0	0	0	4	1
Over 4,095,999	1	0	0	0	0	0	0	0	1
	1926–35								
Entrants	10	—	0	4	2	2	2	0	0
Under 4,000	14	11	3	0	0	0	0	0	0
4,000–15,999	20	11	1	7	1	0	0	0	0
16,000–63,999	30	17	0	1	10	1	0	1	0
64,000–255,999	31	12	0	0	1	13	5	0	0
256,000–1,023,999	19	5	0	0	0	0	11	3	0
1,024,000–4,095,999	6	0	0	0	0	0	1	4	1
Over 4,095,999	2	0	0	0	0	0	0	0	2
	1935–45								
Entrants	15	—	0	2	7	3	3	0	0
Under 4,000	4	4	0	0	0	0	0	0	0
4,000–15,999	12	0	0	5	6	1	0	0	0
16,000–63,999	14	4	0	1	6	3	0	0	0
64,000–255,999	16	0	0	0	0	14	2	0	0
256,000–1,023,999	19	3	0	0	0	0	14	2	0
1,024,000–4,095,999	8	1	0	0	0	0	1	5	1
Over 4,095,999	3	0	0	0	0	0	0	0	3
	1945–54								
Entrants	14	—	1	1	6	2	3	1	0
Under 4,000	0	0	0	0	0	0	0	0	0
4,000–15,999	9	2	0	4	3	0	0	0	0
16,000–63,999	20	1	0	0	14	4	1	0	0
64,000–255,999	21	6	0	0	1	12	2	0	0
256,000–1,023,999	20	3	0	0	0	0	12	5	0
1,024,000–4,095,999	7	0	0	0	0	0	0	3	4
Over 4,095,999	4	0	0	0	0	0	0	0	4

[a] The first column (labeled "total") contains the number of firms in each size class at the beginning of the period. For each beginning-of-period size class (i.e., each row), the remaining columns show the end-of-period size distribution.

TABLE B—TRANSITION MATRICES FOR THE PETROLEUM REFINING INDUSTRY, 1921-27, 1927-37, 1937-47, AND 1947-57[a]

Daily Capacity (Bbls.) at Beginning of the Period	Daily Capacity (Bbls.) at End of the Period							
	Total	Disappearances	Under 1,000	1,000-3,999	4,000-15,999	16,000-63,999	64,000-255,999	Over 255,999
	[Number of firms] 1921-27							
Entrants	207	—	75	92	36	4	0	0
Under 1,000	58	34	13	6	4	1	0	0
1,000-3,999	173	119	3	34	15	2	0	0
4,000-15,999	61	29	1	5	17	9	0	0
16,000-63,999	15	4	0	0	0	7	4	0
64,000-255,999	6	0	0	0	0	0	6	0
Over 255,999	1	0	0	0	0	0	0	1
	1927-37							
Entrants	153	—	44	62	43	3	1	0
Under 1,000	92	74	8	8	2	0	0	0
1,000-3,999	137	94	1	27	14	0	1	0
4,000-15,999	72	40	1	6	19	6	0	0
16,000-63,999	23	11	0	1	2	5	4	0
64,000-255,999	10	0	0	0	0	0	6	4
Over 255,999	1	0	0	0	0	0	0	1
	1937-47							
Entrants	210	—	83	75	43	9	0	0
Under 1,000	54	26	21	6	1	0	0	0
1,000-3,999	104	53	4	34	13	0	0	0
4,000-15,999	80	30	1	7	27	15	0	0
16,000-63,999	14	3	0	0	2	8	1	0
64,000-255,999	12	1	0	0	0	0	8	3
Over 255,999	5	0	0	0	0	0	0	5
	1947-57							
Entrants	90	—	7	33	31	16	3	0
Under 1,000	109	98	4	5	2	0	0	0
1,000-3,999	122	95	0	16	10	1	0	0
4,000-15,999	86	54	0	3	22	7	0	0
16,000-63,999	32	13	0	0	2	12	5	0
64,000-255,999	9	0	0	0	0	0	5	4
Over 255,999	8	0	0	0	0	0	0	8

[a] See note a, Table A. Both domestic and foreign capacity owned by firms are included.

the size of each firm at both points in time. With this information at hand, it was a simple matter to construct each matrix.

Four points should be noted regarding these data: (1) When a firm's name appeared on a list for the first time, we assumed that it entered the industry during the preceding period. Similarly a firm is regarded as having left the industry when its name disappeared from the lists. Although we tried to keep track of mere changes in company names (where changes in ownership were not involved), some were undoubtedly missed and hence the entry and exit rates may be inflated. But on the other hand, they may also be underestimated because some firms may have kept the same names despite a change in ownership. (Of course, for large corporations, changes in ownership occur to some extent all the time and are not very important unless changes in the control of the firm are involved.) Unfortunately, the available data force us to use a firm's name as an indicator of its ownership. But one would certainly expect the resulting rates of entry and exit to be closely related to the actual ones. Of course, if they are proportional on the average, there is no problem. But this is unlikely.

MANSFIELD: THE GROWTH OF FIRMS 1047

(2) When mergers occurred, they were treated as if the largest firm involved in the merger bought the others. That is, the resulting firm was regarded as a continuation of the largest of its components, and the other parties to the merger were treated as if they went out of business. This procedure is arbitrary, but no other seems clearly preferable. Fortunately, it should not affect the results very substantially. Note too that some of the entrants may have "purchased" existing facilities by merging with established firms. (3) Some members of the industry did not provide data regarding their size at some of these points in time, and there was no choice but to omit them during the relevant periods. This should be of little consequence because only a few such cases were encountered. Note that this accounts for the fact that the number entering a particular size class sometimes differs from the number in that size class at the beginning of the next period. (4) The steel data pertain to all firms with ingot capacity (open hearth, bessemer, or electric) and the petroleum data pertain to all firms with crude capacity (operating or shut-down). For some purposes, it might have been preferable to have excluded electric furnaces and shut-down capacity.

Second, we describe the way in which the data in Table 1 regarding Π_{it}, C_{it}, V_{it}^2, and $\bar{S}_{it}/S_{it}$ were derived. To estimate Π_{it}, we needed figures on profits after taxes as a percentage of net worth in each industry. For rubber tires, the data came from the *Statistics of Income*. For petroleum, they came from Epstein [10], De Chazeau and Kahn [9], and the *Statistics of Income*. For steel, they came from Schroeder [26], but some adjustment was made for differences in concept. The data for automobiles came from *Moody's* and pertained to the largest five firms. The 1925–57 data for all manufacturing came from the First National City Bank of N.Y. (as reported in the 1959

TABLE C—TRANSITION MATRICES FOR THE RUBBER TIRE INDUSTRY, 1937–45 AND 1945–52[a]

Number of People Employed at Beginning of the Period	Number Employed at End of the Period								
	Total	Disappearances	Under 40	40–159	160–639	640–2,559	2,560–10,239	10,240–40,959	Over, 40,959
	[Number of firms] 1937–45								
Entrants	22	0	4	12	4	2	0	0	0
Under 40	6	4	0	2	0	0	0	0	0
40–159	13	6	0	3	4	0	0	0	0
160–639	13	2	0	0	5	6	0	0	0
640–2,559	11	2	0	0	0	6	3	0	0
2,560–10,239	2	1	0	0	0	0	1	0	0
10,240–40,959	3	0	0	0	0	0	0	0	3
Over 40,959	1	0	0	0	0	0	0	0	1
	1945–52								
Entrants	39	0	16	15	6	2	0	0	0
Under 40	4	4	0	0	0	0	0	0	0
40–159	17	14	0	2	1	0	0	0	0
160–639	12	3	0	1	6	2	0	0	0
640–2,559	14	5	0	0	1	7	1	0	0
2,560–10,239	6	0	0	0	0	1	6	0	0
10,210–40,959	0	0	0	0	0	0	0	0	0
Over 40,959	4	0	0	0	0	0	0	0	4

[a] See note a, Table A. In each year a few firms had to be excluded because the *Rubber Red Book* provided no employment figures for them.

Petroleum Facts and Figures). The earlier data for all manufacturing came from Epstein [10].

In many respects, the data are rough. An unweighted average of the profit rates of firms above the minimum efficient size would seem appropriate here. But judging by Bain's figures [4], there is little correlation between size and profit rate in steel, petroleum, and tires; and firms above the minimum efficient size account for almost all of the assets. Thus the weighted averages that we use should be fairly good approximations. In autos, there seems to be some correlation of this sort and consequently we use an unweighted average. This results in a much lower figure for autos than the weighted average that is generally published. For 1949–59, the figure seems much too low, but it could be appreciably higher without affecting the results substantially.

To obtain C_{it} in each industry, we multiplied Bain's estimate [4] of the required investment by the ratio of the average size of firm at the beginning of the tth period (measured in terms of capacity in steel and petroleum, production in automobiles, and employment in tires) to the average size of firm in 1945 (steel), 1947 (petroleum), 1949 (autos), or 1945 (tires). (By Bain's estimate we mean the average of the upper and lower limit he gives. It includes initial losses in the case of the automobile industry.) If the ratio of the average size to the minimum efficient size of firm remained constant over time in each industry and if the necessary investment varied in proportion to the minimum efficient size, this would be all right. This is probably as sensible as any of the simple, operational assumptions we could make, but its crudeness is obvious.

Note that C_{it}—even if it were accurately measured—would not necessarily be the minimum investment for an entrant because the typical entrant was below the minimum efficient size. For the same reason, the typical entrant could not expect to earn profits of Π_{it}. But it seems reasonable that the expected profitability of the typical entrant would be closely related to Π_{it}. And since the average size of an entrant is a relatively constant proportion of the minimum efficient size in these cases, it is pretty certain that the average capital requirements would be closely related to C_{it}.

The estimates of V_{it}^2 were obtained from the frequency distributions in Tables A–C and from *Moody's* figures on assets of automobile firms. To estimate the ratio of the average size of firm to the minimum efficient size, we divided Bain's estimate [4] of the minimum efficient size in each industry into the average size of firm in 1947 (petroleum), 1945 (steel and tires), or 1949 (autos). The estimates of the minimum efficient size were 1,000,000 net tons of capacity (steel), 120,000 barrels of capacity (petroleum), $1\frac{1}{2}$ per cent of total employment (tires), and 10 per cent of total production (autos). The average size of firm in each case came from Tables A–C and *Automotive Industries*. Then we assumed that this ratio was constant over time. Note that the minimum efficient size for the production of specialty items (and in certain locations) may be less than this. This may be quite important. For further comments, see note 18. The crudeness of these estimates of $\bar{S}_{it}/\hat{S}_{it}$ is obvious.

Third, we describe the way in which firms were classified by $S_{ij}{}^t$ and $S_{ij}{}^{t+\Delta}/S_{ij}{}^t$ in the χ^2 tests in Table 2. In the tests where deaths were included, the following size classes were used. In steel, we classified firms by their value of $S_{ij}{}^t$ into four classes: 4,000–15,999 tons, 16,000–63,999 tons, 64,000–255,999 tons, and 256,000–4,096,000 tons. In tires, we used four classes: 20–79 men, 80–159 men, 160–639 men, and 640–5,119 men. And in petroleum, there were four classes: 500–999 barrels, 2,000–3,999 barrels, 8,000–15,999 barrels, and 32,000–511,999 barrels. To cut down the computations involved, only firms in these classes were included. Thus, some of the largest and smallest firms were omitted in steel and tires, and some small, medium-sized, and large firms were excluded in petroleum. But had all firms been included, the results would almost certainly have been much the same.

In all cases, the firms in a size class were divided into three groups—those where $S_{ij}{}^{t+\Delta}/S_{ij}{}^t$ was less than .50, between .50 and 1.50, and 1.50 or more. These classes were chosen so that the expected number of firms in each cell of the contingency table would be five or more. (According to a well-known rule of thumb, the expected number in each cell should be this large.) This did not always turn out to be the case, but further work showed that the results would stand up if cells were combined.

With the following exceptions, these same classifications were used in the tests where deaths were excluded. In steel and tires, the two smallest size classes were combined. In some cases, firms were classified into groups where $S_{ij}{}^{t+\Delta}/S_{ij}{}^t$ was less than 1.00, between 1.00 and 2.00, and 2.00 or more. These changes were made to meet the rule of thumb noted above. Despite these changes, the expected number of firms in some cells was not quite five, but the results would not be affected if some cells were combined.

Fourth, we describe the way in which the innovators in Section II B were identified. The first step was to write trade associations and trade journals in each industry and to ask for a list of the important processes and products first introduced in the industry since 1918. Usable questionnaires were filled out and returned by one trade association and three trade journals. There was evidence that the respondents went to considerable pains in preparing them. The number of innovations of each type (process and product) that were provided ranged from about 20 to 40. In all, about 150 innovations were listed in the replies.

The second step was to determine what firm first introduced each innovation commercially and when this took place. To determine the date and to identify the innovator, articles in trade and technical journals were consulted. When doubts arose, letters were sent to equipment producers and members of the industry to determine whether the information was correct. Members of the Carnegie Institute of Technology engineering faculty were also consulted. Ultimately, the required information was obtained for over 80 per cent of the innovations. These data appear in [17].

Finally, we describe the way in which the average annual growth rate of the "other firms" in Table 3 was computed. If the innovator was smaller than the sizes given in the second sentence in note 18, we used the following technique to estimate the average annual growth rate of the other firms of its initial size. We assumed that, for the jth "other firm" in the ith industry, $\ln S_{ij}^{t+\Delta} = a_i + b_i \ln S_{ij}^t + Z_{ij}'''$, where Z_{ij}''' is a random error term. An equation of this form fits the data for the smaller firms quite well. We then obtained least-squares estimates (shown in Table 3) of a_i and b_i; and taking each innovator, we used this regression to estimate the average value of $\ln S_{ij}^{t+\Delta}$ for the "other firms" corresponding to its value of S_{ij}^t. Deducting its value of $\ln S_{ij}^t$ from this computed average value and dividing the result by Δ, we obtain an estimate of the average annual growth rate of "other firms" of the same original size as this innovator.

If the innovator was larger than the sizes given in note 18, we had to use another method because the regressions do not always fit the larger firms very well. In these cases, we used the average annual growth rate of the "other firms" larger than the sizes given in note 18. Finally, to obtain the figures in the second row of Table 3, we took the resulting average growth rate for the "other firms" corresponding to each innovator during the period (whether or not it was above the sizes in note 18) and averaged them.

References

1. I. Adelman, "A Stochastic Process Analysis of the Size Distribution of Firms," *Jour. Am. Stat. Assoc.*, Dec. 1958, *58*, 893-904.
2. M. Adelman, "Differential Rates and Changes in Concentration," *Rev. Econ. Stat.*, Feb. 1959, *41*, 68-69.
3. American Iron and Steel Institute, *Directory of Iron and Steel Works*, New York, 1916, 1926, 1935, 1945, and 1954.
4. J. Bain, *Barriers to New Competition*. Cambridge 1956.
5. J. Bronfenbrenner, "Source and Size of Least-Square Bias in a Two-Equation Model," in W. C. Hood and T. C. Koopmans, ed., *Studies in Econometric Method*. New York 1953.
6. Bureau of Mines, *Petroleum Refineries, including Cracking Plants in the United States*, Washington, Jan. 1, 1937, 1947, and 1957.
7. B. Churchill, "Rise in the Business Population," *Surv. Curr. Bus.*, May 1959, *39*, 15-19.
8. N. Collins and L. Preston, "The Size Structure of Industrial Firms, 1909-58," *Am. Econ. Rev.*, Dec. 1961, *51*, 986-1011.
9. M. De Chazeau and A. Kahn, *Integration and Competition in the Petroleum Industry*. New Haven 1959.
10. R. Epstein, *Industrial Profits in the United States*. New York 1934.
11. C. Ferguson, "The Relationship of Business Size to Stability: An Empirical Approach," *Jour. Ind. Econ.*, Nov. 1960, *9*, 43-62.
12. R. Gibrat, *Les inégalités économiques*. Paris 1931.
13. P. Hart and S. Prais, "The Analysis of Business Concentration: A Statistical Approach," *Jour. Royal Stat. Soc.*, Ser. A, 1956, *119*, 150-81.
14. A. Hoggatt, "A Simulation Study of an Economic Model," in *Contributions to Scientific Research in Management*. Los Angeles 1959.
15. S. Hymer and B. Pashigian, "Firm Size and Rate of Growth" (abstract), *Econometrica*, Apr. 1959, *27*, 315.

16. E. Mansfield, "Technical Change and the Rate of Imitation," *Economet-rica,* Oct. 1961, *29,* 741-66.

17. ————, "Size of Firm, Market Structure, and Innovation," *Jour. Pol. Econ.* (forthcoming).

18. ————, "The Expenditures of the Firm on Research and Development," Cowles Foundation Discussion Paper No. 136.

19. ————, "The Speed of Response of Firms to New Techniques," *Quart. Jour. Econ.* (forthcoming).

20. ———— and C. Hensley, "The Logistic Process: The Stochastic Epidemic Curve and Applications," *Jour. Royal Stat. Soc.* Ser. B, 1960, *22,* 332-37.

21. A. Marshall, *Principles of Economics.* London 1916.

22. J. Miller, "Measures of Monopoly Power and Concentration: Their Economic Significance," *Business Concentration and Price Policy.* Princeton 1955.

23. A. Oxenfeldt, *New Firms and Free Enterprise.* Washington 1943.

24. A. Papandreau and J. Wheeler, *Competition and Its Regulation.* New York 1954.

25. E. Penrose, *The Theory of the Growth of the Firm.* New York 1959.

26. A. Schroeder, *The Growth of the Major Steel Companies.* Baltimore 1953.

27. H. Simon and C. Bonini, "The Size Distribution of Business Firms," *Am. Econ. Rev.,* Sept. 1958, *48,* 607-17.

28. G. Stigler, "Introduction," *Business Concentration and Price Policy.* Princeton 1955.

29. ————, "The Economics of Scale," *Jour. Law and Econ.,* Oct. 1958, *1,* 54-71.

30. R. Triffin, *Monopolistic Competition and General Equilibrium Theory.* Cambridge 1941.

31. H. Vatter, "The Closure of Entry in the American Automobile Industry," *Oxford Econ. Papers,* Oct. 1952, *4,* 213-34.

MANAGEMENT SCIENCE
Vol. 21, No. 12, August 1975
Printed in U.S.A.

THE COSTS OF INDUSTRIAL PRODUCT INNOVATIONS*

EDWIN MANSFIELD† AND JOHN RAPOPORT§ ¶

To help shed new light on the factors associated with the large differences among innovations in the percent of innovation costs devoted to R and D, detailed data were obtained concerning a sample of chemical innovations. A simple econometric model was used to test a number of tentative hypotheses advanced to help explain these differences. The model can explain about half of the observed variation.

1. Introduction

Very little is known about the innovation process within the firm—the process that culminates in the introduction of a new process or product. Despite the obvious importance of this process, and the fact that considerable work is going on in this area,[1] we are still a long way from understanding the innovation process. Even the costs incurred in this process are not understood well. In recent years, several studies have emphasized that research and development expenditures are only a part, and sometimes a small part, of the total costs of an innovation. But we know very little about the factors associated with the percentage of total innovation costs that go for R and D. In other words, why is it that the total costs of innovating are largely R and D costs in the case of some innovations, but largely non-R and D costs in the case of other innovations? To our knowledge, no information has been published on this score. The purpose of this note is to present some econometric results that may help to throw a bit of additional light on this question.

2. The Basic Data

For present purposes, the innovation process is considered to begin when exploratory work is started by the innovator with the particular new product in mind. Thus, it excludes basic research but includes applied research (if any) directed toward the product. The innovation process ends when the new manufactured product is available

---

* Processed by Professor Burton V. Dean, Departmental Editor for Research and Development; received March 1, 1974, revised September 17, 1974. This paper has been with the authors 5 months for revision.

† Professor of Economics at the Wharton School, University of Pennsylvania.

§ Associate Professor of Economics at Mount Holyoke College.

¶ The work on which this paper is based was supported by a grant to Mansfield from the National Science Foundation. Also, some of the work was carried out while he was a Fellow at the Center for Advanced Study in the Behavioral Sciences at Stanford. Preliminary versions of the paper were included in seminars given at Stanford and Johns Hopkins Universities.

[1] For some recent publications in this area, see the Organization for Economic Cooperation and Development, *The Conditions for Success in Industrial Innovation*, Paris, 1971; S. Myers and D. Marquis, *Successful Industrial Innovations*, National Science Foundation, 1969; E. Mansfield, J. Rapoport, J. Schnee, S. Wagner, and M. Hamburger, *Research and Innovation in the Modern Corporation*, W. W. Norton, 1971; and International Economic Association, *Science and Technology in Economic Growth*, Macmillan, 1973. Also, see National Science Foundation, *Proceedings of a Conference on Technology Transfer and Innovation*, Washington, 1967; Office of the Director of Defense Research and Engineering, *Project Hindsight*, 1969; IIT Research Institute, *Technology in Retrospect and Critical Events in Science*, 1968; NRC Materials Advisory Board, *Report of the Ad Hoc Committee on Research-Engineering Interaction*, 1966; and E. Mansfield and S. Wagner, "Organizational and Strategic Factors Associated with Probabilities of Success in Industrial R and D," *Journal of Business*, April 1975.

1380

(at an acceptable quality level and cost) for sale and delivery. Following the procedures of the Panel on Invention and Innovation of the Department of Commerce, as well as our own previous work,[2] we classify the work leading up to the first commercial introduction of a new product into the following stages: applied research, preparation of product specifications, prototype or pilot plant construction, tooling and construction of manufacturing facilities, manufacturing startup, and marketing startup. Of course, there is no presumption that these stages do not overlap, or that they must occur in any particular time sequence.

More specifically, the activities included in each stage are as follows. *Applied research*, as defined by the National Science Foundation (and used here), is "Investigation directed toward the discovery of new scientific knowledge where such knowledge is sought with a particular commercial use in mind."[3] An example of the applied research done on products in our sample (described below) is an investigation to find a cheaper method to synthesize a resin previously synthesized by university chemists. *Preparation of project requirements and basic specifications* often consists partly of routine planning and scheduling which involves close coordination with marketing to increase the probability that the proposed product will be a success commercially. In the chemical industry, this stage contains some bench scale work and applications research. The definition of *prototype or pilot plant design, construction, and testing* seems fairly self-evident. Although the major concern here is the product itself, the work often involves the firm in new technological areas related to manufacture of the product in quantity. Since all of the innovations included in our sample (used in subsequent sections of this paper) are chemicals, we are concerned here only with pilot plants, not with prototypes.

The definition of the preparation of detailed manufacturing drawings, tooling, and the design and construction of manufacturing facilities also seems self-evident. While this may lead to minor changes in the product in order to make it a more suitable object for manufacture, the focus is on the problems of manufacturing rather than on the product itself. This stage may represent a transfer of responsibility from the R and D management to the production management and is quite often characterized by considerable investment in physical capital. *Manufacturing start-up* includes training workers, "debugging" the plant, and production before an acceptable quality level is reached. *Marketing start-up* includes activities like market studies, advertising, establishment of a system of distribution, and training the sales force. Marketing start-up cost includes all expenditure of this nature before the first sale and delivery of the product.

Table 1 shows, for a sample of 38 innovations in the chemical, machinery, and electronics industries, the average and standard deviations of the percent of total innovation costs attributable to each of these six stages. Clearly, as one would expect, there is an enormous amount of variation among innovations in the percent of total costs attributable to each stage. (The standard deviations are eloquent on this score.) The National Science Foundation's definition of research and development accords well with the first three stages listed in Table 1. Thus, on the average, R and D accounted for about 40 percent of the total innovation cost for the sample of chemical innovations, and for about 50 percent of the total innovation costs for the sample of

[2] See U. S. Department of Commerce, *Technological Innovation*, Washington, D.C., 1967; and Mansfield, Rapoport, Schnee, Wagner, and Hamburger, *op. cit.*

[3] National Science Foundation, *Methodology of Statistics on Research and Development*, 1959.

TABLE 1

Percent of Total Cost of Innovation Arising in Each Stage of Innovative Activity

Stage	Chemicals	Machinery	Electronics	Whole Sample
			(percent)	
Applied research				
Mean	17	3	4	10
Standard deviation	17	5	6	
Specifications				
Mean	13	4	3	8
Standard deviation	17	6	3	
Prototype or pilot plant				
Mean	13	41	44	29
Standard deviation	8	17	17	
Tooling and manufacturing facilities				
Mean	41	37	30	37
Standard deviation	29	10	18	
Manufacturing start-up				
Mean	8	4	14	9
Standard deviation	8	6	9	
Marketing start-up				
Mean	7	11	6	8
Standard deviation	12	12	5	

Source: E. Mansfield, J. Rapoport, J. Schnee, S. Wagner, and M. Hamburger, *Research and Innovation in the Modern Corporation*, W. W. Norton, 1971.

machinery innovations and the sample of electronics innovations. In each industry, there is a great deal of variation among innovations in the percent of total innovation costs going for R and D.[4]

To help shed new light on the factors associated with the large differences among innovations in the percent of innovation costs devoted to *R* and *D*, detailed data were obtained concerning 17 chemical innovations completed in the 1960's. Admittedly, this is a small sample, but because a great deal of detailed information had to be collected concerning each innovation, this was as big a sample as the available resources would support. These innovations were introduced by 5 chemical firms, and were primarily polymers for industrial use (such as synthetic elastomers and fibers) and a few organic chemicals (such as starches). The innovations included had all been commercialized (or very nearly so) at the time we obtained the data, and each had been carried out entirely by one firm. Data on the distribution of total cost (among the six stages, defined above) for each innovation were obtained through personal interviews with managers who actually participated in the work on the project. Since firms' accounting records often did not yield data corresponding exactly to the breakdown into stages we used, accounting data were supplemented by estimates of the managers. Other relevant information about the innovations was obtained during the interviews, by a later mail questionnaire, and by follow-up conversations and interviews.

The following statistics provide some idea of the characteristics of the innovations

---

[4] Neither here nor in subsequent sections are we assuming that the observed distribution of costs for each innovation was the distribution planned by the firm at the outset of the project. Obviously, the actual distribution is likely to differ substantially from the planned distribution.

included in the sample: The average total innovation cost was $2,252,000 (the standard deviation being $2,318,000); the average annual expected revenue from the product during the first three years of its life was $5,941,000 (the standard deviation being $13,017,000); and the average number of years of R and D experience of the innovator in the relevant product area was 8.8 (the standard deviation being 9.8). Further, in 35 percent of the cases, the innovation was a response to a similar product by a competitor (and in 65 percent, it was not); in 29 percent of the cases, it was necessary to construct a new pilot plant (and in 71 percent, it was not); in 59 percent of the cases, all or most of the equipment required to produce the product was already available (and in 41 percent, it was not); and in 53 percent of the cases, the firm's workers had considerable experience with the production of this kind of product (and in 47 percent, they did not).

3. Factors Influencing the Percent of Innovation Costs Going For R and D

In our sample of seventeen chemical innovations, R and D costs accounted for 39 percent, on the average, of total innovation costs. But, as in Table 1, there is an enormous amount of variation about this average. Specifically, the percentage of total innovation cost attributable to R and D ranged from 7–71%. Clearly, some innovations were accomplished with a relatively small expenditure on R and D, whereas, for other innovations, the R and D costs are the lion's share of the total innovation costs. What factors are responsible for these great differences? Why is it that R and D bulks large in the costs of some innovations, but is relatively insignificant in others? To help answer these questions, we see how well a number of hypotheses—some suggested by economic theory, some suggested by conversations with leading chemical engineers—can explain the observed variation. Some of these hypotheses are extremely tentative, since the available theory in this area is so weak. We regard them as interesting hypotheses to test, even though we do not feel that, on *a priori* grounds, all of them are equally convincing.

The first hypothesis is that bigger, more important innovations—ones that constitute major new products that enjoy large markets—require, on the average, a larger proportion of their costs to go for R and D. It is easy to point to exceptions, but it is frequently argued that this hypothesis holds on the average. Whereas relatively small improvements can be made without much R and D, it is argued that, on the average, this is not the case for more important innovations. To measure a product's importance, we use its expected annual sales in the first three years of its life. This measure is far from ideal, but it should be good enough for present purposes.[5]

The second hypothesis is that, holding other factors constant, larger firms may devote a larger percentage of total innovation costs to R and D than smaller firms. Although there is bound to be great variation in individual cases, this hypothesis seems reasonable on the average. R and D, because of its uncertain nature, may produce results in areas not directly related to the specific problem at hand. A large firm may feel that it is more likely to be able to utilize such unpredictable spillovers,

---

[5] Expected sales, rather than actual sales, were used because some of the innovations were only entering the market at the time when the data were collected. However, subsequent experience indicates that these expectations were reasonably accurate.

Of course, the choice of three years is arbitrary. We could just as well have used five years or some other period. But three years seems reasonable, at least for these innovations. However, we recognize that, for very novel or far-reaching innovations, this period might underestimate the importance of an innovation.

and thus may be willing to spend more of the total costs on R and D than a smaller firm. For another thing, the available evidence suggests that it often costs a large firm more than a small one to develop the same product.[6] If this is the case, and if the difference between large and small firms in non-R and D costs is smaller, one would expect the percent of total costs attributable to R and D to be higher for the large firms than the small ones.

The third hypothesis is that the extent of the innovator's R and D experience in the relevant technological area is likely to affect the percent of the innovation's costs that go for R and D. Economists have devoted considerable attention to the phenomenon of "learning by doing" in production, but they have been slow to recognize the importance of "learning by doing" in R and D. This is unfortunate, because organizational learning is important in R and D too. In R and D, as in production, the more experience that a firm has in the relevant technological area, the more efficient it is likely to be. Since there is probably much less relationship between a firm's R and D experience in the relevant area and the amount of learning in the areas of tooling and construction of plant, manufacturing start-up, and marketing start-up, one might expect the percent of total costs attributable to R and D to be lower for firms with more R and D experience in the relevant area.

Finally, two other variables that may be relevant are the size of the total innovation costs and whether or not a new pilot plant must be built. As the scale of a project increases, the non-R and D costs, particularly for tooling and construction of manufacturing facilities, may tend to increase more rapidly (in this range) than the R and D costs. Thus, the size of the total innovation costs may have a systematic effect on the percent of total costs attributable to R and D. Similarly, whether or not a new pilot plant must be built may also affect the percent of an innovation's costs that go for R and D. However, it is difficult to predict the direction of this effect. On the one hand, one might expect an innovation where a new pilot plant must be built to have relatively more spent on R and D simply because of the necessity of building a pilot plant. On the other hand, innovations requiring a new pilot plant are likely to be much more ambitious projects where the non-R and D costs are much higher too. Consequently, it is hard to tell whether the net effect of this variable is to reduce or increase the percent of total costs going for R and D.

4. Econometric Results

To see how well these hypotheses can explain the observed variation, we assume that

$$(1) \qquad D_i = \alpha_0 + \alpha_1 R_i + \alpha_2 S_i + \alpha_3 E_i + \alpha_4 T_i + \alpha_5 N_i + z_i,$$

where D_i is the percent of the ith innovation's total costs spent on R and D, R_i is expected annual sales of the ith innovation (over the first three years of its product life), S_i is the annual sales of the firm that was the innovator in the case of the ith innovation, E_i is the number of years of R and D experience in the relevant technological area of this firm, T_i is the total cost of the ith innovation (the sum of the six stages in §2), N_i is a dummy variable that equals 1 if a new pilot plant is built in the

---

[6] See E. Mansfield, *Industrial Research and Technological Innovation*, W. W. Norton for the Cowles Foundation for Research in Economics at Yale University, 1968; A. Cooper, "R and D Is More Efficient in Small Companies," *Harvard Business Review*, June 1964; J. Schmookler, Testimony before the Senate Judiciary Committee, 1965; and E. Mansfield, J. Rapoport, J. Schnee, S. Wagner, and M. Hamburger, *op. cit.*

case of the ith innovation and zero otherwise, and z_i is a random error term. S_i is measured in millions of dollars, while R_i and T_i are measured in thousands of dollars.

Using the data concerning our sample of 17 innovations, we computed least-squares estimates of the α's. The results are:

$$D_i = 37.4 + 0.00076R_i + 0.019S_i - 0.59E_i - 0.0051T_i - 11.9N_i.$$
(2)
$$(3.2) \qquad (3.1) \qquad (1.7) \qquad (2.8) \qquad (1.9)$$

The t-ratios are given in parentheses below each regression coefficient. This regression fits the data reasonably well, $\overline{R}^2$, after adjustment for degrees of freedom, being 0.55. In other words, this regression explains about 55 percent of the variation among these innovations in the percent of total innovation costs devoted to R and D. It is not surprising, of course, that a large proportion (45%) of the variation remains unexplained. In view of the enormous heterogeneity of product innovations in the chemical industry, and the many other factors that influence D_i, we would not expect a very high value of $\overline{R}^2$.

Each of the regression coefficients in (2) has the expected sign (if this was stipulated in advance). In accord with the first hypothesis, the size of a new product's expected annual revenue (R_i) seems to have a major effect on D_i. Specifically, if R_i increases by $13 million (one standard deviation), the percent of total innovation costs devoted to R and D increases, on the average, by about 10 percentage points. Also, the effect of the size of the innovating firm seems to be in accord with the second hypothesis. Judging from equation (2), a $250 million increase in the annual sales of the innovator will result in an increase of about 5 percentage points, on the average, in the percent of total innovation costs devoted to R and D. Since the firms in our sample ranged from $100 million to over $2 billion in annual sales, it is evident that variation in firm size within the range of sizes represented in our sample seems to be associated with substantial differences in the percent of total innovation costs going for R and D.

In accord with the third hypothesis, the extent of the innovating firm's R and D experience in the relevant technological area also seems to have a significant effect. But unlike the other variables, it is significant only at the 10%, not the 5% level. Judging from (2), 10 years of additional experience (one standard deviation) reduce the percent of total innovation costs devoted to R and D by about 6 percentage points, on the average. Also, the results suggest that increases in total innovation costs are associated with reductions in the percent of such costs going to R and D, and that innovations where a new pilot plant is built tend to spend a lower percentage of total costs on R and D. Apparently, in cases where a new pilot plant is built, the added non-R and D costs tend to be bigger, percentagewise, than the amount that the pilot plant adds to the R and D costs.

5. Conclusions

Economists sometimes have assumed that research and development expenditures could be treated as synonymous, or nearly so, with the costs of product innovation. In previous studies, it has been shown that this assumption is a poor one, since R and D expenditures account, on the average, for less than half of the amount spent on a product innovation (in the cases we studied). However, there is an enormous amount of variation among innovations in the percent of total innovation costs that go for R and D. The results of the present study suggest that a substantial proportion of this variation can be explained by the importance of the innovation (as measured by sales volume), the amount of experience the innovator has had in the relevant technological area, the size of the innovating firm, the total innovation costs, and whether or not a new pilot plant must be built.

In view of the smallness of the sample (composed entirely of chemical innovations) and the roughness of the data, these results should be viewed as highly tentative. However, if confirmed by future research, they seem to have several interesting implications. First, if R and D plays a more important role in more major innovations than in less important ones, this means that, if innovations are unweighted by their importance (as so frequently is the case), data concerning the percentage of innovations based to any significant degree on R and D are likely to contain a serious downward bias. Data of this sort have often been used in important policy discussions in this country and abroad concerning the effects of R and D on technological change. Second, if "learning by doing" is as important in R and D as it seems, this fact has implications for competitive relationships among firms, and for barriers to entry, as well as for intrafirm decision-making. If at all possible, it would be interesting, of course, to quantify and analyze at least some aspects of the relevant learning curves. Third, if it is true that large firms tend to devote a higher percentage of total innovation costs to R and D, the official figures on R and D expenditures may exaggerate the extent to which total expenditures on innovation are concentrated in big firms. This, of course, is an interesting question from the point of view of public policy toward the large firm. Finally, the results indicate (for the types of innovations considered here) the extent to which a prospective innovator must expect to supplement its R and D funds in order to bring a new product to market, and some factors associated with the size of this supplement. To the individual firm, this is a matter of considerable importance.

[4]

MANAGEMENT SCIENCE
Vol. 34, No. 10, October 1988
Printed in U.S.A.

THE SPEED AND COST OF INDUSTRIAL INNOVATION IN JAPAN AND THE UNITED STATES: EXTERNAL VS. INTERNAL TECHNOLOGY*

EDWIN MANSFIELD

*Center for Economics and Technology, University of Pennsylvania,
Philadelphia, Pennsylvania 19104-6297*

This study, based on detailed data obtained from carefully selected samples of about 200 Japanese and American firms, seems to be the first comprehensive empirical investigation of the differences between Japan and the United States in innovation cost and time. Whereas the Japanese have substantial advantages in this regard in some industries (notably machinery), they do not seem to have any substantial advantage in others (notably chemicals). Whereas they have great advantages in carrying out innovations based on external technology, they do not seem to have any in carrying out innovations based on internal technology. Japanese firms allocate their resources quite differently than do American firms, a larger percentage of total innovation cost being devoted to tooling and manufacturing equipment and facilities, a smaller percentage being devoted to marketing startup. A large part of America's problem in this regard seems to be due to its apparent inability to match Japan as a quick and effective user of external technology.
(INNOVATION; RESEARCH AND DEVELOPMENT; ECONOMICS)

1. Introduction

The outcome of the intense rivalry that currently exists between Japan and the United States in high-technology industries (like computers, electronics, and biotechnology) will be determined in part by how quickly and economically each nation's firms can develop and commercially introduce the new products and processes that are central to success in these industries. [1] According to IBM's former chief scientist, Japan's "greatest technological strength" vis-a-vis the United States is "the speed with which developments are translated into improved products and processes." [2] Unfortunately, very little systematic investigation has been undertaken to find out how much of an advantage Japan has in this regard, and to identify the factors determining whether this advantage is big or small. This paper, based on detailed data obtained from carefully selected samples of about 200 Japanese and American firms, provides new information on this score, as well as on the spillover effects of R and D investment.

2. Innovation Time and Cost

To begin with, we present a detailed comparison of innovation time and innovation cost in the two countries. By innovation time we mean the length of time elapsing from the beginning of applied research (if there was any) by the innovator on a new product or process to the date of the new product's or process's first commercial introduction. By innovation cost we mean all costs to the innovator of developing and introducing the innovation, including R and D, plant and equipment, and startup costs. In comparing innovation costs, we must recognize that the official exchange rate does not adequately reflect the relative prices of R and D and other inputs in the innovation process in the two countries. Thus, as the Organization for Economic Cooperation and Development

---

* Accepted by Alok K. Chakrabarti; received November 11, 1987. This paper has been with the author 1 month for 1 revision.

[1] See Davidson (1984), Feigenbaum and McCorduck (1984), and Okimoto (1986), among others.

[2] Clark, Hayes, and Lorenz (1985, p. 139).

1157

(1979) and others have pointed out, one must construct an exchange rate reflecting purchasing power parities for resources used in the innovation process. To do so, we obtained data regarding the relative prices of these resources in the two countries.[3]

A random sample of 50 Japanese and 75 American firms in the chemical (including pharmaceuticals), rubber, machinery (including computers), instruments, metals, and electrical equipment industries was selected.[4] The members of this sample account for about one-quarter of all R and D carried out in these industries in both countries. For its own industry, each firm provided an estimate of the average ratio of American to Japanese innovation time and the average ratio of American to Japanese innovation cost for new products and processes introduced in 1985. While these estimates were based on reasonably precise data concerning the firms' own times and costs, they sometimes had to be based on the best judgment of the firms' leading executives concerning their rivals' times and costs. (The data in the following section are free of this problem.) Decisions regarding which innovations were comparable in terms of novelty, importance, and complexity were made by the firms, although some checks were made with others.

Among firms from both countries, there was overwhelming agreement that the Japanese tend to develop and commercially introduce new products and processes more quickly than the Americans, although their advantage in this respect is not as great as is sometimes claimed. Averaged over all industries, the time differential was about 18 percent, according to the Japanese data, or 6 percent, according to the American data (Table 1). However, the picture varies from industry to industry. In some industries, like machinery, both the Japanese and American data indicate that there was a substantial differential. In other

TABLE 1

Ratio of American to Japanese Innovation Time, Based on Data Provided by 50 Japanese and 75 American Firms, 1985

Industry	Japanese Estimates		American Estimates	
	Number of Firms	Mean	Number of Firms	Mean
Chemicals	17	0.96	20	1.04
Rubber	3	1.10	3	1.16*
Machinery	13	1.23***	19	1.17**
Metals	4	1.18	5	0.99
Electrical	8	1.42*	17	1.03
Instruments	5	1.38*	11	1.00
All Industries	50	1.18***	75	1.06**

  * Significantly different from 1.00 at the 0.10 probability level.
 ** Significantly different from 1.00 at the 0.05 probability level.
*** Significantly different from 1.00 at the 0.01 probability level.
Source: see §2.

[3] These data were obtained from a sample of major firms that carry out R and D and related innovative activities in both Japan and the United States. Each firm provided data for 1985 (and other years) concerning the prices in both countries of R and D inputs and other resources used in the innovative process. The resulting exchange rate is based on the mean of the firms' weighted price ratios. Because the firms' experiences were very similar, the sampling errors in this exchange rate are negligible.

[4] The Japanese firms were chosen at random from major members of these industries in *International Dun and Bradstreet*. The American firms were chosen at random from the listing of major firms in each of these industries in *Business Week* (July 9, 1984). Each firm in these samples was contacted, and a questionnaire was sent to the firm's president (or chairman). In some cases, interviews were obtained with the firm's executives. Because of a very intensive and persistent effort (extending in some cases over many months and with the help of influential third parties), data were obtained from practically all of the firms. Thus, there is no significant problem of nonresponse. This is true as well in the other samples described in note 7.

TABLE 2

Ratio of American to Japanese Innovation Cost,ᵃ Based on Data Provided by 50 Japanese and 75 American Firms, 1985

Industry	Japanese Estimates		American Estimates	
	Number of Firms	Mean	Number of Firms	Mean
Chemicals	17	1.14***	20	1.02
Rubber	3	1.22	3	1.16**
Machinery	13	1.28***	19	1.21***
Metals	4	1.10*	5	0.95
Electrical	8	1.32***	17	1.04
Instruments	5	1.40**	11	1.23***
All Industries	50	1.23***	75	1.10***

* Significantly different from 1.00 at the 0.10 probability level.
** Significantly different from 1.00 at the 0.05 probability level.
*** Significantly different from 1.00 at the 0.01 probability level.
Source: see §2.
ᵃ Because official exchange rates do not reflect accurately the relative prices in the two countries of R and D and other inputs used in the innovation process, a special exchange rate was computed based on price data for these inputs provided by a sample of the firms that do R and D in both countries. Thus, the cost ratios presented here are estimates of the differential between Japan and the United States in the cost of developing and commercially introducing a new product or process, when these input prices are held constant. See §2 and footnote 3.

industries, like instruments, the Japanese data indicate that there was a substantial differential, whereas the American data do not. In still other industries, notably chemicals, both the Japanese and American data indicate that there was no large differential.[5]

On the average, Japanese firms also developed and commercially introduced new products and processes more cheaply than American firms (Table 2). Averaged over all industries, the resource cost differential was 23 percent, according to the Japanese data, or 10 percent, according to the American data.[6] Here too, the situation varies from industry to industry. For example, in machinery and instruments, based on both the Japanese and American data, the cost differential seemed substantial; in chemicals, on the other hand, the American data do not indicate that any substantial differential existed.

3. External vs. Internal Technology

To understand the factors responsible for these cost and time differentials we must recognize that some innovations are based largely on external technology (i.e., technology developed outside the innovating firm) while others are based largely on internal technology (i.e., technology developed within the innovating firm). To see whether these cost and time differentials depend on whether innovations are based on internal or external technology, we picked a random sample of 60 major Japanese and American firms in the chemical (defined broadly to include pharmaceuticals and petroleum), machinery (including computer), and electrical equipment and instruments industries. The sample

---

[5] As indicated in Table 1, the mean ratio in Table 1 differs significantly from 1 at the 0.01 probability level for the Japanese sample and at the 0.05 level for the American sample. The fact that the mean ratio is higher for the Japanese than the American sample seems to be due in part to differences in the coverage of the data. The Japanese seemed to give more weight to industrial and technological areas within their industry where these differences were relatively large; the Americans gave more weight to areas where it was relatively small. This is true as well in Table 2.

[6] As indicated in Table 2, the mean ratio in Table 2 differs significantly from 1 at the 0.01 probability level for both the Japanese and American samples.

is composed of 30 matched pairs, where each pair consists of an American and Japanese firm of roughly comparable size in the same industry.[7] Every firm indicated how much time and money it devoted, on the average, to the development and commercialization of each of the new products it introduced during 1975–85, depending on whether the product was based on external or internal technology. According to expert opinion, the new products introduced by each pair of firms were reasonably comparable. Since the Japanese cost figures were converted to dollars on the basis of the special exchange rate discussed in §2, they indicate how much (approximately) the resources used in Japan would have cost in the United States.[8]

Like the estimates in Tables 1 and 2, the results indicate that the Japanese tend to have cost and time advantages over U.S. firms. However, these advantages seem to be confined to innovations based on external technology (where the cost and time differentials are greater than in Tables 1 and 2). Among innovations based on internal technology, there seems to be no significant difference in average cost or time between Japan and the United States.[9] The ratio of innovation cost or time for a new product based on external technology to that for a new product based on internal technology tends to be much lower in Japan than in the United States (Table 3 and 4). Moreover, this is true in each industry as well as for all industries combined.[10]

American firms take almost as long, and spend almost as much money, to carry out an innovation based on external technology as one based on internal technology. In the development part of the innovation process (beginning at the start of R and D and ending when the product is developed), an American innovation based on external technology takes less time and money than one based on internal technology; but in the commer-

---

[7] A random sample of 30 Japanese firms in these industries was selected from the *International Dun and Bradstreet*; then, for each Japanese firm chosen, an American firm was selected at random in the same industry from among firms of roughly comparable size. Each firm in these samples was contacted (frequently more than once), and a questionnaire was sent to the firm's president (or chairman). In some cases, interviews were obtained with the firm's executives.

[8] Four points should be noted regarding the distinction between innovations based on internal technology and those based on external technology. First, for an innovation to be based on internal technology, it is not necessary that no technology stemming from outside the innovating firm be used. Practically all innovations make use of some technology stemming directly or indirectly from outside the firm. What is necessary is that a major portion of the new technology underlying the innovation be developed within the innovating firm. For example, duPont's nylon was an innovation based on internal technology.

Second, for an innovation to be based on external technology, it is not necessary that the innovating firm contribute nothing to the modification or adaptation of the product or process. Frequently, firms that imitate or license innovations from others make minor changes in them. What is necessary is that only a minor portion of the new technology underlying the innovation be developed within the innovating firm. For example, when Sumitomo Chemical licensed high density polyethylene from ICI, this was an innovation based on external technology.

Third, the distinction between innovations based on external technology and those based on internal technology, while frequently used, can sometimes be blurred. There are some cases where the innovator made extensive use of technology stemming from outside the firm and also contributed substantially to the technology that was used. In cases of this sort, the judgment of industry executives and engineers was used to classify the innovations into one or the other category.

Fourth, one would expect it to be quicker and cheaper to carry out an innovation based on external technology than one based on internal technology, because firms carrying out innovations based on external technology often pay less for the technology than it would have cost them to develop it themselves. More will be said on this score when we discuss Tables 3 and 4.

[9] Our finding that the average cost and time for innovations based on internal technology does not differ significantly between the two countries pertains to all industries combined. For individual industries, because the sample size is relatively small, such a test would not have much power. More work should be carried out to increase the sample size in individual industries.

[10] In Tables 3 and 4, the mean difference between the American and Japanese ratios for all industries combined is statistically significant in all six cases, generally at the 0.01 probability level. However, in individual industries, the differences frequently are not significant.

TABLE 3

Ratio of Mean Innovation Time for a New Product Based on External Technology to That for a New Product Based on Internal Technology, 60 Firms, Japan and the United States, 1975–85

Industry and Nationality[a]	Part of Innovation Process[b]		Innovation Time
	Development	Commercialization	
All Industries Combined			
Japan	0.67	0.86	0.72
United States	0.88	1.25	0.98
Chemicals			
Japan	0.63	0.91	0.71
United States	0.74	1.10	0.87
Electrical and Instruments			
Japan	0.61	0.69	0.63
United States	0.99	2.50	1.28
Machinery			
Japan	0.77	0.92	0.82
United States	0.94	1.19	0.99

[a] The sample sizes are: all industries combined, 60; chemicals, 16; electrical and instruments, 16; machinery, 28.

[b] The innovation process is divided here into two parts: development (beginning at the start of R and D and ending when the product is developed) and commercialization (beginning when the product is developed and ending when it is first introduced commercially). The ratio of the mean time (for each part) for a new product based on external technology to that for a new product based on internal technology is given here.

cialization part (beginning when the product is developed and ending when it is first introduced commercially), the time and cost is at least as great as one based on internal technology.

In Japan, on the other hand, firms take about 25 percent less time, and spend about 50 percent less money, to carry out an innovation based on external technology than

TABLE 4

Ratio of Mean Innovation Cost for a New Product Based on External Technology to That for a New Product Based on Internal Technology, 60 Firms, Japan and the United States, 1975–85

Industry and Nationality[a]	Part of Innovation Process[b]		Innovation Cost
	Development	Commercialization	
All Industries Combined			
Japan	0.62	0.41	0.50
United States	0.90	1.00	0.95
Chemicals			
Japan	0.57	0.37	0.45
United States	0.86	0.91	0.89
Electrical and Instruments			
Japan	0.92	0.61	0.76
United States	0.92	0.87	0.89
Machinery			
Japan	0.68	0.55	0.61
United States	0.86	1.59	1.10

[a] See note a, Table 3.

[b] The innovation process is divided here into two parts: development and commercialization. (See note b, Table 3.) The ratio of the mean cost (for each part) for a new product based on external technology to that for a new product based on internal technology is given here.

one based on internal technology. Moreover, this is true in all industries. The contrast between Japanese and American firms in the commercialization part of the innovation process is particularly striking. Whereas in the United States the commercialization of an innovation based on external technology takes more time and about as much money as the commercialization of one based on internal technology, in Japan it takes about 10 percent less time and over 50 percent less money than the commercialization of an internal-technology-based innovation.

Many innovations based on external technology are new products that imitate others in important respects. The relatively higher commercialization cost for innovations based on external technology in the United States than in Japan seems to have been due in part to the fact that the Japanese, in carrying out such innovations, have been more likely than the Americans to make significant technical adaptations of the imitated product and/or to reduce its production costs substantially. The Americans have been more inclined than the Japanese to invest heavily in marketing startup costs in an effort to position such innovations optimally in the market, the emphasis being more on marketing strategies than on technical performance and production cost. (Much more will be said on this score in §5 below.) Naturally, this has resulted in relatively high commercialization costs for such innovations in the United States.

4. Time-Cost Tradeoffs

To see more clearly the nature and extent of the Japanese advantage with respect to innovations based on external technology, consider the well-known time-cost tradeoff function:

$$c = f(t), \tag{1}$$

where c equals the cost of carrying out a particular innovation and t is the time devoted to doing so. According to many studies (for example, Mansfield et al. 1971), innovation time can generally be reduced by increasing innovation cost, the consequence being that $dc/dt < 0$ and $d^2c/dt^2 > 0$ for most innovations. A convenient measure of the sensitivity of cost to changes in time is $-dc/dt \cdot t/c$, the elasticity of innovation cost with respect to innovation time.

To see how the nature of this time-cost tradeoff differs between Japan and the United States, we obtained information from 60 Japanese and American firms (the sample of 30 matched pairs described in §3) regarding the average value of the elasticity of cost with respect to time for both the development and commercialization of their innovations introduced in 1975–1985.[11] The results, classified by industry and by whether the innovation was based on internal or external technology, show a strikingly consistent tendency for this elasticity to be higher in Japan than in the United States. Both for development and for commercialization, this elasticity in Japan tends to be about double what it is in the United States (Table 5).[12]

One important implication of this result is that Japanese firms seem willing to devote a much greater amount of resources than American firms to reduce the time taken to develop and introduce an innovation. On the average, Japanese firms in these industries

---

[11] These data were obtained from each firm's managers and engineers, who estimated for each innovation the effects on development cost or commercialization cost of reductions in development or commercialization time. For a description of the methods used, see Mansfield et al. (1971). For each firm, the elasticity of cost with respect to time was calculated for each of its innovations, and the mean of these elasticities was computed. Table 5 shows the average of these means for the firms in each industry and country.

[12] For all industries combined, the differences between Japan and the United States in Table 5 are usually statistically significant, generally at the 0.01 probability level. However, in individual industries, these differences often are not significant.

TABLE 5

Mean Elasticity of Cost with Respect to Time, Development and Commercialization Parts of the Innovation Process, 60 Firms, Japan and the United States, 1975–85

Industry and Nationality[a]	Internal Technology		External Technology	
	Development	Commercialization	Development	Commercialization
	(percentage cost increase to reduce time by 1 percent)			
All Industries Combined				
Japan	10.4	9.8	8.8	7.3
United States	6.2	4.0	3.6	3.7
Chemicals				
Japan	11.2	14.2	7.8	9.2
United States	2.7	2.5	2.8	3.1
Electrical and Instruments				
Japan	5.2	9.0	3.9	8.9
United States	4.3	3.3	5.7	4.8
Machinery				
Japan	15.7	7.7	14.3	4.7
United States	7.4	4.7	3.3	3.5

[a] See note a, Table 3.

are operating at points on their time-cost tradeoff functions where they are devoting the equivalent of about $9(c/t)$ extra dollars of resources to reduce time by 1 month. On the other hand, American firms are operating at points where they are devoting about $4(c/t)$ extra dollars of resources for such a time reduction. Since c/t is not too different in the two countries, as indicated in Tables 1 and 2, the Japanese seem to be willing to devote about twice as many resources to accomplish such a time reduction.[13] Apparently, this is because they believe that the discounted value of the expected profits (gross of innovation costs) from an innovation tends to decrease more rapidly due to delays in the project than do American firms.

If time-cost tradeoff functions were the same in both countries, this emphasis on time would raise the Japanese resource costs above those of their American rivals. But time-cost tradeoff functions are not the same in Japan as in the United States. For innovations based on external technology, the tradeoff function in Japan for a "typical" innovation (that is, one where the elasticity of cost with respect to time equals the mean in Table 5) is considerably to the left of that in the United States, as shown in panel A of Figure 1. On the other hand, for innovations based on internal technology, the time-cost tradeoff functions for a "typical" innovation are as shown in panel B of Figure 1. For this type of innovation, as indicated in §3, American firms appear to be able to match Japanese

---

[13] To derive the figures in the text, note that in Japan the average value of the four elasticities of cost with respect to time for all industries combined in Table 5 is about 9. Thus, since this elasticity equals $-dc/dt \cdot t/c$, dc/dt must equal about $-9c/t$. In the United States, the average value of the four elasticities in Table 5 for all industries combined is about 4, so dc/dt equals about $-4c/t$. Based on Tables 1 and 2, American firms have innovation times and costs that are about 10 or 20 percent greater than those in Japan, so c/t does not seem very different in the two countries. Note once again that the special exchange rate described in §2, not the official exchange rate, is used here.

For the innovation process as a whole, the elasticity of cost with respect to time equals a weighted average of the elasticity for development and the elasticity for commercialization. If the development time and commercialization time are both reduced by 1 percent, the resulting increase in cost equals $E_C \times C_C + E_D \times C_D$, where E_C is the elasticity for commercialization, C_C is the original commercialization cost, E_D is the elasticity for development, and C_D is the original development cost. Since the original total innovation cost was $C_C + C_D$, it follows that the percentage increase in total innovation cost resulting from this 1 percent reduction in total innovation time equals $[C_C/(C_C + C_D)]E_C + [C_D/(C_C + C_D)]E_D$.

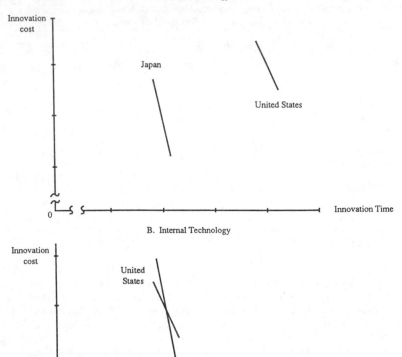

FIGURE 1.   Illustrative Time-Cost Tradeoff Functions, Innovations Based on External and Internal Technology, Japan and the United States.

innovation times when resource costs are the same in the two countries. Thus, if they reduce their innovation time, they may have an advantage over the Japanese since they seem to be positioned to bring about such a time reduction at a smaller extra resource cost than the Japanese.[14]

5.   U.S.-Japanese Differences in the Allocation of Innovation Costs

To explore further the reasons why Japanese firms seem to carry out industrial innovations at less resource cost than do American firms, we obtained information from a sample of 100 Japanese and American firms concerning the ways in which they allocate resources among the following six phases of the innovation process.[15]

---

[14] It is worth noting that the elasticities for U.S. firms in Table 5 tend to be substantially higher than those obtained in Mansfield et al. (1971). This may reflect a greater emphasis on time (relative to cost) in the 1980s than in the 1960s, due to more intense competitive pressures.

[15] This classification of phases of the innovation process comes from Mansfield et al. (1971), and has been used in a number of other studies, including Mansfield (1987). For other relevant studies, see Caves and Uekusa (1976), Guerard, Bean, and Andrews (1987), and Terleckyj and Levy (1985).

1. *Applied Research*, which, according to the National Science Foundation, includes projects that "represent investigation directed to discovery of new scientific knowledge and which have specific commercial objectives with respect to either products or processes." [16]

2. *Preparation of project requirements and basic specifications*, which includes the specification of the product's characteristics, often in coordination with marketing and other non-R and D personnel, as well as planning and scheduling of the project.

3. *Prototype* or *pilot plant*, which includes the design, construction, and testing of a prototype or pilot plant.

4. *Tooling and manufacturing equipment and facilities*, which includes preparation for manufacturing, and the design, construction, and acquisition of manufacturing facilities for the new product, as well as tooling and equipment.

5. *Manufacturing startup*, which includes the training of production workers, the "debugging" of the production facilities, and the resources expended to obtain an acceptable quality level.

6. *Marketing startup*, which includes marketing studies, advertising, sales promotion, and other marketing activities before the sale of any appreciable amount of the new product.

Our sample was chosen from the chemical (including pharmaceuticals), machinery (including computers), electrical equipment, instruments, rubber, and metals industries. It consists of 50 matched pairs, where each pair consists of an American and Japanese firm of roughly comparable size in the same industry.[17] Detailed data were obtained from each firm concerning the average proportion of the total cost of developing and introducing a new product (introduced in 1985) that was incurred in each of the above six stages. Weighting each firm's figures by its size, the results for each industry are shown in Table 6.

TABLE 6

Percentage Distribution of Innovation Costs, 100 Firms, Japan and the United States, 1985

	Percent of Innovation Cost Going for:						
Industry and Nationality[a]	Applied Research	Preparation of Product Specifications	Prototype or Pilot Plant	Tooling and Manufacturing Equipment and Facilities	Manufacturing Startup	Marketing Startup	Total
All Industries Combined							
Japan	14	7	16	44	10	8	100
United States	18	8	17	23	17	17	100
Chemicals							
Japan	18	9	13	42	6	11	100
United States	29	7	13	22	13	17	100
Electrical and Instruments							
Japan	21	7	18	26	18	10	100
United States	16	8	11	26	18	21	100
Machinery							
Japan	6	5	20	58	5	6	100
United States	6	11	23	20	21	18	100
Rubber and Metals							
Japan	9	8	6	66	6	5	100
United States	15	4	15	45	15	6	100

[a] The sample sizes are: all industries combined, 100; chemicals, 36; electrical and instruments, 20; machinery, 30; and rubber and metals, 14.

[16] Sanow (1959, p. 124).

[17] The 50 Japanese firms are the same as those included in the sample in §2. As pointed out in §2, they account for about one-quarter of all R and D in these industries in Japan. The 50 American firms account for a somewhat smaller fraction than this of all R and D in these industries in the United States.

Clearly, Japanese firms, in carrying out an innovation, allocate their resources quite differently than do American firms. In particular, the Japanese devote a much larger percentage of total innovation cost to tooling and manufacturing equipment and facilities than do Americans. Specifically, this percentage is about double that in the United States, and in all but one of these industries in Table 6, there is a large difference of this sort. [18] The emphasis of Japanese firms on process engineering and efficient manufacturing facilities is well known, [19] but never before have data been obtained to indicate how large this difference between Japanese and American firms really is.

American firms, on the other hand, devote a much larger proportion of innovation cost to manufacturing startup than do Japanese firms, which may reflect greater difficulties in the United States in attaining desired quality levels (due partly perhaps to differences in the experience, training, and education of the labor force). Also, according to some Japanese firms, their manufacturing startup costs tend to be relatively low because their engineers work more closely and directly with their workforce than do those in many American firms. [20]

But the biggest and perhaps most illuminating difference pertains to marketing startup (which, to repeat, consists of pre-introduction marketing activities). American firms devote a much larger percentage of total innovation cost to marketing startup than do Japanese firms. [21] In every industry, the percentage of innovation cost devoted to marketing startup in the United States is about double that in Japan. If American firms were able to reduce this percentage to the Japanese level (while holding constant the amounts they spend on other stages of the innovation process), it appears that about 60 percent of the Japanese cost advantage in Table 2 would be eliminated. [22]

6. Summary and Conclusions

Based on this study, which is the first systematic empirical investigation of the differences between the two countries in innovation cost and time, the situation is much more varied and complex than is generally portrayed by the largely anecdotal accounts that have begun to appear. Whereas the Japanese have substantial advantages in this regard in some industries (notably machinery), they do not seem to have any substantial advantage

[18] For all industries combined, the difference between Japan and the United States in the proportion of innovation cost devoted to tooling and manufacturing equipment and facilities is statistically significant at the 0.01 probability level.

[19] For example, see Okimoto (1986) and Riggs (1985).

[20] For all industries combined, the difference between Japanese and American firms in the percentage of innovation cost devoted to manufacturing startup is statistically significant at the 0.05 probability level. According to some observers (in both countries), another reason why this percentage is relatively low in Japan is that Japanese employees in this stage of the innovation process are more likely than their American counterparts to work on the project on their own time. We have no evidence to confirm or deny this.

[21] For all industries combined, this difference is statistically significant at the 0.01 probability level. Two points should be noted concerning this difference. First, to some extent, it may reflect the fact that some Japanese firms are less involved with the marketing, as distinct from the production, of their products than American firms. For example, see Clark (1984). However, even among firms that are closely involved with the marketing function, there seems to be a difference of this sort. Second, the Japanese seem to be particularly adept at innovations suggested by external customers or the firm's own manufacturing department and by suggestions for incremental change from the company's own organization. For such innovations, there may be less need for marketing startup expenditures than for other types of innovations. In sum, because of structural differences between Japanese and American industry (for example, the importance of trading companies in Japan), one must be cautious in interpreting this difference; however, it appears to be much more than a statistical artifact.

[22] According to Table 2, U.S. costs of innovation exceed those in Japan by 10–20 percent, which means that, if U.S. costs were cut by about 15 percent, they would be approximately equal to those in Japan. If American firms reduced the percentage of innovation cost devoted to marketing startup from its current level (17 percent, according to Table 6) to the Japanese level (8 percent), this would reduce the U.S. costs of innovation by about 9 percent. Thus, it appears that about 60 percent of the Japanese cost advantage would be eliminated.

in others (notably chemicals). Whereas they have very great advantages in carrying out innovations based on external technology, they do not seem to have any in carrying out innovations based on internal technology. These results are important, because they put the Japanese challenge to American technological leadership into better perspective.

A large part of America's problem in this regard seems to be due to its apparent inability to match Japan as a quick and effective user of external technology. As Brooks (1983) has warned, "the United States, so long accustomed to leading the world, may have lost the art of creative imitation. . . ."[23] This is not to deny that part of the Japanese advantage may be due to factors like their propensity to overlap various stages of the innovation process, their subcontractor network, and their fewer organizational barriers and better communication between functional departments of firms.[24] But the fact that the Japanese advantage tends to be limited to innovations based on external technology suggests that it is in this area that many central problems lie.[25]

American firms should reexamine the way they carry out such innovations. Recognizing the roughness and limitations of our data,[26] it nonetheless is striking that the cost and time required to carry out innovations based on external technology is so much higher (both in absolute terms and relative to other innovations) in the United States than in Japan. Based both on the data and direct observations of the innovation process, one suspects that many firms safely could reduce the cost and time devoted to marketing startup without impairing the vital interface between R and D and marketing. The organization of firms, including the relationship between R and D, marketing and production, might be altered somewhat to promote the utilization and adaptation of external technology. More efforts might be made by both firms and government agencies to obtain information concerning foreign technology. There is no reason why American firms,

---

[23] Brooks (1983, p. 17).

[24] Other factors stressed by Imai, Nonaka, and Takeuchi are the role of top management as catalyst, the use of self-organizing teams, the promotion of learning, and subtlety of control. For further discussion of these and other factors, see Clark, Hayes, and Lorenz (1985), and Abegglen and Stalk (1985).

We obtained detailed unpublished information from Imai, Nonaka, and Takeuchi concerning the frequency of overlap among adjacent nonmarketing phases of the innovation process (listed in §5) in the sample of innovations they studied. In about $\frac{3}{4}$ of the cases, there was some overlap. The limited amount of data on this score for the United States indicates that, for about $\frac{1}{2}$ of the cases studied, there was some overlap. (See Mansfield et al. 1971.) Thus, the data seem to be in accord with their hypothesis that Japanese firms have been more inclined than American firms to overlap stages of the innovation process, although it is obvious that American firms too do considerable overlapping. Nonetheless, because the data are so sparse, this should not be considered a formal test of this hypothesis.

Another factor, pointed out by Lewis Branscomb in private correspondence, is that, once a new product is shipped, and further improvements need to be made, the manufacturing engineering department in the Japanese plant may make these changes without going back to development. In the United States, the marketing team is likely to go back to the development organization, which would consider whether to make them. If so, they might make the complete changes in documentation for design and production release, and perhaps have quality assurance requalify the product. This takes months and is costly.

[25] The Japanese adeptness at utilizing external technology has often been noted. For example, see Abegglen and Stalk (1985), Baranson (1981), Lynn (1982), and Okimoto (1986). It is worth stressing that part of their success in this regard hinges on the thoroughness and skill with which they monitor foreign technology and determine which types of external technology to utilize. They invest much more in such monitoring than do American firms. See Mansfield (1985).

[26] Before concluding, it should be recognized that, although we have devoted many man-months to the task of making the Japanese and American data in this paper as comparable as possible, and although hundreds of Japanese and American firms, as well as government officials and academic scholars, have helped us enormously, there is no way to eliminate completely the possibility of errors of interpretation by respondents. Thus, while intensive discussions with respondents indicate that there is little chance that the very large and persistent overall differences between the two nations identified here can be attributed to such factors, some of the results for particular industries (particularly those where the sample size is small) should be treated with considerable caution.

which once were very talented and accomplished imitators, cannot improve their performance in this regard.[27]

[27] This paper was presented at the Annual Meeting of the American Economic Association in December 1987. A preliminary version was presented at the Spring 1987 Symposium at Wharton Econometric Forecasting Associates. The research on which it is based was supported by a grant from the Division of Policy Research and Analysis of the National Science Foundation, which, of course, is not responsible for the views expressed here. I am indebted to Rolf Piekarz, Gary Saxonhouse, and Eleanor Thomas for their helpful comments and to the many Japanese and American firms that provided data for this study.

References

ABEGGLEN, J. AND G. STALK, *Kaisha: The Japanese Corporation*, Basic Books, New York, 1985.

BARANSON, J., *The Japanese Challenge to U.S. Industry*, D. C. Heath, Lexington, MA, 1981.

BROOKS, H., Testimony before House Subcommittee on Science, Research, and Technology, *Japanese Technological Advances and Possible United States Responses Using Research Joint Ventures*, 98th Congress, first session, June 29–30, 1983.

CAVES, R. AND M. UEKUSA, *Industrial Organization in Japan*, Brookings, Washington, D.C., 1976.

CLARK, K., R. HAYES AND C. LORENZ (EDS.), *The Uneasy Alliance*, Harvard Business School, Boston, 1985.

CLARK, R., *Aspects of Japanese Commercial Innovation*, The Technical Change Centre, London, November 1984.

DAVIDSON, W., *The Amazing Race*, John Wiley, New York, 1984.

FEIGENBAUM, E. AND P. MCCORDUCK, *The Fifth Generation*, New American Library, New York, 1984.

GUERARD, J., A. BEAN AND S. ANDREWS, "R and D Management and Corporate Financial Policy," *Management Sci.*, 33 (November 1987), 1419–1427.

IMAI, K., I. NONAKA AND H. TAKEUCHI, "Managing the New Product Development Process: How Japanese Companies Learn and Unlearn," in Kim Clark, Robert Hayes, and Christopher Lorenz (Eds.), *The Uneasy Alliance*, Harvard Business School, Boston, 1985.

LYNN, L., *How Japan Innovates*, Westview Press, Boulder, CO, 1982.

MANSFIELD, E., "Innovation, R and D, and Firm Growth in Robotics: Japan and the United States," Symposium on Research and Development, Industrial Change and Economic Policy, University of Karlstad, Sweden, 1987.

———, "Industrial R and D in Japan and the United States: A Comparative Study," *American Economic Review*, 78 (May 1988).

———, "Comments on Productivity Growth and R and D: Japan-U.S. Comparisons," National Bureau of Economic Research, Conference on Income and Wealth, 1985.

———, A. ROMEO, M. SCHWARTZ, D. TEECE, S. WAGNER AND P. BRACH, *Technology Transfer, Productivity, and Economic Policy*, W. W. Norton, New York, 1982.

———, J. RAPOPORT, J. SCHNEE, S. WAGNER AND M. HAMBURGER, *Research and Innovation in the Modern Corporation*, W. W. Norton, New York, 1971.

OKIMOTO, D., "The Japanese Challenge in High Technology," in R. Landau and N. Rosenberg (Eds.), *The Positive Sum Strategy*, National Academy Press, Washington, D.C., 1986.

Organization for Economic Cooperation and Development, *Trends in Industrial R and D, 1967–75*, OECD, Paris, 1979.

RIGGS, H., "Innovation: A U.S.-Japan Perspective," High Technology Research Project, Stanford University, September 1985.

SANOW, K., "Development of Statistics Relating to Research and Development Activities in Private Industry," *Methodology of Statistics on Research and Development*, National Science Foundation, Washington, D.C., 1959.

TERLECKYJ, N. AND D. LEVY, "Trends in Industrial R and D Activities in the United States, Europe, and Japan, 1963–83," Conference on Income and Wealth, 1985.

Technological change in robotics: Japan and the United States

Summary

This paper summarizes very briefly the results of a study comparing the R & D, innovation and diffusion processes with regard to industrial robots in Japan and the United States. Detailed data were collected from carefully selected samples of over 200 Japanese and US firms. The United States seems to be at a disadvantage with respect to innovation time (which is about 20–30 per cent lower in Japan) and innovation cost (about 10 per cent lower). The Japanese advantage in robotics seems to increase as one moves from R & D toward the market.

Introduction

The industrial robot is one of the most important manufacturing innovations of recent times. Japan and the United States, two of the leading producers and users of robots, both compete and cooperate with regard to robotics. Our purpose in this paper is to summarize very briefly a study that compares the R & D, innovation and diffusion processes with regard to robots in the two countries. In particular, we are concerned primarily with the following questions:

1. Do US robot producers develop and introduce new robots as quickly and economically as the Japanese?
2. Do they spend as much on various kinds of research and development as the Japanese?
3. Has the number of firms using industrial robots grown as rapidly in the United States as in Japan?
4. Has the number of robots used by firms grown as rapidly in the United States as in Japan?

Practically all our results are based on data obtained from carefully selected samples of over 200 Japanese and US firms. We use the definition of a robot put forward by the Robotics Industry Association, which says that it is a reprogrammable multi-functional manipulator designed to move material, parts, tools and specialized devices through various programmed motions for the performance of a variety of tasks. In their statistics the Japanese often include manual manipulators and fixed-sequence 'robots' as well. Like most analysts, we do not regard these as robots.

Industrial robots in the United States and Japan

Much of the early work on robotics took place in the United States, and some of the first patents for an industrial robot were developed by George C. Devol Jr in the 1950s.

Devol sold the rights in 1961 to Consolidated Diesel Electric Corporation, which formed a subsidiary (Unimation) which became the leading producer of robots for many years. During the 1960s and 1970s the sales of robots remained very small, although they became more sizeable during the late 1970s, when the auto industry purchased more robots, particularly for spot welding. The 1980s have seen substantial growth in robot sales in the United States, which exceeded $400 million in 1985. However, sales dropped in 1987, due in part to the scaled-back investment plans of General Motors.

Since Unimation's formation many firms have entered the US robot industry. Cincinnati Milacron, DeVilbiss (which sold robots licensed by the Norwegian firm, Trallfa), ASEA (a large Swedish firm) and Prab were relatively early entrants. During the 1980s major firms such as IBM and General Electric, as well as small start-up ones like Automatix and Control Automation, entered the ranks. Moreover, General Motors and Fujitsu Fanuc established a joint venture in 1982 which by 1984 had become the new industry leader. However, in the past couple of years, as expected sales increases have not materialized, some of these firms, such as General Electric and Unimation (which was sold to Westinghouse in 1982), have withdrawn from the market or closed their plants.[1]

In Japan, although some relevant academic research occurred in the 1950s and 1960s, Japanese firms showed little interest in robotics until about 1967, when a subsidiary of AMF brought a Versatron robot to Japan and a robot symposium was held in Tokyo. In 1968 Unimation assigned license rights to Kawasaki Heavy Industries, which became the leading Japanese producer of robots. There was a very great interest in robots in Japan during the late 1960s and early 1970s and many firms entered the industry. At present, the industry is composed of about 150 firms, some very large (Kawasaki, Hitachi and Mitsubishi) and some very small (Dainichi Kiko).[2]

The Japanese robot industry has developed considerable strength. According to the International Trade Commission (1983):[3]

> Research and development in the United States is largely directed at the design of more complex devices ... Japanese producers have directed a sizable share of their effort ... to produce relatively less expensive machines which can be easily diffused through their industries.

By 1983 the US Department of Commerce concluded that: 'The Japanese enjoy undisputed superiority in terms of their producers' experience, capacity, financial strength, and market position.'[4] The Japanese government has been active in developing and supporting robotics, as we shall see below.

The innovation process

To see whether US robot producers develop and introduce new robots as quickly and economically as the Japanese we chose a random sample of 20 US and 15 Japanese robot producers which includes almost 90 per cent of US production and about 20 per cent of all Japanese.[5] Each firm in the sample was asked to estimate the percentage difference, if any, between the average time and cost of developing and commercially introducing a new robot (of comparable novelty, importance and complexity) by Japanese and US firms. Both nations' firms report that the Japanese tend to be faster, by about 30 per cent according to the Japanese or by 20 per cent according to the

Americans. Based on purchasing power parity for resources used in the innovation process,[6] Japanese firms also seem to be more economical innovators than the Americans, the difference being about 10 per cent according to both Japanese and American estimates (see Table 1).

Table 1   Ratio of innovation time and cost in Japan to that in the US robot industry, 1985, as reported by Japanese and US firms in the sample

Nationality of firms providing the estimates	Mean ratio of Japan to USA	
	Innovation time	Innovation cost[a]
Japanese	0.72	0.86
American	0.83	0.92

[a]   The exchange rate used to convert yen into dollars reflects the relative price of R & D inputs (and others used in the innovation process) in Japan and the United States. The data on which this exchange rate is based were obtained from a sample of firms which is large enough so that the sampling errors are negligible (see note 6). As the Organization for Economic Co-operation and Development (1979) and others have stressed, the official exchange rate does not adequately reflect the relative price of R & D inputs (and other inputs used in the innovation process) in the two countries. Consequently, we had to derive and apply this exchange rate in order to estimate the difference between the two countries in the amount of resources used to develop and commercialize a new robot.

Detailed data were also obtained from the firms in this sample concerning the proportion of the total cost of developing and introducing a new product that was incurred in (1) applied research, (2) preparation of project requirements and basic specifications, (3) the design, production and testing of the prototype, (4) tooling and design, construction and acquisition of manufacturing facilities for the new product, (5) manufacturing start-up, and (6) marketing start-up. These six stages are defined to include the entire innovation process.[7] The results indicate that the US firms devote a much larger proportion of innovation cost to marketing start-up – that is, to marketing studies, advertising, sales promotion and other marketing activities before the sale of any appreciable amount of the new product – than do Japanese firms (Table 2). On the other hand, the Japanese devote a much larger percentage of total innovation cost to tooling and manufacturing equipment and facilities than do the Americans.

Surprisingly, if the US firms were to reduce their marketing start-up costs by one-third, which would mean that the percentage of total innovation costs devoted to marketing start-up would still be more than double that in Japan, the Japanese advantage with respect to the total resource cost of innovation in this industry would vanish.[8] One reason why US robot producers have devoted unusually large percentages of total innovation cost to marketing start-up is that the diffusion of robots has been slower than many firms forecasted, and they have been pressed to find and persuade potential customers to purchase them. In Japan, on the other hand, many robot producers have developed robots for their own use, and have not devoted much marketing effort to them in their earlier stages. In other industries, not robots alone, Japanese firms devote relatively fewer resources to marketing start-up than US firms.

The emphasis of Japanese firms on process engineering and efficient manufacturing facilities is reflected in the fact that the percentage of total innovation cost devoted to tooling and manufacturing equipment and facilities seems to be about five times that of the United States. In both countries high-growth robot producers tend to devote a much higher proportion of innovation costs to tooling and manufacturing facilities than do low-growth ones (Table 2), and the proportion devoted to marketing start-up seems to be much lower among high-growth than low-growth robot producers. Based on these data, it appears that the more successful firms in both countries, like the Japanese, tend to emphasize manufacturing in the innovation process, rather than marketing.[9]

R & D expenditures

As in any science-based industry, research and development is of great importance to robot producers. In our sample, US robot producers devoted about 17 per cent of 1985 sales to R & D, while the Japanese firms allocated about 10 per cent (Table 3). However, since Japan's robot sales have been much larger than those of US firms, its total 1985 R & D investment in absolute, real terms may have been greater than that of the US robot industry.[10] Turning to the composition of R & D, detailed data obtained from the sample of firms indicate that the Japanese robot firms devote about as large a percentage of their R & D expenditures to basic and applied research (rather than development) as do US ones (Table 4). Also, there is no significant difference between the US and Japanese firms in the proportion of R & D expenditures reportedly aimed at the development of entirely new products and processes (rather than the improvement or adaptation of existing products or processes).[11] In contrast to many other industries, it appears that the Japanese robot firms are betting as heavily as the Americans on making great advances, not incremental changes, in technology.

Table 2   Composition of innovation cost, Japanese and US robot producers, 1985

Nationality and characteristics of firms[a]	Applied research	Preparation of product specifications	Prototype	Tooling and manufacturing equipment and facilities	Manufacturing start-up	Marketing start-up	Total
Japanese firms	11	16	29	23	12	10	100
Large	10	17	27	23	12	10	100
Small	14	6	48	14	9	9	100
High growth	5	14	30	33	11	7	100
Low growth	19	22	25	7	13	13	100
US firms	10	11	24	4	14	37	100
Large	10	10	21	4	14	41	100
Small	7	16	43	6	13	13	100
High growth	12	13	24	4	12	34	100
Low growth	5	1	13	1	20	60	100

Percentage of innovation cost going for:

[a]   In the United States a small robot producer is one with 1984 sales below $5 million; a large one has 1984 sales of $5 million or more. In Japan a small robot producer is one with 1983 sales below 800 million yen; a large one has 1983 sales of 800 million yen or more.

   In the United States high-growth producers are defined as those that had more than a 50 per cent average annual increase in robot sales in 1982-5; low-growth producers are those that had a 50 per cent increase or less. (Of course, this is a short period, but the robot industry is very young. In one case where data were unavailable for 1982-5, the growth rate had to be based on only part of the period.) In Japan high-growth producers are those that had an average annual growth rate of sales of more than 50 per cent during 1979-84; low-growth producers are those that had an average annual growth rate of 50 per cent or less. (In cases where data were unavailable for 1979-84 the growth rates had to be based on only part of the period.)

   For lack of data, not all of the sample can be classified as 'high growth' or 'low growth'. Joint ventures between US and Japanese firms are omitted, since they are neither purely US nor purely Japanese.

Table 3   Expenditures on research and development as a percentage of sales, Japanese and US robot producers, 1985[a]

	Japan	United States
All firms	10	17
Large	9	17
Small	12	21
High growth	12	30
Low growth	7	9

[a]   See note a, Table 2. Note in particular that joint ventures between Japanese and US firms are omitted because they are neither purely American nor purely Japanese and because it is so difficult to consider them separately from their parent firms.

Given the often-stated assertion that the Japanese are more patient than US firms, it is interesting to note that the proportion of R & D expenditure devoted to relatively long-term projects (those expected to last more than five years) does not differ significantly between the two countries – and the sample proportion is higher in the United States than in Japan. The share of R & D expenditure devoted to new products and product improvements (rather than new processes and process improvements) is higher for Japanese robot firms than for US ones. In most industries this is not the case; instead the Japanese generally emphasize process R & D more than US firms.

In both countries high-growth robot producers tend to be more research-intensive and technologically ambitious in their R & D programmes than low-growth ones. The percentage of sales devoted to R & D was about two or three times as great among high-growth as among low-growth producers (Table 3). The percentage of R & D expenditures devoted to research (rather than development) and that aimed at entirely new products and processes was at least twice as large among high-growth as among low-growth producers (Table 4). In the robot industry the more successful firms seem to devote a larger share of their R & D to more fundamental and technologically ambitious projects, which is likely to have contributed to their success.[12]

Table 4   Composition of R & D expenditures, Japanese and US robot producers, 1985

Nationality and characteristics of firms[a]	Basic research	Applied research	New products and product improvements	Entirely new products and processes	Projects expected to last more than 5 years
		Percentage of R & D expenditures going for:			
Japanese firms	12	23	65	51	10
Large	12	24	65	53	8
Small	11	17	73	10	34
High growth	15	32	73	63	6
Low growth	6	11	51	34	12
US firms	13	21	39	46	17
Large	15	23	41	44	11
Small	2	8	25	56	50
High growth	14	29	48	52	12[b]
Low growth	15	4	22	19	11[b]

[a]   See note a, Tables 2 and 3.
[b]   As pointed out in note a, Table 2, because of lack of data not all of the sample can be classified as 'high growth' or 'low growth'. This explains why both these percentages are below the figure of 17 per cent given in this column for all US firms. Similar situations occur for this reason elsewhere in Tables 2-4.

The imitation process

Although the industrial robot was largely a US invention the rate of imitation for industrial robots in the United States was slow relative to other major industrial inno-vations. Based on data we obtained from a random sample of one hundred major firms[13] it took, on average, about 12 years (from the date of first use in the relevant industry) for half of the major potential users in ten industries – autos, auto parts, electrical equipment, appliances, steel, non-ferrous metals, aerospace, farm machinery, machine tools and other machinery – to begin using robots.[14] In contrast, it took only about five years, on average, for half of the potential users in an industry to begin using numerically controlled machine tools, an important precursor of robots.[15]

In Japan, where US robotics technology began to be transferred in the 1960s, the rate of imitation was faster than in the United States. Based on data we obtained from a random sample of 75 firms, it took, on average, about eight years (from the data of first use in the relevant industry) for half of the major potential users in four industries – autos, electrical equipment, metals and machinery – to begin using robots.[16] In both the United States and Japan the imitation process can be represented reasonably well by a simple econometric model similar to that in Mansfield (1961, 1968) and Mansfield *et al.* (1977). According to the results, Japan's higher rate of imitation can be explained entirely by its later start, which enabled it to utilize earlier experience in the United States and elsewhere.[17]

Since robots tend to be more profitable for firms that can introduce them in relatively large quantities, and for other reasons,[18] one would expect that larger firms in both countries would be quicker, on average, than smaller firms to begin using them. In each country and industry we regressed a firm's year of first use of robots (less 1959) on its sales. In all but one case the regression coefficient has the expected sign, and in about half of the cases it is statistically significant.

By 1985 the average proportion of major firms in these industries using robots was about 70-75 per cent in both Japan and the United States. Based on the estimates of the non-users as to when, if ever, they would begin using robots, it appears that 90 per cent or more of the major firms in practically all these US industries will be using robots by 1990. (Our model is less optimistic in this regard.) In Japan such estimates indicate that the proportion of major Japanese firms in these industries using robots will be about 90 per cent by 1995.[19]

Intrafirm rates of diffusion

Turning from the rate of imitation (the growth over time in the number of firms using robots) to the intrafirm rate of diffusion (the growth over time in the number of robots used by a firm), it seems clear that the intrafirm rate of diffusion has been much greater in Japan than in the United States. In our sample, the number of robots used per 10 000 employees is much higher in Japan than the United States. Tables 5 and 6 show the world robot population, as well as the areas of application in Japan and the United States.

In considerable part, this observed difference in robot utilization between Japan and the United States seems to be due to differences in the minimum rate of return required to justify investing in robots. Whereas the Japanese often invest in robots yielding returns of 20 per cent, US firms frequently insist on 30 per cent or more. This difference in minimum required rates of return has been noted in other studies as well, and may reflect a tendency, cited by Kaplan (1986), for US firms to exaggerate their cost of capital.[20] Based on data we obtained from the Japanese firms in our sample, it seems that if they had applied the same 'hurdle rates' as their US rivals their robot utilization would have fallen by 50 per cent or more.

Also, the relatively large number of robots used by Japanese firms may be due to government programmes designed to promote their use. Low-interest loans have been granted to small and medium-sized firms for the purchase of robots with extra depreciation allowances. The Japanese Robot Leasing Company provides generous leasing terms for robots. The Japanese firms in our sample claim that these programmes have had a relatively minor effect on the rate of diffusion, but it seems obvious that they have had a positive one.[21]

Table 5   World robot population, 1978-82

Nation	1978	1979	1980	1981	1982
Japan	10 095	11 533	14 246	21 684	31 900
United States	2 831	3 340	3 849	4 700	7 232
West Germany	450	b	823	2 301	3 500
Sweden	800	b	1 133	1 700	b
France	b	b	200	620	993
United Kingdom	125	b	371	713	977
Belgium	b	b	b	44	305
Canada	b	b	b	214	273
Italy	b	b	400	450	600
Finland	b	b	40	b	75
Austria	b	b	b	b	70
Norway	b	b	b	b	20
Switzerland	b	b	b	b	200
Taiwan	b	b	b	b	11
Other	b	b	b	b	2 000
Total	16 000	19 000	24 000	35 000	50 000

[a]   Excludes Communist countries.
[b]   Not available.
Source: International Trade Commission (1983).

Table 6   Installed operating industrial robots, by application, Japan and the United States, 1982

	Japan		United States	
Application	Units	Percentage	Units	Percentage
Welding	8 052	25	2 453	39
Painting	1 071	3	490	8
Assembly	6 099	19	73	1
Casting	557	2	875	14
Materials handling	6 797	21	1 300	21
Machine loading and unloading	2 578	8	1 060	17
Other	6 746	21	50	1
Total	31 900	100[a]	6 301	100[a]

[a]   Because of rounding errors, the figures do not sum to the total.
Source: Aron (1983). The basic data come from reports of the Japanese Industrial Robot Association and the Robotics Institute of America.

Conclusions

Our results indicate that, in comparing Japan and the United States with regard to technological change in robotics, it is essential that one consider the R & D, innovation, imitation and intrafirm diffusion processes separately, since the relative performance of the two countries seems to vary considerably depending on which of these processes is taken up. In research and development the US robot producers, while their R & D spending may not be as great as the Japanese in absolute real terms, spend more as a percentage of sales than their Japanese rivals, and technologically ambitious projects seem to bulk as large in their R & D as in that in Japan. Moreover, there is no evidence that US firms are any less efficient than the Japanese in doing the R & D for a new robot; on the contrary, US firms do not seem to have any higher resource costs than do the Japanese.[22] Further, there is no evidence that the quality of R & D output is lower in the United States than in Japan.[23]

Turning to the innovation process, the United States seems to be at a disadvantage with respect to innovation time (which is about 20-30 per cent lower in Japan) and innovation cost (which is about 10 per cent lower in real terms in Japan). To a considerable extent, this disadvantage with regard to the resource cost of innovation reflects the much greater allocation of resources to marketing start-up in the United States than in Japan. Perhaps US firms can cut their large marketing start-up costs without reducing the effectiveness of their new product introductions; the more successful robot producers in both Japan and the United States seem to keep such costs relatively low while devoting a relatively large share of total innovation cost to tooling and manufacturing equipment.

With regard to the imitation process, the number of firms using robots has grown more slowly in the United States than in Japan, but this has been due to Japan's later start. If we compare industries that began to introduce robots at the same time the rate of imitation has been no lower in the United States than in Japan. The large difference between the two countries has occurred in the intrafirm diffusion process. Once they have begun using robots, US firms have been slower to do so in very large numbers than have the Japanese. This seems to have been due in considerable part to their insisting on much higher minimum rates of return to justify investing in robots than have the Japanese. According to Kaplan (1986) and others, US firms have frequently overestimated their true cost of capital, which may help to account for this tendency.

Clearly, the Japanese advantage in robotics seems to increase as one moves from R & D toward the market. Whereas the Japanese seem to be quicker and more efficient innovators, they do not seem to be more effective at R & D, and while they have introduced many more robots than US firms, they have not been quicker to begin using them. If, as many observers claim, US industry has not utilized robots as fully as it should, the principal fault does not seem to lie with US R & D. Instead, this case seems to illustrate the Business-Higher Education Forum's (1983) contention that, in those areas where the United States is falling behind competitively, it is due to problems 'not so much in R & D or inventiveness, but in the commercial application of scientific discoveries and technological advances'.[24]

Acknowledgements

This paper was presented at the annual meetings of the Association of Managerial Economists in December 1987. The research on which it is based was supported by a grant from the Division of Information Science and Technology of the National Science Foundation, which, of course, is not responsible for the views expressed here. Thanks go to Laurence Rosenberg and Charles Brownstein of the Foundation for helpful comments, as well as to the many Japanese and US firms that provided data.

Notes

1. For descriptions of the evolution of the robot industry, see Office of Technology Assessment (1984), Hunt and Hunt (1983), and Miller (forthcoming).
2. See Baranson (1983) and Ayres et al. (1982).
3. International Trade Commission (1983), p.51.
4. US Department of Commerce (1983), p.38.
5. In 1984 almost 90 per cent of all robots produced in the United States were accounted for by our sample. The Japanese sample also contains a wide range of firm sizes. The data were collected through correspondence and interviews. The firms were chosen at random from the lists of robot producers in Aron (1983, 1985) and Prudential-Bache (supplemented by the Thomas Register). Problems of non-response were minor.
6. See Organization for Economic Co-operation and Development (1979). These data were obtained from leading firms that carry out R & D and related innovative activities in relevant fields in both countries. The results for these firms were averaged. Because the interfirm differences turned out to be small, the sampling errors in the resulting R & D exchange rate seem to be negligible.
7. This division of the innovation process was used in Mansfield et al. (1971), where each phase is discussed in more detail.
8. If US firms could reduce marketing start-up costs by about one-third, these costs would be about 25 per cent of total innovation costs (which is more than double the Japanese percentage), and total innovation costs in the United States would be cut by about 12 per cent, which would make them approximately equal to those in Japan (according to Table 1). Of course, this calculation assumes that the costs of phases of the innovation process other than marketing start-up remain constant.
9. More detailed description and analysis of the results summarized in this section are presented in Mansfield (1987a).
10. For robot sales in both countries, see Mansfield (1987a).
11. Of course, it is difficult to distinguish between an entirely new product or process and an improvement of an existing one, so this finding should be viewed with caution. However, it is worth noting that in other industries the Japanese generally report a lower percentage of R & D expenditures aimed at entirely new products and processes than the Americans do.
12. Mansfield (1987a) contains a more detailed account of the findings summarized in this section.
13. A 'major' firm is defined here as one whose 1984 sales exceeded $50 million. In our sample (described in note 14) of major firms each firm not using robots in 1985 was asked whether it would do so by the year 2000. If it said no, it was not included as a potential user. Only 4 per cent of the firms in the sample said no.
14. *Business Week*, 9 July 1984, and the *Thomas Register* provided a list of major firms (1984 sales exceeding $50 million) in these ten industries. A random sample of 100 of these firms was chosen. Each firm in this sample was contacted and a questionnaire dealing with its use (or non-use) of robots was sent to the firm's president (or chairman). In many cases it was necessary to contact the firm again, and in some, interviews were obtained with the firm's executives. Also, published information and other sources were used. Eventually the data were obtained. For further details, see Mansfield (1987b).
15. See Mansfield et al. (1977).
16. A sample of 80 Japanese firms in these industries was chosen from *International Dun and Bradstreet*. The population consisted of the larger firms in each industry, the number being approximately the same as in the population in note 14. Thus the Japanese population is comparable with the American population of firms (excluding the aerospace industry, which is far more important in this regard in the United States than in Japan). The size distribution of firms in the Japanese sample is somewhat different from that in the US sample, but this reflects the differences in the population size distributions. For further details, see Mansfield (1987b).
17. *Ibid.*
18. For other reasons, see Mansfield (1968).
19. See Mansfield (1987b).
20. See Baranson (1983) and Office of Technology Assessment (1984). Also, the cost of capital may be higher in the US.

21. For a more detailed account of these findings, see Mansfield (1987b). Other factors that are often cited are Japan's system of lifetime employment, the fact that Japanese labour unions are not primarily craft ones but industrial unions or those organized on a company basis, the Japanese fear during the early 1970s of a labour shortage due to demographic changes, the propensity of US firms to under-estimate the returns from robots by focusing almost exclusively on their effects on labour costs and the fact that the senior management of many large US firms are dominated by people with non-engineering, non-manufacturing backgrounds. Obviously, there is no way to tell with precision how much of the observed Japanese-American gap in robot utilization each of these factors can explain.

22. R & D consists of applied research, preparation of product specifications and prototype in Table 2. Thus according to Table 2, it accounts for 56 per cent of the cost of developing and commercially introducing a new robot in Japan and 45 per cent of this cost in the United States. According to Table 1, the resource cost of developing and commercially introducing a new robot in Japan is about 89 per cent of that in the United States. Consequently, the resource cost of the R & D for a new robot in the United States must average about $0.45 \div (0.89 \times 0.56)$, or about 90 per cent of that in Japan for a comparable new robot. Of course, these figures are approximate.

23. See, for example, US Department of Commerce (1983).

24. Business-Higher Education Forum (1983), pp. 20-21.

References

Aron, P. (1983), *The Robot Scene in Japan: an Update*, New York: Daiwa Securities.

Aron, P. (1985), *The Robot Scene in Japan: the Second Update*, New York: Daiwa Securities.

Ayres, R., L. Lynn and S. Miller (1982), 'Technology transfer in robotics between the U.S. and Japan'. In C. Uyehara (ed.), *Technological Exchange: The U.S.-Japanese Experience*, Washington, DC: University Press of America.

Baranson, J. (1983), *Robots in Manufacturing*, Mt Airy, Maryland: Lomond.

Business-Higher Education Forum (1983), *America's Competitive Challenge*, Washington, DC: Business-Higher Education Forum.

Hunt, H.A. and T. Hunt (1983), *Human Resource Implications of Robotics*, Kalamazoo, Michigan: W.E. Upjohn Institute.

International Trade Commission (1983), *Competitive Position of U.S. Producers of Robotics in Domestic and World Markets*, Washington, DC: Government Printing Office.

Japan Industrial Robot Association (1982), *The Robotics Industry of Japan*, Tokyo: Fuji Corporation.

Kaplan, R. (1986), 'Must CIM be justified by faith alone?' *Harvard Business Review* **64**, March, 329-38.

Mansfield, E. (1961), 'Technical change and the rate of imitation', *Econometrica* **29**, October, 741-66.

Mansfield, E. (1968), *Industrial Research and Technological Innovation*, New York: W.W. Norton for the Cowles Foundation for Research in Economics at Yale University.

Mansfield, E. et al. (1971), *Research and Innovation in the Modern Corporation*, New York: W.W. Norton.

Mansfield, E. et al. (1977), *The Production and Application of New Industrial Technology*, New York: W.W. Norton.

Mansfield, E. (1987a), 'Innovation, R and D, and firm growth in robotics: Japan and the United States'. Symposium on Research and Development, Industrial Change, and Public Policy, University of Karlstad, Sweden.

Mansfield, E. (1987b), *The diffusion of industrial robots in Japan and the United States*, Center for Economics and Technology, University of Pennsylvania.

Mansfield, E. (1988), 'Industrial R and D in Japan and the United States: a comparative study', *American Economic Review* **78**, May, 2238.

Mansfield, E. (forthcoming), 'The speed and cost of industrial innovation in Japan and the United States: external vs. internal technology', *Management Science*.

Miller, S. (forthcoming), *Impacts of Robotics on Manufacturing Labor and Costs*, Madison: University of Wisconsin.

Office of Technology Assessment (1984), *Computerized Manufacturing Automation: Employment, Automation, and the Workplace*, Washington, DC: US Government Printing Office.

Organization for Economic Co-operation and Development (1983), *The Impact of Industrial Robots on the Manufacturing Industries of Member Firms*, Paris: OECD.

US Department of Commerce (1983), *The Robotics Industry*, Washington, DC: US Government Printing Office.

6

Japan and the World Economy 4 (1992) 1–16
North-Holland

1

Flexible manufacturing systems

Economic effects in Japan, United States, and Western Europe

Edwin Mansfield *

University of Pennsylvania, Philadelphia, PA, USA

Received June 1990, final version received March 1991

Abstract: This paper presents and analyzes detailed data obtained from over 200 firms in Japan, the United States, and Western Europe concerning the economic effects of flexible manufacturing systems, and compares the effectiveness and profitability of these systems in various countries. Such a comparison should be of widespread interest, particularly since some leading American experts, like Jaikumar (1986), have charged that Japanese firms use their flexible manufacturing systems much more effectively than do their U.S. rivals.

Keywords: Flexible manufacturing systems, productivity, minimum efficient size of plant, research and development.

1. Introduction

Flexible manufacturing systems are widely regarded as being among the most important modern innovations in manufacturing technology. According to the U.S. Department of Commerce, flexible manufacturing systems allow 'a wide variety of parts [to] be manufactured in random order with few or no people involved, while the system provides monitoring for correction of deviation from design requirements. The FMS concept has provided the ability to respond to product variation in lower volume production runs while

---

* The research on which this paper is based was supported by a grant from the Division of Information Science and Technology of the National Science Foundation. My thanks go to Laurence Rosenberg of the Foundation for helpful comments and to the more than 200 American, Japanese, and European firms that provided the basic data. This paper was presented at the Conference on International Technological Cooperation and Competition held at New York University on April 4–5, 1990. Ajay Maindiratta, as well as other conference participants, provided helpful comments. Also, parts of this paper were presented at the 1990 annual meetings of the American Economic Association.
Correspondence to: Edwin Mansfield, University of Pennsylvania, Philadelphia, PA 19104, USA

remaining in a position to manufacture in a cost-effective and competitive manner'. [1]

Flexible manufacturing systems tend to be built around a core of machine tools. Automation of the system occurs through the integration of materials handling and inspection. A numerical or programmable controller controls each work station, and a supervisory control oversees management at the systems level. Central computer control over real-time routing, production scheduling, and load balancing distinguishes flexible manufacturing systems from flexible manufacturing cells. [2]

While flexible manufacturing systems undoubtedly are an important aspect of industrial automation, relatively little is known about their economic effects, in part because they are relatively new. Information on this score has been provided by Jaikumar (1986), Miller (1989), Bessant and Haywood (1986), Warndorf and Merchant (1986), and Randa (1989). However, it is widely agreed that much more data on this score is needed, particularly since expert opinion in this area has not been uniform. Some observers have been much more impressed than others with the effectiveness of flexible manufacturing systems (and with their impact on the organization of manufacturing firms). The purposes of this paper are to present and analyze for the first time detailed new data obtained from over 200 firms in Japan, the United States, and Western Europe concerning the economic effects of flexible manufacturing systems, and to compare the effectiveness and profitability of these systems in various countries. Such a comparison should be of widespread interest, particularly since some leading American experts, like Jaikumar (1986), have charged that Japanese firms use their flexible manufacturing systems much more effectively than do their U.S. rivals.

2. Extent of use of flexible manufacturing systems

At the outset, it is worth pointing out that flexible manufacturing systems, which were first introduced in about 1970, have gained widespread acceptance. In Japan, the United States, and Western Europe (defined for present purposes as France, Italy, the United Kingdom, and West Germany com-

---

[1] U.S. Department of Commerce (1985), p. vii. Throughout this paper, a flexible manufacturing system is defined as follows: A flexible manufacturing system is a production unit capable of producing a range of discrete products with a minimum of manual intervention; it consists of production equipment workstations (machine tools or other equipment for fabrication, assembly, or treatment) linked by a materials-handling system to move parts from one workstation to another, and it operates as an integrated system under full programmable control. This is an adaptation of the definition developed by the International Institution for Production Engineering Research; it was used by the Office of Technology Assessment (1984).

[2] For detailed descriptions of flexible manufacturing systems, see Economic Commission of Europe (1986), U.S. Department of Commerce (1985), and U.S. Office of Technology Assessment (1984). For a variety of case studies, including SCAMP, Vought Aero Products, General Electric, and Fanuc, see Greenwood (1988).

bined), over 40 percent of the firms with more than 10,000 employees in the automobile, electrical equipment, machinery, and aerospace industries seemed to have begun using such systems by 1987. The percentage using such systems seemed to be substantially higher in Japan than in the United States or Western Europe, and in the aerospace and automobile industries than in the machinery or electrical equipment industries. [3]

Nonetheless, the rate of diffusion of flexible manufacturing systems seems to have been relatively slow. From the date of first use in a particular industry, it seems to have taken about 5 years, on the average, for one-quarter of the major firms in these industries to begin using such systems. Compared with other significant recent industrial innovations, the rate of imitation for flexible manufacturing systems seems low. For example, about half of the major potential users of numerically controlled machine tools had begun using them within 5 years after the date of first use in a particular industry. Even the industrial robot, which has spread more slowly than most innovations for which we have data, seems to have had a higher rate of imitation in many industries than flexible manufacturing systems. [4]

Users of flexible manufacturing systems tend to be much larger firms than non-users. This was true as well for numerically controlled machine tools, industrial robots, and many other innovations. Large firms would be expected to begin using flexible manufacturing systems more quickly than small firms because they have more resources and are better able to take the risks involved than their smaller rivals. Since a typical flexible manufacturing system (FMS) costs several million dollars, it is obvious than many small firms are not able to introduce them.

To estimate the future rate of diffusion, we asked a sample of nonusers in each industry and country when, if ever, they would begin using FMS, and used the findings to forecast the growth of the percentage of firms using FMS in each industry and area. Also, a simple econometric model was formulated to forecast the percentage of firms using FMS. According to the results, a

---

[3] A list of firms with over 10,000 employees in each of these industries in each country was obtained from International Dun and Bradstreet. Based on EEC data, U.S. Department of Commerce data, IIASA data, and data we obtained from the firms themselves, estimates were made of the percentage of these firms in each industry and country that had introduced flexible manufacturing systems by 1987. The results are rough because not all firms may have used the definition we specified, and for other reasons. But this seems to be one of the most complete surveys of this sort carried out to date. See Mansfield (1990).

[4] The length of time that it took for about one-quarter of the major potential users to begin using each of the following innovations was: 2 years (diesel locomotive), 5 years (centralized traffic control), 4 years (car retarders), 4 years (continuous wide-strip mill), 10 years (by-product coke oven), 11 years (continuous annealing), 1 year (shuttle car), 4 years (trackless mobile loader), 2 years (continuous mining machine), 1 year (tin container), 4 years (high-speed bottle filler), and 4 years (palletloading machine). See Mansfield (1968). For data concerning the diffusion of numerically controlled machine tools and robots, see Mansfield et al. (1977) and Mansfield (1989). For data concerning FMS, see Mansfield (1990).

considerable majority of the major firms in these industries in Japan, the United States, and Western Europe are likely to have installed flexible manufacturing systems by the year 2000. [5]

3. Effects of FMS on costs, lead time, and product quality in the United States: Evidence from 30 systems

Most metalworking manufacturing is done in batch production. Flexible manufacturing systems are best suited for firms with mid-volume production of a family of related parts. An important advantage of FMS is flexibility, which enables the firm to respond quickly to frequent changes in product design and production requirements. Also, FMS can increase machine utilization, and reduce work-in-process inventories. Computer control can help to organize the production system so that the proper amount of output is produced at the right time to meet demand. Fewer machines and less floor space may be required, and direct labor costs may be cut. Also, lead times may be reduced, and product quality may be enhanced by FMS. [6]

To investigate the extent to which these advantages of flexible manufacturing systems are actually being realized in practice in the United States, we chose a random sample of 30 flexible manufacturing systems in four industries – machinery, aerospace, electrical equipment, and automobiles. Detailed information was obtained from the personnel that supervise each of these systems. (The specific people were those regarded by each firm's top management as most knowledgeable in this regard.) This information was obtained in late 1988 on the basis of mail questionnaires and interviews. [7] Supplementary data were obtained in 1989, and a variety of analyses were carried out in 1989 and early 1990.

On the average, flexible manufacturing systems seem to have cut work-in-process inventories in half (table 1), a figure that is quite consistent with the rough estimate by the Manufacturing Studies Board of the National Research Council, [8] and somewhat higher than that given by the U.S. Department of Commerce (1985). In the United Kingdom, the percentage reduction in work-in-process inventory is even larger, according to Bessant and Hay-

---

[5] Mansfield (1990).

[6] For detailed descriptions of the economic advantages of flexible manufacturing systems, see Economic Commission for Europe (1986), Greenwood (1988), Jaikumar (1986), U.S. Department of Commerce (1985), and U.S. Office of Technology Assessment (1984).

[7] Based on the data in the U.S. Department of Commerce (1985), Economic Commission of Europe (1986), and our own surveys of FMS suppliers and users, we had a reasonably complete list of FMS users. A sample of 30 users was chosen, and each firm was asked to identify the engineers and managers who were most knowledgeable concerning its FMS. These people were contacted by telephone and were sent mail questionnaires. There was little or no non-response. Many of the responses were rounded to the nearest 5 percentage points.

[8] For the Manufacturing Studies Board's estimates, see Warndorf and Merchant (1986), Table 1.

Table 1
Effects of flexible manufacturing systems on costs, lead time, machine utilization, and product
quality, median of 30 installations, United States, 1988.

Effect of flexible manufacturing system	Median
Percent reduction in:	
Direct labor costs	50
Indirect labor costs	20
Materials costs	0
Work-in-process inventories	50
Floor space	35
Lead time from product design to initial production	20
Lead time from receipt of order of shipment	50
Percent increase in:	
Machine utilization rate	48
Product quality (yield of acceptable product)	20

Source: See section 3 and note 7.

wood (1986), based on a small sample. With regard to labor costs, the
percentage reduction is also substantial and about the same as unpublished
estimates by a West German machine tool builder for West European firms
(but less than this machine tool builder's estimates for Japanese firms). [9]
Also, the results are similar to those of Tchijov and Sheinin (1989), based on
a sample of 74 systems (many in Eastern Europe). [10]

Flexible manufacturing systems result in about a 50 percent increase in the
machine utilization rate (the ratio of actual metal-cutting time to time
available for metal cutting), which is not too different from the results of
Bessant and Haywood (1986) for the United Kingdom. Floor space is reduced
by about 40 percent, on the average, but materials costs are not affected. The
lead time from receipt of an order to shipment has been reduced by about 50
percent, according to our sample. This result is approximately equal to the
rough estimate by the Manufacturing Studies Board of the National Research Council, [11] and is lower than estimates by Bessant and Haywood
(1986) for the United Kingdom, by the West German machine tool builder,
and by Tchijov and Sheinin (1989) for a sample of 45 systems (many in
Eastern Europe). The lead time from product design to initial production is
also estimated to be reduced by about 20 percent. In addition, product
quality (as measured by yield of acceptable product) rose by about 20
percent, which is substantial.

[9] One of the leading West German machine tool builders made estimates of percentage
reduction in personnel in Western Europe and Japan, based on published and unpublished
data. The firm's chairman kindly made these estimates (which were prepared for the firm's
internal use) available to us. In part, these estimates were based on 'Flexible Ferlegungssys-
teme in Europa: Ehrfahrungen der Anwender', VDI-Z, September 1985.
[10] Tchijov and Sheinin (1989).
[11] See Warndorf and Merchant (1986), Table 1.

4. Development, installation, and utilization of flexible manufacturing systems

Before a flexible manufacturing system can produce any of the advantages cited above, it must be developed and installed. Our results indicate that, on the average, it takes American firms almost three years – and about 20,000 hours of labor – to develop a system (table 2). Comparing these figures for system development time and cost with those found by Jaikumar (1986), whose figures pertained to 1984, it appears that between 1984 and 1988 American firms may have been able to reduce their investment in labor and time to develop such a system. However, system development time and labor hours still seem to be higher in the United States than in Japan or West Germany. Jaikumar found that the Japanese take about 1.5 years and 6,000 hours of labor to develop a system, and unpublished data from a German machine tool builder estimated that West German firms take about 14,000 hours of labor.

Jaikumar (1986) and others have charged that 'U.S. companies used FMS the wrong way – for high-volume production of a few parts rather than for high-variety production of many parts at low cost per unit'. [12] Our results indicate that, on the average, U.S. firms produce about 15 types of parts on an FMS, which is greater than the figure (10) Jaikumar obtained in 1984, but less than the figure (93) he obtained then for Japanese firms. Also, it is less than the figure (82) that the West German machine tool builder reported for West German firms. Thus, American firms seem to be increasing the variety of parts produced, but are still not producing as a wide a variety of parts as their German of Japanese rivals. Moreover, although the annual volume per part (775) is lower than Jaikumar reported, it still is far higher than his estimate (258) for Japanese firms.

However, as one might expect, questions have arisen concerning Jaikumar's charges. Ayres and Ranta (1989) have suggested that 'it seems possible that he was inadvertently comparing apples and oranges', [13] since his Japanese sample was heavily weighted toward machine tool production, whereas his U.S. sample was heavily weighted toward high-volume producers of standardized items of heavy equipment. Because of the difficulties in obtaining comparable data in studies of this sort, one must be cautious about interpreting differences of this sort as evidence of relative inefficiency.

American firms have also been criticized for not exploiting opportunities to introduce new products. Our results indicate that, on the average, about 6 new parts are produced annually, which is well above the figure (1) that Jaikumar obtained in 1984. However, it still is well below the figure (22) he obtained for the Japanese. Thus, here too American firms seem to have

---

[12]   Jaikumar (1986), p. 69.
[13]   Ayres and Ranta (1989), p. 423.

Table 2
Development time, characteristics of output, and utilization of flexible manufacturing systems,
median of 30 installations, 1988.

Item	Median
System development time (months)	31
System development manhours (thousands)	20
Number of types of parts produced on FMS	15
Annual volume per part	775
Average number of parts produced per day	55
Number of new parts produced annually	6
Average metal cutting time (hours per day)	15
Utilization rate [a]	70

[a] Ratio of actual metal-cutting time to time available for metal cutting during two shifts, expressed as a percentage.

Source: See section 4.

increased the variety and flexibility of their operations, but still are not at the Japanese level.

Still another criticism of U.S. firms has been that their flexible manufacturing systems have not been reliable. In 1984, the average utilization rate – defined as metal-cutting time as a percentage of total time over two shifts – was estimated to be 52 percent, as compared to 84 percent in Japan. Our results indicate that the U.S. figure rose to 70 percent in 1988, which is still lower than the Japanese figure or the West German machine tool builder's estimate (86 percent) for German firms. But the increase in this regard during 1984–88 seems substantial.

5. Effects of flexible manufacturing systems on productivity and profits in Japan, the United States, and Western Europe

To obtain more detailed data concerning the effects of flexible manufacturing systems on productivity and profits, we constructed a random sample of 78 firms that used such systems in 1988, 17 of these firms being Japanese, 15 being American, and 46 being West European. Eleven of these firms were in the automobile industry; six were in the aerospace industry; 33 were in the machinery industry; and 28 were in the electrical equipment industry. [14] Information was obtained concerning the effects of flexible manufacturing systems on productivity and profits in each of these firms. In many cases, this

[14] This sample was chosen from a list of firms reported (by the Economic Commission for Europe (1986), the U.S. Department of Commerce (1985), and various FMS suppliers and others) to have been using FMS. A sample of 80 firms was chosen, but two refused to provide any information. The sample sizes in various industries and areas were determined by attempting to allocate the sample optimally (that is, with sample size being proportional to the total number of firms times the relevant standard deviation).

Table 3

Percentage of firms regarding flexible manufacturing systems as a success, and increase in labor productivity due to flexible manufacturing systems, four industries, Japan, United States, and Western Europe, [a] 1987.

Area or industry	Percentage of firms regarding FMS as successful	Percent increase in labor productivity
Japan	100	137
United States	85	55
Western Europe	90	57
Automobile	67	42
Electrical equipment	92	96
Machinery	97	68
Aerospace	100	76

[a] Western Europe includes France, Italy, United Kingdom, and West Germany.

Source: See section 5.

information was gotten through correspondence, but frequently it was obtained in personal interviews.

The first point to note is that the bulk of these firms regard their flexible manufacturing systems as a success. All of the Japanese firms, 90 percent of the Western European firms, and 85 percent of the American firms reported this to be the case (table 3). One reason for the firms' enthusiasm was that flexible manufacturing systems have increased labor productivity substantially (table 3). The Japanese firms report a doubling of output per worker; American and Western European firms report about a 60 percent increase. In the aerospace, machinery, and electrical equipment industries, the increase tends to be greater than in the automobile industry. However, since these figures pertain only to direct labor, which frequently accounts for only a small percentage of total costs, this is only one of many reasons for the firms' positive assessments. [15]

While most firms seem to regard their flexible manufacturing systems as a success, this does not mean that their first such systems generally have yielded an estimated rate of return in excess of that normally required for investments of this sort. As would be expected, a firm's first flexible manufacturing system has tended to be less profitable than subsequent systems. Only about 40 percent of firms' first systems have earned a higher-than-normally-required estimated rate of return, whereas about 40 percent have earned an estimated rate of return below the minimum required rate of return, and 20 percent have earned an estimated return barely equal to the minimum

[15] As pointed out by Hayes, Wheelwright, and Clark (1988), 'the cost of direct labor in a typical high-technology company today seldom exceeds 10 percent of total costs; increasingly it is under 5 percent, as are depreciation charges. Indirect factory costs – particularly materials control, quality assurance, maintenance and process engineering, and software development – have been growing rapidly, on the other hand, and in many companies now add up to five to ten times direct labor costs' (pp. 137–138).

Table 4

Average estimated and anticipated rates of return from investments in flexible manufacturing systems, four industries, Japan, United States, and Western Europe [a].

Area or industry	Estimated rate of return from firms' first systems [b]	Anticipated rate of return from firms' first systems [c]	Estimated rate of return from all systems [b]	Minimum required rate of return
Japan	33	45	38	24
United States	26	33	29	27
Western Europe	31	32	33	26
Automobiles	18	29	23	23
Electrical equipment	35	37	37	28
Machinery	34	35	35	27
Aerospace	24	30	26	21

[a] Western Europe includes France, Italy, United Kingdom, and West Germany. These data pertain to the sample of 78 firms described in Section 5. Not all of the firms provided complete data, so the coverage differs somewhat from column to column of the table.

[b] The estimated rate of return is the rate of return that, according to the firm's principal executives (and their staffs), the firm has received from its investment in FMS. These estimates are rough because some of these systems have not been in operation for more than a few years, and because of the inherent difficulties in measuring the returns from an FMS. (See note 18.) Also, because of international differences in accounting practices, these estimates may not be entirely comparable from country to country. (However, the firms we interviewed did not feel that there were any obvious biases in this regard.) Recognizing these problems, the firms' top executives (who should have a reasonably objective and broad view) regarded these figures as their best estimates, based on studies and analyses carried out in their firms to date.

[c] FMS. Obviously, it may contain biases of many kinds and may conceal wide differences of opinion among individual executives and engineers regarding the prospective profitability of the investment. Nonetheless, it is a rough measure of how optimistic firms seemed to be about the profitability of their first FMS.

Source: See section 4.

required rate. Based on these estimates by the users, a firm's first FMS has tended to be less profitable (relative to the minimum required rate of return) than most other major twentieth-century manufacturing innovations for which we have data. [16]

---

[16] According to Table 4, the average estimated return from firms' first systems (about 30 percent) was approximately 15 percent above the average minimum required rate of return (26 percent). For the twelve innovations listed in note 4, the average rate of return from the first installations was about 85 percent above the average minimum required rate of return in the United States. Even in the case of industrial robots in the United States, the average rate of return from firms' first robots was about 26 percent above the average minimum required rate of return. See Mansfield (1989).

For about 10 percent of the firms for which we have data, the firm anticipated that its first FMS would earn less than the rate of return normally required for investments of this sort. Nonetheless, these firms installed the FMS because of what they hoped to learn and the potential value of the experience gained.

Because flexible manufacturing systems are very complex, and prompt substantial organizational changes, one would expect that users would require a period of time to learn how to use them. Since a firm's experience with one FMS is likely to improve its utilization and operation of subsequent FMS's, the rate of return from a firm's first FMS would be expected to be lower than the rate of return from its subsequent FMS's. Based on our findings, this appears to be true (table 4). In all industries and areas, the average estimated rate of return from the total investment in flexible manufacturing systems exceeds the average estimated rate of return from firms' initial investments in such systems.

6. Estimated and anticipated profitability of flexible manufacturing systems

The total investment in flexible manufacturing systems in these industries seems to have been less profitable in the United States than in Japan or Western Europe (table 4). This accords with our findings that productivity increase in Japan due to FMS has been greater than in the United States, and is of particular interest in light of the criticisms of American utilization of FMS by Jaikumar (1986) and others. Combining our data for all areas (Japan, the United States, and Western Europe), the resulting average rate of return is quite similar to that obtained by Tchijov and Sheinin (1989) for a sample of 44 systems (many in Eastern Europe). [17] However, their sample is not randomly chosen, and Tchijov and Sheinin believe that their estimates are biased upward because firms obtaining relatively low returns from FMS were less likely to respond than those obtaining relatively high returns from it. This problem does not arise in the present study because the sample is randomly chosen and the nonresponse rate is minimal.

In all areas, flexible manufacturing systems seem to have been less profitable in the automobile industry than in the aerospace, electrical equipment, or machinery industries (table 4). This accords with our findings in the previous section that only two-thirds of the auto firms in our sample regard FMS as a success, and that productivity increases due to flexible manufacturing systems have been smaller in automobiles than in the other industries. According to some observers, this is related to the fact that the auto companies tend to produce items in large volumes where FMS has a relatively hard time competing with other production techniques. Of course, in evaluating these and other results in this section, it is important to bear in mind that conventional estimates of the rate of return often suffer from a variety of limitations when applied to FMS. [18]

---

[17] Tchijov and Sheinin (1989).

[18] Flexible manufacturing systems provide many benefits – higher quality, more flexibility, less inventory and floor space, and lower throughput times, among others – that frequently are ignored in the customary methods of evaluating investments of this sort. Some of these benefits can be very difficult to evaluate in dollar terms. See, for example, Kaplan (1986).

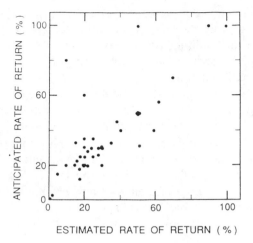

Fig. 1. Relationship between anticipated and estimated rate of return from firms' first flexible manufacturing systems, four industries, Japan, United States, and Western Europe.

Where possible, we obtained data from each firm concerning the anticipated rate of return from its investment in its first flexible manufacturing system. [19] On the average, the rate of return from the first flexible manufacturing system was overestimated by about one-fifth – or about 6 to 7 percentage points (table 4). Japanese firms have tended to be more optimistic in this regard than firms in other countries, and the electrical equipment and machinery industries have been more optimistic than the automobile or aerospace industries. There is no evidence that the degree of optimism has been less for systems installed more recently than for those installed when FMS was relatively new.

To measure the relationship between the anticipated and estimated rate of return from the investment in a flexible manufacturing system, a regression was calculated, the result being:

$$A_i = 9.43 + 0.85 \ E_i \qquad\qquad (1)$$
$$(2.32) \quad (7.90)$$

where A_i is the anticipated rate of return from the ith system and E_i is the estimate of the actual rate of return from this system. (See fig. 1.) The figures in parentheses are t-statistics. While the relationship is not very close ($r^2 = 0.58$), the correlation is higher than that found much earlier by Carter and Williams (1958) for a sample of British investments in innovative processes and products, the value of r^2 in their sample being only about 0.02. In

[19] Data of this sort could be obtained from 63 of the firms in the sample (15 firms in the United States, 9 firms in Japan, and 39 firms in Europe). For a more detailed description of these data and their limitations, see note c, Table 4.

large part, this difference between the value of r^2 in their sample and its value in our sample probably reflects the improvements between the 1950s and the 1980s in firms' abilities to forecast the rate of return from investments of this sort. In their sample, many of the firms were reported to be rather inexperienced in this regard.

Among firms that have obtained a relatively high rate of return from their FMS, the anticipated rate of return has tended to be overly pessimistic; whereas among those that have obtained a relatively low rate of return, the anticipated rate of return has tended to be overly optimistic. These results are similar to those obtained by Beardsley and Mansfield (1978) for the new products and processes introduced by one of the United States' largest firms. This firm underestimated the profitability of new products and processes that turned out to be very profitable and overestimated the profitability of those that were not relatively profitable. It seems likely that a pattern of this sort will be found in many circumstances.

7. Effects of flexible manufacturing systems on minimum efficient scale and capital requirements

As pointed out above, flexible manufacturing systems reduce the costs of batch production, thus narrowing the gap between the unit cost of producing intermediate and large numbers of a given item. According to many observers, FMS tends to change the shape of a firm's long-run average cost curve, as shown in fig. 2. [20] Although it seems likely that flexible manufacturing systems will have effects on the structure of some major industries, little empirical research has been carried out to determine what these effects will be. To help answer this question, we obtained estimates from a random sample of 75 Japanese firms and 100 U.S. firms of the effects of flexible manufacturing systems on the minimum efficient size of plant and the minimum efficient size of firm (both measured in terms of output) in their industry. [21]

Based on the results, shown in table 5, the average estimated reduction in the minimum efficient size of plant will be about the same in both Japan and

---

[20] Flexible manufacturing systems are suitable for manufacturing processes with a medium number of parts (about 4 to 500) and a medium production volume (about 20 to 20,000). See U.S. Department of Commerce (1985). For fewer parts and higher production volume, transfer lines are most suitable. For a large number of parts and relatively small production, stand-alone machines are most suitable. Although Figure 2 presents the traditional view, this view is not without its critics. Thus, Ranta and Tchijov (1989) believe that FMS is also suitable for high volumes.

[21] The industrial composition of this sample is somewhat different from our earlier sample, since metals are included. Also, the sample is large enough so that American industries can be broken down more finely than in Table 4. The frame for the American sample was the Business Week listing of major firms in these industries. The frame for the Japanese sample was the International Dun and Bradstreet listing of major firms in these industries. For a more detailed description of these samples, see Mansfield (1989).

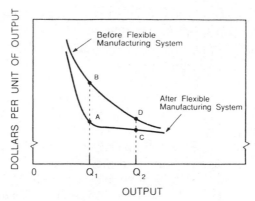

Fig. 2. Long-run average cost curve, before and after introduction of flexible manufacturing systems (see footnote 20).

the United States – about 15 percent. Moreover, in both countries, the estimated reduction will be greater in automobiles and electrical equipment than in most other industries. However, the estimated effect of flexible manufacturing systems on the minimum efficient size of firm will be less than

Table 5

Estimated effects of flexible manufacturing systems on minimum efficient scale and capital requirements, ten industries, Japan and the United States (percent).

	Reduction in minimum efficient size of plant	Reduction in minimum efficient size of firm	Increase in capital requirement for plant of minimum efficient size
United States			
Autos	20	11	14
Auto parts	21	17	15
Electrical	20	6	29
Appliances	10	0	50
Nonferrous metals	13	7	29
Steel	10	3	7
Aerospace	9	5	20
Farm machinery	21	19	23
Machine tools	18	8	19
Mean	15	8	21
Japan			
Autos	18	17	26
Machinery	10	4	49
Metals	11	8	44
Electrical	21	24	65
Mean	13	11	49

Source: See section 7.

on the minimum efficient size of plant. In both countries, it will be about 10 percent, according to these firms.

If these estimates are at all close to correct, it does not appear that flexible manufacturing systems will have a very major impact on the size distribution of firms in these industries. While a 10 percent cut in the minimum efficient size of firm may result in some reduction in industrial concentration, this reduction is not likely to be large. Moreover, in the United States and perhaps to a greater extent in Japan, flexible manufacturing systems will mean a considerable increase (about 20 percent in the U.S., about 50 percent in Japan) in capital requirements for a plant of minimum efficient scale, which will tend to raise barriers to entry (table 5).

Overall, both Japanese and American firms seem to feel that the effects of flexible manufacturing systems on industrial structure will be much less striking than Jaikumar (1986) or Piore and Sabel (1984) foresee. [22] However, this may be due in part to the fact that the firms were estimating the effects in the next decade or two. Over a longer time horizon, the effects may be greater.

8. Conclusions

Based on data obtained from a substantial sample of Japanese, American, and Western European users, it appears that flexible manufacturing systems are generally reported to be a success. (The percentage of firms reporting FMS was not a success was higher in the automobile industry than in the electrical equipment, machinery, or aerospace industries.) Nonetheless, according to these users, estimated rates of return from their investments in their first flexible manufacturing systems have tended to fall short of anticipations; and although, on the average, these investments seem to have yielded more than the minimum required rate of return, this has not been true for most individual users. [23] However, as so frequently occurs, learning has improved the situation: as firms have learned how to operate these systems more effectively, these estimated rates of return have tended to increase.

---

[22] According to Piore and Sabel (1984), flexible manufacturing systems should be most applicable to the specialized needs of small scale, small batch producers who will be given a competitive advantage by this new technology. Jaikumar (1986) states that: 'The minimum efficient scale for FMS operations is a cell of roughly six machines and fewer than a half dozen people' (p. 76).

[23] Table 4 provides averages for all firms concerning estimated and minimum rates of return, but for some of these firms only one or the other of these rates of return is available. (See note a, Table 4.) If we include only those firms where both are available, the results indicate that the difference between estimated and minimum rates of return in Japan tends to be smaller than in Table 4. Our statement in the text that the estimated rate of return has not exceeded the minimum rate of return for most users is based on only those firms where both rates of return are available. Also, each of the geographical areas (Japan, United States, and Western Europe) is weighted equally.

The average estimated rate of return from the investment in flexible manufacturing systems appears to have been substantially lower in the United States than in Japan. (Western Europe seems to have ranked in the middle in this regard.) Although this is consistent with earlier studies that concluded that American firms have not used these systems as effectively as the Japanese, it is important to recognize that the Japanese systems may not have been entirely comparable with those in the United States. Thus, this finding should be interpreted with caution.

U.S. firms continue to spend more time and money to develop and install a flexible manufacturing system than in Japan and Germany; they continue to produce fewer parts (and higher annual volumes per part) than in Japan or Germany; they continue to introduce fewer new parts than in Japan; they continue to have a smaller percentage of systems that are untended than in Japan; and they continue to have lower utilization rates than in Japan. If, as the critics believe (but some others question), these differences indicate that U.S. firms are not using flexible manufacturing systems as effectively as their foreign rivals do, our results indicate that these gaps have not been closed, but that American performance has improved.

However, one gap that has not narrowed at all is the difference between Japanese and American firms in the percentage of workers assigned to operate and maintain flexible manufacturing systems that are college-educated engineers. In the United States, we found this percentage to be about 8 percent, exactly the same as it was reported to be in 1984. In Japan, this figure has been estimated to be over 40 percent. Despite the critics' contention that American firms should increase the proportion of the work-force that are college-trained engineers, no such increase seems to have occurred, at least in our sample.

Finally, although there have been many predictions by leading scholars that flexible manufacturing systems will have striking effects on the structure of industry, this does not seem to jibe with firms' estimates of the effects of FMS on minimum efficient size of firm. Both Japanese and American firms estimate that flexible manufacturing systems will result in about a 10 percent reduction in minimum efficient size in the next decade or two. If this were to occur, it would be unlikely to cause dramatic changes in the size distribution of firms. However, it is important to recognize that these estimates pertain only to the next decade or two; over a longer period of time, the effects may be considerably greater.

References

Ayres, R. and J. Ranta, 1989, Factors governing the evolution and diffusion of CIM, in J. Ranta, ed., Trends and impacts of computer integrated manufacturing (International Institute for Applied Systems Analysis, Laxenburg) 405–430.

Beardsley, G. and E. Mansfield, 1978, A note on the accuracy of industrial forecasts of the profitability of new products and processes, Journal of Business 51, 127–135.

Bessant, J. and B. Haywood, 1986, Flexibility in manufacturing systems, Omega 6, 465–473.

Carter, C. and B. Williams, 1958, Investment in innovation (Oxford University Press, London).

Economic Commission for Europe, 1986, Recent trends in flexible manufacturing (United Nations, New York).

Gerwin, D., 1981, Control and evaluation in the innovation process: The case of flexible manufacturing systems, IEEE Transactions on Engineering Management 35, 90–100.

Greenwood, N., 1988, Implementing flexible manufacturing systems (Wiley, New York).

Hayes, R., S. Wheelwright and K. Clark, 1988, Dynamic manufacturing (The Free Press, New York).

Jaikumar, R., 1986, Postindustrial manufacturing, Harvard Business Review 64, 69–76.

Kaplan, R., 1986, Must CIM be justified by faith alone? Harvard Business Review 64, 87–95.

Kelley, M., 1988, Technical, economic, and organizational factors influencing the propensity to adopt programmable automation among U.S. manufacturers, Working paper 88-54 (School of Urban and Public Affairs, Carnegie-Mellon University, Pittsburgh, PA).

Mansfield, E., 1969, Industrial research and technological innovation (W.W. Norton for the Cowles Foundation for Research in Economics and Yale University, New York).

Mansfield, E., 1988a, Industrial R&D in Japan and the United States: A comparative study, American Economic Review 78, 223–228.

Mansfield, E., 1988b, Industrial innovation in Japan and the United States, Science 241, 1769–1774.

Mansfield, E., 1988c, The speed and cost of industrial innovation in Japan and the United States: External vs. internal technology, Management Science 34, 1157–1168.

Mansfield, E., 1989, The diffusion of industrial robots in Japan and the United States, Research Policy 18, 183–192.

Mansfield, E., 1991, The diffusion of flexible manufacturing systems in Japan, Europe, and the United States (Center for Economics and Technology, University of Pennsylvania, Philadelphia, PA).

Mansfield, E. et al., 1977, The production and application of new industrial technology (W.W. Norton, New York).

Manufacturing Studies Board CAD/CAM Interface Committee, 1984, Computer integration of engineering design and production (National Academy Press, Washington, DC).

Miller, S., 1989, Impacts of industrial robotics (University of Wisconsin Press, Madison, WI).

Piore, M. and C. Sabel, 1984, The second industrial divide: Possibilities for prosperity (Basic Books, New York).

Ranta, J. and I. Tchijov, 1989, Economics and success factors of flexible manufacturing systems, in: J. Ranta, ed., Trends and impacts of computer integrated manufacturing (International Institute for Applied Systems Analysis, Laxenburg) 311–354.

Tchijov, I. and R. Scheinin, 1989, Flexible manufacturing systems: Current diffusion and main advantages, in: J. Ranta, ed., Trends and impacts of computer integrated manufacturing (International Institute for Applied Systems Analysis, Laxenburg) 221–248.

U.S. Department of Commerce, 1985, A competitive assessment of the U.S. flexible manufacturing systems industry (Government Printing Office, Washington, DC).

U.S. Office of Technology Assessment, 1984, Computerized manufacturing automation: Employment, education, and the workplace (Government Printing Office, Washington, DC).

Warndorf, P. and M.E. Merchant, Development and future trends in computer-integrated manufacturing in the U.S.A., International Journal of Technology Management 1, 161–178.

PART II

INDUSTRIAL RESEARCH
AND DEVELOPMENT

[7]

Basic Research and Productivity Increase in Manufacturing

By EDWIN MANSFIELD*

Basic research is defined by the National Science Foundation (NSF) as "original investigation for the advancement of scientific knowledge...which do[es] not have immediate commercial objectives" (1959, p. 124). A hotly debated topic among economists, scientists, technologists, and policymakers[1] is: Does basic research, as contrasted with applied research and development, make a significant contribution to an industry's or firm's rate of technological innovation and productivity change? Although economic studies (see Zvi Griliches, 1980; my 1968 book and my 1980 paper, Nestor Terleckyj) indicate that R&D expenditures have been directly related to its rate of productivity change, they have been unable to shed light on this question, because no attempt has been made to disaggregate R&D. (See my 1977 paper.) One purpose of this paper is to fill this void. Specifically, the paper attempts to determine whether an industry's or firm's rate of productivity change in recent years has been related to the amount of basic research it performed, when other relevant variables (such as its rate of expenditure on applied R&D) are held constant.

A second purpose of this paper is to present data obtained from 119 firms concerning past and prospective changes in the

composition of their R&D expenditures. In recent years, there has been widespread feeling that American industry has reduced the proportion of its R&D expenditures going for relatively basic, long-term, and risky projects. However, very few data are available regarding the extent to which such changes in the composition of industrial R&D expenditures have taken place. And no information whatsoever seems to be available concerning firms' expectations regarding future changes of this sort. My results seem to be the first data on this subject, about which there is currently so much discussion.

I. Interindustry Differences in the Rate of Productivity Increase: The Model

The first step is to analyze the relationship between an industry's rate of productivity increase and the amount of basic research it performed. The model used here is essentially the same as that employed by Griliches, Terleckyj, and myself, among others, except that research and development is disaggregated into two parts: basic research, and applied research and development. In a particular industry, the production function is assumed to be

$$(1) \qquad Q_t = A e^{\lambda t} R_{tb}^{\alpha 1} R_{ta}^{\alpha 2} L_t^{\nu} K_t^{1-\nu}$$

where Q_t is the industry's value-added in year t, R_{tb} is the industry's stock of basic research capital, R_{ta} is the industry's stock of applied R&D capital, L_t is the industry's labor input, and K_t is the industry's stock of physical capital in year t.[2] Thus, the annual

*Professor of economics, University of Pennsylvania. This paper is based on work supported by a grant from the National Science Foundation. Of course, the Foundation takes no responsibility for the views expressed here. My thanks go to Z. Griliches, L. Lederman, R. Nelson, and K. Shell for comments on an earlier draft, and to J. Kendrick for providing me with unpublished data.

[1] For two influential studies, see Illinois Institute of Technology Research Institute and Chalmers Sherwin and Raymond Isenson. Of course, the mere fact that industry carries out some basic research does not prove that it makes a significant contribution to innovation and productivity change. Also, see my coauthored book, 1977, and Richard Nelson.

[2] The concept of a stock of research capital has been used by most investigators in this field. (See Griliches 1973 and 1980; my 1968 book; Terleckyj.) Our definitions of R_{tb} and R_{ta} are in accord with those used in previous work. Specifically, the stock of basic research capital in year t equals $\Sigma_i w_{bi} X_{t-i}$, where X_{t-i} is the

rate of change of total factor productivity is

$$\rho_t = \lambda + \alpha_1 \frac{dR_{tb}/dt}{R_{tb}} + \alpha_2 \frac{dR_{ta}/dt}{R_{ta}}$$

Since $\alpha_1 \dfrac{dR_{tb}/dt}{R_{tb}} = \dfrac{\partial Q_t}{\partial R_{tb}} \cdot \dfrac{dR_{tb}/dt}{Q_t}$

and $\alpha_2 \dfrac{dR_{ta}/dt}{R_{ta}} = \dfrac{\partial Q_t}{\partial R_{ta}} \cdot \dfrac{dR_{ta}/dt}{Q_t}$

$$(2) \quad \rho_t = \lambda + \phi_0 \frac{dR_{tb}/dt}{Q_t} + \phi_1 \frac{dR_{ta}/dt}{Q_t}$$

where $\phi_0 = \partial Q_t / \partial R_{tb}$ and $\phi_1 = \partial Q_t / R_{ta}$.

Because the rate of growth of each industry's stock of R&D capital (both basic and applied) cannot be measured directly, I assume, as Griliches and Terleckyj did, that an industry's expenditure on R&D during year t is approximately equal to that year's change in the industry's stock of R&D capital. For this assumption to hold, the depreciation of the R&D capital and the lag in the effect of this investment must be small enough to be ignored.[3] Although the assumption of no lags is a useful starting point, I relax this assumption later. (See fn. 7.) According to John Kendrick, Terleckyj, and others, an industry's annual rate of change of total factor productivity also depends on the extent to which the industry's workers are unionized.[4] To avoid specifica-

expenditure by the industry on basic research in year $t - i$, and w_{bi} is the proportion of this expenditure that is still productive in year t. The stock of applied R&D capital in year t equals $\Sigma_i w_{ai} A_{t-i}$, where A_{t-i} is the expenditure by the industry on applied R&D in year $t - i$, and w_{ai} is the proportion of this expenditure that is still productive in year t.

[3]The rationale given by Griliches and Terleckyj for ignoring depreciation is that, because so little was spent on R&D prior to World War II and because the rate of growth of R&D expenditures in the 1950's was so high, the amount of depreciation that would have been able to build up during the period covered by our data should be small. Relatively little is known about the length of the relevant lags, although some data on this score are presented in my 1968 book and my 1980 paper.

[4]See Kendrick and Terleckyj. Another variable that Terleckyj found to be statistically significant in some specifications was the percent of the industry's sales to nongovernment buyers. I included this variable in those equations where he found it was significant. For the results, see fn. a of Table 1.

tion errors, I therefore include u_t, the percent of the industry's workers that are union members, as an additional independent variable in equation (2). Thus, the resulting equation is

$$(3) \quad \rho_t = \lambda + \phi_0 \frac{X_t}{Q_t} + \phi_1 \frac{A_t}{Q_t} + \phi_2 u_t$$

where X_t is the industry's expenditure on basic research in year t, and A_t is the industry's expenditure on applied R&D in year t.

During the period to which my data pertain, there seems to have been only a limited amount of variation in an industry's value of X_t/Q_t, A_t/Q_t, and u_t. Thus, as a first approximation, it seems reasonable to suppose that $X_t/Q_t = B$, $A_t/Q_t = D$, and $u_t = u$. Then, if an industry's values of λ, ϕ_0, ϕ_1, and ϕ_2 are statistically independent of its values of B, D, and u, it follows that

$$(4) \quad \rho_i = \bar{\lambda} + \bar{\phi}_0 B_i + \bar{\phi}_1 D_i + \bar{\phi}_2 u_i + z_i$$

where ρ_i is the annual rate of change of total factor productivity in the ith industry during this period; B_i, D_i, and u_i are the values of B, D, and u in the ith industry, $\bar{\lambda}$, $\bar{\phi}_0$, $\bar{\phi}_1$, and $\bar{\phi}_2$ are the average values of λ, ϕ_0, ϕ_1, and ϕ_2 in all relevant industries, and z_i is a random error term.[5]

II. Econometric Results

To what extent can equation (4) explain the differences among manufacturing industries in the rate of increase of total factor productivity? To answer this question, we must have data concerning ρ_i, B_i, D_i, and u_i. Kendrick has provided data concerning ρ_i for the twenty 2-digit SIC manufacturing industries during 1948–66. Following Terleckyj, who has used a similar sort of model to analyze Kendrick's data, each of the independent variables (other

[5]With regard to A_t/Q_t and X_t/Q_t, the earliest comparable data are for 1953. Comparing an industry's value of A_t/Q_t in 1953 with that in 1966, I find that there is a high correlation ($r = .91$) between them, and that the intertemporal variation in A_t/Q_t is much smaller than the interindustry variation in it. Similar results were found for X_t/Q_t.

TABLE 1—RESULTS OF REGRESSION TO EXPLAIN RATES OF PRODUCTIVITY INCREASE
IN TWENTY MANUFACTURING INDUSTRIES, 1948–66[a]

Constant	Independent Variables[b]								
	B_i	D_i	U_i	D_{pi}	D_{gi}	I_i	I_{pi}	Y_i	$\bar{R}^2$
4.80	1.49	.068	−.056	–	–	–	–	–	.63
	(3.34)	(2.75)	(3.90)						
4.74	1.33	–	−.055	.105	.055	–	–	–	.63
	(1.51)		(3.54)	(0.59)	(0.80)				
4.37	1.66	−.084	−.055	–	–	.54	–	–	.71
	(4.55)	(1.59)	(4.73)			(3.10)			
4.28	1.50	−.18	−.054	–	–	–	.74	–	.80
	(4.94)	(0.71)	(5.57)				(4.41)		
4.46	.285	.084	−.061	–	–	–	–	.065	.86
	(0.81)	(5.17)	(6.37)					(4.80)	
4.83	.682	–	−.064	−.023	.122	–	–	0.68	.87
	(1.27)		(6.32)	(0.21)	(2.88)			(4.90)	
4.46	.572	.005	−.059	–	–	.27	–	.054	.86
	(1.67)	(.14)	(7.02)			(2.07)		(4.16)	
4.42	.665	.035	−.058	–	–	–	.37	.045	.86
	(1.85)	(1.29)	(6.81)				(2.11)	(2.90)	

[a] Besides these regressions, I calculated all of Terleckyj's equations in his Tables 4–9 with B_i and Y_i added (and with the nonsignificant non-R&D variables in his equations omitted). In practically all cases, the regression coefficient of B_i is significant when it alone is added. When both B_i and Y_i are added, the regression coefficient of Y_i is always highly significant, but the regression coefficient of B_i is significant in only one-third of the equations. The estimated coefficients of the independent variables are generally similar to those shown here.

[b] All of the independent variables, as well as the dependent variable, are expressed as percentages. The number in parentheses below each regression coefficient is its t-value.

than u_i, which pertains to 1953) is measured as of 1958. To measure B_i, I calculated the ratio of each industry's expenditure on basic research to its value-added in 1958, based on data published by the National Science Foundation and the Commerce Department.[6] Terleckyj has provided data concerning D_i and u_i. Using these data, I regressed ρ_i on B_i, D_i, and u_i, with the results shown in Table 1. All three independent variables turn out to be highly significant, and over

[6] The data regarding B_i are based on the basic research expenditures reported in the 1961 edition of *Research and Development in Industry*. Note that both government- and company-financed basic research are included. In two cases, the NSF provided data regarding two of the industies combined. I allocated the basic research expenditures between the two industries in proportion to their applied R&D expenditures (as reported in Terleckyj). This procedure is very unlikely to result in any serious error, since these industries do very little basic research. If an industry did no applied R&D in 1958, according to Terleckyj, and the NSF provided no indication that it carried out any basic research, I assumed that its basic research expenditures were zero in 1958.

60 percent of the variation among industries in the rates of productivity increase are explained by the equation.[7]

[7] The effects of R&D often occur with a lag, and the lag for basic research is generally thought to be much longer than for applied R&D. Because so little is known about the length of these lags, previous work along this line has sometimes (but not always) ignored them; but once we separate basic research from applied R&D, it is hazardous to continue this procedure, since the lags in the effects of basic research may be quite long. If an expenditure on basic research is included in the stock of basic research capital only after a lag of θ_1 years, and if an expenditure on applied R&D is included in the stock of applied R&D capital only after θ_2 years, equation (3) must be modified as follows:

$$\rho_t = \lambda + \phi_0 \frac{X_{t-\theta_1}}{Q_t} + \phi_1 \frac{A_{t-\theta_2}}{Q_t} + \phi_2 u_t$$

If r_1 is the average annual rate of growth of the industry's value-added between year $t-\theta_1$ and year t, and if r_2 is the average annual rate of growth of the industry's value-added between year $t-\theta_2$ and year t, it follows that

$$\rho_t = \lambda + \phi_3 \frac{X_{t-\theta_1}}{Q_{t-\theta_1}} + \phi_4 \frac{A_{t-\theta_2}}{Q_{t-\theta_2}} + \phi_2 u_t \qquad \text{(over)}$$

To see how robust these results are, I experimented with some other specifications of the regression equation. First, I divided the total amount of applied R&D into two parts: the amount that is privately financed, and the amount that is financed by the government. This means that two independent variables, D_{pi} (the amount of privately financed applied R&D divided by value-added) and D_{Gi} (the amount of government-financed applied R&D divided by value-added), must be substituted for D_i. As shown in Table 1, this substitution has relatively little effect on the estimate of $\bar{\phi}_0$,

---

where $\phi_3 = \phi_0 + (1 + r_1)^{\theta 1}$ and $\phi_4 = \phi_1 + (1 + r_2)^{\theta 2}$. If the independent variables in this equation remain relatively constant in the relevant period, and if an industry's values of λ, ϕ_2, ϕ_3, and ϕ_4 are statistically independent of the values of these independent variables,

$$\rho_i = \bar{\lambda} + \bar{\phi}_3 B_i'' + \bar{\phi}_4 D_i'' + \bar{\phi}_2 u_i + z_i$$

where B_i'' is the value of $X_{t-\theta 1}/Q_{t-\theta 1}$ and D_i'' is the value of $A_{t-\theta 2}/Q_{t-\theta 2}$ in the ith industry during the relevant period. Although we do not know θ_1 and θ_2 with much accuracy, it is very likely that there is a high correlation between B_i'' and B_i, as well as between D_i'' and D_i. For as far back as reasonably accurate data exist, industries with relatively high ratios of basic research to value-added in one year have tended to have relatively high ratios in other years, and industries with relatively high ratios of applied R&D to value-added in one year have tended to have relatively high ratios in other years. The coefficient of correlation between an industry's ratio of applied R&D expenditures to value-added in 1953 and its ratio in 1975 is 0.93. The coefficient of correlation between an industry's ratio of basic research expenditures to value-added in 1953 and its ratio in 1975 is 0.85. Even if the value of θ_1 or θ_2 varies from industry to industry, there is likely to be a high correlation between B_i'' and B_i and between D_i'' and D_i. Thus, B_i and D_i can be regarded as proxies for B_i'' and D_i''. Viewed in this way, my regression equations, since they are based on these proxies rather than on B_i'' and D_i'', cannot be used to estimate the rates of return from basic research or from applied R&D, unless one can estimate the unknown values of θ_1 and θ_2, as well as the relationship between these proxies and the variables for which they stand. However, the results are useful in testing whether ϕ_0 equals zero, since, if this is the case, the regression coefficient of B_i in the regressions should be zero. Thus, despite the presence of these lags, my results are useful in testing whether an industry's or firm's rate of productivity change has been affected by the amount of basic research it performed, when its rate of expenditure on applied R&D is held constant.

although it reduces its statistical significance.

Second, I added to equation (3) a fourth independent variable I_i, which measures the amount of R&D that is embodied in an industry's purchased inputs (divided by its value-added). Terleckyj has provided estimates of this variable for these twenty industries. As shown in Table 1, when this variable is added, it is highly significant, but its inclusion has little effect on the size or statistical significance of the estimate of $\bar{\phi}_0$. Similarly, if this variable is defined to include only privately financed R&D, the results are essentially the same, as shown in Table 1 (where this variable is denoted by I_{pi}).

These findings seem to indicate a strong relationship between the amount of basic research carried out by an industry and the industry's rate of productivity increase during 1948–66. However, one wonders whether, since the distinction between basic research and applied research is often nebulous, this relationship may not reflect the fact that industries that carry out relatively large amounts of long-term R&D tend to have relatively high rates of productivity increase. In other words, basic research may be a proxy for long-term R&D. To shed some light on this question, I added another variable, Y_i (the percent of the industry's firms that expected their R&D expenditures in 1958 to pay off in no less than six years), to the four regressions discussed above.[8] As shown in Table 1, the results suggest that much of the apparent effect of basic research may really be due to long-term R&D. When this additional variable is introduced, its effect is highly significant in every case,

---

[8] Data concerning Y_i were obtained from McGraw Hill's *Business' Plans for New Plants and Equipment, 1958–1961,* p. 8. The figure for primary metals is the average of that given for "iron and steel" and for "nonferrous metals." The figure for transportation equipment is the average of that given for "autos" and that given for "transportation equipment." The figure for fabricated metal products and instruments is that given for "other metalworking." Since three of the industries carried out no applied R&D expenditures in 1958 according to Terleckyj, no data regarding Y_i exist for these industries.

whereas the effect of B_i becomes smaller and often statistically nonsignificant.

In addition, to extend the time period to which the data pertain, I used unpublished data by Kendrick to calculate ρ_i for these twenty manufacturing industries during 1948–76. When these values of ρ_i are used in Table 1, the magnitude of the regression coefficient of B_i—and the number of specifications where it is statistically significant —is about the same as in Table 1. However, the regression equations do not fit nearly as well, probably due in part to the increased importance during 1966–76 of regulatory considerations and a variety of other factors not included in the model. Also, the regression coefficients of Y_i are no longer statistically significant. This is not surprising because there have been considerable changes since 1958 (the year to which Y_i pertains) in the extent to which various industries have focused their *R&D* on long-term work. Much more will be said on this score in Section IV.[9]

III. Interfirm Differences in the Rate of Productivity Increase

Besides investigating the relationship between basic research and productivity increase at the industry level, I also investigated this relationship at the firm level. Once again, let us assume that equation (1) holds, but now Q_t is the firm's valued-added in year t, R_{tb} is the firm's stock of basic research capital, R_{ta} is the firm's stock of applied *R&D* capital, and so forth. Making the same assumptions as in Section I, it

---

[9]Kendrick kindly provided me with estimates of total factor productivity in each industry during 1948–76. These estimates will appear in his forthcoming book. I calculated the annual percentage rate of growth of total factor productivity between 1948 and the year since 1966 when total factor productivity reached a maximum. (If total factor productivity is less than in a previous year, the industry is probably not operating on its production function, and the inclusion of such an observation may result in misleading results.) The year when it reaches a maximum is almost always 1976 or 1973. When the resulting values of ρ_i are inserted in the regressions in Table 1, the regression coefficient of B_i is statistically significant at the .05 level in about the same proportion of cases as in Table 1.

---

follows that

$$(5) \qquad \rho_i' = \bar{\lambda}' + \bar{\phi}_0' B_i' + \bar{\phi}_1' D_i' + z_i'$$

where ρ_i' is the annual rate of change of total factor productivity in the ith firm; B_i' and D_i' are the ratio of basic research expenditure to value-added and the ratio of applied *R&D* expenditure to value-added in the ith firm; and $\bar{\lambda}'$, $\bar{\phi}_0'$, $\bar{\phi}_1'$, and z_i' are analogous (at the firm level) to $\bar{\lambda}$, $\bar{\phi}_0$, $\bar{\phi}_1$, and z_i. Equation (4) is analogous to equation (3) except that u_i is excluded because it has the same value for all firms in the industry.[10]

To see how well this model fits, and to estimate $\bar{\phi}_0'$ and $\bar{\phi}_1'$, I obtained data concerning value-added and employment during 1960–76, and data concerning investment in plant and equipment during 1920–76 for ten major petroleum firms and for six major chemical firms.[11] The stock of physical capital was estimated annually for each firm during 1960–76. To obtain such an estimate for a particular year, the investment data for each firm for previous years were deflated, depreciated (using the Jack Faucett-Bureau of Labor Statistics (BLS) depreciation rates for plant and equipment in chemicals and petroleum refining), and summed. Using

---

[10]Of course, I could have included a variable measuring interfirm differences in the extent of unionization, but this did not seem worthwhile, because the interfirm differences in this regard seemed small.

[11]The data concerning value-added and employment were obtained from *Moody's Industrial Manual* and from the annual reports of the firms. The figures regarding value-added were deflated by the Bureau of Economic Analysis's implicit deflator for the industry. Most of the data concerning investment in plant and equipment come from annual reports and *Moody's*. However, for the earliest years, it was often necessary to estimate a firm's investment in plant and equipment during certain years by assuming it was proportional to the change in the firm's total assets. Although these estimates for the early years are crude, the results should be influenced very little by whatever errors they contain, since the investment figures for the early years have relatively little weight in the capital stock figures. This is because most of the plant and equipment acquired in the early years were depreciated by 1960. In the case of the petroleum firms, the analysis was carried only up to 1971, not 1976, because of the gyrations in oil prices and the unsettled conditions in the industry in recent years.

these data concerning each firm's stock of physical capital each year, together with the data concerning each firm's (deflated) value-added and employment each year, I estimated the annual rate of total factor productivity change for each firm during 1960–76.[12] In addition to these estimates of ρ_i', we need estimates of B_i' and D_i' for each of these firms. As a by-product of previous research, I had these data for all of these firms for 1964 or for 1965.[13]

To estimate the parameters of equation (5), I regressed each firm's value of ρ_1' on its values of B_i' and D_i', the result being

(6) $\rho_i' = 2.15 + 1.78 B_i' + 0.10 D_i'$
           (7.51)   (2.08)   (0.86)

$$\bar{R}^2 = 0.58$$

where the *t*-statistics are shown in parentheses below the regression coefficients, and

---

[12] The investment figures were deflated by price deflators provided by the BLS. Then the Faucett-BLS depreciation rates were applied, and the results were summed to obtain the firm's capital stock each year. Then, for each firm, I computed $g_t = lnQ_t - blnL_t - (1 - b)lnK_t$, where Q_t is the firm's deflated value-added in year t, L_t is its employment in year t, K_t is its capital stock in year t, and b is its average proportion of value-added going for wages during 1960–76. Finally, I regressed g_t on t, the resulting regression coefficient being the estimate of ρ_i'. Years when the firm's value-added was less than in some previous year were omitted because the firm was apparently operating well below its capacity. Clearly, in an analysis of this sort, the data should apply to periods when the firm is operating reasonably close to capacity. The data described in this and the previous footnote were obtained, and the calculations were made, by Nancy Fox as part of her work toward a doctoral dissertation at the University of Pennsylvania.

[13] Some of these data were described in my coauthored book, 1971. The rest come from an unpublished survey carried out by Henry Armour and David Teece. To check whether the ratio of applied *R&D* expenditures to value-added remained relatively constant during the relevant period, I compared the values of this ratio in 1976 and (about) 1964 for the six chemical firms. In most firms, the 1976 ratio was within 25 percent of the 1964 ratio. The interyear differences tend to be much smaller than the interfirm differences. There was a high correlation between a firm's 1976 ratio and its 1964 ratio. With regard to the ratio of basic research expenditures to value-added, the results are much the same.

where both the dependent and independent variables are expressed as percentages. To determine whether there were interindustry differences between the chemical and petroleum firms, I introduced as an additional independent variable a dummy variable that equals 1 if the firm is in the chemical industry and 0 if it is in the petroleum industry. This dummy variable was not statistically significant, so it was omitted from equation (6).[14]

The results are surprisingly similar to those obtained at the industry level. There is a statistically significant tendency for a firm's rate of productivity increase during 1960–76 to be directly related to how much basic research it carried out in 1964, when the amount spent on applied *R&D* is held constant. Moreover, the regression coefficient of B_i' in equation (6) is not too different from the regression coefficient of B_i in equation (4).

Previous studies (for example, Griliches, 1980) have used such regression coefficients as estimates of the private rate of return from *R&D*. For well-known reasons, some of which are discussed in footnote 7, estimates of this sort should be treated with considerable caution. Nonetheless, it is interesting to see how an estimate of this sort based on these data compares with previous estimates, since so little is known about the changes that have occurred in recent years in the profitability of *R&D*. (Practically all previous work of this kind pertains to the early 1960's.) To obtain such an estimate, I regress ρ_i' on $(B_i' + D_i')$, the result being

(7) $\rho_i' = 2.2 + .275 (B_i' + D_i')$
              (7.06)   (4.08)

$$\bar{R}^2 = .49$$

which implies that the rate of return from all *R&D* (basic and applied) was about 27 percent in 1960–76 in these chemical and petroleum firms. This estimate is lower than corresponding estimates (using the same technique and the same industries) for the

---

[14] The same result was obtained in my 1968 book on the basis of earlier data.

early 1960's, a result that is consistent with the reduced rate of growth of R&D expenditures by industry during the early 1970's and with opinions expressed by many R&D managers.[15]

IV. Recent Changes in the Composition of Industrial R&D Expenditures

In recent years, there has been a widespread feeling that industry has been devoting a smaller share of its R&D expenditures to basic research, long-term projects, and risky and ambitious projects. Unfortunately, however, little or no data have been available on this score. To make some progress toward filling this gap, I obtained information from 119 firms concerning the changes that have occurred in this regard between 1967 and 1977, and changes they expect between 1977 and 1980. The firms included in my sample, all of which spent over $10 million on R&D in 1976, accounted for about one-half of all industrial R&D expenditures in the United States in 1976. Although this sample has its shortcomings, it is certainly among the most comprehensive surveys of this type ever carried out.[16]

The results presented in Table 2 indicate that the proportion of R&D expenditures devoted to basic research declined between 1967 and 1977 in practically every industry.

[15] In 1960, the estimated rate of return in these industries averaged about 30 percent or more (see my 1968 book). In the early 1960's, it was about 40 percent, according to Griliches, 1980. Of course, all of these estimates neglect lags, and should be treated with considerable caution.

[16] Data were obtained (through correspondence or interviews) from practically all of the major chemical firms, from about three-quarters of the major aerospace, automotive, petroleum, metals, and office equipment and computer firms, from about two-thirds of the major rubber, soap, and machinery firms, from about one-half of the major drug, food, and instruments firms, and from about one-quarter of the major electronics and electrical equipment firms. By a major firm, I mean one that spent over $10 million on R&D in 1976, according to the survey in Business Week, June 27, 1977. The data were obtained in practically all cases from the firm's vice president of research and development. One obvious limitation of the sample is that it focuses entirely on large firms. For an interesting recent study which deals with some of the topics discussed here, see Howard Nason et al.

In the aerospace, metals, electrical equipment, office equipment and computer, chemical, drug, and rubber industries, this proportion dropped substantially. In the sample as a whole, the proportion fell about one-fourth, from 5.6 percent in 1967 to 4.1 percent in 1977. According to the firms' forecasts, there is no evidence that this drop will continue during 1977–80, but neither is there any evidence that the proportion will rise very much. For the sample as a whole, the proportion is expected to be about 4.3 percent in 1980.[17]

In four-fifths of the industries, there was also a decline between 1967 and 1977 in the proportion of R&D expenditures devoted to relatively risky projects (specifically, ones with less than a fifty-fifty estimated chance of success). In some industries, like metals, chemicals, aircraft, drugs, and rubber, this reduction has been rather large. Between 1977 and 1980, there will be some increase overall in the proportion devoted to relatively risky projects, according to the firm's forecasts, with the result that the average proportion for the sample as a whole is expected to get closer to its 1967 level.

Despite the decrease in the proportion of R&D expenditures devoted to basic research, the proportion devoted to relatively long-term projects (specifically, those lasting five or more years) did not decline appreciably between 1967 and 1977 in the sample as a whole. In some industries, like aircraft,

[17] According to NSF's figures, 4.7 percent of company-financed R&D expenditures in manufacturing went for basic research in 1975 (the most recent year for which NSF has published data). This is reasonably close to my 1977 figure of 4.1 percent. In 1968, NSF put this percentage at 6.9 percent, whereas my 1967 figure is 5.6 percent. For nine industries in 1977 and seven industries in 1967, I could compare my percentage with NSF's percentage. I found that my percentages are positively correlated with NSF's, but that they do not always agree closely. This is not surprising, since my definition of each of these industries differs somewhat from NSF's and NSF's coverage is more comprehensive than mine. Nonetheless, there is close agreement with regard to the change in this percentage in all manufacturing. NSF's data indicate a decrease of 32 percent in this percentage between 1968 and 1975, and my data indicate a decrease of 27 percent between 1967 and 1977. For the NSF data, see Research and Development in Industry, 1975 and 1978.

TABLE 2—PERCENTAGE OF COMPANY-FINANCED *R&D* EXPENDITURE GOING FOR BASIC, LONG-TERM
AND RELATIVELY RISKY PROJECTS: 1967; 1977; 1980[a]

Industry	Basic Research			Projects Lasting Five or More Years			Projects Aimed at Entirely New Pro-ducts and Processes			Projects with Less than 50-50 Estimated Chance of Success		
	1967	1977	1980	1967	1977	1980	1967	1977	1980	1967	1977	1980
Metals	6.2	2.4	2.4	26	22	22	28	18	19	18	11	12
Chemicals	7.3	5.9	5.8	43	39	39	37	33	31	37	30	27
Aerospace	8.5	1.7	1.7	31	24	24	35	26	28	35	27	29
Automobiles	0.3	0.2	0.3	18	20	23	15	16	–	47	45	45
Petroleum	9.1	8.1	9.7	26	27	29	21	25	26	24	23	24
Drugs	20.7	16.4	15.3	63	66	63	76	68	65	46	40	38
Food	2.6	4.1	4.3	16	16	22	18	22	25	19	18	20
Instruments	3.7	3.3	3.3	40	40	41	24	22	22	11	9	10
Soap and Cosmetics	3.4	3.9	3.6	23	30	37	38	48	55	43	55	55
Machinery	4.2	3.6	3.4	34	31	32	23	18	20	8	5	5
Electronics and Electrical Equipment	6.4	4.6	4.8	10	14	14	37	45	47	3	5	5
Office Equipment and Computers	3.5	1.8	–	55	55	–	60	60	–	9	9	–
Stone, Clay and Glass	8.0	7.1	8.1	35	43	38	37	28	27	28	24	21
Rubber	2.7	1.7	1.7	9	5	4	32	28	28	37	27	22
Miscellaneous	5.1	2.5	3.5	30	27	27	21	22	27	18	13	17
Total	5.6	4.1	4.3	34	34	–	36	34	34	28	25	27

[a] The 1980 figures are the firms' forecasts. Some 1980 figures are not entirely comparable with earlier ones because some firms did not provide 1980 forecasts; in cases where the lack of comparability is serious, no 1980 figure is given.

chemicals, metals, and rubber, there was a substantial decline; but in other industries, like drugs, there was an increase in this proportion. In most industries, the firms forecast that the proportion of *R&D* expenditures devoted to relatively long-term projects will increase somewhat between 1977 and 1980.[18] The proportion of *R&D* expenditures aimed at entirely new products and processes (rather than improvements and modifications of existing products and processes) declined somewhat between 1967 and 1977.[19] Again, there are marked differences among industries in the amount

[18] For other data regarding the proportion of firms' *R&D* expenditures that goes for relatively long-term projects, see my coauthored book, 1971, and my 1980 paper. These data are quite consistent with the results in Table 2.

[19] The distinction between an entirely new product or process and an improved or modified product or process is often arbitrary (although it is often used). So long as each respondent uses the same definition for one year as for another year, the results should help to

and direction of change. Between 1977 and 1980, little change was expected to occur in this proportion in most industries.

A multiple regression analysis provides no evidence of any relationship between a firm's size, profitability, or percentage of *R&D* expenditures devoted to sales, on the one hand, and the change in the proportion of the firm's *R&D* expenditures devoted to basic research between 1967 and 1977 (or expected to occur between 1977 and 1980), on the other. Moreover, there is no relationship between these three variables and the change in the proportion of the firm's *R&D* expenditures devoted to relatively risky projects, or to relatively long-term projects, or to projects aimed at entirely new products

portray the changes that have occurred over time in a given industry. But a comparison in this regard of one industry with another may be misleading since the definitions used in one industry may be quite different from those used in another industry.

and processes.[20] Further, there is only a very weak relationship, if any, between the change in the proportion of a firm's *R&D* expenditures devoted to basic research, and the change in the proportion devoted to relatively risky projects, relatively long-term projects, or projects aimed at entirely new products or processes.[21]

Besides obtaining data from these 119 firms, I also asked those that have cut back on the proportion of their *R&D* expenditures going for basic research and relatively risky and long-term projects why such a change has occurred. The reason most frequently given was the increase in government regulations, which has reduced the profitability of more fundamental and longer-term projects. This reason was advanced particularly often by the chemical and drug firms.[22] Another reason advanced by some of the respondents was that breakthroughs are more difficult to achieve than in the past, because the field has been more thoroughly worked over. Also, high rates of inflation were cited.

---

[20] I ran four regressions, the dependent variables being (a) the change between 1967 and 1977 in the proportion of a firm's *R&D* expenditures devoted to basic research, (b) the change between 1967 and 1977 in the proportion devoted to projects where there was less than a 50-50 estimated chance of success, (c) the change between 1967 and 1977 in the proportion devoted to projects lasting five or more years, and (d) the change between 1967 and 1977 in the proportion aimed at entirely new products or processes. Each of these dependent variables was regressed on the firm's sales in 1976, its ratio of *R&D* expenditures to sales in 1976, its ratio of profits to net worth in 1976, and industry dummy variables. Other than some of the dummy variables, none of the independent variables in any of these multiple regressions was statistically significant.

[21] I regressed three dependent variables—the change between 1967 and 1977 in the proportion of a firm's *R&D* expenditures devoted to projects lasting five or more years, the change in the proportion aimed at entirely new products or processes, and the change in the proportion devoted to projects where there was less than a 50-50 estimated chance of success—on the change between 1967 and 1977 in the proportion devoted to basic research. Although the sample size exceeded 100, in only one case was the regression statistically significant, and in this case, r^2 was only .06.

[22] About 80 percent of the relevant chemical firms and practically all of the relevant drug firms cited this reason.

V. Conclusions

My results indicate that there is a statistically significant and direct relationship between the amount of basic research carried out by an industry or firm and its rate of increase of total factor productivity, when its expenditures on applied *R&D* are held constant. To some extent, this may reflect a tendency for basic research findings to be exploited more fully by the industries and firms that were responsible for them. Or it may reflect a tendency for applied *R&D* to be more effective when carried out in conjunction with some basic research. (See William Price and Lawrence Bass.) Whether the relevant distinction is between basic and applied research is by no means clear; there is some evidence that basic research may be acting to some extent as a proxy for long-term *R&D*. Holding constant the amount spent on both applied *R&D* and basic research, an industry's rate of productivity increase during 1948–66 seems to be directly and significantly related to the extent to which its *R&D* was long term. This appears to be the first systematic evidence that the composition, as well as the size, of an industry's or firm's *R&D* expenditures affects its rate of productivity increase.

My findings also indicate that the composition of many industries' *R&D* expenditures has changed in the last decade. Practically all industries have cut the proportion of their *R&D* expenditures going for basic research. Most industries have cut the proportion going for relatively risky projects. Some, but not most, industries have cut the proportion going for relatively long-term projects.[23] Particularly in the chemical, aerospace, and rubber industries, it appears that such changes may put a damper on the

---

[23] To some extent, this may be misleading if the length of projects is increased by regulatory and other such factors. In this case, the proportion spent on what formerly would have been regarded as long-term projects may have declined, even though this does not show up in the data because of the general lengthening of projects. The drug industry is an example where regulatory factors seem to have prompted a general lengthening of projects.

rate of productivity increase.[24] But without much more accurate data concerning the lags in the effects of R&D, it is difficult to say how quickly these effects will be felt.

In conclusion, the limitations of this study should be noted. In particular, the model adopted in Section I is highly simplified, and the data in Sections II and III often are rough. Even in Section IV, where the data pertain to about one-half of all R&D by U.S. manufacturing companies, there are bound to be sampling errors, since not all firms are included. For these and other reasons, my findings must be regarded as tentative. Much more work is needed in this area. For example, it is important that we try to determine the extent to which the observed relationship between the composition of an industry's or firm's R&D expenditures and its rate of productivity change is due to the influence of other factors on both variables.[25] Nonetheless, despite its limitations, I believe that this study is of considerable interest, since it is the first attempt to disaggregate R&D expenditures (which are notoriously heterogeneous) and to investigate the effects of the composition of an industry's or firm's R&D expenditures on its rate of productivity increase.

[24]Besides this damper due to changes in the composition of R&D, there may be a damper on the rate of productivity increase in these industries because of the decrease during the last decade in the ratio of basic research expenditures to value-added and in the ratio of applied R&D expenditures to value-added.

[25]It is possible that industries and firms with high rates of productivity growth tend to spend relatively large amounts on basic research, but that their high rates of productivity growth are not due to these expenditures. Much more work is required before one can be entirely confident of the way in which this observed relationship should be interpreted.

REFERENCES

K. Arrow, "Economic Welfare and the Allocation of Resources for Invention," in *The Rate and Direction of Inventive Activity: Economic and Social Factors*, Universities-Nat. Bur. Econ. Res. conference series, Princeton 1962.

Z. Griliches, "Research Expenditures and Growth Accounting," in B. R. Williams, ed., *Science and Technology in Economic Growth*, London 1973.

_____, "Returns to Research and Development Expenditures in the Private Sector," in John W. Kendrick and Beatrice N. Vaccara, eds., *New Developments in Productivity Measurement*, Nat. Bur. Econ. Res. Stud. in Income and Wealth, Vol. 44, New York 1980.

John Kendrick, *Post War Productivity Trends in the United States, 1948–69*, New York 1973.

_____, *Productivity in the United States*, forthcoming.

Edwin Mansfield, *Industrial Research and Technology Innovation*, New York 1968.

_____, "Comments on Returns to Research and Development Expenditures," in John W. Kendrick and Beatrice N. Vaccara, eds., *New Developments in Productivity Measurement*, Nat. Bur. Econ. Res. Stud. in Income and Wealth, Vol. 44, New York 1980.

_____, "Research and Development, Productivity Change, and Public Policy," *Colloquium on Research and Development and Productivity*, National Science Foundation 1977.

_____, "Technology and Productivity in the United States," Conference on Postwar Changes in American Economy, Nat. Bur. Econ. Res. 1980.

_____ et al., *Research and Innovation in the Modern Corporation*, New York 1971.

_____ et al., *The Production and Application of New Industrial Technology*, New York 1977.

Howard Nason, Joseph Steger, and G. Manners, *Support of Basic Research by Industry*, Washington 1978.

R. Nelson, "The Simple Economics of Basic Scientific Research," *J. Polit. Econ.*, June 1959, *67*, 297–306.

W. Price and L. Bass, "Scientific Research and the Innovative Process," *Science*, May 16, 1969, *169*, 802–06.

C. Sherwin and R. Isenson, *First Interim Report on Project Hindsight*, Office of Defense Research and Engineering, Washington 1966.

Nestor Terleckyj, *Effects of R and D on the Productivity Growth of Industries*, Washington 1974.

Illinois Institute of Technology Research Institute, *Technology in Retrospect and Critical Events in Science,* rept. to the National Science Foundation, Washington 1969.

McGraw-Hill Economics Department, *Business Plans for New Plants and Equipment, 1958 –1961,* New York 1962.

Moody's Industrial Manual, New York, various issues.

National Science Foundation, *Methodology of Statistics on Research and Development,* Washington 1959.

_____, *Research and Development in Industry,* Washington, various issues.

Reprinted from

THE AMERICAN ECONOMIC REVIEW

8

TECHNOLOGICAL CHANGES: STIMULI, CONSTRAINTS, RETURNS

RATES OF RETURN FROM INDUSTRIAL RESEARCH AND DEVELOPMENT*

By Edwin Mansfield

University of Pennsylvania

I. *Introduction*

Although recent years have seen a notable increase in the amount of attention devoted to the economics of research and development, no attempt has been made to use econometric techniques to estimate the marginal rate of return from R and D expenditures in individual firms and manufacturing industries.[1] The enormous difficulties, both conceptual and practical, in making estimates of this sort are all too obvious. Nonetheless, it is important that the task be begun, since business firms and government agencies badly need better measures of the return from R and D.

This paper presents some results which are both preliminary and tentative. Having cursed the dark loudly and publicly,[2] my purpose here is to stimulate discussion of the problem and to light a few candles, limited though their power may be. Section II shows how the marginal rate of return from R and D expenditures can be estimated, assuming that a simple model of production holds and that all technical change is organizational. Section III presents numerical results for a small number of manufacturing firms and industries. Section IV shows how such estimates can be obtained, assuming that all technical change is capital-embodied, and Section V presents numerical results based on this assumption. Section VI discusses the findings and concludes the paper.

II. *Organizational Technical Change: Model*

To begin with, I assume that all technical change is organizational

* The work on which this paper is based was supported by a grant from the National Science Foundation and by the Ford Foundation Committee on Technological Change and Economic Growth, of which I'm a member. Previous versions of the paper were presented at the Cowles Foundation for Research in Economics at Yale University and the Brookings Conference on Public Expenditures. My thanks go to N. Auspitz, C. Phillips, and J. Smith for assistance, and to A. Ando, S. Koizumi, and R. Solow for comments on an earlier draft. Because of space limitations, it was necessary to delete parts of the paper. Mimeographed copies of the complete paper are available from the author on request.

[1] For agricultural research, Griliches [2] [3] has made some estimates of the rate of return. Ewell [1] has made some rough estimates for the entire economy. However, no estimates have been made for particular manufacturing industries or firms. For some estimates of payout periods, see [9].

[2] See Mansfield [6].

and that the production function for a particular firm is

$$(1) \qquad Q(t) = A e^{a_1 t} \left[\int_{-\infty}^{t} e^{-\lambda(t-g)} R(g) dg \right]^{a_2} L^{\alpha}(t) K^{1-\alpha}(t),$$

where $Q(t)$ is the output rate (in 1960 prices) at time t, $L(t)$ is the labor input at time t, $K(t)$ is the stock of capital (1929 prices) employed at time t, $R(g)$ is the rate of expenditure (1960 prices) on R and D by this firm at time g, λ is the annual rate of "depreciation" of an investment in R and D, a_1 is the rate of technical change that would occur even if R and D expenditures (net of "depreciation") by this firm were to cease, a_2 is the elasticity of output with respect to cumulated past net R and D expenditures, A and α are parameters, and time is measured in years from 1960.

Five points should be noted regarding equation (1). First, it recognizes that the firm's efficiency depends on its previous R and D expenditures, as well as on the inventive activity of other firms and nonprofit institutions (the effect of the latter being incorporated in a_1).[3] Second, it allows for the possibility that an investment in R and D, like that in plant and equipment, depreciates over time, because of the obsolescence of research findings and designs.[4] Third, it makes the usual assumption that holding constant the level of previous R and D expenditures (which determines the level of technology at a given point in time), there are constant returns to scale with respect to labor and capital. Fourth, A and α can vary from firm to firm, and a_1 and a_2 can vary from industry to industry.[5] Fifth, the little evidence that is available seems to support equation (1). A study [11] of seventeen chemical firms indicates that this type of production function fits well and that the coefficients are generally statistically significant and of expected size. This evidence is hardly conclusive, but it is all we have.[6]

Next, assume that, for the period up to 1960,

$$(2) \qquad R(g) = R_o e^{(\rho-\sigma)g},$$

[3] For other papers that assume that current output is a function of cumulated past R and D expenditures, see Minasian [10] [11] and Kurz [4]. Apparently, this is the first model that uses a depreciation factor and includes "imported" technical change.

[4] One implication of this model, as it stands, is that the firm must do some R and D just to maintain its efficiency at a constant level. Since it takes some R and D simply to move along a given production function in response to changing factor prices, etc., this may not be too unrealistic. If one believes that this is not the case, he can set λ equal to zero. This makes little difference in the subsequent analysis.

[5] We assume that a_1 and a_2 are the same for firms within the same industry, but this assumption can be relaxed if one part of an industry seemed to differ significantly from another part. In Sections III and V, we assume that a_2 is the same in chemicals as in petroleum. Because the industries are similar in many respects, this seems reasonable. Of course, if more data were available, it would not be necessary to make this assumption.

[6] Note that Minasian's results [11] are based on the assumption that λ and σ equal zero and that his data on R and D expenditures do not go back very far. Moreover, because of the correlation between time and the sum of previous R and D expenditures, his estimates are not very precise when both of these variables are included in the production function. Nonetheless, his study, which is the only one of this sort that has been done to date, seems to point toward the use of equation (1) as a first approximation. For further comments see note 9.

where R_o is the firm's R and D expenditures in 1960, ρ is the rate of increase of R and D expenditures in current dollars, and σ is the rate of price increase of R and D, as well as an allowance for noncomparability of R and D figures over time. According to the available data, R and D expenditures in current dollars rose (approximately) exponentially in most firms during 1927–60. It seems reasonable to assume as a first approximation that R and D expenditures in constant dollars did so, too.

Given these assumptions, what would have been the marginal rate of return from an additional amount spent in 1960 on R and D, assuming that R and D expenditures after 1960 would continue to conform to equation (2)? If an additional expenditure of ϵ had been made on R and D in 1960, the output at a subsequent time t would have been

$$(3) \qquad Q(t) = A e^{a_1 t}\left(\frac{R_o e^{(\rho-\sigma)t}}{\rho - \sigma + \lambda} + \epsilon e^{-\lambda t}\right)^{a_2} L^\alpha(t) K^{1-\alpha}(t),$$

and

$$(4) \qquad \frac{\partial Q(t)}{\partial \epsilon}\bigg|_{\epsilon=0} = a_2 A e^{(a_1-\lambda)t}\left(\frac{R_o e^{(\rho-\sigma)t}}{\rho - \sigma + \lambda}\right)^{a_2-1} L^\alpha(t) K^{1-\alpha}(t).$$

Thus, if $L(t) = L_o e^{lt}$ and $K(t) = K_o e^{kt}$, it follows that

$$(5) \qquad \int_0^\infty \frac{\partial Q(t)}{\partial \epsilon}\bigg|_{\epsilon=0} e^{-rt}dt$$

$$= a_2 A \left(\frac{R_o}{\rho - \sigma + \lambda}\right)^{a_2-1} L_o^\alpha K_o^{1-\alpha}$$

$$\neq \int_0^\infty e^{t[a_1-\lambda-r+(a_2-1)(\rho+\sigma)-\alpha l+(1-\alpha)k]}dt$$

$$= a_2(\rho - \sigma + \lambda)\frac{Q}{R_o}$$

$$\cdot [r + \lambda - a_1 - (a_2 - 1)(\rho - \sigma) - \alpha l - (1 - \alpha)k]^{-1},$$

where Q is the 1960 value of $Q(t)$. We assume that the price of the product will remain constant from 1960 on, and that the elasticity of supply of the R and D inputs to the firm is infinitely elastic. Consequently, since both $Q(t)$ and $R(g)$ are expressed in 1960 prices, we set the right-hand side of equation (5) equal to one, solve for r, and find that

(6) $\quad r^1 = a_2(\rho - \sigma + \lambda)\dfrac{Q}{R_o} + a_1 - \lambda + (a_2 - 1)(\rho - \sigma) + \alpha l + (1 - \alpha)k,$

where r^1 is the marginal rate of return from the extra expenditure in 1960 on R and D.

III. *Organizational Technical Change: Empirical Results*

To illustrate how equation (6) can be used to estimate the marginal rate of return from R and D, I did a pilot study of ten chemical and petroleum firms and ten manufacturing industries. First, let us consider the case of the ten firms. From correspondence with the firms, annual reports, and *Moody's*, I obtain estimates for each firm of α, R_o, ρ, and Q. Assuming that the value of labor's marginal product is set equal to its wage, I use labor's average share of value added in the firm (during 1946–62) as an estimate of α. To estimate Q and R_o, I use data regarding the firm's value added and R and D expenditures in 1960. To estimate ρ, I use the slope of the regression of the natural logarithm of the firm's R and D expenditures (current dollars) on time during 1945–58.

The next step is to estimate $b' = a_1 + a_2(\rho - \sigma)$. Letting

(7) $\qquad\qquad \dot{V}/V = \dot{Q}/Q - \alpha \dot{L}/L - (1 - \alpha)\dot{K}/K,$

it follows from equations (1) and (2) that

(8) $\qquad\qquad ln\ V(t) = \text{constant} + b't.$

For each firm, I obtained data regarding $Q(t)$, $L(t)$, and $K(t)$ for 1946–62.[7] Letting $V = 1$ in 1946, I calculated $V(t)$ for each subsequent year, regressed $ln\ V(t)$ on t, and used the resulting regression coefficient as an estimate of b'. Since the model applies only to periods when the firm is operating at full capacity, I omitted years when output was less than some previous year.

Next, given an independent estimate of a_2, I estimate a_1, assuming that a_2 is the same for all of these firms but that a_1 may differ from industry to industry. Since

(9) $\qquad\qquad \hat{b}' = [a_1 - a_2\sigma] + a_2\rho + z,$

---

[7] Note that the data on value added contain an error, which was judged to be too small to be worth correcting. By mistake, they are net of R and D expenditures. However, since R and D expenditures are a very small and relatively constant percentage of value added in these firms (about 5 percent), their omission is very unlikely to have an important effect on the findings. Note too that our estimate of α is very rough. We assume that labor's marginal product is set equal to its wage. (Of course, we could assume that physical capital's marginal product is set equal to its price. The resulting estimate of α would be the same.) However, we cannot assume that the marginal products of both labor and capital are set equal to their prices, because this would leave nothing as compensation for the investment in R and D. Of course, if this assumption seems too unrealistic, there are other ways that α could be estimated.

where $\hat{b}'$ is our estimate of b' and z is the sampling error it contains, it follows that

$$a_1 = [\hat{b}' - a_2\rho] + a_2\sigma + z.$$

An independent estimate [15] of a_2, based on data for seventeen chemical firms, is .11, the standard error being .01. To check this estimate,[8] I regressed b on ρ, and found that the regression coefficient, .12, was very close to .11, the difference not being statistically significant. Setting a_2 equal to .11,[9] the average value of $(\hat{b}' - a_2\rho)$ for our ten firms is .013, and there is no evidence that it differs significantly between industries. Thus; omitting z,

(10) $a_1 = .013 + .11\sigma.$

Finally, inserting these estimates of a_1 and a_2, together with the estimates of α, ρ, R_o, and Q, into equation (6) and assuming that $\alpha l + (1-\alpha)k = .02$ for all firms, we obtain the estimates of r', given assumed values of σ and λ. The results are shown in Table 1.

Let's turn to the ten two-digit manufacturing industries in Table 2. The model in Section II can be reinterpreted on an industry-wide basis, $Q(t)$, $L(t)$, etc., being regarded as industry aggregates rather than figures for individual firms. Based on this interpretation, estimates of α, ρ, Q, R_o, and b' were obtained for each industry by methods similar to those used for the firms. However, since a_2 would be expected to vary considerably from one industry to another, I cannot estimate a_2 and a_1 in the way I did for the firms, unless data are available for a number of relatively homogeneous industries. Having data for only a small number of industries, I rewrite equation (6) as

(11) $r' = \dfrac{Q}{R_o} b' \left(1 - x + \dfrac{a_2}{b'}\lambda\right) + b' - \lambda - \rho + \sigma + \alpha l + (1-\alpha)k,$

where $x = (a_1/b)$ is the proportion of the industry's technical change not due to its own R and D. Then I set a_2 equal to zero, insert the estimates of α, ρ, Q, R_o, and b' into equation (11), assume that $\alpha l + (1-\alpha)k = .02$, and obtain the results shown in Table 2. It can easily be seen that these results are lower bounds on the marginal rates of return.

---

[8] We can obtain our own estimate of a_2 by regressing b' on ρ, since z should be uncorrelated with ρ. To allow for interindustry differences in a_1, one can allow the intercept to differ between industries. However, it turns out that these differences are not statistically significant.

[9] Note two things. First, since the two estimates are largely independent, it would be better to average Minasian's estimate of a_2 and ours rather than to use his alone. However, the two estimates are so close that this would make no difference. Second, it may be objected that Minasian's estimate of .11 is inappropriate here because it is based on the assumption that a_1 is zero. However, if we use the estimate he obtains when he relaxes this assumption, together with our results, we get almost exactly the same answer. Specifically, if we average his estimate (.08) and ours (.12), we get .10. Moreover, although each of these estimates has a substantial standard error, the average is statistically significant.

TABLE 1

Estimates of b and b' and Marginal Rates of Return from R and D Expenditures,
Ten Chemical and Petroleum Firms

FIRM	ESTIMATES		RATES OF RETURN							
			Capital-Embodied				Organizational			
	b	b'	$\sigma=.04$ $\lambda=.04$	$\sigma=.04$ $\lambda=.07$	$\sigma=.07$ $\lambda=.04$	$\sigma=.07$ $\lambda=.07$	$\sigma=.04$ $\lambda=.04$	$\sigma=.04$ $\lambda=.07$	$\sigma=.07$ $\lambda=.04$	$\sigma=.07$ $\lambda=.07$
C1	.0051	.0035	.12	.18	.03	.12	.04	.04	.04	.04
C2	.0624	.0239	.25	.26	.25	.25	.02	.01	.02	.02
C3	.0200	.0260	.42	.46	.38	.42	.10	.11	.09	.10
C4	.0354	.0141	.33	.36	.29	.33	.14	.17	.12	.14
C5	.0534	*	.53	.58	.47	.53	.06	.06	.05	.06
P1	.0212	.0033	.24	.25	.20	.24	.13	.16	.11	.13
P2	.0594	.0191	.57	.72	.49	.57	.25	.33	.17	.25
P3	.0656	.0317	.64	.70	.56	.64	.51	.63	.40	.51
P4	.0947	.0107	.92	.99	.82	.92	.79	.96	.63	.79
P5	.0877	.0182	.73	.78	.67	.73	.31	.37	.26	.31

* Less than zero.
SOURCE: See Sections III and V.

IV. *Capital-Embodied Technical Change: Model*

Before discussing the results of Section III, let us consider an alternative model based on the supposition that technical change is capital-embodied, not organizational, and see the extent to which the results differ from those in Section III. For capital installed at time v which is still in existence at time t, the production function for a particular firm is assumed to be

$$(12) \qquad Q_v(t) = A e^{a_1 v} \left[\int_{-\infty}^{v} e^{-\lambda(v-g)} R(g) dg \right]^{a_2} L_v^{\alpha}(t) K_v^{1-\alpha}(t),$$

where $Q_v(t)$ is the output rate (in 1960 prices) at time t from such capital and $L_v(t)$ is the rate of labor input being combined with this capital at time t. Of course, A, a_1, and a_2 are not the same as in Sections II–III.

Next, assume that all capital in a particular firm, regardless of vintage, depreciates at an annual rate of δ and that the firm's labor force is allocated efficiently among various vintages of capital. Given this assumption, one can show that

$$(13) \quad Q(t) = A L^{\alpha}(t) \left\{ e^{-\delta t} \int_{-\infty}^{t} e^{(a_1/(1-\alpha)+\delta)v} \right.$$

$$\left. \cdot \left(\int_{-\infty}^{v} e^{-\lambda(v-g)} R(g) dg \right)^{a_2/(1-\alpha)} I(v) dv \right\}^{1-\alpha}$$

TABLE 2

ESTIMATES OF b AND b' AND LOWER BOUNDS ON THE MARGINAL RATES OF RETURN FROM R AND D EXPENDITURES, TEN MANUFACTURING INDUSTRIES

INDUSTRY	ESTIMATES		RATES OF RETURN							
			Capital-Embodied				Organizational			
	b	b'	$\sigma=.04$ $\lambda=.04$	$\sigma=.04$ $\lambda=.07$	$\sigma=.07$ $\lambda=.04$	$\sigma=.07$ $\lambda=.07$	$\sigma=.04$ $\lambda=.04$	$\sigma=.04$ $\lambda=.07$	$\sigma=.07$ $\lambda=.04$	$\sigma=.07$ $\lambda=.07$
						$x=.25$				
Chemicals.........	.037	.035	.03	.03	.04	.03	.24	.21	.27	.24
Machinery.........	*	.020	†	†	†	†	.01	−.02	.04	.01
Food..............	.047	.014	.58	.57	.58	.58	1.77	1.74	1.80	1.77
Paper.............	.034	.023	.26	.26	.27	.26	1.51	1.48	1.53	1.50
Instruments.......	.083	.010	.07	.07	.07	.07	−.07	−.10	−.04	−.07
Electrical equipment	.036	.037	.04	.04	.04	.04	.07	.04	.10	.07
Stone, clay, and glass	.015	.025	.08	.08	.08	.08	.81	.78	.84	.81
Furniture..........	.019	.010	.37	.37	.38	.37	2.49	2.46	2.52	2.49
Apparel...........	.030	.009	.98	.97	.99	.98	3.38	3.35	3.41	3.38
Motor vehicles.....	.086	.024	.04	.04	.05	.04	.01	−.02	.04	.01
						$x=.50$				
Chemicals.........	.037	.035	.02	.02	.02	.02	.14	.11	.17	.14
Machinery.........	*	.020	†	†	†	†	−.04	−.07	−.01	−.04
Food..............	.047	.014	.43	.42	.43	.43	1.15	1.12	1.18	1.15
Paper.............	.034	.023	.19	.18	.19	.19	.98	.95	1.01	.98
Instruments	.083	.010	.05	.05	.05	.05	−.08	−.11	−.05	−.08
Electrical equipment	.036	.037	.03	.02	.03	.03	.01	−.02	.04	.01
Stone, clay, and glass	.015	.025	.11	.05	.06	.11	.52	.49	.55	.52
Furniture..........	.019	.010	.27	.26	.27	.27	1.64	1.61	1.67	1.64
Apparel...........	.030	.009	.75	.74	.74	.75	2.23	2.20	2.26	2.23
Motor vehicles.....	.086	.024	.03	.03	.03	.03	−.04	−.07	−.01	−.04
						$x=.90$				
Chemicals.........	.037	.035	.00	.00	.00	.00	−.03	−.06	.00	−.03
Machinery.........	*	.020	†	†	†	†	−.10	−.13	−.07	−.10
Food..............	.047	.014	.11	.11	.11	.11	.17	.14	.20	.17
Paper.............	.034	.023	.04	.04	.04	.04	.13	.10	.16	.13
Instruments.......	.083	.010	.01	.01	.01	.01	−.10	−.13	−.07	−.10
Electrical equipment	.036	.037	.01	.01	.01	.01	−.08	−.11	.05	−.08
Stone, clay, and glass	.015	.025	.01	.01	.01	.01	.05	.02	.08	.05
Furniture..........	.019	.010	.06	.07	.06	.06	.26	.23	.29	.26
Apparel...........	.030	.009	.22	.23	.22	.22	.38	.35	.41	.38
Motor vehicles.....	.086	.024	.01	.01	.01	.01	−.12	−.15	−.09	−.12

* Due to sampling errors, this estimate violates the a priori constraint that $b>0$.
† No estimate can be made because the estimate of b is negative.
SOURCE: See Sections III and V.

where $I(v)$ is the gross investment in plant and equipment (1929 prices) by the firm at time v. Of course, δ varies from industry to industry, but I assume that it is the same for all firms in the same industry. Finally, I assume once again that equation (2) holds up to 1960.

Given this alternative model, what would have been the marginal rate of return from an additional amount spent in 1960 on R and D, assuming that R and D expenditures after 1960 would continue to conform to equation (2)? If an additional expenditure of ϵ had been made on R and D in 1960, the output at a subsequent time t would have been

$$(14) \quad Q(t) = A L^\alpha(t) \left\{ e^{-\delta t} \left(\int_{-\infty}^{0} e^{[a_1 + a_2(\rho-\sigma)]/(1-\alpha)\,v} I(v) dv \right) \right.$$

$$\cdot \left(\frac{R_o}{\lambda + \rho - \sigma} \right)^{a_2/(1-\alpha)}$$

$$\left. + e^{-\delta t} \int_{0}^{t} e^{[\delta + a_1/(1-\alpha)]v} \left[\frac{R_o e^{(\rho-\sigma)v}}{\lambda + \rho - \sigma} + \epsilon e^{-\lambda v} \right]^{a_2/(1-\alpha)} dv \right\}^{1-\alpha}.$$

Let $Q_0(t)$ be the output rate at time t if $\epsilon = 0$, and let

$$(15) \qquad J_o(t) = e^{-\delta t} \int_{-\infty}^{t} e^{[\delta + (a_1 + a_2[\rho-\sigma])/(1-\alpha)]v} I(v) dv.$$

That is, $J_0(t)$ is the "effective" stock of capital [13] [15] at time t if $\epsilon = 0$. Assuming that $I(v) = I e^{iv}$ from 1960 on, it follows that

$$(16) \quad \frac{\partial Q(t)}{\partial \epsilon} \bigg|_{\epsilon=0} = a_2(\lambda + \rho - \sigma) \frac{Q_o(t)}{J_o(t)} \frac{I}{R_o}$$

$$\cdot \left[\frac{e^{[i-\lambda + a_1/(1-\alpha) + (a_2/(1-\alpha)-1)(\rho-\sigma)]t} - e^{-\delta t}}{\delta - \lambda + i + \dfrac{a_1}{1-\alpha} + \left(\dfrac{a_2}{1-\alpha} - 1 \right)(\rho - \sigma)} \right]$$

where I is gross investment in plant and equipment in 1960. Assuming for simplicity that $Q_o(t)/J_o(t) = Q/J$, where Q and J pertain to 1960, we have

$$(17) \quad \int_{0}^{\infty} \frac{\partial Q(t)}{\partial \epsilon} \bigg|_{\epsilon=0} e^{-rt} dt$$

$$= \frac{a_2(\lambda + \rho - \sigma) Q I}{\left[\delta - \lambda + i + \dfrac{a_1}{1-\alpha} + \left(\dfrac{a_2}{1-\alpha} - 1 \right)(\rho - \sigma) \right] J R_o}$$

$$\times \left\{ \int_{0}^{\infty} e^{[-r+i-\lambda + a_1/(1-\alpha) + (a_2/(1-\alpha)-1)(\rho-\sigma)]t} dt - \int_{0}^{\infty} e^{-(\delta+r)t} dt \right\}.$$

$$(18) \quad = a_2 \frac{(\lambda + \rho - \sigma)}{(\delta + r)} \frac{Q}{J} \frac{I}{R_o}$$

$$\cdot \left[r + \lambda - i - \frac{a_1}{1-\alpha} - \left(\frac{a_2}{1-\alpha} - 1 \right)(\rho - \sigma) \right]^{-1}$$

where r is assumed to exceed

$$i - \lambda + \frac{a_1}{1-\alpha} + \left(\frac{a_2}{1-\alpha} - 1\right)(\rho - \sigma).$$

Setting the right-hand side of equation (18) equal to one and solving for r, we have

$$(19) \quad (r^* + \delta)\left[r^* + \lambda - i - \frac{a_1}{1-\alpha} - \left(\frac{a_2}{1-\alpha} - 1\right)(\rho - \sigma)\right]$$

$$= a_2(\lambda + \rho - \sigma)\frac{Q}{J}\frac{I}{R_o},$$

where r^* is the rate of return from the extra amount spent in 1960 on R and D.[10]

V. Capital-Embodied Technical Change: Empirical Results

To illustrate how equation (19) can be used to estimate r^*, I again consider the ten chemical and petroleum firms and the ten manufacturing industries. To estimate I for each firm, I obtained data regarding its investment in plant and equipment (1929 dollars) in 1960. The slope of the regression of $ln\ I(v)$ on v during 1946–62 is used as a rough estimate of i. As an estimate of δ, I use the reciprocal of the length of life of plant and equipment in the industry, assuming that plant has a 45 year life and that the average life of equipment is given by the Treasury's 1962 *Depreciation Guidelines and Rules*. To estimate J, the deflated book value of the firm's 1960 fixed assets was multiplied by Phelps's estimate [13] of the ratio of "effective" to "old-style" capital in the business sector of the economy.

The next step is to estimate $b = a_1 + a_2(\rho - \sigma)$ for each firm. If the assumptions in the previous section hold,

$$(20) \quad (1-\alpha)\ ln\ \left\{[W(t) - W(t-1) + \delta W(t)]/I(t)\right\}$$

$$= ln\left[A\left(\frac{R_o}{\lambda + \rho - \sigma}\right)^{a_2}\right] + bt,$$

where $W(t) = Q^{1/(1-\alpha)}(t)/L^{\alpha/(1-\alpha)}(t)$. Thus, in each firm, I calculate the value of the left-hand side of equation (20) for each year during 1946–62, using the estimates of α and δ described above and the data provided by the firms regarding $Q(t)$, $L(t)$, and $I(t)$. Then I regress this value on t, and use the regression coefficient, $\hat{b}$, as an estimate of b. As in Section III, I omitted years when output was less than some previous year.

[10] In most cases, a good approximation for r^* is $\sqrt{a_2(\lambda+\rho-\sigma)IQ/R_oJ}$.

Next, I estimate a_1 and a_2, assuming that a_2 is the same for all firms but that a_1 may differ between industries. The regression of $\hat{b}$ on ρ is

$$(21) \qquad\qquad \hat{b} = -\,.024 + .673\,\rho,$$

$$(.242)$$

the correlation coefficient (adjusted for degrees of freedom) being .61, and there is no evidence that a_1 differs between the industries. Thus, our estimate of a_2 is .673 and our estimate of a_1 is $-.024 + .673\sigma$. Finally, inserting these estimates, together with the estimates of δ, α, ρ, i, I, R_o, Q, and J, into equation (19), we obtain estimates of r^*, given assumed values of σ and λ. The results are shown in Table 1.

Turning to the two-digit manufacturing industries, we again reinterpret the model in terms of industry-wide aggregates. Estimates of δ, I, i, and J were obtained by methods similar to those used for the firms. Rewriting equation (19) as

$$(22) \quad (r^* + \delta)\left(r^* - \frac{b}{1-\alpha} + \lambda - i + \rho - \sigma\right)$$

$$= b\left(1 - x + \frac{a_2\lambda}{b}\right)\frac{I}{R_o}\frac{Q}{J},$$

I set a_2 equal to zero, insert the estimates of δ, I, R_0, Q, J, i, α, and b into equation (22), and obtain the results shown in Table 2. Like the comparable results in Section III, they are lower bounds on the rate of return rather than estimates of the rate of return. Without data for more industries, we cannot obtain the latter.

VI. *Discussion and Conclusion*

In view of their roughness it would be unwise to read too much into the results in Tables 1 and 2. However, several points are worth noting. First, like the results of previous studies the estimates in Table 1 tend to be very high. Among the petroleum firms, regardless of whether technical change was capital-embodied or organizational, the marginal rates of return average about 40–60 percent. Among the chemical firms, they average about 30 percent if technical change is capital-embodied, but only about 7 percent if it is organizational. Even if the elasticity of supply to the firm of R and D inputs is less than infinite, as Machlup asserts, the rates of return remain high, so long as the elasticity remains within seemingly reasonable bounds.[11]

---

[11] If true, these high marginal rates of return may persist because of the riskiness of R and D activities or because firms are ignorant of the true returns. For further discussion, see below. However, if there is a lag in the effect of R and D expenditures on the production function, our estimates in Tables 1 and 2 overestimate the true rate of returns. If one knows the length of the lag, the necessary adjustment can be made quite easily. For example, in the case of organizational technical change, it turns out that our estimates in Table 1 (with σ and λ equal to .04) are about 20 percent too high if the lag is one year. Obviously, this may be important.

Second, comparing these results with the few estimates of this sort that have been published by other economists, it appears that although our estimates seem very high they are generally much lower than those obtained by others. However, comparing our results with data I obtained from a number of large chemical and petroleum firms regarding the expected profitability of their current R and D projects, it appears that our estimates are considerably higher than the firms'. To some extent, the latter difference is due to differences in concept and to sampling errors and other inadequacies in our estimates. But to the extent that this difference is real and our estimates are closer to the truth, it suggests an underinvestment in R and D, particularly among the petroleum firms.[12]

Third, the estimates in Table 1 suggest that the marginal rate of return was directly related to a firm's size in chemicals but inversely related to it in petroleum. To the extent that these differences, which seem to persist for all values of λ and σ in Table 1 and for capital-embodied and organizational technical progress, are real, they suggest that a transfer of R and D inputs from the smaller chemical firms to the largest ones and from the largest petroleum firms to the somewhat smaller ones might be desirable.

Fourth, the lower bounds in Table 2 suggest that, even if x is as large as .90, the marginal rate of return exceeded 15 percent in the apparel industry, regardless of whether technical change was organizational or capital-embodied. If it was organizational, the same was true for food and furniture. Although they are by no means unambiguous, these results suggest that there may have been an underinvestment in R and D in some of these industries.[13]

Fifth, whether technical change is capital-embodied or organizational, there is evidence of diminishing return to scale from cumulated net R and D expenditures in chemicals and petroleum. If technical change is organizational, our results, like Minasian's [11], suggest that the average effect of a 1 percent increase in cumulated net R and D expenditures is a .1 percent increase in current output. If technical change is capital-embodied, its effect is a .7 percent increase in current output.

Sixth, since the rate of technical change is measured by b if technical change is capital-embodied (and by b' if it is organizational), Table 1 provides the first published estimates of the rates of technical change during the postwar period in particular firms. These estimates indicate that a firm's rate of technical progress is directly related to the rate of

[12] For results based on other studies, see [1] [2] [3] and [7]. The data regarding the firms' expectations pertain to eight firms and were obtained by interviews and correspondence. These data, together with similar information collected during the next few months, will be used in a paper I am writing with Michael Hamburger on industrial R and D expenditures.
[13] Of course, this presumes that x does in fact lie between .25 and .90 in all industries. This is reasonable, but by no means indisputable.

growth of its R and D expenditures, as would be expected on the basis of our model.[14] However, there is no evidence that such frequently-used variables as the firm's ratio of R and D expenditures to sales or its growth rate exert an important influence on its rate of technical change.[15]

Seventh, Table 2 provides new estimates of the rate of capital-embodied technical progress in various manufacturing industries. According to these estimates, technology advanced most rapidly in motor vehicles and instruments and least rapidly in machinery, glass, and furniture. As would be expected, the estimated rate of technical change generally exceeds the estimated rate of organizational technical change. However, there is relatively little correlation between them.

In conclusion, these results should be viewed with considerable caution, for at least three reasons. First, they are based on a number of highly simplified assumptions: that uncertainty can be ignored, that technical change is cost-reducing,[16] that all technical change is neutral, that the production function is Cobb-Douglas, and that, to use Phelps's phrase [12], capital is putty, not hard-baked clay. Second, the estimates in Tables 1 and 2 contain substantial sampling errors.[17] Third, they are incomplete estimates of the social rate of return, since they do not take account of the effects of increased R and D expenditures in one industry or firm on productivity in another industry or firm. The social rates of return may be higher than ours.

Nonetheless, I believe that the results represent a useful first step toward the formulation of operational techniques to measure the returns from R and D, and I hope that others will be encouraged to join in the work toward this end.

REFERENCES

1. R. Ewell, "Role of Research in Economic Growth," *Chemical Engineering News*, July, 1955.
2. Z. Griliches, "Research Expenditures, Education, and the Aggregate Agricultural Production Function," *A.E.R.*, Dec., 1964.

[14] Note three things: (1) When industry-wide data are used rather than firm data, there is also a positive relationship between b (or b') and ρ. (2) In practically all cases, regardless of whether the data pertain to firms or industries and whether b or b' is used, this positive relationship is statistically significant, the exception being the case where firm data are used and technical change is assumed to be organizational. (3) It is possible that an identification problem exists in all of these relationships and that b or b' influences ρ. However, the tests that have been made to determine whether some other variable, like a firm's (or industry's) rate of growth, is responsible for the variation in both b or b' and ρ, have not indicated that this is the case. See note 15.

[15] Both the ratio of R and D expenditures to sales in 1960 and the rate of growth of sales during 1945–58 were used as additional independent variables in equation (21) and the corresponding regression in the case of organizational technical change. Neither was statistically significant. The rate of growth of profits during 1945–58 was used, too, with similar results. When industry-wide data are used instead of firm data, the results are the same. For some relevant discussion, see [16]. Note that, according to the model, the rate of technical change does not depend on λ.

[16] Of course, this helps to explain our choice of the petroleum and chemical industries, both of which direct a great deal of their R and D at new processes.

[17] The sampling errors in the averages reported in the first paragraph of Section VI are much smaller than those in the individual numbers in Table 1.

3. ———, "Research Costs and Social Returns: Hybrid Corn and Related Innovations," *J.P.E.*, Oct., 1958.
4. M. Kurz, "Research and Development, Technical Change, and the Competitive Mechanism" (Inst. of Math. Studies in the Soc. Sci., Stanford, 1962).
5. E. Mansfield, "Industrial Research and Development Expenditures: Determinants, Prospects, and Relation to Size of Firm and Inventive Output," *J.P.E.*, Aug., 1964.
6. ———, "The Economics of Research and Development: A Survey of Issues, Findings, and Needed Future Research," *Univ. of Pennsylvania Conference on Technological Change and Government Regulation of Industry* (Irwin, forthcoming).
7. ———, and R. Brandenburg, "The Allocation, Characteristics, and Success of the Firm's R and D Portfolio: A Case Study," *Ford Foundation Conference on Technical Change* (forthcoming).
8. ———, "Innovation and Technical Change in the Railroad Industry," *Transportation Economics* (Columbia for N.B.E.R., 1965).
9. McGraw-Hill Economics Department, *Business Plans for New Plant and Equipment*, annual.
10. J. Minasian, "The Economics of Research and Development," *The Rate and Direction of Inventive Activity* (Princeton, 1962).
11. ———, "Technical Change and Production Functions" (unpublished paper presented at the fall, 1961, meetings of the Econometric Society).
12. E. Phelps, "Substitution, Fixed Proportions, Growth, and Distribution," *Int. Econ. Rev.*, Sept., 1963.
13. ———, "The New View of Investment: A Neoclassical Analysis," *Q.J.E.*, Nov., 1962.
14. R. Solow, "Capital, Labor, and Income in Manufacturing," *The Behavior of Income Shares* (Princeton, 1964).
15. ———, "Investment and Technical Progress," *Mathematical Methods in the Social Sciences* (Stanford, 1959).
16. N. Terleckij, "Sources of Productivity Advance" (Ph.D. thesis, Columbia, 1960).

9

INDUSTRIAL RESEARCH AND DEVELOPMENT: CHARACTERISTICS, COSTS, AND DIFFUSION OF RESULTS*

By Edwin Mansfield
University of Pennsylvania

I. *Introduction*

In view of the size of the current R and D effort in the United States[1] and its effect on other economic variables like the rate of technological change, the rate of investment, and the rate of economic growth, it is important that we obtain a better understanding of the nature and characteristics of the R and D programs carried out by industry, the factors that seem to be associated with the cost of individual R and D projects, and the process by which the results of R and D become adopted and accepted. This paper summarizes very briefly some results of a number of related empirical studies of these topics.

II. *Characteristics of R and D Programs*

The first study, by Michael Hamburger and I,[2] is concerned with the characteristics of industrial research and development. Despite the attention that this area has received in recent years, little is known about the characteristics of the activities that firms call "research and development." This lack of information has been a hindrance to progress in this area,

since, without a reasonable amount of information on this score, it is difficult to formulate or evaluate models relating R and D expenditures to other economic variables. In an attempt to shed additional light on this subject, we studied the characteristics of the R and D programs carried out in 1964 by twenty-two major firms in the chemical and petroleum industries—two industries that are very important performers of R and D.

The results indicate at least four things. First, they show that the bulk of the R and D projects carried out by these firms is relatively safe from a technical point of view. In practically all firms in our sample, most of the projects were regarded as having better than a fifty-fifty chance of technical success.[3] Second, only a small

* The studies described in this paper were supported by the National Science Foundation, the Ford Foundation, and the Small Business Administration. I want to express my appreciation to them for generous financial support.

[1] In 1966, industry alone performed about $15 billion of research and development. For a discussion of the growth of R and D expenditures in the postwar (and earlier) period, see Edwin Mansfield, *The Economics of Technological Change* (Norton, 1968), Chaps. 3 and 6.

[2] Edwin Mansfield and Michael Hamburger, "A Study of Research and Development in the Chemical and Petroleum Industries" (unpublished paper, 1968). Only a few of our results can be presented in the time available here.

[3] Of course, it might be objected that these estimates are biased upward because the R and D personnel are trying to sell projects. But we have data from related studies for some firms that allow us to compare estimated probabilities of success with actual probabilities of success. The results indicate that, although there may be some upward bias, it is not very large on the average. For example, in one firm, the average estimated probability of technical success was about 80 percent whereas the actual percentage of projects that were technically successful was about 75. In another firm, these figures were both about 80. Of course, projects that were not carried out as intended, or that were dropped for commercial reasons, were omitted to provide a fair comparison. A project is defined to be a technical success if it attains its technical objectives in the budgeted time and within the budgeted cost; otherwise it is defined to be a technical failure. Of course, such a simple classification can be misleading. For example a project may not attain its technical objective but it may nonetheless result in very valuable information. Despite these disadvantages, it seemed worthwhile to gather data concerning the estimated probability of technical success, since this estimate is commonly used by firms as a rough measure of the riskiness of a project from a technical angle, and it is likely to be as good a measure of this sort as one can obtain in a survey.

65

percentage of the money spent by these firms goes for basic research. On the average 9 percent of their R and D expenditures were devoted to basic research, 45 percent were devoted to applied research, and 46 percent were devoted to development.[4] Third, most of the R and D projects are expected to be quite profitable if they are technically successful, the median expected rate of return for a firm's projects generally being about 30 percent.[5] Fourth, the bulk of the R and D projects are expected to be finished and to have an effect on profits in five years or less.

These findings seem to support the hypothesis advanced by Hamberg[6] and others, that the bulk of the R and D carried out by large corporations is relatively safe and aimed at fairly modest advances in the state of the art. Models or policies based on the popular supposition that the bulk of the research and development in the industrial laboratory is very risky, far-out work aimed at really major inventions are likely to be misconceived and misleading. This is an important point, both for analysis and policy.

The results also indicate that, in each industry, there is a great deal of interfirm diversity in the characteristics of the R

and D programs.[7] For example, some chemical firms devote 18 percent of their R and D expenditures to basic research, whereas others devote none. Some chemical firms spend $47,000 on R and D per scientist and engineer, whereas others spend $25,000. The median expected rate of return is about 40 percent for some chemical firms and less than 20 percent for others. The median length of time to completion is about two years for some chemical firms and about four years for others. Only in the case of the median estimated probability of technical success of projects is the interfirm variation in each industry relatively small. In all but three firms it lies between 50 and 62 percent in chemicals; in all firms, it lies between 70 and 83 percent in petroleum.[8]

III. Size of Firm and Characteristics of R and D Programs

Some of this variation among firms in the characteristics of their R and D programs can of course be explained by differences in size of firm.[9] In particular, one would suppose that the largest firms would devote a larger proportion of their R and D expenditures to more basic, more risky, and longer-term R and D projects than their smaller competitors. Our data for the chemical and petroleum industries bear out these hypotheses. For example, consider a chemical firm with sales that

[4] We used the National Science Foundation's definitions of basic research, applied research, and development. For example, see *Basic Research, Applied Research, and Development in Industry, 1962* (NSF, 1965).

[5] Note that these estimates are conditional on the project's being technically successful. The unconditional estimates would, of course, be lower.

[6] Daniel Hamberg, "Invention in the Industrial Research Laboratory," *J.P.E.*, Apr., 1963.

[7] Of course, some of this variation could be due to differences among firms in the interpretation of the definitions of research and development, basic research, applied research, development, scientist, engineer, and so on. We questioned a number of the respondents to be sure that they were fully aware of the definitions and that they interpreted them properly. We could find no evidence that they were interpreting the definitions in significantly different ways.

[8] Note that we are concerned here only with the technical risks. Since technical success by no means insures commercial success, the total risks are considerably greater than indicated by the probabilities of technical success. But this does not alter the fact that the bulk of the projects tends to be relatively safe from a technical angle. For similar data for a large electrical equipment manufacturer, see Edwin Mansfield, *Industrial Research and Technological Innovation* (Norton, for the Cowles Foundation for Research in Economics, 1968), Chap. 3.

[9] For studies of the effect of firm size on total R and D expenditures, see Edwin Mansfield, *Industrial Research and Technological Innovation, op. cit.;* and Richard Nelson, Merton Peck and Edward Kalachek, *Technology, Economic Growth, and Public Policy* (Brookings, 1967).

are one-tenth of the sales of the largest firm in the sample. Such a firm devotes to basic research a percentage of total R and D expenditures that is about one-third of the percentage devoted by the largest firm in the sample. Similarly, such a firm has a median probability of technical success that is about 20 percent higher, and a median length of time to completion that is about 15 percent lower, than the largest firm in the sample.

However, it is very important to note that, although the largest chemical firm in the sample differs significantly from the relatively small firms in these respects, the difference between the largest firm and the average firm that is about one-half of its size, is generally small, if it exists at all. With regard to the percentage of total R and D expenditures devoted to basic research, the difference is only a couple of percentage points. With regard to the median probability of technical success and the median length of time to completion, the median probability is higher (not lower), and the median length of time is lower (not higher), in the largest firm in the sample than in a firm that is one-half its size. The results are much the same for the petroleum firms. Only in the case of the median length of time to completion is there a substantial difference between the largest petroleum firm in the sample and the average firm of about one-half its size.

Thus, the results indicate that firm size is associated with a substantial amount of the interfirm variation in these characteristics. They also indicate that, although the differences between the largest firms in the sample and the relatively small firms are sometimes quite large, the differences between the largest firms and firms of one-half their size are seldom large, if they exist at all. To the extent that the sample is trustworthy, the results suggest that, in these industries at least, firms as large as the largest firms in the

sample are not required to insure that the existing amount of R and D of a more basic, risky, and long-term nature is carried out. Firms that are about one-half as large as the largest firms in the sample invest about the same percent of their R and D budget in more basic, risky, and long-term projects as do the largest firms in the sample. This too is an important point.[10]

IV. *The Costs of Development*

Let's turn from the characteristics of a firm's R and D program to the characteristics of an individual R and D project. An important, and extremely difficult, question is: what determines how much it costs to develop a new product? Some work bearing on this question is being carried out by Jerome Schnee,[11] who has obtained detailed data concerning about sixty development projects conducted by one major ethical drug firm between 1950 and 1967. Specifically, he has information concerning the costs of clinical testing and product formulation for each drug, and he is interested in determining whether it is possible to explain a reasonable amount of

---

[10] It is important to note that we do not have complete data for all of the largest firms in these industries. Although there is no obvious bias in one direction or the other, the results pertain to only a sample of the firms, and it is always possible that this sample is unrepresentative in important ways. However, a reasonably large proportion of the firms are included, over 50 percent of the chemical firms with 1963 sales of $100 millions or more and over 50 percent of the petroleum firms with 1963 sales of $500 millions or more being included. Of course, nothing can be deduced from these results concerning other industries. Whether or not the same kind of results hold for other industries can only be determined by obtaining this sort of data for them.

[11] Schnee is working on a doctoral dissertation at the University of Pennsylvania. The results described in this section pertain to only part of his work and are tentative, since the project is still under way. The only other econometric studies of the determinants of development costs (of which I am aware) have been carried out at the RAND Corporation and pertain only to military development. Unfortunately, many of them are classified.

the variation among drugs in these costs by the characteristics of the product being developed, the development strategy, and so on.[12]

Three types of development projects are treated separately, since the nature of the development work is quite different in each type. These three categories are development projects that are aimed at (1) new chemical entities, (2) compounded products, and (3) alternate dosage forms. In each category, it is hypothesized that the costs depend on the number of dosage forms (tablets, oral liquid, nasal spray, etc.) being developed, which dosage forms are being developed, the therapeutic classification of the drug, and the spectrum of the drug's activity.[13] Also it is hypothesized that there has been an upward trend in costs during this period, due to inflation and changes (partly reflecting FDA regulation) in development procedures.[14] In

addition, it is hypothesized that the costs will depend on the priority of the project and on whether or not parallel development efforts are employed. Finally, a variable similar to that used by Peck and Scherer[15] and Marschak, Glennan and Summers[16] to measure the extent of the advance in the state of the art was also included, more or less as an experiment.[17]

In each category, a regression based on these variables can explain a substantial portion of the observed variation in costs, R^2 being 0.93 for new chemical entities, 0.67 for compounded products and 0.90 for alternate dosage forms. In part, of course, these high correlations may be due to the fact that the data pertain to only one firm. Not all of the independent variables turn out to be statistically significant. Among new chemical entities, the number of dosage forms, the priority attached to the project, and calendar year are significant variables. Among compounded products, the spectrum of activity, the state of the art advance, calendar

[12] Although the costs of clinical testing of the compound and of product formulation are important parts of the total R and D costs pertaining to a drug, they are not all of the R and D costs associated with a particular drug. There are large costs that are usually incurred before the right compound is found. This should be borne in mind in interpreting the results.

[13] Dummy variables are used to represent which dosage forms are being developed and the therapeutic classification of the drug. The "spectrum of activity" refers to the range of a drug's biological activity and is measured by a dummy variable showing whether the drug is being developed for more than one therapeutic market. Some of these variables were omitted in particular categories. Among new chemical entities, the variable representing which dosage form was being developed was omitted because it seemed much less important than the number of dosage forms and to conserve degrees of freedom. Among alternate dosage forms, the spectrum of activity was omitted since they all were developed for a single market. One would expect that, other things equal, development cost would increase with the number of dosage forms and with the extent of the spectrum of activity. Also, some types of dosage forms are more expensive than others to develop.

[14] The calendar year is used as an independent variable. With regard to the FDA, 1962 amendments to the Food, Drug and Cosmetic Act strengthened the regulatory authority of the FDA over the clinical testing of new drugs and outlined minimum re-

quirements for studies to demonstrate the efficacy and safety of a new drug.

[15] Merton Peck and F. M. Scherer, *The Weapons Acquisition Process* (Harvard, 1962).

[16] Thomas Marschak, Thomas Glennan, and Robert Summers, *Strategy for R and D* (Springer-Verlag, 1967).

[17] This variable represented a rough judgment of scientists and project managers familiar with these drugs. Essentially, the procedure used to obtain these judgments was like that used by Summers and Peck and Scherer. Obviously this variable is crude, which may help to explain why it is not always statistically significant. One would expect, of course, that projects attempting large advances in the state of the art would cost more than less ambitious projects. Dummy variables are used to indicate whether parallel development efforts were used and whether the project was given high priority by top management. Data concerning these variables could be obtained from the firm's records. On a priori grounds, it is difficult to predict the effect of the priority variable since costs tend to be high if there is a great emphasis on time reduction and also if there is very little emphasis on time reduction. The results, where significant, suggest that high priority projects are cheaper. The expected effects of the use of parallel development efforts are discussed below.

year, the therapeutic classification, and the use of parallel development efforts are significant variables. Among alternate dosage forms, the type and number of dosage forms, the therapeutic classification, the state of the art advance, and calendar year are significant variables.

The results concerning the effects on costs of using parallel development efforts are quite interesting. Based on the theory underlying the use of parallel efforts, one would expect that parallel efforts would be more likely to reduce costs for new chemical entities than for compounded products or new dosage forms, since the uncertainty as to the optimal approach tends to be much greater in the former case. The results are consistent with this hypothesis, the estimated effect of parallel efforts being to increase costs among alternate dosage forms and compounded products and to decrease costs among new chemical entities. However, the effect of this variable is statistically significant only among compounded products.[18]

V. *Diffusion of the Results of Research and Development*

The results of industrial R and D, to be economically important, must be accepted and used. The final study I shall discuss is concerned with this diffusion process. Continuing along lines set forth in previous studies, I have carried out an investigation of the diffusion of numerical control in the tool and die industry, the purpose being to see how rapidly this innovation is spreading, the kinds of firms that are relatively quick to adopt it, the reasons given by firms for not using it, and

the opinions of firm owners concerning the impact of the innovation on the structure of the industry.[19]

Numerical control—a way of operating machine tools by means of numerical instructions on tapes or cards—is certainly one of the most important innovations in this century. According to one leading research institute, numerical control "is the most significant new development in manufacturing technology since Henry Ford introduced the concept of the assembly line."[20] One of the industries most affected by this innovation is the tool and die industry. This industry is composed of a very large number of small firms, which means that we have the opportunity to study the diffusion of an innovation in an industry where there is very little concentration and where the organization of decision making in the firm is relatively simple. Other diffusion studies concerned with manufacturing have dealt chiefly with more concentrated industries.

To estimate the growth over time in the percent of tool and die firms using numerical control, a mail survey was carried out of the membership of the National Tool, Die, and Precision Machining Association.[21] The results indicate that

---

[18] For discussion of the effect of parallel development efforts, see Burton Klein, "The Decision Making Problem in Development," *The Rate and Direction of Inventive Activity* (N.B.E.R., 1962); Richard Nelson, "Uncertainty, Learning, and the Economics of Parallel Research and Development Efforts," *Rev. of Econ. and Statis.*, 1961; and Marschak's work in Marschak, Glennan, and Summers, *op. cit.*

[19] Only a few of the findings can be presented in the available time. For a more complete discussion, see Edwin Mansfield, "Numerical Control in the Tool and Die Industry: The Diffusion of a Major Technological Innovation" (unpublished paper, 1968). For a review of the literature, see E. Mansfield, *The Economics of Technological Change, op. cit.*, Chap. 4.

[20] Illinois Institute of Technology Research Institute, *Technological Change: Its Impact on Metropolitan Chicago* (1964), p. 1.

[21] Note that all of the findings pertain only to the approximately 1,000 members of the Association, since the costs of extending the frame beyond the Association membership were out of the question. The Association members account for the bulk of the industry's output. Figures for all members of the Association for 1967 and 1968 were available from the Association's *Directory*, so these figures contain no sampling error. A carefully selected sample of firms was interviewed. The results, which are unbiased, are in close agreement with the results of the mail survey.

less than 1 percent of the firms had begun using numerical control before 1961. By the beginning of 1966, the percentage had grown to 10 percent; and by the beginning of 1968, 20 percent of the firms were using numerical control. Allowing for differences in the profitability of using the innovation and the size of investment required, this innovation seems to be spreading more rapidly than innovations in other industries for which data are available. This is a noteworthy finding, because it supports the view that, all other things equal, innovations tend to spread more rapidly in less concentrated industries.[22]

VI. *Characteristics of Early Users*

There are a good many reasons for expecting the larger tool and die firms to be quicker than the smaller ones to introduce numerical control. For example, the larger firms are more likely to have the financial resources to enable them to experiment, and they are more likely to have the technical know-how and the managerial qualities that are important in determining a firm's speed of response to a new technique. This hypothesis is borne out by my results. The median employment of firms using numerical control at the beginning of 1968 was about seventy, while the median employment of nonusers was about twenty-five. Moreover, among the users of numerical control, there is a significant inverse relationship between the size of a firm and the year when it began using numerical control.[23]

Other variables that would be expected to influence whether or not a firm adopted numerical control before 1968 is the education and age of the firm's president. Better educated entrepreneurs are likely to be in a better position to understand the issues regarding numerical control, to have the flexibility of mind to use it, and to be in contact with technical and university centers and the relevant literature. Younger entrepreneurs would be more likely to make the break with the past, their emotional attachments to old skills and old technology being weaker and their willingness to take risks probably being greater than their older rivals. The data are consistent with these hypotheses. Most of the users (for which we have data) are college graduates while most of the nonusers finished high school or less; the median age of the users was about forty-eight while the median age of the nonusers was about fifty-five. However, when a multiple regression is run (age and education being independent variables, the dependent variable being a dummy variable showing whether or not a firm used numerical control before 1968), the effect of education is statistically significant, but the effect of age is not.

A carefully selected sample of twenty-eight firms without numerical control was interviewed to determine why they were not using it. Practically all claimed that it would not be profitable for them at present, the primary reason being that they do one-of-a-kind work. (About 20 percent of the firms planned to begin using it in the next year or two.) However, about 30

---

[22] This finding is in agreement with my previous results, which pertain to four other industries. They indicate that, holding constant the profitability of the innovation and the size of the investment, the rate of imitation tends to be greater in less concentrated industries. However, there were too few industries to be at all sure the relationship was not due to chance. See E. Mansfield, *Industrial Research and Technological Innovation, op. cit.*, Chap. 7.

[23] To some extent, this relationship is probably due to a difference between the growth rates of users and

nonusers of numerical control, users probably having had higher growth rates. But this can explain only part of the relationship, there being evidence that, when they began using numerical control, the early users tended to be larger than the nonusers. Of course, the fact that the larger firms tend to be quicker than the small firms to begin using an innovation does not contradict in any way the finding that the rate of imitation tends to be faster in less concentrated industries.

percent of the managers, by their own account, had important gaps in their knowledge and understanding of numerical control. About 10 percent of the firm owners, being close to retirement, had decided to stick with conventional methods until they retired—or until they were put out of business. Judging by the interviews and other evidence, the diffusion process seems to have been slowed perceptibly by misunderstanding of the innovation and resistance to change.[24]

VII. *Conclusion*

In conclusion, organized scientific and inventive activity is a relatively new, and very important, factor in the modern economy. This paper has presented a brief summary of the results of several empirical studies of industrial research and development, these studies focusing on its characteristics, cost, and diffusion. Some of the principal findings are the following: First, the bulk of the R and D projects carried out by a sample of major chemical and petroleum firms seems relatively safe from a technical point of view, most projects having better than a fifty-fifty chance of technical success. This supports the hypothesis advanced by some economists that the bulk of the R and D carried out by large corporations is relatively safe and aimed at fairly modest advances in the state of the art.

Second, the largest firms in the sample devote a larger proportion of their R and D expenditures to more basic, more risky, and longer-term projects than their smaller competitors. However, although the differences between the largest firms in the sample and relatively small firms are sometimes quite large, the difference between the largest firms and firms of one-half their size are seldom large, if they exist at all. To the extent that the sample is trustworthy, the results suggest that, in these industries at least, firms as large as the largest firms in the sample are not required to insure that the existing amount of R and D of a more basic, risky, and long-term nature is carried out. Firms that are one-half as large as the largest firms in the sample invest about the same percent of their R and D budget in more basic, risky, and long-term projects as do the largest firms in the sample.

Third, a detailed study of about sixty development projects carried out in a large ethical drug firm indicates that the cost of developing a particular product is related to the therapeutic classification of the product, its spectrum of activity, and the number and type of dosage forms. It is also related to the priority attached to the development project and to whether or not parallel development efforts are used, at least in some product categories. This seems to be the only econometric study of the determinants of development costs in the civilian economy that has been carried out to date. Much more work is needed.

Fourth, a study of the diffusion of numerical control in the tool and die industry indicates that, allowing for differences in profitability and size of investment, this innovation seems to be spreading more rapidly than innovations in other industries for which data are available. This finding tends to support the hypothesis that innovations generally spread more rapidly in less concentrated industries. The early users of numerical control tend to be the larger tool and die firms. Also, whether or not a firm is using numerical control seems to be related to the age and education of the firm's owner; but when both age and education are introduced simultaneously, only the effect of education is significant.

---

[24] Nonetheless, as noted in Section V, the imitation process seems to be going on relatively rapidly. Thus, these drags on the rate of imitation may be less important than in other cases for which we have data.

10

THE JOURNAL OF BUSINESS

The Graduate School of Business of the University of Chicago

VOL. XXXIX   *OCTOBER 1966*   *No. 4*

THE ALLOCATION, CHARACTERISTICS, AND OUTCOME OF THE FIRM'S RESEARCH AND DEVELOPMENT PORTFOLIO: A CASE STUDY*

EDWIN MANSFIELD† AND RICHARD BRANDENBURG‡

I. INTRODUCTION

DESPITE the remarkable increase in recent years in the amount of attention devoted to the economics of research and development (R and D), there have been surprisingly few detailed studies of the R and D activities of the firm. Consequently, although we know something about the factors influencing the firm's total expenditures on R and D [15], little is known about the allocation of funds among projects, the characteristics of the projects that are undertaken, and the probable outcome of these projects.[1] In view of the importance of these matters, there is clearly a need for research in depth by economists and others to help fill the present void.

This paper reports the findings of a case study of the R and D portfolio of the central research laboratory of one of the nation's largest firms, a prominent equipment manufacturer. The study, which took two years, is the most detailed treatment to date of the allocation, characteristics, and outcome of a firm's R and D expenditures. Data were obtained regarding seventy major projects, and numerous interviews were obtained with officials at various levels of the firm. Like all case studies, the results are limited by the fact that they pertain only to one firm, but, where possible, the findings were checked against preliminary results for other firms.[2]

* This paper was presented in 1965 at the First World Congress of the Econometric Society in Rome. The work on which it is based was supported by a grant from the National Science Foundation and by the Ford Foundation Committee on Technological Change and Economic Growth, of which Mansfield is a member. Brandenburg's contribution was supported largely by a contract with the National Science Foundation. Our thanks go to C. Phillips and N. Auspitz for assistance and to the company for data, interviews, and co-operation in every way.

† Professor of economics, University of Pennsylvania.

‡ Assistant dean, Graduate School of Industrial Administration, Carnegie Institute of Technology.

[1] Although there is a growing literature proposing techniques for R and D project selection, it appears that such procedures have been difficult to implement. E.g., see Baker and Pound [2]. Further, little descriptive work has been done. See Brandenburg [3] for a first step along these lines.

[2] Mansfield, together with Michael Hamburger, is carrying out a study of the characteristics of the R and D portfolios of chemical and petroleum firms. Although the results are not yet ready for publication, the work is far enough along to provide some indication of the representativeness of some of the

The plan of the paper is as follows. Section II describes the process by which R and D proposals and budgets were generated and evaluated within this laboratory. Section III presents and tests a simple model to explain the expenditures proposed for a particular project. Section IV contains a similar model to explain the modifications made by the laboratory management in the proposed level of expenditures. Section V discusses the implications of the results. Section VI describes the characteristics of the projects that were accepted. Sections VII–VIII analyze the outcomes of these projects and the extent to which the firm was able to predict their technical success or failure. Section IX concludes the paper.

II. THE DECISION PROCESS
WITHIN THE FIRM

The central research laboratory of the firm we studied is organized into departments concerned with the study of materials, equipment, basic science, and technology.[3] The bulk of the laboratory's expenditures, totaling about $20 million annually, is for applied R and D, only about 10 per cent being for basic research. Excluding basic research, about 60 per cent of the laboratory's expenditures is on "new business" projects which attempt to develop entirely new products and almost all of which stem from the laboratory. The remaining 40 per cent of the expenditures (excluding basic research) is on projects suggested by operating divisions of the firm, which

findings presented below. Rubenstein [25] and Rubenstein and Hannenberg [26] have also presented some relevant material.

[3] Examples of these departments are "materials science," "metallurgy and ceramics technology," "science and mathematics," and "equipment science."

request particular product improvements and new processes.

This section describes how the laboratory's portfolio of applied R and D projects was chosen in 1963,[4] the first step in this process being a rough screening by the laboratory management of various project proposals. With regard to projects proposed by the divisions, this screening began in the summer of 1962, when the laboratory asked the divisions for proposals for 1963. For each research proposal, a division was requested to estimate (1) the probability of commercial success of the project (if technically successful), (2) the extra profit to the firm if the project was commercially successful, and (3) the investment required to put the research results into practice.[5] These proposals were then sent to the managers of the relevant laboratory departments, who made preliminary estimates of the cost of doing the R and D and the corresponding chance of technical success. Combining the information provided by the division and the department manager, the laboratory's project-evaluation group, a small group of project analysts that report to

[4] Throughout the paper, we are concerned for obvious reasons with applied R and D, not basic research. The paper contains data regarding 1964 as well as 1963. The procedure for selecting projects was somewhat different in 1964.

[5] Note three things. First, in rating projects, the firm seemed to act as if there were only two outcomes of the project—"technical success" or "technical failure." If it was a technical success, there was again assumed to be only two outcomes—"commercial success" or "commercial failure." A technical failure produces no useful information; a commercial failure produces no profits. Needless to say, the model of the world implicit in this rating scheme was exceedingly simple—as the relevant executives recognized. Second, the profit figures were gross of the costs involved in putting the research results into practice, i.e., the investment required. Third, other questions were also asked the division, but the three mentioned in the text seemed to be the most important.

the laboratory management, computed a "figure of merit" for each proposal and rated it A, B, or C.[6] The project-evaluation group also computed a figure of merit for each "new business" project, using estimates of potential market and production costs for the product which the project would try to develop, and rated it as A, B, or C.

The second step in the decision-making process involved the formulation of a proposed R and D portfolio by each department of the laboratory. The department manager received all division requests and new business proposals that fell within his department's responsibility, together with the rating of each project. The laboratory management recommended that the A proposals be given top priority and that the C proposals be avoided, but beyond such loose guidelines, the department manager was free to formulate whatever set of projects seemed best to him. After considerable deliberation, each department manager sent the laboratory management a list of projects that he wanted to carry out. These projects were designed to be largely independent entities.[7] For each proj-

[6] For each project, the figure of merit equaled $qtrG/(E + D)$, where q is the project-evaluation group's estimate of the extra annual profit if the project is technically and commercially successful, t is their estimate of the number of years that this profit stream will continue, G is their estimate of the probability of commercial success, r is the department manager's preliminary estimate of the probability of technical success, E is his preliminary estimate of the cost of the R and D, and D is the division's estimate of the cost of putting the research result into practice. If $M > 4$, the proposal was rated A; if $4 \geq M \geq 2$, the project was rated B; and if $M < 2$, the project was rated C.

[7] I.e., to the extent possible, the projects are defined so as to reduce their interdependence. E.g., parallel paths to the same objectives are considered parts of the same project, not separate projects. Nonetheless, some interdependence remains and is recognized by the project-evaluation group and the laboratory management.

ect, the department manager proposed a level of expenditure and estimated the probability of technical success. In the next section, this proposed level of expenditure is called C^* and the estimated probability of success is called P^*.

The final step in the decision-making process involved the modification of each department's proposals by the laboratory and corporate management. The laboratory management evaluated each project proposed by the department manager, decided whether to accept or reject it, and suggested a level of expenditures on each project that it accepted. (This level of expenditures is referred to as C_M^* in Sec. IV.) A list of the projects that survived this stage of the process was submitted to the corporate management, together with the proposed expenditures on each one. The corporate management then set the level of total expenditures at the laboratory. Finally, since the level set by corporate management was too small to finance all of the projects on the list, some were dropped and others had their budgets modified.

III. THE PROPOSED LEVEL OF EXPENDITURES ON AN R AND D PROJECT

What determined how much money was allocated to a particular R and D project? To help sort out the relevant factors, it is convenient to break this question into two parts: first, what determined the amount that the department manager proposed to spend on the project? Second, what determined the extent to which the laboratory management modified the department manager's proposal? This section, which is concerned with the first question, constructs and tests a simple model to explain the department manager's proposed level of expenditures. Section IV takes up the second question.

At the outset, two points should be noted. First, the simple models presented in Sections III–IV are not meant to be descriptions, in any literal sense, of the decision-making process. In fact, of course, the relevant managers do not go through the process visualized by the models, but this is not important, so long as they act as if they do. Second, if the models are to be testable, they must be formulated in terms of concepts that correspond to those for which the firm generates data. In the previous section, we saw that the principal pieces of information generated within the firm are estimates of a project's expected profitability and its probability of success. It seems natural to build our models around these concepts, both because they are important and because data are available for them.

Returning to the department manager, we begin by assuming that he believes that the probability that a project is successfully completed between time t and time $t + \Delta$ is $\beta C\Delta$, where C is the rate of expenditure on the project, β is a parameter that varies from project to project, and t is measured in years. If this extremely simple model holds,[8] it can

be shown that

$$P = 1 - e^{-\beta C}, \qquad (1)$$

where P is the probability that the project will be successfully completed during the year. Thus, the expected discounted profit from the project is

$$\pi = (1 - e^{-\beta C})X - C, \qquad (2)$$

where X is the estimated discounted profit if the project is technically successful.[9]

Next assume that the department manager has in mind some total budget for his department and that he fixes C so as to maximize the sum of the expected discounted profits from all his projects, subject to this constraint. Assuming that the projects are independent, he sets

$$\frac{\partial \pi}{\partial C^*} = \beta e^{-\beta C^*} X - 1 = \lambda, \qquad (3)$$

where λ is the marginal expected discounted profit from an extra dollar spent in his department and C^* is the amount of money that he proposes to spend on the project. Consequently,

$$C^* = \frac{\ln[\beta X/(1+\lambda)]}{\beta}. \qquad (4)$$

To test this model, we make two additional assumptions. First, we assume that the department manager's estimate of X is determined by X_D, the division's estimate of the discounted profits (net of division costs) if the project is successful.[10] In particular, suppose that

$$X = a_0 X_D^{a_1} Z, \qquad (5)$$

---

[8] Taking a particular project, it seems obvious that the probability of completing the project in a given time interval is an increasing function of the length of the time interval and the annual rate of expenditure on the project. Moreover, it is also obvious that the probability tends to zero as either of these variables tends to zero. Given these conditions, the simplest assumption that meets them is that the probability is proportional to the product of the two variables. This model is a reasonable approximation for R and D where the probability of success, holding the time interval and the rate of expenditures constant, does not vary greatly with time. In effect, it views R and D as a search process where the ground previously explored is always so small, relative to the total, that the probability of success varies little within a reasonably short span of time. Although not all R and D is of this type, this model is perhaps as good a first approximation as any of comparable simplicity.

[9] According to the model, the department manager assumes that, if a project receives a budget of C for the coming year, it will spend it all—even if success is reached before the end of the year. As a first approximation, this probably does relatively little violence to reality. Also, we follow the practice, implicit in the firm's rating scheme, of assuming that a project which is not a technical success results in no profits, now or in the future.

[10] We restrict our attention to projects proposed by an operating division. The reader will recall from

where the a's are the same for all projects and Z is a random-error term. Second, we assume that λ, a non-observable variable that undoubtedly differs from department manager to department manager, is statistically independent of X_D.

Given these assumptions, the model predicts that

$$\ln\left(\frac{C^*}{1-P^*}\right) - \ln\left[\ln\left(\frac{1}{1-P^*}\right)\right] \quad (6)$$
$$= \phi + a_1 \ln X_D + Z^1,$$

where ϕ equals $\ln a_0$ plus the average value of $\ln[1/(1+\lambda)]$, P^* is the probability of technical success associated with the level of expenditure (C^*) proposed by the department manager, and Z^1 is an error term that equals Z plus the deviation of $\ln[1/(1+\lambda)]$ from its average value. To obtain equation (6), note that

$$\beta = \frac{\ln[1/(1-P^*)]}{C^*},$$

substitute this expression for β into equation (4), and then substitute the expression for X in equation (5) into the result.

To test the model, we gathered data regarding C^*, P^*, and X_D for eleven major projects;[11] and, using equation (6), we obtained least-squares estimates of ϕ and a_1. The resulting regression,

$$\ln\left(\frac{C^*}{1-P^*}\right) - \ln\left[\ln\left(\frac{1}{1-P^*}\right)\right]$$
$$= 4.13 + .21 \ln X_D, \quad (7)$$
$$(0.44) \quad (.06)$$

is quite consistent with the model, the regression coefficient having the predicted sign and being statistically significant. About 50 per cent of the variation in the dependent variable can be explained. Thus, the results, though extremely tentative, seem to support the model reasonably well.[12]

IV. MODIFICATIONS BY THE LABORATORY MANAGEMENT

The previous section was concerned with the level of expenditures proposed by the department manager. To determine the extent to which the laboratory management modified these proposals, data were obtained regarding the disposition of seventy-two projects during 1963 and 1964.[13] The results, shown in

---

Sec. II that the division was required to provide information regarding the probability of commercial success, the extra profit if the project was commercially successful, and the investment required. Using an interest rate of 0.10, we obtained X_D by discounting back the expected profits if the project was technically successful.

[11] The sample size was reduced by the necessity to omit projects with some government financing (since the model obviously does not apply to them) and by the expense of gathering the detailed data underlying the estimates of X_D. See n. 27 for other considerations. Although the number of projects is small, they account for quite a large dollar expenditure.

[12] Note five things. (1) For given values of X_D, eq. (7) provides an expected relationship between C^* and P^*; to predict C^*, one must know P^*. Of course, this does not lessen the usefulness of eq. (7) as a test of the model. (2) There may be an identification problem in eq. (7), since the department managers, in dealing with divisions, sometimes are able to influence X_D so as to rationalize certain values of C^*. (3) We eliminated β from eqs. (6) and (7) because, whereas C^* and P^* are variables actually measured and used by the firm, β does not exist outside of the model. It stems entirely from the assumption in eq. (1). (4) Interviews with laboratory executives indicate that they agreed with many of the basic ideas underlying the model, although not necessarily with the details. (5) All tests in this paper use the .05 significance level.

[13] These seventy-two applied research and development projects accounted for about $5 million of the laboratory's budget. The relevant data are in Panel A of Table 1. However Panel B is also of interest. One might argue that we should be concerned with the level of expenditure finally approved by the laboratory, rather than C_M^*. However, we suspect that the same model would work in either case.

Table 1, indicate that the modifications were generally substantial. For example, among projects designed to satisfy division requests in 1963, about one-half experienced an alteration of 20 per cent or more.

However, it is recognized that the laboratory management has different information regarding X and a different value of λ. Thus,

$$C_M^* = \frac{\ln\left[\beta X_M/(1+\lambda_M)\right]}{\beta}, \quad (8)$$

TABLE 1

CHANGES BY THE LABORATORY MANAGEMENT IN THE PROPOSED
BUDGETS OF SEVENTY-TWO R AND D PROJECTS

RATIO	NO. OF PROPOSED PROJECTS			PERCENTAGE OF PROPOSED EXPENDITURES			PERCENTAGE OF BUDGETED EXPENDITURES		
	Division Requests (1963)	Division Requests (1964)	New Business (1963)	Division Requests (1963)	Division Requests (1964)	New Business (1963)	Division Requests (1963)	Division Requests (1964)	New Business (1963)
A. Ratio of Expenditures Initially Approved* by Laboratory Management to That Proposed by Department Manager									
0.00–0.39......	3	5	6	13	38	42	0	16	0
0.40–0.79......	7	4	4	24	24	32	19	20	15
0.80–1.19......	20	8	4	47	36	23	61	53	72
1.20–1.59......	2	0	1	2	0	3	3	0	13
1.60 and over....	6	2	0	14	1	0	17	10	0
Total†........	38	19	15	100	100	100	100	100	100
B. Ratio of Expenditures Finally Approved‡ by Laboratory Management to That Approved Initially by Them									
0.00–0.39......	1	0	5	2	0	53	1	0	7
0.40–0.79......	5	4	1	9	15	12	7	18	8
0.80–1.19......	29	10	2	89	61	29	92	61	81
1.20–1.59......	0	2	1	0	14	5	0	13	0
1.60 and over....	0	2	1	0	10	1	0	7	4
Total†........	35	18	10	100	100	100	100	100	100

* By "initially approved" we mean approved before the corporate management sets the laboratory's total budget.
† Because of rounding errors the percentages do not always sum to 100.
‡ By "finally approved" we mean approved after the corporate management has set the laboratory's total budget.

To explain the extent of the modification, we construct a model which is quite similar to that in Section III. We assume that the laboratory management, like the department manager, believes that equation (1) holds and that it, too, attempts to maximize expected profits subject to a budget constraint.

where. C_M^* is the level of expenditure approved by the laboratory manager, X_M is his estimate of X, and λ_M is the marginal expected discounted profits from an extra dollar spent in the laboratory. Combining equations (4) and (8), the percentage change made by the laboratory management in a given project's budget is

$$\frac{C_M^* - C^*}{C^*} = \left[\ln \left(\frac{X_M}{X} \right) \right.$$

$$\left. + \ln \left(\frac{1+\lambda}{1+\lambda_M} \right) \right] \left[\ln \left(\frac{\beta X}{1+\lambda} \right) \right]^{-1}$$

$$= - \left[\ln \left(\frac{X_M}{X} \right) \right.$$

$$\left. + \ln \left(\frac{1+\lambda}{1+\lambda_M} \right) \right] [\ln (1 - P^*)]^{-1}.$$ (9)

To test this model, we make two additional assumptions. First, the laboratory management is assumed to set the value of X_M on the basis of X_ρ, the project-evaluation group's estimate of the discounted profits (net of division costs) if the project is successful.[14] In particular, suppose that

$$X_M = B_0 X_\rho^{B_1} Z'',$$ (10)

where the B's are the same for all projects and Z'' is a random-error term. Second, we assume that the deviations of the unobservable variable, $\ln [(1 + \lambda)/(1 + \lambda_M)]$, from its average value, σ, can be treated as a random-error term. Given these assumptions,

$$\frac{C_M^* - C^*}{C^*}$$

$$= \frac{\ln(a_0/B_0) - \sigma + a_1 \ln X_D - B_1 \ln X_\rho + Z'''}{\ln(1 - P^*)},$$

where Z''' is a random-error term. Finally, letting $\ln (a_0/B_0) - \sigma = \theta$, we have

$$\left(\frac{C_M^* - C^*}{C^*} \right) \ln(1 - P^*)$$

$$= \theta + a_1 \ln X_D - B_1 \ln X_\rho + Z'''.$$ (11)

To test the model, we collected data regarding X_ρ and C_M^*, as well as X_D, P^*, and C^*, for ten major projects,[15] and obtained least-squares estimates of θ, a_1, and B_1. The resulting regression,

$$\left(\frac{C_M^* - C^*}{C^*} \right) \ln(1 - P^*) = - \underset{(0.88)}{1.74}$$

$$+ \underset{(.16)}{.46} \ln X_D - \underset{(.17)}{.22} \ln X_\rho,$$ (12)

is quite consistent with the model, the regression coefficients having the expected sign and all but one being statistically significant. About 44 per cent of the variation in the dependent variable can be explained. Also, in accord with the theory, the regression coefficient of $\ln X_D$ in equation (7) does not differ significantly from that in equation (12). Thus, the available data, although far less extensive than one would like, seem to support the model.[16]

V. IMPLICATIONS OF THE RESULTS

To the extent that the results of this pilot study are borne out by further investigation, they have several implications. First, they suggest that, despite its

[14] The project-evaluation group, like the division, made estimates of the profitability of a project. The department manager saw only the division estimates, whereas the laboratory management generally saw only the estimates prepared by the project-evaluation group. Occasionally, the laboratory management also saw the division estimates, which normally are less conservative than the project-evaluation group's. Of course, if the laboratory management's value of X_M is a linear function (in logs) of both X_ρ and X_D, it would not affect the results.

[15] Although the sample size is small it should be remembered that these projects account for a large dollar expenditure. Note, too, that the costs involved in expanding the sample were quite large.

[16] Interviews with laboratory executives indicated that many of them agreed with the basic ideas behind the model. However, as would be expected, they did not necessarily agree with some of the simplifying assumptions. See Sec. V.

obvious limitations,[17] the assumption of expected profit maximization is of considerable use in understanding the allocation of R and D funds. Needless to say, this does not mean that various "noneconomic" factors, which are discussed in the following paragraph, are unimportant. However, it does mean that a substantial portion of the observed allocation of funds can be explained by a purely "economic" model of the most old-fashioned variety. This point is important in formulating public policy regarding R and D and in attempting to predict firm behavior. It makes a great deal of difference whether we assume that a firm's R and D portfolio is dictated largely by organizational factors and by variables other than profit which play an important role in the goal structure of the decision-maker—or whether we assume that profit expectations are at least as important as such "non-economic" variables.[18]

Second, the results suggest that, although profit expectations are important, they can explain only about half of the observed allocation of funds.[19] Interviews with company executives and scientists indicate that the following factors are particularly important in explaining the rest.[20] (1) Decisions made by company scientists reflect their scientific and professional goals, which are not always consistent with the strictly commercial objectives of the firm.[21] (2) The laboratory management is influenced by the necessity to maintain good relations with various operating executives who have an interest in promoting projects in their areas.[22] (3) At each level of the decision process, the estimates received by the decision-maker are increased, decreased, given less weight or more weight, depending on the source of the estimate and its probable accuracy.[23] This aspect of the decision process obviously increases the variance of Z and Z'', thus increasing the unexplained variation. (4) Because of the way projects tend to be judged within the firm, there is a tendency to concentrate on

[17] Some of the most obvious limitations of the model are its neglect of organizational variables, risk aversion, the nature of information flows, and the role of variables other than profit in the goal structure of the decision-maker.

[18] By "non-economic" factors, we merely mean those not usually considered in the traditional theory of the firm. Note that the results suggest that the firm tends to invest in projects that it *believes* to be very profitable. Whether they are *actually* very profitable is unknown. See n. 48.

[19] This assumes that P^* is held constant. Then, judging from the correlation coefficients in eqs. (7) and (12), about half of the variation in $\ln C^*$ or $(C_M^* - C^*)/C^*$ can be explained by these equations. Of course, it is not necessary to hold P^* constant. One could shift the terms in eqs. (7) and (12) that involve P^* to the other side of these equations, thus making C^* and C_M^* a function of P^* and the other variables. Then one could compute the percentage of the variation in C^* or C_M^* that is explained. However, this is unlikely to change the results very much. Of course, the fact that C^* and P^* are determined at the same time does not make it wrong to use P^* as an independent variable which influences C^*.

[20] Of course, some of the unexplained variation is simply due to the fact that eq. (1) is only a first approximation, that there is some interdependence among projects (see n. 26), and that, even if eq. (1) held, the laboratory management's estimate of β would not always coincide with the department manager's. Moreover, in the long run, some of the factors discussed in this paragraph of the text may be quite consistent with profit maximization.

[21] The conflicts between management and scientists, arising from different traditions and goals, have often been pointed out. See, e.g., Marcson [19] and Mansfield [18]. E.g., the laboratory department manager is influenced by the talents, experience, and interests of the members of his department, the budgets for some projects being increased to accommodate the scientific interests of certain scientists or to give others something to do in a slack period.

[22] For one thing, these executives help to determine the laboratory budget.

[23] Cost estimates are generally taken more seriously than revenue estimates, and estimates by a distinguished scientist are taken more seriously than those by a novice.

projects where it is likely that success can be claimed at the end of the year, even if other, more adventurous projects promise higher expected returns to the company. (5) Most important of all, some scientists and department managers are much more effective than others in arguing for their proposals, in mobilizing support for them in the operating divisions, and in "selling" them to the laboratory management.

Third, the results provide new insight into the intrafirm generation and use of information. Both the department manager and the laboratory management rely on others to generate the estimates of X that determine their decisions. Apparently, both tend to discount extremely high or extremely low estimates, a_1 and B_1 being significantly less than one.[24] Thus, both put themselves less far out on a limb with regard to any project. It would be very interesting to know whether the same kind of bias exists in other parts of the firm—and in other firms.

Finally, the limitations of the models in Sections III–IV should be noted. First, the assumption that π is the criterion function—and that equation (1) holds—is very rough.[25] Second, there is sometimes

an interdependence among projects that is ignored.[26] Third, as noted above, many important factors are omitted because of measurement problems—the interest, training, and experience of the research staff, "political" pressures and relations with the operating divisions, and the interests and ambitions of the department manager and the laboratory management. Fourth, the data underlying equations (7) and (12)—and the model—pertain almost entirely to the development end of the R and D spectrum.[27] Fifth, because of difficulties in obtaining satisfactory data, the empirical results in Section IV are based on a non-random sample of projects, which may be biased somewhat in favor of the model.[28] Sixth, the models take as given the set of project proposals that the department man-

---

[24] This assumes that, *on the average*, the estimate of X used by either of these decision-makers is approximately equal to that which is given to them. This seems reasonable.

[25] The limitations of eq. (1) have been discussed in n. 8. As for the use of π as the criterion function, it should be noted that this assumes that the decision-maker is neither a risk-averter nor a risk-lover. (E.g., see Markowitz [21].) Contrary to this assumption, it seems likely that many of the relevant decision-makers are risk-averters. Also, the use of π assumes that a project is either a technical success or a technical failure and that the latter results in a dead loss of C. This seems to be in accord with the firm's rating scheme, but it is clearly a naïve assumption. Also, the models in Secs. III–IV do not apply to projects where a small amount is invested in order to determine the feasibility of a certain approach. Of course, the firm does buy infor-

mation in this way, but most of its bigger, more advanced projects are not viewed in this light. Instead, they are viewed as gambles with certain fairly definite commercial advantages as payoffs. Note that the models in Secs. III–IV are static in the sense that they do not take account of the fact that projects may be postponed to future periods. In Marglin's terminology [20], they are "myopic." However, in the present context, this is no deficiency. It seems to reflect the actual decision-making process.

[26] The probability that one project will be successful may depend on the probability that another is successful, because they draw on a common pool of manpower and/or the results of one project are helpful in carrying out the other. But if the relevant utility function were linear (as assumed), this would make no difference. However, one project's value of X may depend on that of another project, and this would make a difference.

[27] Obviously, the "non-economic" variables are much more important at the research end of the spectrum.

[28] We chose one-year projects to avoid ambiguities due to the use of a one-year budgetary period. In the case of longer-term projects, a cutback in next year's expenditures may represent only a transfer of funds from the next year to the more distant future, but no change in the project's total budget. Also, we were forced to include only those projects where the necessary data could be obtained. It may well be that such projects are more likely than others to conform to the model.

ager or the laboratory management consider.[29] Seventh, the assumption that the department manager and the laboratory management have the same value of β is very rough.[30] Eighth, note once again that the models in Sections III–IV are not meant to be detailed descriptions of the decision-making process. In fact, the relevant managers do not go through the process of estimating the β's and maximizing π, but this is not important, so long as they act as if they do.

VI. CHARACTERISTICS OF THE FIRM'S R AND D PORTFOLIO

It is often claimed [10, 11] that the bulk of the R and D carried out by large corporations is relatively short term, safe, and aimed at fairly modest advances in the state of the art. If true, this hypothesis has important implications regarding the role of the large firm in promoting technical progress. How long

[29] There is no explicit discussion of the factors influencing the generation of new project proposals and the decision to review the status of old ones. Obviously, the types of projects that are proposed (in a serious way) are influenced by the relative power of the technical and R and D personnel as contrasted with that of the operating divisions. See n. 21. Most projects are reviewed when budgets and other such statements must be prepared. Of course, a particularly careful and quick review is triggered by a marked change in a project's progress, a large change in the resources it will require, or the occurrence of some event influencing strongly the importance of the project.

[30] Fortunately, if the laboratory management reduced all of the department managers' β's by the same proportion, the analysis would be unaffected. The department manager's estimate of β may be biased upward because of overoptimism or because he believes that it is good strategy in selling projects to underestimate their true costs. Suppose that the laboratory management divides these estimates of β for all projects by k. Then,

term were the projects carried out in the central research laboratory of this large firm? How great were the technical risks that were taken? To find out, we obtained data regarding the characteristics of seventy applied R and D projects carried out in 1963 or 1964. Executives of the firm seemed to regard these projects, which accounted for about $5 million of the firm's R and D budget, as being reasonably representative.[31] Tables 2–4 show the results, based on equal weights for all projects, weights reflecting the size of the expenditures proposed for a project by the department manager, and weights reflecting the size of the expenditures budgeted for a project.

Most projects were expected to be completed in less than four years (Table 2), and the time interval between project completion and the application of the results was seldom expected to be more than one year (Table 3). Expectations of this sort are generally optimistic; according to company officials, the elimination of this bias would increase the figures in Tables 2 and 3 by about 50 per cent. If one follows Hamberg [10] and defines short-term projects to be those taking five years or less, the bulk of the projects were short term, even if this bias were eliminated.[32] However, this definition of

where U represents $\ln [\beta/k (1 + \lambda_M)]/k - \ln [\beta/(1 + \lambda)]$. Substituting the expressions in eqs. (5) and (10), we obtain an expression like eq. (11), except that the regression coefficient of $\ln X_\rho$ is B_1/k rather than B_1.

[31] However, they did seem to think that the sample of 1963 new business projects was somewhat biased toward short-range projects.

[32] These results do not seem atypical. We have similar data for several large petroleum and chemi-

$$\frac{C_M^* - C^*}{C^*} = \frac{\ln[\beta X_M/k(1+\lambda_M)]/k - \ln[\beta X/(1+\lambda)]}{\ln[\beta X/(1+\lambda)]}$$

$$-\left(\frac{C_M^* - C^*}{C^*}\right) \ln(1 - P^*) = \frac{1}{k} \ln X_M - \ln X + U,$$

a short-term project may be too stringent. If three years, rather than five, were used as a cutoff point, a very substantial percentage of the projects would be long term.

cal firms. For three petroleum firms, projects that were expected to be completed and have an effect on profits in less than five years were 80, 65, and 50 per cent of the total. For the chemical firm, such projects were 90 per cent of the total. These figures pertain to 1964.

Most of the projects do not involve very great technical risks. In about three-fourths of the cases, the estimated probability of technical success exceeds .80 (Table 4). In part, this undoubtedly reflects the optimism so often found among professional researchers and the necessity to sell projects, but interviews with various executives of the firm indicate that, if this bias were removed, the

TABLE 2

NUMBER OF YEARS ELAPSING BETWEEN BEGINNING AND ESTIMATED
COMPLETION DATE,* SIXTY-EIGHT R AND D PROJECTS

No. of Years	No. of Projects			Percentage of Proposed Expenditures			Percentage of Budgeted Expenditures		
	Division Requests (1963)	Division Requests (1964)	New Business (1963)	Division Requests (1963)	Division Requests (1964)	New Business (1963)	Division Requests (1963)	Division Requests (1964)	New Business (1963)
Less than 2.0.....	6	14	1	13	77	0	10	89	4
2.0–3.9........	13	1	6	37	23	52	28	11	96
4.0–5.9........	8	0	5	18	0	24	21	0	0
6.0–7.9........	1	0	2	5	0	20	8	0	0
8.0–9.9........	2	0	1	3	0	3	5	0	0
10.0 and over....	8	0	0	23	0	0	28	0	0
Total†.......	38	15	15	100	100	100	100	100	100

* This is the completion date estimated by the department manager in 1963 or 1964 and not necessarily the completion date that was estimated when the project was begun.
† Because of rounding errors, the figures in the last six columns may not always sum to 100.

TABLE 3

ESTIMATED NUMBER OF MONTHS ELAPSING BETWEEN COMPLETION OF THE
PROJECT AND APPLICATION OF THE INVENTION,* TWENTY-SEVEN
R AND D PROJECTS

No. of Months	No. of Projects		Percentage of Proposed Expenditures		Percentage of Budgeted Expenditures	
	Division Requests (1963)	Division Requests (1964)	Division Requests (1963)	Division Requests (1964)	Division Requests (1963)	Division Requests (1964)
Less than 6.0......	8	7	65	43	68	46
6.0–11.9..........	2	5	21	33	27	29
12.0–17.9.........	1	2	11	16	0	20
18.0 or more......	1	1	3	8	3	5
Total†..........	12	15	100	100	100	100

* These estimates were made by the project-evaluation group.
† Because of rounding errors, the figures in the last four columns may not always sum to 100.

bulk of the estimates would still be well above .50. Additional evidence to this effect is presented in the following section of this paper, which describes the outcome of these projects. However, since technical success by no means insures commercial success, the total risks are considerably greater than is indicated by Table 4.[33]

To what extent does the laboratory management, in choosing among alternative proposals, discriminate against long-term, risky proposals? If the labo-

laboratory management. A comparison of the frequency distributions yields no evidence of such discrimination (Tables 2–4). However, interview studies seem to suggest that the laboratory management does discriminate in this way.[34]

Finally, consider the estimated profitability of the R and D projects, if successful. Griliches [9] has shown that the rate of return from successful agricultural inventions was very high. Enos [7] has obtained similar results for petroleum refining. According to Table 5, the rate

TABLE 4

ESTIMATED PROBABILITY OF TECHNICAL SUCCESS,* SEVENTY R AND D PROJECTS

ESTIMATED PROBABILITY	No. of Projects			PERCENTAGE OF PROPOSED EXPENDITURES			PERCENTAGE OF BUDGETED EXPENDITURES		
	Division Requests (1963)	Division Requests (1964)	New Business (1963)	Division Requests (1963)	Division Requests (1964)	New Business (1963)	Division Requests (1963)	Division Requests (1964)	New Business (1963)
.90–1.00........	15	6	7	33	24	54	36	24	21
.80– .89........	12	8	1	39	63	6	45	58	7
.70– .79........	6	3	5	17	12	34	10	18	72
.60– .69........	0	0	0	0	0	0	0	0	0
.50– .59........	4	0	1	8	0	4	5	0	0
Less than .50....	1	0	1	3	0	2	4	0	0
Total†.......	38	17	15	100	100	100	100	100	100

* These estimates were made by the department managers before beginning the projects.
† Because of rounding errors, the figures in the last six columns may not always sum to 100.

ratory management tends to cut the proposed expenditures for long-term, risky projects more than for short-term, safe projects, the frequency distribution of projects, weighted by the size of the expenditures proposed by the department manager, should be more "long term" and "risky" than the frequency distribution of projects, weighted by the size of the expenditures budgeted by the

[33] These results are similar to those regarding several large petroleum firms. For three petroleum firms, projects with expected probabilities of success exceeding .75 were 60, 56, and 50 per cent of the total. However, for the chemical firm, such projects were only 15 per cent of the total.

of return from these R and D projects would be about as high as those in agriculture and petroleum refining, if they too were successful. In practically all of the cases, the estimated rate of return exceeds 100 per cent.[35]

[34] Obviously, the department managers may propose projects of this sort because they think that these are the types of projects that the laboratory management wants. The data in Tables 2–4 cannot get at this sort of an effect.

[35] Of course, this presumes that the project is successful. But, as Griliches [9] points out, the rate of return on a successful project may be of interest, since "it may be useful to break down the probable rate of return into two components: the rate of return if the development turns out to be a success

To sum up, it appears that most projects are expected to be completed in four years or less, the results are expected to be applied only a few months later, and the estimated probability of technical success averages about .80. If successful, the rate of return from the investment in R and D is expected to be very high. In interpreting these results, note that the central research laboratory of a large science-based firm tends to be more heavily committed to long-term, risky R and D than most industrial laboratories. Thus, the R and D portfolio described here is probably less conservative and short term than that of most large firms.[36]

VII. OUTCOME OF THE R AND D PROJECTS

Whereas previous sections were concerned with the allocation of the R and D budget and the characteristics of the projects that were attempted, the rest of this paper is concerned with the outcome of these projects. What proportion was technically successful? What were the principal reasons for failure? To what extent did the actual expenditures on a project correspond with the budgeted expenditures? How accurate were the firm's predictions of the probability of

success? Data are presented for the first time to help answer these questions.

To begin with, consider the proportion of the projects described in Section VI that turned out to be successful. By a "success," we mean a project where, according to the judgment of the project-evaluation group, the stated goals were met in the expected length of time.[37] According to Table 6, about one-half of the projects were successful, the rest

TABLE 5

ESTIMATED RATE OF RETURN FROM R AND D PROJECTS IF TECHNICALLY SUCCESSFUL, ELEVEN PROJECTS,* 1963

	No. of Projects	
RATE OF RETURN (PER CENT)	Division Estimates	Project-Evaluation Group's Estimates
Less than 0........	0	1
0– 99...........	2	6
100–199...........	2	1
200–299...........	2	1
300 or more........	5	2
Total..........	11	11

* The rates of return were computed on the basis of estimates generated by the divisions and the project-evaluation group.

either being delayed or dropped. Among those that were delayed, the average slippage factor (the revised time to completion divided by the original estimated time to completion) was about 1.30.

The proportion of failures is consider-

and the probability that it will be a success." Note, too, that the estimates in Table 5 seem higher than those for several large petroleum and chemical firms. In part, this may be due to the fact that the estimates in Table 5 are rates of return on the extra investment required to finish the projects. Naturally, the rate of return on the total investment is lower. Also, these figures are estimates of the private rate of return, not the social rate of return. (Griliches estimates the latter.) For estimates of the marginal rate of return in petroleum and chemicals, see Mansfield [16].

[36] For some discussion of the role of the large firm in stimulating technical progress, see Hamberg [10], Jewkes, Sawers, and Stillerman [11], and Mansfield [14, 17].

[37] The project-evaluation group reviewed the records of each of the projects carefully. In view of its position in the laboratory organization and the fact that the review was conducted for the laboratory management, there is no reason to suspect any appreciable bias in its findings. Of course, this is only one possible definition of success. Others could have been used. Moreover, we could have employed a richer classification than the simple dichotomy of success or failure. However, this procedure seems to be a sensible first step.

ably higher than would be expected on the basis of the estimated probabilities of success in Table 4. Apparently, the primary reason is that about one-third of the projects were not carried out in the way the department manager proposed. In 18 per cent of the projects, manpower was diverted to higher-priority projects;[38] in 9 per cent, the objective of the project was changed; and in 13 per cent, various miscellaneous factors (such as a key scientist quitting the firm) prevented the project from being carried out as planned. In only 16 per cent of the

TABLE 6

Outcome of Forty-Five R and D Projects,* 1963

Item	Technically Successful Projects	Reasons for Failure†				
		Manpower Diverted to Higher-Priority Projects	Objectives Changed	Unforeseen Technical Difficulties	Other	Total
Percentage of:						
Projects	44	18	9	16	13	100
Budgeted expenditures.	53	12	9	19	7	100
Actual expenditures...	51	10	10	20	7	100
Slippage in schedule:‡						
Mean	....	1.26	1.69	1.07	1.46	....
S.D.	....	0.36	0.62	0.19	....	....

* At the end of 1963, the project-evaluation group rated all projects as "successful," "partially successful," or "unsuccessful." The latter two classes are lumped together here.

† Note that these reasons were given by the project-evaluation group, not the department manager. Some of the reasons included under "other" are the inability to hire personnel, the fact that a key scientist quit, and the termination of a project because it no longer seemed justified commercially.

‡ The 1964 estimate of the time interval from the beginning to the end of the project, divided by the 1963 estimate.

TABLE 7

Ratio of Actual Expenditures to Final Budget Approved by Laboratory Management, Forty-five R and D Projects, 1963

Ratio	No. of Proposed Projects		Percentage of Budgeted Expenditures	
	Division Requests	New Business	Division Requests	New Business
0.00–0.39	2	0	1	0
0.40–0.79	19	2	45	17
0.80–1.19	14	2	50	77
1.20–1.59	2	1	2	7
1.60 and over...	2	1	2	0
Total*	39	6	100	100

* Because of rounding errors, the figures in the last two columns may not always sum to 100.

projects was failure due to unforeseen technical difficulties (Table 6).[39]

The changes in the staffing, nature, and objectives of the projects are reflected in the ratio of actual to budgeted expenditures (Table 7). In about one-half of the cases, actual expenditures were more than 20 per cent below the budget, generally because manpower could not be obtained or had been diverted elsewhere. In about 15 per cent of the cases, actual expenditures exceeded

[38] These projects with higher priorities often were government-financed projects on which the laboratory was working or new projects suggested after the R and D portfolio was tentatively fixed.

[39] Note that there was no evidence that the other reasons for failure, e.g., diversion of manpower, existed after, or as a consequence of, unexpected technical difficulties.

the budget by 20 per cent or more, often because the objective of the project was changed.

These results are of interest for at least four reasons. First, they provide further evidence that the bulk of the applied R and D carried out in this laboratory involves relatively small technical risks. Including only those cases where the project was carried out as planned, the chance of success averaged about .75. Second, they help to explain why the laboratory seldom uses parallel R and D efforts, which are based on the assumption that technical uncertainties are very great.[40] Third, they shed new light on the extent to which project failure and slippage are "man-made rather than caused by an ill-natured technology" [27, p. 498], the importance of this question being pointed out by Klein [12], Scherer [27], and others.[41] Finally, they show for the first time the extent of the slippage in commercial R and D and the way it depends on the cause of the delay.[42]

[40] More accurately, parallel R and D efforts rest on the assumption that a great deal can be learned relatively quickly regarding the costs of alternative development paths. However, if there is little un-certainty to begin with, there is likely to be relative-ly little learning either. Note that these results do not contradict Klein's [12] contention that parallel R and D efforts should be carried out in military de-velopment. He is concerned with cases where large advances are being sought in the state of the art. Consequently, the uncertainties are undoubtedly much greater.

[41] This question is important in interpreting the figures regarding failure rates and slippages in schedule, which are used repeatedly to measure the extent of the uncertainty in R and D. Judging from our results, these figures exaggerate considerably the extent of the technical risks involved.

[42] Marshall and Meckling [22] present data re-garding slippages in military R and D, but no data have been available until now regarding commercial R and D. Apparently, the average slippage is some-what smaller (1.3 vs. 1.5) than in military work. Ac-cording to Table 6, the slippage tended to be greatest when the objective of the project had changed and least when technical difficulties were encountered.

VIII. ACCURACY OF ESTIMATED PROBABILITIES OF SUCCESS

How accurate are the estimates of the probability of success made before the projects were started? This is a very important question, because the tech-niques recommended by economists and operations researchers [3, 6, 8, 23, 24] for selecting R and D projects depend on the use of such estimates. If it is impossible to make reasonably accurate estimates, techniques that are relatively sensitive to errors in the estimates should be avoided, even if they have other features that seem desirable.[43]

To find out how accurate the estimates (i.e., P^*) were, we construct a statistical discriminant function to predict whether or not a project was successful on the basis of its value of P^*. This function is optimal in the sense that, under specified conditions,[44] it minimizes the expected costs resulting from incorrect prediction. To estimate this discriminant function, we define a variable, U, where

$$U = \frac{n_1}{n_1 + n_2} \qquad (13a)$$

if the project is not a success,

$$U = \frac{n_2}{n_1 + n_2} \qquad (13b)$$

if the project is a success, n_1 is the num-ber of successes, and n_2 is the number of failures. Then we regress U on P^*, the result being

$$U = -0.6655 + .0084\ P^* . \qquad (14)$$
$$(.0044)$$

[43] Unfortunately, the discussions of selection techniques seldom, if ever, contain any treatment of the sensitivity of the results to errors of this kind.

[44] This assumes that the a priori probability of a success is 0.5 and that the cost of each type of error is the same. See Anderson [1]. These conditions are only approximately fulfilled, but if better approxi-mations were used the results would be about the same.

Since projects that were not carried out as planned are obviously not relevant here, the results are based on the remaining twenty-five projects.[45]

If a project's value of U calculated from equation (14) exceeds zero, one should predict success; if not, one should predict failure. This rule makes optimal use of the data on P^*. How accurate is it? The fact that the regression coefficient of P^* in equation (14) is statistically significant indicates that P^* is of some use in predicting success or failure.[46] However, it does not seem to be of much use, since it predicts incorrectly in 36 per cent of the cases on which equation (14) is based.

Of course, P^* may be more useful as a predictor if various other factors are held constant. To find out how much improvement there is, we included the age and experience of the department manager and the type of project (cost reduction, product improvement, consulting) as additional explanatory variables. Unfortunately, there was no evidence that their inclusion made any difference, since none of these variables turned out to be statistically significant factors in the discriminant function.

To sum up, although there is a direct relationship between the estimated probability of success and the outcome of a project, it is too weak to permit very accurate predictions. Using a statistical discriminant function, the probability of error is about .36.

IX. SUMMARY AND CONCLUSIONS

This paper reports the findings of a detailed, two-year case study of the allocation, characteristics, and outcome

[45] We include "partial successes" with "success" here. There are so few that it makes no difference which way they are treated.

[46] Note that a one-tailed test is appropriate here.

of the R and D portfolio of the central research laboratory in one of the nation's largest firms. We examine the process by which resources are allocated among projects and investigate the way in which estimates pertaining to proposed projects are adjusted and reinterpreted at various points in the multistage evaluation process used by the firm. In addition, we study the characteristics of both the projects that are accepted and the estimates that are used.

The major results are as follows: First, the assumption of expected profit maximization seems to be of use in explaining the allocation of funds among applied R and D projects. The size of the budget proposed for a project can be explained fairly well by a model that assumes that proposed spending is increased to the point where the increase in the probability of success is no longer worth its cost. The alterations made by the laboratory management in the proposed budget also can be explained fairly well by a similar model. However, these findings are extremely tentative, since the sample of projects is quite small and some other model may provide an even better explanation.

Second, although expected profit maximization can explain about half of the variation in the allocation of funds, about half remains unexplained. Four factors seem to account for much of this unexplained variation. (1) Holding expected profit constant, safe projects are preferred over risky ones. (2) Some attempt is made to satisfy scientific as well as commercial objectives, the consequence being that some projects are justified more on the basis of scientific interest than expected profit. (3) Projects differ considerably in the amount of pressure applied by operating executives to have them carried out. (4) Some scientists and department managers are much more effective than others in arguing for their proposals and in mobilizing support for them.

Third, a detailed description of the laboratory's applied R and D projects seems to indicate that most are expected to be completed in four years or less, and the results are expected to be applied only a few months later. The estimated probability of technical success averages about .80; and if the projects are successful, the estimated rate of return from the investment in the R and D is extremely high. These results are not very different from some preliminary findings pertaining to several large firms in the chemical and petroleum industries.

Fourth, failure rates and slippages in schedule, which are used repeatedly to measure the extent of the uncertainty in R and D, seem to exaggerate very greatly the extent of the technical uncertainties involved. About one-half of this laboratory's projects did not achieve their technical objectives on time. However, about two-thirds of these "failures" resulted from changes in objectives or the transfer of personnel to other projects. In only about one-third of these cases was there any evidence that "failure" was due to technical difficulties. Thus, whereas the unadjusted failure rate would indicate that the average probability of technical success was about .50, it was really about .75.

Fifth, a comparison of the estimate of the probability of a project's technical success (made prior to the beginning of the project) with the outcome of the project indicates that such estimates have some predictive value, but not much. A discriminant function based on these estimates predicted correctly in only 64 per cent of the cases. This finding should be useful in the formulation and evaluation of various R and D budget-allocation techniques, practically all of which rely on such estimates. Up to this point, no information was available regarding their accuracy.[47]

Despite their limitations, which are detailed above, these findings should be useful to economists interested in industrial organization, operations research, and the microeconomics of technical change. At this point such economists must begin to look beyond the figures on total R and D spending, which are notoriously difficult to interpret, and determine the sorts of projects that are being carried out, the factors determining the allocation of funds among them, and their eventual outcomes. Hopefully, this paper will encourage further work of this kind.

[47] Because of the difficulties in measuring the returns from an R and D project and the fact that too little time has elapsed to gauge even roughly the success of many of these projects, we do not and cannot present information on actual profit outcomes of projects or characteristics of projects that were successful in terms of return on investment. This is an important limitation, since technical success does not necessarily imply commercial success.

REFERENCES

1. Anderson, T. *An Introduction to Multivariate Statistical Analysis.* New York: John Wiley & Sons, 1958.
2. Baker, N., and Pound, W. "R and D Project Selection: Where We Stand." Paper presented at the joint TIMS-ORSA Meeting, Minneapolis, October, 1964.
3. Brandenburg, R. "Research and Development Project Selection." Ph.D. thesis, Cornell University, 1964.
4. Carter, C., and Williams, B. *Industry and Technical Progress.* New York: Oxford University Press, 1957.

5. Carter, C., and Williams, B. *Science in Industry*. New York: Oxford University Press, 1959.

6. Dean, B., and Sangupta, S. "Research Budgeting and Project Selection," *IRE Transactions on Engineering Management* (December, 1962).

7. Enos, J. *Petroleum Progress and Profits*. Cambridge, Mass.: M.I.T. Press, 1962.

8. Freeman, R. J. "A Stochastic Model for Determining the Size and Allocation of the Research Budget," *IRE Transactions on Engineering Management* (March, 1960).

9. Griliches, Z. "Research Costs and Social Returns: Hybrid Corn and Related Innovations," *Journal of Political Economy* (October, 1958).

10. Hamberg, D. "Invention in the Industrial Research Laboratory," *Journal of Political Economy* (April, 1963).

11. Jewkes, J., Sawers, D., and Stillerman, R. *The Sources of Invention*. New York: St. Martin's Press, 1959.

12. Klein, B. "The Decision Making Problem in Development," *The Rate and Direction of Inventive Activity*. New York: National Bureau of Economic Research, 1962.

13. Malcolm, D., Rosebloom, J., Clark, C., and Fagar, W. "Application of a Technique for R and D Project Evaluation," *Operations Research* (September, 1959).

14. Mansfield, E. "Size of Firm, Market Structure, and Innovation," *Journal of Political Economy* (December, 1963).

15. ———. "Industrial R and D Expenditures: Determinants, Prospects, and Relation to Size of Firm and Inventive Output," *ibid.* (August, 1964).

16. ———. "Rates of Return from Industrial Research and Development," *American Economic Review* (May, 1965).

17. ———. "The Economics of Research and Development: A Survey of Issues, Findings, and Needed Future Research," *Patents and Progress*. Homewood, Ill.: Richard D. Irwin, Inc., 1966.

18. ———. "Technical Change and the Management of Research and Development," *The Economics of Technical Change*. New York: W. W. Norton & Co., 1966.

19. Marcson, S. *The Scientist in American Industry*. New York: Harper & Row, Publishers, 1960.

20. Marglin, S. *Approaches to Dynamic Investment Planning*. Amsterdam: North-Holland Publishing Co., 1963.

21. Markowitz, H. *Portfolio Selection*. New York: John Wiley & Sons, 1959.

22. Marshall, A., and Meckling, W. "Predictability of Costs, Time and Success of Development," *The Rate and Direction of Inventive Activity*. New York: National Bureau of Economic Research, 1962.

23. Mottley, C., and Newton, R. "The Selection of Projects for Industrial Research," *Operations Research* (November, 1959).

24. Pound, W. H. "Research Project Selection: Testing a Model in the Field," *IRE Transactions on Engineering Management* (March, 1964).

25. Rubenstein, A. "Rate of Organizational Change, Corporate Decentralization, and the Constraints on Research and Development in the Firm." Paper presented at the Institute of Management Science, June, 1959.

26. Rubenstein, A., and Hannenberg, R. "Idea Flow and Project Selection in Several Industrial Research and Development Laboratories." Paper presented at 1962 Ohio State University Conference on Research and Development.

27. Scherer, F. "Comment," *The Rate and Direction of Inventive Activity*. New York: National Bureau of Economic Research, 1962.

[11]

Edwin Mansfield* and Samuel Wagner†

Organizational and Strategic Factors Associated with Probabilities of Success in Industrial R & D‡

I. INTRODUCTION

An enormous amount has been written concerning the management of industrial research and development. Yet much of this literature is so vague and qualitative that it is hard to verify, or to apply, the hypotheses that are put forth. In this paper, we present the results of some econometric and statistical studies carried out to test a number of hypotheses concerning the effects of various organizational and strategic factors on a firm's probabilities of success in its R & D program. The results, based on data from 20 major firms in the chemical, drug, petroleum, and electronics industries, should promote a better understanding of the nature and management of industrial R & D.

We begin by defining three probabilities of success. Then we study the effects of several organizational and strategic factors on each of these probabilities of success, this study being based on data from 16 of the firms. Next, we look more intensively at the effect of two factors: the degree of integration between R & D and marketing, and the degree of formality and quantification of the R & D project selection system. This study is based on very detailed data from three of the firms. Finally, we investigate the extent to which there may be an underutilization of R & D results due to inadequate understanding and receptivity in other parts of the firm. This study is based on data from 18 of the firms.

II. PROBABILITIES OF SUCCESS: DEFINITION AND MEASUREMENT

In this paper, we are concerned entirely with three probabilities: the probability of technical completion, the probability of commercialization (given technical completion), and the probability of economic success (given commercialization). The *probability of technical completion* is the probability that an R & D project will achieve its *technical* objectives. The *probability of commercialization (given technical completion)* is the probability that a technically complete R & D project will be commercialized—that is, that there will be a full-scale marketing or application of the new or improved product or process beyond a test-market or pilot-plant trial. The *proba-*

* Professor of economics, Wharton School, University of Pennsylvania.
† Associate professor of management, Temple University.
‡ The work on which this paper is based was supported by a grant to the first author from the National Science Foundation; some of the work was also carried out while he was a Fellow at the Center for Advanced Study in the Behavioral Sciences, Stanford, California. Preliminary versions of the paper were presented at seminars at Johns Hopkins, Stanford, and Georgetown Universities.

179

bility of economic success (given commercialization) is the probability that a commercialized R & D project will yield a rate of return (on the R & D costs plus any additional investment made to introduce the innovation) in excess of what was available from other (non–R & D) investment alternatives. Note that the product of these probabilities equals the probability that an R & D project begun by the firm will be an economic success. Also, note that basic research is not included here (for obvious reasons) and that the bulk of the projects are development projects.

Probabilities of this sort are commonly used to measure the riskiness of a firm's R & D program, as well as how well it manages and utilizes its R & D resources. Clearly, these probabilities are by no means ideal measures; indeed, they suffer from a number of well-known difficulties.[1] But in a field where measurement is so difficult, it seems worthwhile to try to determine how much light interfirm differences in these probabilities can shed on differences among firms in the nature of their R & D portfolios and in the quality of their R & D managements. In this paper, we carry out what seems to be the first systematic study of interfirm differences in these probabilities. On the basis of intensive interviews with 20 major firms, we obtained estimates of each of these probabilities for practically all of the

---

1. These probabilities indicate the percentage of projects—or percentage of R & D dollars, since, as we shall see below, the projects are weighted by their cost—that went for completed or successful projects. Although they are of interest, these probabilities may be misleading if firms with low values of these probabilities tend to obtain a much higher average rate of return from economically successful projects than firms (in the same industry) with high values of these probabilities. Existing evidence is too weak to tell us definitely whether this is the case, but, on the basis of the estimates of the average rate of return from economically successful projects obtained from the firms, there is no evidence that this was true among the firms in our sample.

To see how these probabilities are related to a firm's return from its R & D investment, let N be the number of R & D projects begun by a firm in a particular period, N_t be the number that are technically completed, N_c be the number commercialized, and N_s be the number of economic successes. If R_B is the average cost of an R & D project that is begun but not technically completed, R_t is the average cost of an R & D project that is technically completed but not commercialized, and R_c is the average cost (R & D and other) of a project that is commercialized, then the total investment in R & D and commercialization of R & D results is: $I = NR_B + N_t(R_t - R_B) + N_c(R_c - R_t)$, and the total annual return from this investment equals $\pi = N_s\pi_s$, where π_s is the average annual profit per economic success. (We assume for simplicity that the average return from economic failures is zero.) Letting P_t equal the probability of technical completion, P_c equal the probability of commercialization (given technical completion), and P_s equal the probability of economic success (given commercialization), it is clear that $P_t = N_t/N$, $P_c = N_c/N_t$, and $P_s = N_s/N_c$. Consequently, $I = N[R_B + P_t(R_t - R_B) + P_tP_c(R_c - R_t)]$, and $\pi = NP_tP_cP_s\pi_s$. Thus, $\pi = (IP_tP_cP_s\pi_s)/[R_B + P_t(R_t - R_B) + P_tP_c(R_c - R_t)]$. Holding constant I, π_s, R_T, R_B, and R_C, it is obvious that π increases with P_t, P_c, and P_s.

Note, however, that the probabilities we use are generally weighted by project cost (see n. 2 below). Thus, under the conditions described above, $\pi^* = I^*P^*_tP^*_cP^*_s\pi^*_s$, where π^* is the average annual return from the investment in R & D, P^*_t is the proportion of R and D expenditures spent on technically completed projects, P^*_c is the proportion of the amount spent on technically completed projects that is spent on commercialized projects, P^*_s is the proportion of the amount spent on commercialized projects that is spent on economically successful projects, I^* is the total investment in R & D, and π^*_s is the average rate of return from a dollar spent on an economically successful project. Obviously, if I^* and π^*_s are held constant, π^* increases with P^*_t, P^*_c, and P^*_s.

firms. In calculating these probabilities, projects were weighted by their cost, since otherwise the results might be unduly influenced by very small projects.

Table 1 shows the frequency distribution of each of these probabilities during 1968–71 for 16 firms in our sample.[2] (The other firms did not provide all the data we requested.) These data show that there is great variability among firms in these probabilities. In some firms, the probability of technical completion is as high as .94; in other firms, it is as low as .05. In some firms,

Table 1

Estimated Probability of Technical Completion, Commercialization (Given Technical Completion), and Economic Success (Given Commercialization), 1968–71

	Probability of (No. of Firms):		
Probability	Technical Completion	Commercialization	Economic Success
.90 and over..................	2	3	3
.80–.89......................	4	1	1
.70–.79......................	3	4	2
.60–.69......................	1	3	4
.50–.59......................	0	3	1
.40–.49......................	1	0	0
.30–.39......................	1	0	0
Less than .30................	4	2	0
Total......................	16	16	11*
Average probability..........	.57	.65	.74

* Estimates could be obtained for only 11 firms.

the probability of commercialization (given technical completion) approaches 1.00; in other firms, it is as low as .12. In some firms, the probability of economic success (given commercialization) approaches 1.00; in other firms, it is as low as .50. Even in the same industry, each of these

2. Note several things concerning the sample. (1) Many of these "firms" are major divisions of a large firm, not entire firms. There are advantages, of course, in having the data pertain to less heterogeneous groupings. (2) In the regressions in Section IV, not all of the 20 firms could be included because not all provided data on each of the relevant independent and dependent variables. Those that could be included in eq. (4) are included in col. 1 of table 1, those that could be included in eq. (5) are included in col. 2 of table 1, and those that could be included in eq. (6) are included in col. 3 of table 1. (3) Tables 2, 3, and 4 are based on those firms that could be included in eq. (4).

The average probability of technical completion is very similar to that which we found in earlier studies of 19 industrial laboratories, the latter being .57. Also, the average probability of commercialization (given technical completion) is quite similar to that for three laboratories we studied before, the latter being .55. However, the probability of economic success is higher than for the three firms included in a previous study, the latter being .38. See E. Mansfield et al., *Research and Innovation in the Modern Corporation* (New York: W. W. Norton & Co., 1971).

Note, too, that projects are weighted here, but not in table 6, by the size of their R & D expenditures. The results are essentially the same if unweighted data are used instead.

probabilities can be much higher in one firm than in another. These inter-firm differences are of interest and importance. An adequate understanding of the factors responsible for these differences would almost surely promote a better understanding of interfirm differences in the nature, riskiness, and productivity of R & D.

III. A SIMPLE MODEL

To help explain these interfirm differences, we construct a simple econometric model, which hypothesizes that these three probabilities are influenced by the following three variables: First, we would expect that all three of these probabilities would be affected by how quickly R & D projects are evaluated from the point of view of potential market and profit. Some firms

Table 2
Typical Expenditure on an R & D
Project before Studies of Market and
Profit Potential, 16 Firms, 1970

Expenditure ($000)	No. of Firms
Less than 10	7
10–24	3
25–49	1
50–99	2
100–149	1
150–99	1
200 and over	1
Total	16

allow R & D projects to proceed much farther than do other firms before the potential profitability of the project is studied. Table 2 shows that, on the average, the firms in our sample permitted about $40,000 to be spent on an R & D project before such a study was made. But there was a great deal of interfirm variability in this respect. Some firms allowed $200,000 to be spent before such a study, whereas other firms spent little or nothing before it.[3]

In general, there are many arguments for integrating technological considerations with economic considerations relatively early in the game.

3. By a "study" or "evaluation" of the potential market and profitability of the R & D project, we mean a serious attempt by competent professionals to carry out such a task. Such a study need not be very elaborate or expensive, but it must be made by people who are reasonably disinterested and competent, and it must be more than a token effort. Among the firms in table 2, there is relatively little correlation between a firm's size (as measured by sales) and the amount of money that typically can be spent on an R & D project before studies are made of market and profit potential. Specifically, R^2 equals .11. Moreover, there is even less correlation between the total amount spent annually on R & D by the firm (or relevant part of the firm) and the amount of money that typically can be spent on an R & D project before studies are made of market and profit potentiality.

For some relevant analysis of the relationship between R & D costs and the total costs of an innovation, see E. Mansfield and J. Rapoport, "A Note on the Cost of Product Innovation," *Management Science* (in press).

Unfortunately, one suspects that many firms do not integrate these factors early enough, the result being that many projects with very little potential economic payoff are started and continued too long. And because this is the case, the probability of technical completion is lowered, since more projects are started which are stopped short of technical completion because of poor profit prospects.[4] Also, the probability of commercialization (given technical completion) is lowered because more projects are completed technically before it is recognized that their profit outlook is poor. And the probability of economic success (given commercialization) is lowered, since the firm's portfolio of R & D projects tends to be more poorly geared to economic realities and conditions than would otherwise be the case.

Second, we would expect two of these probabilities to be affected by the percentage of a firm's R & D expenditures that go for "demand-pull,"

Table 3
Percentage of R & D Expenditures Devoted to Demand-Pull Projects, 16 Firms, 1968–71

%	No. of Firms
90 and over	8
80–89	1
70–79	2
60–69	2
50–59	1
40–49	1
Less than 40	1
Total	16

rather than "technology-push" projects. Put somewhat crudely, demand-pull projects are designed to satisfy a felt market or management need (or to solve a recognized production problem), whereas technology-push projects are designed to find specific uses or markets for promising technology or for a potential product or process. This dichotomy—which, of course, is sometimes extremely blurred in particular cases—is frequently used to characterize R & D projects. Table 3 shows that, on the average, about three-quarters of the development projects carried out by the 16 firms in our sample were regarded by the firms as primarily demand-pull, not technology-push.[5] But there is considerable variation among firms in

4. Of course, it may also be that the probability of technical completion will increase because more projects will be carried to technical completion before being stopped because of poor prospects. But it seems unlikely that this effect will outweigh that cited in the text, except in unusual cases.

5. This percentage is almost precisely the same as the average percentage obtained by Carter and Williams, Goldhar, Langrish et al., and Myers and Marquis. See K. Pavitt, *The Conditions for Success in Technological Innovation* (Paris: Organization for Economic Cooperation and Development, 1971). Also see N. Baker, J. Siegman, and A. Rubenstein, "The Effects of Perceived Needs and Means on the Generation of Ideas for Industrial R and D Projects," *IEEE Transactions on Engineering Management* (December 1967).

this percentage. In some firms in the sample, it is as high as 100 percent, whereas in other firms, it is as low as 20 percent.

In general, we would expect the probabilities of technical completion and of commercialization to be higher in firms that devote more of their R & D resources to demand-pull projects, rather than technology-push projects. The probability of technical completion would be expected to be higher for demand-pull projects because it is less difficult and risky to complete a project where the problem or need is reasonably well specified than one where the need or market must be found or created. Similarly, we would expect that the probability of commercialization (given technical completion) would be higher for a demand-pull project, since if technical

Table 4

Percentage of R & D Projects in Which the Basic Idea Stemmed from the R & D Department, 16 Firms, 1968–71

%	No. of Firms
90 and over.......................	3
80–89............................	1
70–79............................	5
60–69............................	4
50–59............................	0
40–49............................	1
30–39............................	1
Less than 30.....................	1
Total........................	16

completion is attained, it is much more likely that a market really exists for the innovation and that other parts of the firm will accept and utilize the R & D results. With regard to the probability of economic success (given commercialization), it is less obvious that this factor will be of importance. Once projects have passed all of the tests required before a firm decides to go ahead with commercialization, it is not obvious that demand-pull projects are any better (or worse) bets than technology-push projects.[6]

Third, one might expect some of these probabilities to be influenced by the extent to which the firm's R & D portfolio is based on ideas coming from the R & D department, as distinct from the marketing department and other parts of the firm (or its suppliers and customers). Of course, it is not easy—or sometimes even possible—to identify exactly where particular ideas have come from; and in some cases, there is no single source. Table 4 shows the estimates made by our sample of 16 firms. On the average, about

6. However, to the extent that technology-push projects tend to be more ambitious and aimed at larger potential payoffs, the probability of economic success (given commercialization) may decrease as the percentage of R & D expenditures devoted to demand-pull projects increases. But the data provide no evidence of this.

two-thirds of the R & D projects stemmed from the R & D department.[7] However, there is considerable variation among firms in this percentage. In some firms, about 95 percent of the projects stemmed from the R & D department, whereas in other firms, about 20 percent of the projects stemmed from this source.

In general, one might expect that firms with a relatively high percentage of R & D projects from the R & D department would have a relatively low probability of technical completion. This is because the R & D department tends to be attracted by, and interested in, projects that are technically more demanding, more ambitious, and more risky from a technical viewpoint than those suggested by the marketing and other departments. Also, the projects stemming from the R & D department may be less firmly based on market realities than those submitted by the marketing (and other) departments, so they may be more likely to be stopped short of technical completion because of lack of potential profitability. On the other hand, because the R & D department understands the technical aspects of R & D projects so well, it tends to be a better judge than other departments of what is technically feasible. Thus, one might argue that a high percentage of R & D projects from the R & D department might be associated with a relative high probability of technical completion.[8] It is difficult to judge the relative importance of these conflicting tendencies. We shall test the hypothesis that, on the average, the former factors more than offset the latter, although, on a priori grounds, this is by no means obvious.

One might also expect the probability of economic success (given commercialization) to be higher among firms with a relatively high percentage of R & D projects from the R & D department. Basically, this is because the projects stemming from the R & D department tend to be more ambitious and more fundamental than those stemming from the marketing and other departments. If they can be completed technically and if they pass the commercial tests that precede the decision to commercialize, one might expect them to be more likely to pay off handsomely. (Of course, whether the increase in the probability of market success [given commercialization] is big enough to offset the decrease in the probability of technical completion can vary from case to case.) As in the case of the hypothesis presented in the previous paragraph, there are factors running counter to this hypothesis. For example, one might argue that projects stemming

7. The average percentage in table 4 is remarkably close to the results we obtained in an earlier survey, the average in the earlier study being 62 percent (see Mansfield et al.). In part, this may be due to the fact that about half of the firms included in this study were also included in the previous survey. It may also be worth pointing out that, among the firms in table 4, there is only a low correlation between the percentage of projects stemming from the R & D department and the percentage of R & D expenditures devoted to demand-pull projects. However, as would be expected, what correlation there is is negative.

8. It should be recognized, however, that, if the idea for a project originates outside the R & D department and the R & D department feels that it is not technically feasible, the project generally will not be accepted. Thus, the fact that a relatively large percentage of projects stems from outside the R & D department does not mean that the R & D department does not regard them as feasible.

principally from outside the R & D department tend to be better geared to the realities of the market. As in the previous paragraph, we feel that this is an interesting hypothesis to test, even though we are by no means committed to its validity.[9]

IV. TESTS OF THE MODEL

Summarizing the hypotheses described in the previous section, we assume that

$$T_i = \alpha_0 - \alpha_1 A_i + \alpha_2 N_i - \alpha_3 R_i + z_i , \qquad (1)$$

$$C_i = \alpha_4 - \alpha_5 A_i + \alpha_6 N_i + z'_i , \qquad (2)$$

$$M_i = \alpha_7 - \alpha_8 A_i + \alpha_9 R_i + z''_i , \qquad (3)$$

where T_i is the probability of technical completion for the ith firm, C_i is the probability of commercialization (given technical completion) for the ith firm, M_i is the probability of economic success (given commercialization) for the ith firm, A_i is the amount (in thousands of dollars) that can be spent on an R & D project in the ith firm before studies are made of market and potential profit, N_i is the percentage of the ith firm's R & D expenditures that go for demand-pull rather than technology-push projects, R_i is the percentage of the ith firm's R & D projects that stem from the R & D department, and z_i, z'_i, and z''_i are random error terms. The intercepts— α_0, α_4, and α_7—may vary, of course, from industry to industry, reflecting the differences among industries in risk and other relevant factors.

To test these hypotheses, we use least squares to estimate the α's, the results being

$$T_i = \begin{Bmatrix} 49.7 \\ 23.9 \end{Bmatrix} - .21 A_i + .92 N_i - .71 R_i , \qquad (4)$$
$$\quad\quad\quad (2.82) \quad (4.92) \quad (3.53)$$

$$C_i = \begin{Bmatrix} 32.6 \\ 65.6 \end{Bmatrix} - .23 A_i + .48 N_i , \qquad (5)$$
$$\quad\quad\quad (2.69) \quad (2.53)$$

$$M_i = 53.2 - .17 A_i + .41 R_i . \qquad (6)$$
$$\quad\quad (2.46) \quad (1.79)$$

In equation (4), the top figure in brackets pertains to the 12 nondrug firms, and the bottom figure pertains to the four drug firms. In equation (5), the top figure in brackets pertains to the 14 nonelectronic firms, and the bottom figure pertains to the two electronics firms. Such interindustry differences seem quite sensible in light of previous studies.[10]

---

9. Also, the probability of commercialization (given technical completion) may be associated with the percentage of projects stemming from the R & D department, but there is no evidence that this is the case.

10. In previous studies, we found that the probability of technical completion tends to be lower in the drug industry than in the others; this seems to be due to the nature

The results are in accord with our hypotheses. All of the regression coefficients have the expected signs and are statistically significant. Moreover, these equations can explain a substantial proportion of the variation in the three probabilities, T_i, C_i, and M_i. Specifically, equation (4) explains about 80 percent of the variation in T_i, $\bar{R}^2$—corrected for degrees of freedom—being about .78. Equation (5) explains about one-half of the variation C_i, $\bar{R}^2$—corrected for degrees of freedom—being about .54. And equation (6) explains about 40 percent of the variation in M_i, $\bar{R}^2$—corrected for degrees of freedom—being about .38.

Of course, we would not expect these equations to account for practically all the variation in these probabilities, since many important variables must be omitted because there is no adequate way to measure them. Among these omitted variables is the quality of a firm's scientists and engineers. To a great extent, the effects of such variables are contained in the random-error terms, z_i, z'_i, and z''_i. Since our data pertain only to major firms, which are reasonably homogeneous with respect to variables like the kinds of work they are doing and the quality of their personnel, the variation of the random-error terms would not be expected to swamp the explained variation, but it would be expected to be big enough to keep $\bar{R}^2$ at moderate levels.

V.   IMPLICATIONS OF THE RESULTS

To the extent that firms want to increase these probabilities of success, our findings seem to suggest the desirability of early investigations of the profit potential of R & D projects. According to equations (4)–(6), one can increase T_i, C_i, or M_i by about four percentage points simply by decreasing A_i by $20,000. Of course, this is too bald an interpretation of the results. To a considerable extent, A_i is an index which is associated with many other characteristics of a firm's organization and behavior. It is a surrogate for how rapidly the firm attempts to gauge the profit potential of an R & D project—or put the other way around, it is a surrogate for how long the firm will let a project go on without looking carefully at its profit potential. Also, our results may be due in part to a correlation between a firm's preferences with regard to risk and its value of A_i.[11]

But recognizing these considerations, it nonetheless seems likely that one major reason for our results is that better-managed firms—which, *all*

---

of pharmaceutical research and the inherent risks (and rewards) (see Mansfield et al.). As for the relatively high probability of commercialization (given technical completion) in the electronics industry, this may be because fewer major steps following technical completion must be carried out in electronics to commercialize an innovation. Note that industry dummy variables were tried and discarded in all three equations—(4), (5), and (6). All of the dummies were statistically nonsignificant except for the one pertaining to drugs in eq. (4) and the one pertaining to electronics in eq. (5). Also, note that T_i, C_i, and M_i are percentages, not proportions.

11. We made some attempt to test this hypothesis in interviews with the firms, and the results seemed to indicate that it is not true. But nonetheless the possibility should be borne in mind that this hypothesis partially explains the observed effect of A_i.

other things equal, tend to have higher values of these probabilities—generally have relatively small values of A_i. After all, unless marketing and profit considerations are brought into the picture relatively early in the game, it is inevitable that much R & D will be wasted because it will be directed at problems that, although technically interesting, are not commercially worthwhile. Successful innovation entails the fulfillment of both technological and economic objectives. Unless both are considered at a relatively early stage, the chance of success is reduced.

Turning to the observed effects of N_i on these probabilities, it is important to stress that our results do not indicate that a firm should necessarily increase its value of N_i. It is quite likely that technology-push projects tend to be more risky than demand-pull projects. Thus, firms with less aversion to risk may invest a larger proportion of their R & D expenditures in such projects. Since their probabilities of success are relatively low, we may find a relationship of the sort indicated by equations (4) and (5). However, if this is the case, this relationship does not indicate necessarily that these firms are inefficient or irrational. It may indicate only that they are willing to take bigger risks than the others. (In addition, it may indicate that the results of technology-push projects are harder to sell to marketing, production, and other parts of the firm than those of demand-pull projects.)

Our findings also seem to indicate that there is a trade-off between the probability of technical completion and the probability of economic success (given commercialization). Holding other factors constant, the probability of technical completion goes down as the firm invests a larger percentage of its R & D expenditures in technically more ambitious and fundamental projects. This seems to be a major reason why, in equation (4), the probability of technical completion decreases as more of the R & D portfolio stems from the R & D department. On the other hand, the probability of economic success (given commercialization) seems to increase as the firm invests a larger percentage of its R & D expenditures in technically more ambitious and fundamental projects. This seems to be a major reason why, in equation (6), the probability of economic success (given commercialization) increases as more of the R & D portfolio stems from the R & D department.

It is important that firms recognize that this trade-off exists, and that they decide on rational grounds how far they want to go in reducing one probability to increase the other. At present, one has the impression that many firms are reluctant to reduce the probability of technical completion, even though such a reduction would be more than offset by increases in the probability of economic success (given commercialization). In other words, some firms carry out many relatively trivial projects in which the probability of technical completion is high but the potential profit is low. They might do better to devote a bigger share of their R & D expenditures to technically more ambitious projects in which the probability of technical success is lower but the potential profit is higher. In recent years, some major firms have begun to move in this direction.

VI. INTEGRATION BETWEEN MARKET-
ING AND R & D, PROJECT SELEC-
TION SYSTEMS, AND PROBA-
BILITIES OF SUCCESS

Let us turn now to a more detailed study of the effects of a firm's organization and the nature of its R & D project selection system on its probabilities of success. To begin with, we put forth two hypotheses concerning the effects of these factors. First, we would expect the extent of the communication and cooperation between the marketing and R & D departments to influence some of the probabilities discussed in previous sections. Judging from the results of past research by ourselves and others,[12] successful innovation depends in an important way on R & D being integrated with marketing. The R & D department must be able and willing to respond to the marketing department's needs, and marketing personnel should be involved in R & D project selection. In contrast, the R & D department in some firms has been quite remote from the marketing department and has marched to the beat of quite a different drummer, the result being that the R & D output has been more poorly mated with market conditions than would otherwise have been the case.

More specifically, we would expect that closer integration of R & D and marketing would result in a higher probability of commercialization (given technical completion). One reason why projects are technically completed but not commercialized is that the market for the potential new product turns out to be inadequate. Closer integration of marketing and R & D would make it more likely that such projects would be stopped prior to technical completion. Whether a closer integration of R & D with marketing would affect the probability of technical completion is not clear. On the one hand, it might mean that fewer projects with relatively poor profit potential would be selected, with the result that a smaller proportion would be terminated for nontechnical reasons prior to technical completion. On the other hand, because fewer projects would be taken all the way to technical completion and then shelved because of poor profit prospects, it might mean that this proportion would increase. Similarly, the effect of closer integration on the probability of economic success (given commercialization) is not clear. It might mean that marketing would be better able to exploit new products, thus raising this probability. Or it might result in an R & D portfolio composed of a larger proportion of less ambitious projects— which, if technically successful, have a relatively small payoff. This might lower this probability.

Second, we would expect that some of these probabilities of success

12. See C. Freeman, "A Study of Success and Failure in Industrial Innovation," and E. Mansfield, "Determinants of the Speed of Application of New Technology," both in the International Economic Association's *Science and Technology in Economic Growth* (London: Macmillan Co., 1973). Also see P. Lawrence and J. Lorsch, "New Management Job: The Integrator," *Harvard Business Review* (November 1967); Lawrence and Lorsch, "Differentiation and Integration in Complex Organizations," *Administrative Science Quarterly* (June 1967); and Mansfield et al. (n. 2 above).

may be influenced by the way in which R and D projects are selected. In recent years, there has been a tendency for firms to utilize formal, quantitative project selection techniques based on estimated rates of return, payout periods, and other such criteria. These techniques may use the results of the studies of market and profit potential discussed in Section III (assuming that the latter studies are carried out before the relevant projects are begun), but they may not be the same as the latter studies, since they tend to involve much more formal estimation and numerical manipulation, and they tend to have much more ambitious objectives. We would expect that the use of such quantitative project selection techniques may increase the probability of commercialization (given technical completion). Such techniques are designed to promote a more careful and complete evaluation of a project's commercial potential. It seems likely that their use will result in the choice of an R & D portfolio that is better geared to the realities of the marketplace. If so, the probability of commercialization (given technical completion) should increase, since fewer projects will be technically completed and then shelved because of poor profit potential.

On the other hand, we suspect that the use of such techniques may result in a decrease in the probability of economic success (given commercialization). The basic reason for such an effect is that the use of such techniques may tend to push a firm's R & D portfolio in the direction of less ambitious projects with more modest potential payoff. Since it is much easier to estimate the returns from such projects, it is also easier to get them through a screen based on quantitative selection techniques. But if they can be technically completed and commercialized, the more ambitious and fundamental projects with the really big potential payoffs are much more likely to be economic successes. Thus, we would expect that the use of such techniques may reduce the probability of economic success (given commercialization). Finally, the effect of such techniques on the probability of technical completion is not clear. On the one hand, the probability may increase because the use of such techniques may result in a less (technically) risky R & D portfolio. On the other hand, a larger proportion of projects that would otherwise be carried to technical completion and then shelved for nontechnical reasons may be stopped prior to technical completion.

VII. EXPERIMENTAL DESIGN AND TESTS OF HYPOTHESES

To test these hypotheses, we use data concerning three firms, designated A, B, and C. These three firms were chosen because they belonged to the same two-digit industry (chemicals and allied products), were of roughly the same size, and spent very close to the same amount annually on R & D. However, during the 1960s, they experienced quite different sorts of reorganizations. In each firm, a reorganization changed the extent to which R & D and marketing were integrated, and, at the same time, a significant change was made in the formality and degree of quantification of the project selection system. Table 5 shows the direction of both the reorganization and the change in project selection system in each firm. As you can see, the reorganizations resulted in a closer integration of marketing and R & D in firms A and C, but in less integration of marketing and R & D in firm B. At the same time, the reorganizations resulted in a more formal and quantitative project selection system in firms A and B, and a less formal and quantitative project selection system in firm C.[13]

These three firms provided us with data concerning more than 330 individual R & D projects that occurred over a period from 3–7 years before the reorganization to 5–8 years after it. In each firm, we computed the probability of technical completion, the probability of commercialization (given technical completion), and the probability of economic success (given commercialization) for the period before the reorganization and for

Table 5

Changes in Degree of Integration of R & D and Marketing and in Degree of Formality and Quantification of Project Selection System, Firms A, B, and C

	Change in Project Selection System	
Change in Relationship between R & D and Marketing	Informal and Nonquantitative to Formal and Quantitative	Formal and Quantitative to Informal and Nonquantitative
Closer integration......	Firm A	Firm C
Less integration........	Firm B	. . .

the period after the reorganization. A comparison of each probability's value before the reorganization with its value afterward should provide some information concerning the effects of the reorganization. However, such comparisons are complicated by the fact that two changes—in the

13. All three firms are among *Fortune*'s 500 largest industrial corporations. Two of them were very close in terms of sales; the third was larger. During the relevant time period, they spent almost precisely the same amount on R & D. In each of these firms, it was evident that the integration between marketing and R & D changed as indicated in table 5. In firms A and C, the managements felt that marketing had too small a role in the R & D program management, and the R & D department was reorganized to make R & D more responsive to the needs of marketing. Communication channels and networks were established between them, and marketing's input to R & D decision making increased substantially. On the other hand, in firm B, R & D became much more independent from marketing as a consequence of the reorganization. It tended to establish its own criteria and priorities regarding projects without paying nearly as much attention to marketing as before the reorganization. At the same time, changes took place in the firms' project selection techniques. Before the reorganizations, no formal project evaluation was undertaken in either firm A or firm B. In each firm, projects apparently were selected on the basis of the intuitive judgment of a selection committee, there being little detailed analysis of expected benefits and costs and only a passing comparison with other projects. After the reorganization, a quantitative project selection system—based on estimates of project cost, duration, and probability of technical completion and market estimates of sales and product life—was instituted in both firms. In firm C, on the other hand, the project selection system became less formal and less quantified after the reorganization, partly by neglect and partly by design. A short while after the reorganization, project selection at firm C became highly subjective and informal.

extent of integration of marketing and R & D, and in the project selection system—occurred simultaneously. We would like to extract what information we can concerning the effect of each separate type of change.

To accomplish this, we make paired comparisons between the firms. Firms A and B experienced similar changes in project selection systems, but opposite changes in the degree of integration between marketing and R & D. Thus, to test whether closer integration resulted in a higher probability of commercialization (given technical completion), we see whether this probability increased more (or decreased less) in firm A (which experienced closer integration) than in firm B (which experienced less integration). Any such difference cannot be due to the change in project selection system, since this change was essentially the same in both firms. Of course, a difference of this sort, if it exists, may be due to other causes than the change in the degree of integration between marketing and R & D, since we cannot hold all other variables constant. But it is worthwhile to determine whether the data are in accord with our hypotheses.

Turning to the effect of the project selection system, firms A and C experienced similar changes in the degree of integration between marketing and R & D, but opposite changes in the nature of the project selection system. Thus, to test whether a more quantitative project selection system increases the probability of commercialization (given technical completion), we see whether these probabilities increased more in firm A than in firm C. And to test whether a more quantitative project selection system decreases the probability of economic success (given commercialization), we see whether this probability increased less (or decreased more) in firm A than in firm C. Any such differences cannot be due to the change in the degree of integration between R & D and marketing, since this change was essentially the same in both firms. Again, such differences may be due to other causes than the change in project selection systems, there being no way to hold all other factors constant. But it is of interest to see whether differences exist and whether they are in accord with our hypotheses.

Finally, note that both hypotheses in Section VI imply that there will be an increase in firm A in the probability of commercialization (given technical completion). Why? Because firm A experienced both a closer integration between marketing and R & D and a more quantitative project selection system. According to our hypotheses, each of these changes should increase this probability. Also, both hypotheses imply that there will be a decrease in firm B in the probability of economic success (given commercialization). Why? Because firm B experienced both a looser integration between marketing and R & D and a more quantitative project selection system. According to our hypotheses, each of these changes should decrease this probability. Of course, these tests are not very powerful, because other factors cannot be held constant. But nonetheless it is of interest to see whether the observed differences are in accord with these expectations.[14]

14. When this part of the study was designed, we intended to obtain data concerning firms that experienced no change in organization or project selection system during

VIII. EMPIRICAL RESULTS

Table 6 shows the effects of the reorganization of each firm on its probability of technical completion, its probability of commercialization (given technical completion), and its probability of economic success (given commercialization). The evidence is very much in accord with our hypotheses in Section VI. As we would expect, the probability of commercialization (given technical completion) increased more in firm A than in firm B, and the difference is large and statistically significant.[15] With regard to the

Table 6

Probability of Technical Completion, Commercialization (Given Technical Completion), and Economic Success (Given Commercialization), before and after Reorganization, Firms A, B, and C

Probability of	Before Reorgani- zation (P_1)	After Reorgani- zation (P_2)	$(P_2 - P_1)$	$(P_{2a} - P_{1a}) - (P_{2b} - P_{1b})$[a]	$(P_{2a} - P_{1a}) - (P_{2c} - P_{1c})$[b]
Economic success.....	...	...	...	+.02	−.25**
A................	.55	.75	+.20	...	...
B................	.39	.57	+.18	...	...
C................	.30	.75	+.45**	...	...
Commercialization....	...	...	...	+.60**	+.25**
A................	.65	1.00	+.35*	...	...
B................	.72	.47	−.25	...	...
C................	.49	.59	+.10	...	...
Technical completion.	...	...	...	+.18	−.07
A................	.61	.65	+.04	...	...
B................	.68	.54	−.14	...	...
C................	.52	.63	+.11	...	...

[a] Difference associated with closer integration of marketing with R & D.
[b] Difference associated with more quantitative project selection system.
* Significant at .10 level.
** Significant at .05 level (one-tailed tests).

probability of technical completion and the probability of economic success (given commercialization), the differences are smaller and not statistically significant. Thus, the results suggest that a closer integration of marketing and R & D tends to increase the probability of commercialization (given

---

this period, these firms being a control group. But no suitable firms could be found, and this idea was abandoned.

15. Let Pij be the value of the probability in the ith period $(i = 1, 2)$ in the jth firm $(j = a, b, c)$. To test the significance of the difference between $(P_{2a} - P_{1a})$ and $(P_{2b} - P_{1b})$, we use the following statistic:

$$[(P_{2a} - P_{1a}) - (P_{2b} - P_{1b})] \Big/ \sqrt{\frac{P_{1a}Q_{1a}}{N_{1a}} + \frac{P_{2a}Q_{2a}}{N_{2a}} + \frac{P_{1b}Q_{1b}}{N_{1b}} + \frac{P_{2b}Q_{2b}}{N_{2b}}},$$

where $Q = (1 - P)$ and N is the relevant number of observations. Since the P's—and the differences in the P's—are statistically independent, this statistic should be distributed approximately as a unit normal variable if the null hypothesis is true.

technical completion). It may also have an effect on the other two probabilities, but neither the data nor our hypotheses provide any strong indication of the nature of this effect.

With regard to our second hypothesis in Section VI, the evidence
seems to indicate that quantitative project selection systems tend to increase the probability of commercialization (given technical completion)
and to decrease the probability of economic success (given commercialization). In accord with our hypotheses, the probability of commercialization
(given technical completion) increased more in firm A than in firm C, and
the probability of economic success (given commercialization) increased less
in firm A than in firm C. Both of these differences are statistically significant.
The effect of a more quantitative project selection system on the probability
of technical completion is not statistically significant. Thus, the results
suggest that a more quantitative project selection system tends to increase
the probability of commercialization (given technical completion) and to
reduce the probability of economic success (given commercialization), but
there is no evidence that it influences the probability of technical completion.

Finally, let us see whether, in accord with our hypotheses, an increase
occurred in firm A in the probability of commercialization (given technical
completion). As shown in table 6, this increase occurred and is statistically
significant. On the other hand, the probability of economic success (given
commercialization) did not decrease in firm B, although our hypotheses
imply such a decrease. However, the observed change in this probability
is not statistically significant; and, as noted in the previous section, this
test is not very powerful, since other variables are not held constant.

IX. LIMITATIONS AND IMPLICATIONS

The data presented in table 6 seem to be quite consistent with our hypotheses, but since they pertain to only a few firms, and so many factors are un-
controlled, they can hardly be regarded as conclusive. Nonetheless, since
this seems to be the first quantitative exploration of these issues, it may be
worthwhile to point out two implications of the hypotheses in Section VI,
assuming that these hypotheses continue to be borne out by further study.
First, the importance of integrating the marketing and R & D departments
is underlined and emphasized. The evidence presented here is quite in line
with our previous results, and with Project Sappho.[16] Successful product
innovation requires the coupling of marketing and technology. This coupling
is difficult, particularly in a large organization where the marketing people
and the R & D people tend to be separated. In cases where the marketing
people are involved in R & D project selection, and where the R & D
department's work is geared in considerable measure (but not entirely, of
course) to marketing's perceived opportunities and needs, the productivity
of R & D seems higher, and its riskiness seems lower, than in cases where
there is less integration of R & D with marketing. (Of course, to the extent
that more integration means a lower average return from economically

16. See the references in n. 12 above.

successful projects, these benefits may be partially or totally offset, but there is no evidence that this is the case.)[17]

Second, formal quantitative project selection techniques, as currently applied, seem to have at least two effects, one positive and one negative. The positive effect is that they tend to increase the probability of commercialization (given technical completion). This would be expected, since these techniques force a more careful evaluation of each project's commercial potential. The negative effect seems to be that they reduce the probability of economic success (given commercialization). To the extent that they push a firm's R & D portfolio in the direction of less ambitious projects with

Table 7

Ratio of Value of Probability if R & D Results Were Fully Utilized to Actual Value, 18 Firms

Ratio	Probability of (No. of Firms):		
	Technical Completion	Commercialization	Economic Success
1.00–1.04.	12	8	5
1.05–1.09.	2	2	3
1.10–1.14.	3	1	0
1.15–1.19.	0	0	3
1.20–1.24.	0	0	0
1.25–1.29.	1	3	1
1.30–1.39.	0	0	1
1.40–1.49.	0	1	0
1.50 and over.	0	2	2
Total.	18	17	15
Mean ratio.	1.10	1.26	1.16

more modest potential payoff,[18] this too would be expected. Firms should recognize that both effects may occur, and that whether the positive effect outweighs the negative one is likely to differ from case to case.

X.   UNDERUTILIZATION OF R & D
RESULTS

Finally, it is important to recognize that these probabilities of success depend heavily on how receptive other parts of the firm are to the results obtained by the R & D department. To get some idea of the importance of this factor, R & D executives of 20 major firms in the chemical, drug, petroleum, and electronics industries were asked to estimate what percentage of the R & D projects terminated for nontechnical reasons prior to technical completion would have been economic successes if their firm's marketing and production people had properly grasped their potential. As shown in table 7, the probability of technical completion would have been

17. See n. 1 above.
18. In fact, there is considerable evidence that the firms in this sample that did switch to quantitative project selection techniques tended subsequently to reduce the proportion of their R & D portfolio aimed at relatively ambitious technical advances.

about 10 percent higher, on the average, under these circumstances, according to the estimates of the 18 firms that provided data.

Second, they were asked to estimate the percentage of technically completed projects that were not commercialized which would have been economic successes if marketing and production had properly grasped their potential. As shown in table 7, the probability of commercialization (given technical completion) would have been about 26 percent higher, on the average, under these circumstances, according to the estimates. Third, they were asked to estimate the percentage of the unsuccessful commercialized projects that would have been economic successes if marketing and production had done a proper job in exploiting them. As shown in table 7, the probability of economic success (given commercialization) would have been about 16 percent higher, on the average, under these circumstances, according to the estimates.

If these estimates are at all close to the mark, they indicate that the productivity of industrial R & D would be enhanced greatly by a better and fuller utilization of existing R & D findings. Under recent circumstances, about 32 percent of the R & D projects started by these 18 firms turned out to be economic successes. According to the estimates of these executives, if marketing and production had properly utilized them, about 50 percent of the R & D projects started by these 18 firms would have been economic successes. Thus, based on this rough measure, the success rate would have increased by over 50 percent if the results of R & D had been fully and properly utilized.

Of course, it may be objected (quite properly) that R & D executives are likely to have a biased view of the extent to which the results of R & D are underutilized. To get some idea of the probable bias, we asked a number of marketing or production executives in the same firms to answer the same questions. The results indicated that the non–R & D executives agree with the R & D executives. Indeed, their estimates of the extent to which R & D results are underutilized for these reasons tend to be somewhat higher than the estimates made by the R & D executives.

Recognizing that this problem exists, firms have tried a number of devices and strategies to promote a fuller use of R & D findings. They have tried to get marketing and production to work closely with R & D in the choice of R & D projects. They have tried to promote frequent and extensive communication between R & D and other departments. They have moved personnel back and forth across the interface between the R & D department and other departments. And they have established new-products committees and new-products departments. Unquestionably, these devices have helped a great deal. (For example, there is some evidence that, according to the estimates made by the firms in the sample, R & D results tend to be more fully utilized in firms with new-products committees.)[19]

19. Using standard regression techniques, we find that the percentage of a firm's technically completed, but not commercialized, R & D projects that would have been economic successes if marketing and production had properly grasped their potential

However, our results indicate that there is still a rather serious under-utilization by firms of their R & D results. Apparently, the rate of techno-logical change could be increased significantly—without substantial increases in R and D expenditures—if firms could make fuller use of the R & D results that they are already turning out.[20]

XI.   SUMMARY AND CONCLUSIONS

Four general conclusions seem to stem from our findings. First, there are very large differences among firms in the probability of technical completion, the probability of commercialization (given technical completion), and the probability of economic success (given commercialization) of their R & D projects. Even in the same industry, these probabilities can be much higher in one firm than in another. Among other things, these differences reflect the fact that the R & D portfolios of some firms are inherently more risky than those of others, and that some firms are more efficient than others in carrying out, managing, and utilizing R & D.

Second, on the basis of data from 16 major firms, there is considerable evidence that all three of these probabilities are influenced by how quickly R & D projects are evaluated from the point of view of economic potential. To the extent that firms want to increase these probabilities, they might consider an earlier investigation of the profit potential of projects. Some firms tend to allow projects to run on too long before evaluating their economic (as distinct from their technological) potential. Also, there is considerable evidence that the probability of commercialization (given technical completion) is directly related to the degree to which R & D and marketing are integrated. It seems likely that this reflects the fact that, in some firms, the R & D department has not always worked very

---

(according to the R & D executives) is directly related to the percentage of projects stemming from the R & D department and smaller if a firm has a new-products committee than otherwise. The percentage of a firm's commercialized, but not economically success-ful, R & D projects that would have been economically successful if marketing and pro-duction had done a better job of exploiting them (according to the R & D executives) is directly related to the proportion of the firm's R & D expenditures going for demand-pull projects, inversely related to the firm's probability of economic success (given commercial-ization), and smaller if a firm has a new-products committee or department than otherwise. The percentage of a firm's R & D projects that were terminated prior to technical comple-tion for nontechnical reasons which would have been economic successes if the marketing and production people had properly grasped their potential (according to the R & D executives) is directly related to the percentage of projects stemming from the R & D department and smaller if a firm has a new-products committee or department than otherwise. All of these results are statistically significant. The sign of each of the regression coefficients seems reasonable, with one possible exception: we might have expected the proportion of expenditures going for demand-pull projects to have the opposite effect (in the second sentence in this footnote).

20. Of course, it must be recognized that R & D findings that are not put to use by a firm may be utilized by the same firm or another firm at a later date, and perhaps in a somewhat different form. It should not be assumed that these findings are lost. However, delay can be costly—both to the firm and to society. Also, since the R & D and non–R & D executives were not asked to indicate which particular R & D findings were under-utilized, it is not clear that the two groups agree on this score. All that can be determined from our results is that they seem to agree concerning the magnitude of the problem.

closely with the marketing department, the result being that the R & D output has not been very well mated with market realities.

Third, there is evidence that the use of quantitative project selection techniques seems to increase the probability of commercialization (given technical completion). Also, increases in the proportion of projects stemming from outside the R & D department seem to be associated with increases in the probability of technical completion. However, both of these factors also tend to reduce the probability of economic success (given commercialization), apparently because they push the firm's R & D portfolio in the direction of technically less ambitious projects with more modest payoffs. Whether, on balance, such changes are good or bad will vary from case to case, but it is important to recognize that such a trade-off may exist. Also, there is evidence that the probabilities of technical completion and of commercialization (given technical completion) tend to be lower in firms that devote a relatively large percentage of their R & D expenditures to technology-push projects rather than to demand-pull projects. To a large extent, this may be due to the fact that such projects are inherently more risky and that other parts of the firm are less likely to accept and utilize the results of such projects.

Fourth, it is important to recognize that these probabilities depend heavily on how receptive other parts of the firm are to the firm's R & D results. According to executives (both inside and outside R & D) of 18 major firms, the probability of technical completion would have been about 10 percent higher, on the average, if the marketing and production people had properly grasped the potential of the projects. Also, the probability of commercialization (given technical completion) would have been about 26 percent higher, and the probability of economic success (given commercialization) would have been about 16 percent higher, on the average, if marketing and production had done a proper job of exploiting them. Clearly, the productivity of industrial R & D would be greatly enhanced by a fuller utilization within the firm of its R & D results. On the basis of these results, it appears that the rate of technological change could be increased materially, without any substantial increase in R & D expenditures, if intrafirm barriers to the utilization of R & D results could be reduced.

In conclusion, it is very important that the limitations of this study be recognized. The data pertain to only 20 firms, and, as indicated in previous sections, they are rough in many respects. Also, the hypotheses tested are sometimes rather crude. Clearly, the present study is only a beginning, and the results must be regarded as tentative. However, we hope that the findings will be of interest, and that they will encourage others to pursue quantitative studies in this area. Without such studies, much of the literature concerning the management of industrial research and development will remain vague, qualitative, and difficult to verify or apply.

12

Industrial $R\&D$ in Japan and the United States:
A Comparative Study

By Edwin Mansfield*

Given that Japan has become America's principal rival in many high-technology industries, it obviously is important from both an analytical and policy viewpoint to compare the extent, nature, organization, and effectiveness of the research and development ($R\&D$) activities of Japanese firms with those of comparable American firms. This paper summarizes the results of a study, based both on published data and on data collected directly from a carefully selected sample of 200 Japanese and American firms, comparing the size and composition of firms' $R\&D$ expenditures in both countries, as well as the sources of their industrial $R\&D$ projects. In addition, I study the relationship between the extent of the industrial $R\&D$ in each country, on the one hand, and the rate of productivity increase, on the other hand, with particular emphasis on the differences between these countries in the effects of applied $R\&D$ and basic research.

I. Industrial $R\&D$ and Productivity Growth

Economists are particularly interested in the relationship between industrial $R\&D$ and productivity growth. For the United States, there have been many studies of this topic, whereas for Japan there have been very few. This section presents the results of a study for Japan, the model and methods used being

similar to those employed in earlier studies by Griliches, Terleckyj, and myself. (See my 1980 article.) In a particular industry, the production function is assumed to be

$$(1) \qquad Q_t = Ae^{\lambda t}R_t^{a}L_t^{r}K_t^{1-r},$$

where Q_t is the industry's value-added in year t, R_t is the industry's stock of $R\&D$ capital, L_t is the industry's labor input, and K_t is the industry's capital input. Thus, the annual rate of change of total factor productivity is

$$(2) \qquad \rho_t = \lambda + \Phi((dR/dt)/Q_t).$$

where $\Phi = \partial Q_t/\partial R_t$.

Because the rate of growth of each industry's stock of $R\&D$ capital cannot be measured directly, I assume, as other studies frequently have, that an industry's expenditure on $R\&D$ during year t is equal to the change in the industry's stock of $R\&D$ capital then. If an industry's values λ and Φ are statistically independent of its ratio of $R\&D$ expenditure to value-added, it follows that

$$(3) \qquad \rho_i = \bar{\lambda} + \bar{\Phi}r_i + z_i,$$

where ρ_i is the annual rate of change of total factor productivity in the ith industry, r_i is the ratio of $R\&D$ expenditure to value-added in this industry, $\bar{\lambda}$ and $\bar{\Phi}$ are the average values of λ and Φ in all relevant industries, and z_i is a random error term.[1]

*Director, Center for Economics and Technology, University of Pennsylvania, Philadelphia, PA 19104. The research on which this paper is based was supported by a grant from the Division of Policy Research and Analysis of the National Science Foundation. I am indebted to Rolf Piekarz, Gary Saxonhouse, and Eleanor Thomas for helpful comments, as well as to the 200 Japanese and American firms that provided much of the basic data. I also thank Masahiro Kuroda, Keio University, as well as the OECD, for providing me with unpublished data. A more complete version of this paper describing the analysis and results in more detail is available from the author.

[1] The only previous study (that I know of) using industry-level data to estimate the relationship between $R\&D$ and productivity growth in Japan is Hiroyuki Odagiri (1985). Zvi Griliches and Jacques Mairesse (1985) have used firm-level data, and Pierre Mohnen, M. Ishaq Nadiri, and Ingmar Prucha (1985) have used manufacturing sector data for this purpose. There have been no attempts to disaggregate $R\&D$, the principal focus of attention here.

TABLE 1–REGRESSION COEFFICIENTS TO EXPLAIN
RATES OF PRODUCTIVITY INCREASE,
2-DIGIT MANUFACTURING INDUSTRIES,
JAPAN AND THE UNITED STATES

| r_i | Independent Variables[a] | | | R^2 |
	I_i	A_i	B_i	
	Japan (1960–79)[b]			
0.42	–	–	–	0.34
(2.78)				
0.33	0.05	–	–	0.38
(1.88)	(0.91)			
–	0.05	0.54	−1.52	0.40
	(0.95)	(1.59)	(0.58)	
–	–	0.60	−1.23	0.36
		(1.84)	(0.48)	
	United States (1948–66)[c]			
–	–	0.07	1.49	0.63
		(2.75)	(3.34)	

[a] I_i is the proportion of technology import agreements in the ith industry, A_i is the ratio of applied $R\&D$ expenditure to value-added in the ith industry, and B_i is the ratio of basic research expenditure to value-added in the ith industry. The number in parentheses below each regression coefficient is its t-value.

[b] The Japanese industries included are the same as those used in Odagiri, except that (i) textiles and apparel, and (ii) motor vehicles and other transportation equipment are not combined. Thus, the sample size is 17.

[c] Another variable included in the U.S. regression is the percent of an industry's workers that are unionized. Many investigators have found this variable to be significant in the United States, but Odagiri reports that it has not been significant in Japan. Frequently, in models of this sort, the amount of $R\&D$ that is embodied in an industry's purchased inputs (divided by its value-added) is used as another explanatory variable. My article (1980) found that it was significant in the United States, but Odagiri's results suggest that it is not significant in Japan.

To estimate this model, I used Kuroda's data concerning ρ_i for 2-digit manufacturing industries in Japan for 1960–79 and his data concerning 1972 value-added in these industries, together with OECD data concerning 1972 $R\&D$ expenditures, to calculate r_i. The least squares estimate of $\bar{\Phi}$, shown in Table 1, indicates that, in Japan, an industry's rate of productivity growth was significantly related to its ratio of $R\&D$ expenditure to value-added during this period. Since previous studies often have used estimates of $\bar{\Phi}$ as measures of the rate of return from $R\&D$, it is interesting to note that, if such an interpretation is adopted, the rate of return was about 42 percent, which is relatively high. However, as many of us have stressed, such measures of the rate of return

from $R\&D$ are exceedingly crude, particularly for industry-level data.[2]

Because $R\&D$-intensive industries have tended to be the biggest importers of foreign technology, some of the apparent effect of domestic $R\&D$ on productivity increase may really have been the effect of imported technology. (As is well known, Japan's relatively rapid rate of technological change has been due largely to the importation of foreign technology.) To see whether this is the case, I introduced as an additional variable in equation (3) the proportion of technology import agreements during 1950–65 in the ith industry. As expected, the regression coefficient of r_i falls when this variable is introduced, but not by much. It still is about 33 percent, which is relatively high.

II. Basic Research vs. Applied $R\&D$

In the United States, the variation among industries (and firms) in ρ_i can be explained more completely if basic research expenditure is distinguished from applied research and development expenditure in equation (3). To see whether this was true in Japan as well, I used two variables—the ratio of applied $R\&D$ expenditure to value-added and the ratio of basic research expenditure to value-added—in place of r_i in equation (3). As shown in Table 1, the ratio of basic research to value-added does not have a statistically significant effect on ρ_i. However, the estimated regression coefficient of the ratio of applied research and development to value-added is about 60 percent, which is quite large.

It is interesting to compare these regression results for Japan with my earlier results for the United States (reproduced in part in

[2] The effects of $R\&D$ often occur with a lag (which for basic research can be quite long). Because so little is known about these lags, it is very difficult to include them properly in a model of this sort (see my 1980 article). Also, a variety of other problems and limitations have been identified, many of which are less serious for firm-level than industry-level data. Despite these criticisms, these measures have been used repeatedly to estimate rates of return.

Table 1). If we ignore the many reasons why these regression coefficients are likely to be very crude measures of rates of return, such a comparison suggests that American firms have obtained higher returns from basic research than the Japanese, whereas the Japanese have obtained higher returns from applied $R \& D$ than the Americans. Such a result seems reasonable. Because Japan has been able to draw at relatively small cost on a rich stock of foreign technology that was more advanced than its own, and because a relatively small percentage of Japan's industrial $R \& D$ has been financed by the government (and has gone largely for noncommercial purposes), it is entirely reasonable that the rate of return from applied $R \& D$ may have been higher in Japan than in the United States. Also, Japan's emphasis on process rather than product technology (discussed in Section III) may have enhanced the payoff from its applied $R \& D$. Because of differences between the two countries in the extent of the external benefits to industrial basic research from university research, it is also reasonable that the rate of return from industrial basic research may have been lower in Japan than in the United States. In the United States, there often have been close working relationships between basic researchers in industry and their colleagues in the universities. In Japan, university research seems to have played a lesser role (and seems to have been less highly regarded) than in the United States.

III. Industrial $R \& D$: Intensity and Composition

If it is true that the rate of return from applied $R \& D$ in Japan has been relatively high, one can readily understand why the $R \& D$ intensity of manufacturing firms has increased more rapidly in Japan than in the United States. In 1986, company-financed $R \& D$ expenditures were about 2.7 percent of sales in Japan, in comparison with about 2.8 percent in 1985 in the United States. In 1970, the corresponding figures were 1.3 percent for Japan and 2.2 percent for the United States. In all industries other than machinery, instruments, paper, and petroleum, Japan has narrowed the gap substan-

tially. In some industries (food, textiles, metals, and rubber) Japan now leads; in other industries (paper, petroleum, machinery, and instruments) the United States now leads; and in the rest there is a relatively small difference in $R \& D$ intensity.

Since data on total $R \& D$ expenditures, while useful, are difficult to interpret because $R \& D$ projects are so heterogeneous, I collected data concerning the composition of their $R \& D$ expenditures from a carefully selected sample of Japanese and American firms. Fifty Japanese firms were chosen at random in the chemical, electrical equipment, instrument, machinery, rubber, and metals industries, and for each Japanese firm we picked at random an American firm of the same industry and approximate size. The firms in our sample carry out about 25 percent of the $R \& D$ in each country in these industries. Detailed information was procured from each of these 100 firms (50 matched pairs) concerning the percentage of its 1985 $R \& D$ expenditures devoted to 1) basic research, 2) applied research, 3) product (rather than process) technology, 4) projects aimed at entirely new products and processes, 5) projects with less than a 0.5 estimated chance of success, and 6) projects expected to last longer than 5 years.

Based on the results, the Japanese seem to devote about as large a percentage of their $R \& D$ expenditures to relatively risky and long-term projects as do American firms (Table 2). This differs greatly from the early 1970's, when Merton Peck and Shuji Tamura (1976) characterized Japanese industrial $R \& D$ as composed very largely of "low-risk and short-term projects." Nonetheless, it would be a mistake to think that Japanese and American industrial $R \& D$ have become essentially the same. Whereas American firms report that almost half of their $R \& D$ expenditures are going for projects aimed at entirely new products and processes, Japanese firms report that only about one-third of their $R \& D$ expenditures go for this purpose. (Outside the chemical industry, where there is little difference in this regard, the gap is even wider.) Of course, this is in accord with a great deal of anecdotal information to the effect that the Japanese devote

TABLE 2—COMPOSITION OF R&D EXPENDITURES,
100 FIRMS (50 MATCHED PAIRS),
JAPAN AND THE UNITED STATES, 1985[a]

Percent of R&D Expenditures Devoted to:	Japan	United States
Basic Research	10	8
Applied Research	27	23
Products (rather than processes)	36	68
Entirely New Products and Processes	32	47
Projects with less than 0.5 Estimated Chance of Success	26	28
Projects Expected to Last Longer than 5 Years	38	38

[a] The number of firms in each industry is chemicals (including drugs), 36; electrical and instruments, 20; machinery (including computers), 30; and rubber and metals, 14.

more of their R&D resources to the improvement and adaptation of existing products and processes (rather than to the development of entirely new products and processes) than do American firms.

Even more striking is the difference between Japanese and American firms in their allocation of R&D resources between projects aimed at improved *product* technology and projects aimed at improved *process* technology. The American firms in my sample devote about two-thirds of their R&D expenditures to improved product technology (new products and product changes) and about one-third to improved process technology (new processes and process changes). Among the Japanese firms, on the other hand, the proportions are reversed, two-thirds going for improved process technology and one-third going for improved product technology. Harking back to my results in Section II, Japan's greater emphasis on process technology probably accounts in part for its relatively high estimated value of $\bar{\phi}$, since process R&D tends to have a bigger effect on an industry's own rate of productivity increase than does product R&D.[3]

[3] From the point of view of the economy as a whole, a large proportion of the resources allocated to product technology in the United States really goes for processes,

These results shed new light on a major issue concerning industrial R&D in the United States. Many observers have criticized American industry for neglecting process innovation. As the President's Commission on Industrial Competitiveness puts it, "It does us little good to design state-of-the-art products, if within a short time our foreign competitors can manufacture them more cheaply" (1985, p. 20). Contrary to the common impression that U.S. firms have in recent years begun to react to such criticism by paying more attention to process innovation than in the past, my results do not indicate that there was any perceptible increase between 1976 and 1985 in the proportion of their R&D expenditures devoted to new or improved processes. Thus, in terms of the allocation of their R&D funds, American firms do not seem to have put more emphasis on processes, despite this criticism.

IV. Industrial R&D: Sources and Size of Firm

Some important differences between the industrial R&D efforts in Japan and the United States can be highlighted by looking at the sources of R&D projects in the two countries. Detailed data on this score were obtained from a random sample of 65 American and 35 Japanese firms in the chemical, electrical equipment, machinery, motor vehicle, instruments, and metals industries.[4] The results (in Table 3) indicate

since one firm's products frequently are parts of another firm's processes. Consequently, this difference between Japan and the United States reflects a difference in how much of the process R&D for a given product is carried out by the producers of the product and how much is done by equipment producers and other suppliers of the producers of the product. As many authors have stressed, there can be disadvantages in leaving this sort of R&D to the latter firms. (Also, differences in industry and firm structure are relevant.) Many studies indicate that process R&D has a bigger effect on productivity than does product R&D. However, many of the effects on productivity resulting from new products occur in the industries using them, not in those selling them, and there are difficulties in taking proper account of quality changes, as well as other problems in measuring the benefits from new products.

[4] The American firms were chosen at random from the listing of major firms in these industries in *Business Week*, July 9, 1984. The Japanese firms were chosen at

TABLE 3—SOURCES OF R&D PROJECTS, 100 FIRMS, JAPAN AND UNITED STATES, 1985

Industry/ Country[a]	Percent of R&D Projects Suggested by:			
	R&D	Marketing	Production	Customers
Total				
Japan	47	18	15	15
U.S.	58	21	9	9
Chemicals				
Japan	49	23	15	3
U.S.	45	25	14	8
Electrical				
Japan	47	21	5	27
U.S.	90	7	1	1
Machinery				
Japan	44	22	11	20
U.S.	56	21	4	18
Autos, Instruments, and Metals				
Japan	48	8	26	13
U.S.	51	25	12	11

[a] The sample sizes are all industries combined, 100; chemicals, 26; electrical, 20; machinery, 26; and autos, instruments, and metals, 28.

that Japanese firms base about one-third of their R&D projects on suggestions from their production personnel and customers, whereas only about one-sixth of American projects stem from these sources. The greater importance of production personnel as sources of R&D projects in Japan is a reflection of their greater emphasis (described in Section III) on process technology. The greater importance of customers as sources of R&D projects in Japan stems from the very close relations there, noted by Henry Riggs (1985) and others, between firms and their customers. What is especially noteworthy is that both production personnel and customers tend to be users of a firm's R&D results, and that the Japanese seem to give users a more important role than do Americans in shaping their R&D programs.

Particularly in the electrical equipment industry, American firms tend to base a larger percentage of their R&D projects on suggestions from R&D personnel than do Japanese firms. This is in accord with Riggs' hypothesis that, whereas Japanese firms are better able to carry out advances inspired or driven by users, American firms are better able than their Japanese rivals "to capitalize on opportunities...which are derived from, or inspired by, technology (the research laboratory)..." (p. 10). Also, it is consistent with Masohiko Aoki's belief that American firms put more emphasis than do Japanese firms on the "scientific efforts of professionally trained researchers in R&D under the entrepreneurial direction of top management" (1986, p. 981).

Another difference between Japan and the United States pertains to R&D expenditures aimed at entirely new products and processes. In the United States, increases in firm size tend to be associated with less than proportionate increases in the amount spent on such R&D. In Japan, on the other hand, increases in firm size tend to be associated with more than proportionate increases in the amount spent on such R&D. Thus, relative to smaller firms, the largest firms tend to carry out a disproportionately greater amount of this very ambitious R&D in Japan than in the United States. This may be one reason why small and moderate-sized firms in Japan seem to have contributed less to innovation than their counterparts in the United States.

V. Conclusions

Many observers are impressed by the efficiency of Japanese industrial R&D. Indeed, the president of the Semiconductor Research Corporation has gone so far as to state that: "The United States may never match Japan's R&D efficiency." (See L. Sumney and R. Burger 1987, p. 40.) If one is willing to interpret the regression coefficients in Table 1 as rates of return, my results are consistent with the contention that applied R&D in Japan has yielded a higher return than in the United States. This contention seems reasonable, given Japan's greater emphasis on commercial (rather than government-financed) projects and its reliance on advanced technology from the West, which could be adapted and improved at relatively low cost. But this is only part of the story. My findings provide for the first time data showing the great extent to which Japan has focused on process technology, which according to many experts has tended to be neglected in the United States. Also, I show elsewhere (forthcoming) that Japanese firms

random from *International Dun and Bradstreet.* These same frames were used for the samples in Table 2.

seem to have been much faster and more efficient imitators than American firms. Almost certainly, these factors too have contributed to the effectiveness of applied R&D in Japan.

On the other hand, there is no evidence that basic research has been relatively fruitful in Japan. Moreover, based on the findings in my forthcoming paper, there is no evidence that Japanese firms have been faster or more efficient innovators than American firms in cases where the innovation has been based on internal, rather than external, technology. Apparently, the Japanese advantage has been confined largely to applied R&D, particularly R&D concerned with the adaptation and improvement of existing technology.

Faced with the Japanese technological challenge, American firms might respond by putting more resources into process R&D, which would make it more difficult for Japanese firms and others to appropriate a large share of the benefits from American product innovations. Also, American firms might increase their own capacity to imitate quickly, efficiently, and creatively. If they respond effectively, there is no reason why the United States cannot increase the economic returns from its industrial R&D, although it is inevitable—and by no means undesirable, both from the point of view of the United States and of the world as a whole—that many of the economic benefits from this R&D will continue to accrue to other nations.

REFERENCES

Aoki, Masohiko, "Horizontal vs. Vertical Information Structure of the Firm," *American Economic Review*, December 1986, 76, 971–83.

Griliches, Zvi and Mairesse, Jacques, "R&D and Productivity Growth: Comparing Japanese and U.S. Manufacturing Firms,"

NBER Working Paper, 1985.

Jorgenson, D., Kuroda, M. and Nishimizu, M., "Japan-U.S. Industry-Level Productivity Comparison, 1960–79," Conference on Research in Income and Wealth, 1985.

Mansfield, Edwin, "The Speed and Cost of Industrial Innovation in Japan and the United States: External vs. Internal Technology," *Management Science*, forthcoming.

_____, (1987a) "The Diffusion of Industrial Robots in Japan and the United States," Center for Economics and Technology, University of Pennsylvania, 1987.

_____, (1987b) "Firm Growth, Innovation, and R and D in Robotics: Japan and the United States," Symposium on Research and Development, Industrial Change, and Economic Policy, University of Karlstad, Sweden, 1987.

_____, "Basic Research and Productivity Increase in Manufacturing," *American Economic Review*, December 1980, 70, 863–73.

Mohnen, Pierre, Nadiri, M. I. and Prucha, Ingmar, "R and D, Production Structure, and Rates of Return in the U.S., Japanese, and German Manufacturing Sectors," *European Economic Review*, 1986, 30, 749–71.

Odagiri, Hiroyuki, "Research Activity, Output Growth, and Productivity Increase in Japanese Manufacturing Industries," *Research Policy*, 1985, 14, 117–30.

Peck, Merton and Tamura, Shuji, "Technology," in H. Patrick and H. Rosovsky, eds., *Asia's New Giant*, Washington: The Brookings Institution, 1976.

Riggs, Henry, "Innovation: A U.S.–Japan Perspective," Stanford University High-Technology Research Project, September 1985.

Sumney, L. and Burger, R., "A Semiconductor Strategy," *Issues in Science and Technology*, Summer 1987, 3, 32–41.

President's Commission on Industrial Competitiveness, *Global Competition: The New Reality*, Washington: USGPO, 1985.

PART III

TECHNOLOGICAL FORECASTING

13

15 Technological Forecasting

E. Mansfield

I. INTRODUCTION

The past decade has seen a spectacular increase in the amount of attention devoted to technological forecasting by social scientists, management scientists, and others involved in R & D planning, industrial management, defence problems, environmental protection, technology assessment, and a host of other areas. Books and articles in considerable number have appeared on the subject.[1] New journals devoted entirely to this subject have been born.[2] Firms and research organisations specialising in the subject have sprouted in various parts of the United States – and the world. Given the impressive amount of activity in this area, the time seems ripe to survey and appraise what has been going on. In particular, what is meant by 'technological forecasting'? What sorts of techniques and models have the technological forecasters developed? How accurate are these techniques and models? To what extent are they used? What are the problems and defects in existing techniques and models, and how can they be improved? My purpose in this paper is to answer these questions as best as I can within the space available.

It is customary in the literature on technological forecasting to distinguish between *exploratory technological forecasting* and *normative technological forecasting*. Exploratory technological forecasting attempts to predict the technological state-of-the-art that will be attained and used at future points in time if certain conditions – such as levels of research support – are met. On the other hand, normative technological forecasting attempts to specify a rational allocation of resources – research and development personnel, facilities, and so forth – among alternative uses in an attempt to influence the rate and direction of technological change within a firm, a government organisation, or the country as a whole. Needless to say, these two broad classes of technological forecasts are closely

[1] Among the most prominent texts on this subject are E. Jantsch, *Technological Forecasting in Perspective* (O.E.C.D., 1967); J. Bright, *Technological Forecasting for Industry and Government* (Prentice–Hall, 1968); M. Cetron, *Technological Forecasting: A Practical Approach* (Gordon and Breach, 1969); and R. Ayres, *Technological Forecasting and Long-Range Planning* (McGraw–Hill, 1969).

[2] Examples are *Technological Forecasting and Social Change* and *Futures*. Also, articles on this subject are found in journals like *R and D Management, Research Policy, Technology Assessment*, and *Long Range Planning*.

related. However, in keeping with most discussions of this subject, I shall treat these two classes separately. Sections II–VI deal primarily with exploratory technological forecasting, Sections VII–X deal primarily with normative technological forecasting, and Section XI provides some concluding remarks concerning both types of technological forecasting.

II. INTUITIVE AND DELPHI METHODS

It is widely agreed that technology is a relatively difficult variable to forecast, because there is so much uncertainty concerning what will be produced by R & D efforts, and concerning what breakthroughs will occur, and when. How do the people engaged in technological forecasting go about making their forecasts? According to various surveys, as well as the leading texts on technological forecasting, simple intuitive projections seem to play a very important role in exploratory technological forecasting.[1] For example, suppose that a firm or government agency wants to forecast the maximum speed of commercial aircraft in 1985. One way of obtaining such a forecast is simply to ask an expert, or group of experts, to guess as best they can what the maximum speed will be at that time. Certainly, this approach is straightforward enough and relatively cheap. But it runs into a number of difficulties. First, technologists are no more in agreement about the future than economists are, the result being that the answer is likely to vary, depending on the choice of expert. Second, even when based on the opinion of distinguished experts, such forecasts can contain large errors. For example, Vannevar Bush predicted in 1945 that a 3,000 mile rocket would 'be impossible for many years'.[2]

To cope with some of the problems involved in simply asking a group of experts for a consensus guess, Helmer and Gordon, while at the RAND Corporation formulated a technique, known as the Delphi method, which attempts to utilise expert opinion more effectively. For example, to forecast the maximum speed of commercial aircraft in 1985, users of the Delphi method would ask a number of experts to formulate separate and independent estimates. Then the median and inter-quartile range of the estimates would be communicated to each of the experts, and they would be asked to reconsider their previous answers and revise them if they wanted to.

---

[1] For some results of a survey of firms to determine the sorts of technological forecasting techniques in use, see M. Cetron and C. Ralph, *Industrial Applications of Technological Forecasting* (Wiley, 1971).

[2] For other examples see E. Mansfield, *The Economics of Technological Change* (Norton, 1968) pp. 38-40.

Then those people whose answers lie outside the inter-quartile range would be asked to state why they disagree to this extent from the other members of the group. Then their replies would be circulated among the group, and the members would be asked once again to make a forecast. This iterative process would continue until there was a reasonable convergence of the individual forecasts.

The Delphi method has been used in fields as diverse as defence, pharmaceuticals, political science, and educational technology. According to its developers, it is a useful tool for technological forecasting. However, it is important to recognise the obvious fact that the results of the Delphi method can be no better than the foresight of the individual experts. And as noted above, this foresight can be very imperfect. Moreover, by relying so heavily on a consensus, the Delphi method assumes that collective judgement is better than individual judgement. This is a dangerous assumption, as evidenced by the many important technological advances that have been made by individuals and groups that acted contrary to prevailing majority – and elite – opinion.[1]

III. TREND EXTRAPOLATION AND LEAD-LAG RELATIONSHIPS

Another technique that plays an important role in exploratory technological forecasting is simple trend extrapolation. For example, to forecast the maximum speed of commercial aircraft in 1985, one could obtain a time series of the maximum speed of such aircraft at various points in history, and project the historical trend into the future. In fact, this simple sort of extrapolation technique has been used in the U.S. Department of Defense, where much of the work on technological forecasting originated.[2] It has also been used in commercial work of various kinds. Of course, economists themselves

---

[1] See the articles by O. Helmer and T. Gordon in J. Bright, op. cit. Also, see T. Gordon and O. Helmer, *Report on a Long-Range Forecasting Study*, RAND Corporation Report P-2982 (Sep 1964).

Another well-known technique based on subjective estimates is the 'cross-impact method', also pioneered by Gordon and Helmer. According to this method, one estimates the effects of one event on the probability of occurrence of other events. Then one goes through a Monte Carlo process to estimate the unconditional probabilities of occurrence of various events. See T. Gordon and H. Becker, 'The Cross-Impact Approach to Technology Assessment', *Research Management* (July 1972); and N. Dalkey, 'An Elements Cross-Impact Model', *Technological Forecasting and Social Change* (1972).

[2] For example, see R. Lenz, 'Practical Application of Technical Trend Forecasting', in M. Cetron and J. Goldhar, *The Science of Managing Organized Technology* (Gordon and Breach, 1970), and R. Lenz 'Technological Forecasting Methodology', in Cetron and Ralph, op. cit.

have long used such techniques. For example, about twenty years ago, John Kendrick discussed the use of such crude techniques to forecast productivity change in the American economy.[1]

The problem with naïve extrapolation techniques of this sort is that, unless the fundamental factors determining the technological parameter in question operate much as they have in the past, previous trends will not necessarily be a good guide to the future. For example, a host of factors, including the allocation of R & D resources and the pressure of environmental concerns, may see to it that the maximum speed of commercial aircraft increases at quite a different rate than it has in the immediate past. Or take the case of productivity increase. There is considerable evidence that productivity increase has not occurred at a constant rate in the United States. The moral, well known to economists, is that a naïve projection of historical trends is a dangerous business, particularly when long-term forecasts are being made.

Besides trend extrapolation, the technological forecasters have adopted another old favourite of the economic forecasters – lead–lag relationships. For example, to forecast the maximum speed of commercial aircraft in 1985, one could plot the maximum speed of commercial aircraft against the maximum speed of military aircraft. Finding that commercial speeds have lagged military speeds, one might be able to use this relationship to make the desired forecast.[2] Of course, here too the problem is that the historical relationship may not continue into the future.

IV. THE USE OF INPUT–OUTPUT MODELS

The available evidence indicates that most exploratory technical forecasts, both in industry and in government, are based on the simple intuitive methods and extrapolation techniques described in the previous two sections. In addition, however, there has been some experimentation with at least three types of somewhat more sophisticated types of exploratory forecasting techniques: input–output models, production models containing R & D expenditures, and diffusion models. To begin with, let us consider the use of input–output models. There has been some experimentation with the projection of input–output structures into the future. In order to make such projections, one must forecast both the input requirements of future techniques and the rate of diffusion of future

[1] J. Kendrick, 'National Productivity and Its Long-Term Projection', in National Bureau of Economic Research, *Long-Range Economic Projection* (Princeton, 1954).
[2] For example, see Lenz, op. cit.

M.

techniques, since the input-output coefficients will be a weighted average of existing and future techniques, the weights depending on the rate of diffusion.

In this section, we shall focus attention on the estimation of the input requirements for future techniques, since the estimation of the rate of diffusion is discussed in Section VI. One way that economists have tried to forecast input-output coefficients in a particular industry is to assume that new technologies have a weight proportional to investment in new capacity. By observing the changes in the industry's average input-output structure, and its expenditures on new plant and equipment, one can estimate what the input-output coefficients for the new 'layer' of capital must have been. Then, to make short-term projections, one can assume that the coefficients for the new 'layer' will remain constant, and increase the weight given to these coefficients (in proportion to expected invest-investment). This method, used by the Harvard Economic Research Project, is crude at best. All that its users claim is that it gives 'ballpark' estimates.[1]

Another way of projecting input-output structures is through the use of expert opinion. For example, Battelle Memorial Institute and Scientific American are sponsoring a study of this sort, the object being to estimate inter-industry purchases, including labour requirements, per dollar of output for a 'typical' new plant to go onstream in 1975.[2] About 100 industries are included in the study. As recognised by the study's authors, these projections are plagued by the same sorts of difficulties we cited in Section II. Moreover, there are other problems as well. For one thing, the industrial classification employed in the input-output model is broader than the product categories that the technologists making the forecasts are used to dealing with. For another thing, it is difficult to include qualitative changes, like new products, within the input-output framework. At present, the use of input-output analysis in connection with technological forecasting is still in its infancy. All that can be said is that it represents a promising area for future research.

V. PRODUCTION MODELS CONTAINING R & D EXPENDITURES

Next, let's consider the use of production models containing R & D expenditures. In recent years, a number of economists, including

[1] A. Carter, 'Technological Forecasting and Input-Output Analysis', *Technological Forecasting and Social Change* (1970) pp. 331-45.
[2] Ibid.

Solow,[1] Denison,[2] Griliches[3] and myself,[4] have attempted to formulate econometric models of production in which research and development plays a role. These models are over-simplified and incomplete in many respects. Yet they provide reasonably persuasive evidence that R & D has a significant effect on the rate of productivity increase in the industries and time periods that have been studied. For example, in his study of agriculture, Griliches investigated the relationship in various years between output per farm in a given state and the amounts of land, labour, fertiliser, and machinery per farm, as well as average education and expenditures on research and extension in a given state. The results indicate that, holding other inputs constant, output was related in a statistically significant way to the amount spent on research and extension. Turning to manufacturing, a study of my own, based on data regarding ten large chemical and petroleum firms and ten manufacturing industries, indicated that the measured rate of productivity change was related in a statistically significant way to the rate of growth of cumulated R & D expenditures made by the firm or industry.

These models can be used for technological forecasting. In particular, they can be used to forecast the effects on productivity or output of a certain investment in research and development at various points in time.[5] Moreover, they can be used to forecast future requirements for labour and other inputs.[6] Of course, they cannot be used to forecast the precise nature of the technology that will result from an investment in R & D. But they can provide some idea of the input–output relationships that this technology will permit – and for many purposes these relationships are what really count. For example, if we can be reasonably sure that a given investment in R & D will result in a certain reduction in cost (or in the use of certain crucial inputs), this may be all that is really relevant in making

[1] R. Solow, 'Technical Change and the Aggregate Production Function', *Review of Economics and Statistics* (Aug 1957).

[2] E. Denison, *The Sources of Growth in the United States*, Committee for Economic Development (1962).

[3] Z. Griliches, 'Research Expenditures, Education, and the Aggregate Agricultural Production Function', *American Economic Review* (Dec 1964).

[4] E. Mansfield, *Industrial Research and Technological Innovation* (W. W. Norton for the Cowles Foundation for Research in Economics at Yale University, 1968).

[5] Somewhat similar models have been used in defence. For example, see C. Trozzo, 'Productivity of Defense R D T and E', Institute for Defense Analysis, Paper P–825 (Oct 1971). Also see R. Isenson, 'Technological Forecasting Lessons from Project Hindsight', in Bright, op. cit.

[6] For example see E. Mansfield, 'Innovation and Technical Change in the Railroad Industry', in National Bureau of Economic Research, *Transportation Economics* (Columbia University Press, 1965).

certain decisions. The precise nature of the new technology may not matter much.

It might be noted that some of our government agencies have become interested in these models in recent years. Specifically, these models suggest that the marginal rate of return from certain types of civilian R & D is very high, and that we may be under-investing in such R & D. It is difficult, of course, to tell how much influence these models had on the recent decisions by the American government to experiment with various devices to encourage additional R & D in various civilian areas. But I know that they were one of the influences at work. However, lest anyone gets the impression that these models are sufficiently dependable to play a dominant role in influencing such decisions, let me add that they are extremely crude and subject to considerable error. In a recent paper, I set forth a rather detailed evaluation of these models and a list of relevant areas and topics that, in my opinion, are in need of further research.[1] Much more work needs to be done.

VI. DIFFUSION MODELS

Finally, let's consider the use of diffusion models. In the past fifteen years, a number of studies have been made of the diffusion of innovations. The results suggest that it is possible, on the basis of fairly simple econometric models, to explain fairly well the differences among industrial innovations in their rate of diffusion. In 1961, I presented a simple model – based on variables like the profitability of the innovation, the size of the investment required to adopt the innovation, and the organisation of the industry of potential users – to explain differences in the rate at which innovations spread.[2] This model explained the rates of diffusion of a dozen major innovations in the United States very well. Moreover, subsequent work has shown that it is also useful in explaining the rates of diffusion of other innovations – and in other countries.[3]

[1] See E. Mansfield, 'Contribution of Research and Development to Economic Growth in the United States', *Science*, 8 Feb 1972. Also see the papers by Griliches, Minasian, Terleckij, Fellner and Nelson cited there.

[2] E. Mansfield, 'Technical Change and the Rate of Imitation', *Econometrica* (Oct 1961). Also see Z. Griliches, 'Hybrid Corn: An Exploration in the Economics of Technological Change', *Econometrica* (Oct 1957), and E. Rogers, *Diffusion of Innovations* (the Free Press, 1962).

[3] See E. Mansfield, J. Rapoport, J. Schnee, S. Wagner and M. Hamburger, *Research and Innovation in the Modern Corporation* (Norton, 1971), R. Hsia, 'Technological Change in the Industrial Growth of Hong Kong', in B. R. Williams (ed.), *Science and Technology in Economic Growth* (Macmillan, London, 1973), and the unpublished doctoral dissertations of F. Husic and A. Romeo, both carried out at the University of Pennsylvania.

Models of this sort can be used for technological forecasting. For many purposes, it is extremely important to know how rapidly a new technique will displace an old one. Obviously, this is of crucial importance to the firm marketing the new technique. But it may be of great importance to other groups as well. For example, government agencies are sometimes concerned with the extent to which labour will be displaced and the way in which particular areas will be affected. Also, labour unions and competing firms have a great interest in this question. For many purposes, the important consideration is not when an entirely new process or product will be invented in the future. Instead, it is how rapidly one can expect the new processes and products that have already been invented to diffuse. Certainly, in view of the long time lags in many sectors of the economy, this often is all that matters in the short run – and the intermediate run as well.

Diffusion models have found a variety of uses in technological forecasting. My own model has been used to forecast the rate of diffusion of numerically controlled machine tools in the tool and die industry.[1] Subsequent events indicate that, so far at least, these forecasts, made for a government agency, have been quite accurate.[2] In addition, this model has been used by a number of firms in a variety of industries. For example, a leading chemical firm has been experimenting with the use of this model to forecast the market penetration of its new products. And a leading aircraft engine manufacturer has used this model in its internal planning.[3] Of course, the fact that this model has been used does not mean that it is other than a simple first approximation. We are continually refining it and testing it on a wider and wider variety of technological and product areas. We are still far from having a satisfactory understanding of the diffusion process.

VII. NORMATIVE TECHNOLOGICAL FORECASTING

As pointed out in Section II, normative technological forecasting attempts to specify a rational allocation of R & D resources. More specifically, most of the literature on normative technological fore-

[1] It might also be noted that the 'substitution model' used by some technological forecasters is similar to models developed by economists: Apparently, some technological forecasters, unaware of the economics literature, do not realise that the parameters of their models can be explained by economic models.

[2] E. Mansfield, 'Determinants of the Speed of Application of New Technology', in B. R. Williams, op. cit.

[3] A. Wade Blackman, 'The Rate of Innovation in the Commercial Aircraft Jet Engine Market', *Technological Forecasting and Social Change* (1971).

casting is concerned with the choice of R & D projects. A variety of models have been developed to help solve this problem. These models vary enormously in sophistication, some relying on the crudest sorts of ranking procedures, some employing fairly straight-forward adaptations of capital budgeting techniques, some using linear programming, some using dynamic programming, and some using Bayesian decision theory. Among the best known of these techniques are PROFILE (Programmed Functional Indices for Laboratory Evaluation) and QUEST (Quantitative Utility Estimates for Science and Technology), both of which were developed for the U.S. Navy, and PATTERN (Planning Assistance Through Technical Evaluation of Relevance Numbers), developed by Honeywell.[1]

For present purposes, it is sufficient to present a relatively simple programming model to illustrate the nature of normative technological forecasting. Suppose that a firm has a list of n possible R & D projects that it might carry out and that the ith project would cost C_i dollars to carry out. Moreover, the ith project is estimated to have a probability of success of P_i, and if successful, it will result in a profit (gross of R & D costs) of π_i. Then, if the firm can spend no more than C dollars on R & D, its problem can be represented as follows:

Maximise
$$\sum_{i=1}^{n} X_i(P_i \pi_i - C_i),$$

where
$$\sum_{i=1}^{n} X_i C_i \leqslant C$$

and
$$X_i = 0, 1.$$

In other words, the firm's problem is to choose the X_i – where $X_i = 1$ if the ith project is accepted and 0 if it is rejected – in such a way that the expected value of profit is maximised, subject to the constraint that the total amount spent on R & D be no more than C. This, of course, is an integer programming problem.[1]

Of course, this is a relatively simple model. It is possible to make this model more realistic by recognising that the firm may be interested in parameters of the probability distribution of profit other

[1] See M. Cetron, R. Isenson, J. Johnson, A. Nutt and H. Wells, *Technical Resource Management Quantitative Methods* (M.I.T., 1969), as well as the works cited in n. 1, p. 334 and n. 1, p. 335 above.

[1] This model is somewhat similar to one proposed by R. Freeman, 'A Stochastic Model for Determining the Size and Allocation of the Research Budget', *IEEE Transactions on Engineering Management* (Mar 1960).

than the expected value. It is possible to recognise that, in most cases, there are a variety of expenditure levels at which a project can be carried out. It is possible to recognise that the impact of one project may depend on the outcome of another project. If one is willing to cope with the complexities and data requirements that result, it is possible to extend this model in many directions. But for present purposes, this simple model is a suitable illustration.[1]

VIII. THE APPLICATION OF NORMATIVE TECHNOLOGICAL FORECASTING

It is difficult to measure with accuracy the extent to which normative technological forecasting is being used in the United States. Our own surveys indicate that a large proportion of the laboratories – particularly the larger laboratories – in the chemical, drug, and electronics industries are using some form of quantitative project selection technique. But it is difficult to tell how significant such techniques are in the decision-making process. In some laboratories, they are taken much more seriously than in others. Indeed, one suspects strongly that in some laboratories these techniques are little more than window dressing, the real determinants of project selection – professional hunch, intra-firm politics, as well as a host of other factors – being at work behind the facade.[2]

However, one thing appears to be clear: the more sophisticated types of normative technological forecasting models are not being used very extensively. For example, Cetron and Ralph report that only 20 per cent of the firms responding to their survey had tested or used linear programming models and that only about 10 per cent had tested or used more complicated techniques like PROFILE, QUEST or PATTERN.[3] And for a variety of reasons, I suspect that these figures are over-estimates for American industry as a whole. In the American government, there has been considerable attention devoted to normative technological forecasting, particularly in the Department of Defense. But it is difficult to tell with any certainty the extent to which these models have actually been applied.

There are a number of reasons why the more sophisticated normative technological forecasting models have not found extensive use. First, even the more sophisticated models are often over-

---

[1] For more complex models, see the references in n. 1, p. 334 above.

[2] Mansfield, Rapoport, Schnee, Wagner and Hamburger, op. cit.

[3] Cetron and Ralph, op. cit. Also see N. Baker and W. Pound, 'R and D Project Selection: Where We Stand', *IEEE Transactions on Engineering Management* (June 1964).

simplified in important respects. For example, many models fail to recognise that R & D is a process of buying information, that 'unsuccessful' projects can provide much valuable information, and that the problem is one of sequential decision-making under uncertainty. Thus, they fall into the sorts of traps that the RAND studies of military R & D describe so well.[1] Second, application of the more sophisticated normative technological forecasting is not cheap. For example, Jantsch has estimated that the cost of setting up a PATTERN model is about $250,000 and that the cost of 'maintaining' the model is about $50,000 per year. Needless to say, many techniques do not cost nearly this much, but they are far from costless. Third, and perhaps most important, these models are based on estimates that are extremely unreliable, as we shall see in the following section.[2]

IX. ACCURACY OF ESTIMATES

Practically any normative technological forecasting model requires estimates of the cost of carrying out a prospective R & D project, the time that it will take, the probability that it will achieve certain results, and the value of these results, if achieved. Unfortunately, these estimates tend to be quite inaccurate. In the military field, it is well known that there tend to be large over-runs in R & D costs and lesser over-runs in R & D time. For example, Peck and Scherer found that for a sample of twelve airplane and missile development projects, the average ratio of actual to estimated cost was 3.2, and the average ratio of actual to estimated time was 1·4.[3] In civilian fields, there seems to be more optimism concerning the accuracy of these estimates, with a surprising number of R & D managers regarding such estimates as good or excellent. However, the available evidence indicates that these estimates are almost as bad for civilian as for military work when reasonably large technical advances are attempted.

Even when firms doing commercial work attempt relatively minor advances, these estimates tend to be considerably wide of the mark.

[1] T. Marschak, T. Glennan and R. Summers, *Strategy for R and D* (Springer Verlag, 1967).

[2] For a hard-hitting critique of the technological forecasting methods proposed in the works cited in n. 1, p. 334, n. 1, p. 335 and n. 1, p. 342, see E. Roberts, 'Exploratory and Normative Technological Forecasting: A Critical Appraisal', paper presented at the NATO Defence Research Group's Seminar on Technological Forecasting, 12–14 Nov 1968. Roberts describes some of the principal reasons why these methods have not found extensive use.

[3] M. Peck and F. Scherer, *The Weapons Acquisition Process* (Harvard University Press, 1962).

For example, in a proprietary drug firm we studied, the average ratio of actual to estimated development cost was 2.1, and the average ratio of actual to estimated development time was 2.9. Moreover, the standard deviation of the cost ratio was 3.2, and the standard deviation of the time ratio was 1.6. Clearly, these estimates of development cost and time were very inaccurate. Studies of the accuracy of estimates of the probability of technical success indicate that they too are not very trustworthy. For example, in the proprietary drug firm cited above, although the estimated probabilities of technical completion are of some use in predicting which projects will be completed and which will not, they are not of much use. Indeed, they do not do much better than one would expect by chance. To top it all off, it is generally agreed that the value of the R & D results, if achieved, is even harder to predict than the other things noted above. For example, the extent and duration of the market for a new product is very difficult to forecast.[1]

Given the large biases and errors in the estimates that are used in normative technological forecasting models, it is no wonder that managers have not been quick to adopt them. Indeed, as noted above, there is some evidence that managers may be more optimistic than they have a right to be about the accuracy of some of these estimates. If they had a better idea of how bad these estimates tended to be, they might be even more reluctant to place any dependence on them. With regard to these errors and biases, it should be noted that, to a considerable extent, they are not merely a product of uncertainty. It would be naïve to close one's eyes to the fact that these estimates are used to allocate the firm's or agency's resources. Consciously or unconsciously, cost and time estimates may be biased downward – and estimates of the value of research results may be biased upward – to 'sell' projects to management. This factor, as well as the uncertainties inherent in research and development, is responsible for the large errors in these estimates.

X. EXPERIMENTS TO IMPROVE THE ESTIMATES AND TO EXTEND THE MODELS

How can these estimates be improved? To try to find out, my co-workers and I have carried out several studies of the development and innovative process, particularly in the pharmaceutical and chemical industries, to see the extent to which econometric models

---

[1] For the results underlying this paragraph of the text, see Mansfield, Rapoport, Schnee, Wagner and Hamburger, op. cit. Also see D. Meadows, 'Estimate Accuracy and Project Selection Models in Industrial Research', *Industrial Management Review* (Spring 1968).

M*

can be used to forecast development cost. Needless to say, development cost is only one of many things that one would like to forecast, but it seemed to be a reasonable place to begin. The results have proved encouraging to date. For example, an attempt was made to explain a new drug's development cost by the nature of the new drug (product category, type and number of dosage forms, and spectrum of activity), the extent of the technological advance, the use of parallel development efforts, the priority attached to the project, and a trend term. When the accuracy of this model's forecasts was compared with the accuracy of the estimates made at the outset of each project by the firm, we found that, for most types of projects, the model-generated forecasts were more accurate than the firm's forecasts.[1]

In addition, econometric studies have been carried out to determine how long it takes to develop various types of products and to determine the extent of the non-R & D costs that are involved in successful product innovation in various industries. For example, models have been constructed to explain the percentage of the total costs of a product innovation that is incurred in the following stages of the innovation process: (1) applied research, (2) specification of product specifications, (3) prototype or pilot-plant design, construction and testing, (4) production planning, tooling, and construction and installation of manufacturing facilities, (5) manufacturing start-up, and (6) marketing start-up. These models may be of use in providing certain kinds of estimates needed in normative technological forecasting. They may also be of use in exploratory technological forecasting. For one thing, they demonstrate the important fact that major innovations generally take quite a long time to go from conceptualisation to commercial introduction. For example, the average time interval between the discovery of a new drug and its first commercial introduction in the United States seems to have been about five years – and this lag appears to be shorter than the lag in other industries.[2]

Despite the fact that research is going on to improve existing

---

[1] Most of the results in this section of the paper are described in more detail in ibid.

[2] Also see F. Lynn, 'An Investigation of the Rate of Development and Diffusion of Technology in Our Modern Industrial Society', *Report of the National Commission on Technology, Automation, and Economic Progress* (Washington, D.C., 1966), and C. Freeman, 'Research and Development in Electronic Capital Goods', *National Institute Economic Review* (Nov 1965).

These relatively long lags are also important in connection with technological assessment. For example see National Academy of Sciences, *Technology: Processes of Assessment and Choice*, Committee on Science and Astronautics, U.S. House of Representatives (July 1969), and National Academy of Engineering, *A Study of Technology Assessment*, Committee on Science and Astronautics, U.S. House of Representatives (July 1969).

estimates, it seems doubtful that we will ever be able to forecast the relevant variables very accurately. Thus, more emphasis should be placed on various kinds of sensitivity analysis to show the effects on the results of errors in the estimates. For example, returning to the model in Section VII, one could obtain data concerning the frequency distributions of the errors in C_i, P_i and π_i in the past. Then one could use these frequency distributions to generate a set of 'errors' that could be used to modify the estimates of C_i, P_i and π_i for each of the projects under consideration. Then one could solve the model a number of times, each solution corresponding to a random drawing of 'errors' from the historical frequency distributions. Finally, one could compute for each project the proportion of the cases where it was included in the optimal solution. A comparison among projects of the resulting proportions would indicate how sure one could be that various projects should be carried out.

XI. TECHNOLOGICAL FORECASTING: A BRIEF APPRAISAL

In conclusion, it seems fair to characterise the present state-of-the-art in technological forecasting as follows: First, most of the techniques commonly used for exploratory forecasting seem crude, even by the standards of the social and management sciences. In view of this crudeness, it seems unlikely that the results can be at all accurate. But as matters stand, one cannot even be sure of this, since there have been no studies measuring the track record of various kinds of technological forecasting techniques. Such studies seem to be called for. It would be useful to have some idea of how well these techniques have performed under various circumstances, and of which sorts of techniques seem to do better under particular kinds of circumstances. Without such information, it is hard for anyone to make decisions concerning the types of exploratory forecasting activities that are worth carrying out.

Second, although the crudeness of most existing techniques may be lamentable, there is no doubt that technological forecasting is a necessary part of the decision-making process in firms and government agencies. Just as there is no way to avoid forecasting the economic future – explicitly or implicitly – so there is no way to avoid forecasting the technological future. But this does not mean that it is necessarily worthwhile for a firm or government agency to support any formal work in technological forecasting. Whether or not it is worthwhile to support such work depends on whether – under the particular set of circumstances facing the firm or agency – the potential gains seem to outweight the costs.[1] And given the lack of reliable data regarding the likely gains from various kinds of technological forecasting, this is not an easy comparison to make.

Third, there is a great need for studies leading toward a better understanding of the process of technological change. Until the fundamental processes are somewhat better understood, it seems unlikely that much improvement will occur in exploratory forecasting techniques. The area that is perhaps best understood at present is the diffusion process – and this is the area where forecasting currently seems most effective. Needless to say, I am not suggesting that a moratorium be declared on technological forecasting until we understand the basic processes more thoroughly. What I am suggesting is that more emphasis be placed by researchers and practitioners on the accumulation of the basic knowledge that is required if this field is to become more of a science and less of an art.

Fourth, if normative technological forecasting is to become of widespread use, it is important that better methods be developed to estimate development cost, time, the probability of success, and the value of the outcome if achieved. At present, such estimates tend to be so biased and error-ridden that it is difficult to place much dependence on the results. There is some evidence that econometric models of the development process may result in improved estimates, but it will be some time before we will have any real idea of how far we can go along this route. In view of the inaccuracy of these estimates, organisations that use normative technological forecasting techniques would be well advised to carry out sensitivity analyses to see the effect of such errors on the results. And they would be well advised to see how big the errors in these estimates have been in the recent past – since there seems to be some tendency to underestimate their size.

Fifth, despite the problems in normative technological forecasting, it may be worthwhile for an organisation to devote some effort to such forecasting. After all, if the model is roughly correct – which admittedly is a big 'if', judging from some of the models that have been proposed – the model focuses attention on the relevant variables and forces people to think about them. Even if it is very difficult to come up with accurate estimates of these variables, an exercise of this sort can be worthwhile. (It is easy to underestimate the usefulness of such exercises, unless you have seen the way that some organisations actually work.) However, if such exercises are

---

[1] Thus, Quinn is, of course, quite correct in stressing that technological forecasts need not be completely, or even very accurate to be useful. The correct test is whether their value exceeds their cost. See J. Quinn, 'Technological Forecasting', *Harvard Business Review* (Mar 1967).

to have any real impact, the work of the technological forecasters must be integrated properly with the decisions of the planners and the managers. Too often, the work of the technological forecasters is largely ignored in the decision-making process. If this work is worth doing at all, it should be related and coupled with long-range planning and decision-making.[1]

Finally, it is important to recognise that technological forecasting, if done right, involves much more than just science and engineering. One cannot estimate the probability that a particular technology will come into being on the basis of technological considerations alone. Economic, social, and political considerations often play an equally important role. Moreover, one cannot decide how an organisation's technological resources should be allocated and utilised on the basis of technological considerations alone. Clearly, economic, social, political, and other considerations are involved here as well. Thus, regardless of what sort of mechanism a firm or agency uses to supply its technological forecasts – whether that mechanism be a formal group or an informal one, and whether it uses intuitive or more objective techniques – it is important that the mechanism be properly tuned in to the economic, social, and political environment, as well as to the relevant science and technology.

[1] See P. Thurston, 'Make TF Serve Corporate Planning', *Harvard Business Review* (Sep 1971), J: Dory and R. Lord, 'Does TF Really Work?', *Harvard Business Review* (Nov 1970), and Quinn, op. cit.

14

George Beardsley
California Polytechnic State University

Edwin Mansfield
University of Pennsylvania

A Note on the Accuracy of Industrial Forecasts of the Profitability of New Products and Processes*

Introduction

In making decisions about investments in new products and processes, firms must make forecasts of the profitability of alternative projects. Although several studies have been made of the accuracy of firms' estimates of R & D costs,[1] very little information is available concerning the accuracy of estimates of the profitability of investments in new products and processes.[2] In this paper, we present detailed empirical results of this sort concerning all of the major innovations developed by one of the nation's largest firms in 1960–64. These results should be of use to both researchers and policymakers concerned with technological innovation.

Changes over Time in Forecasting Errors

Our basic data pertain to a multibillion-dollar corporation in an industry that spends about the average percentage of sales on R & D. Because

Very little information is available concerning the accuracy of estimates of the profitability of investments in new products and processes. In this paper we present detailed empirical results on this score concerning all of the major innovations developed by one of the nation's largest firms in 1960–64. Because these data have been systematically and carefully updated by the firm, they provide a relatively unique opportunity to study how quickly forecasts of this sort converge on their true value. Also, we analyze the accuracy of the initial forecasts, both for new processes and new products, and discuss their possible implications for private and public policy.

* The work underlying this paper was supported by a grant to Mansfield from the Office of National R & D Assessment of the National Science Foundation. We are very much indebted to the cooperating firm for providing us with the basic data.

1. See Marschak, Glennan, and Summers 1967; Meadows 1968; and Mansfield et al. 1971.

2. One of the few studies of this sort that has been carried out is Tull (1967), whose study, although very useful, deals only with products (not processes) and provides no information concerning changes over time in the accuracy of a firm's forecast.

(*Journal of Business*, 1978, vol. 51, no. 1)
© 1978 by The University of Chicago
0021-9398/78/5101-0002$01.38

of its vast size, its R & D establishment is among the biggest in the country. Since 1960, this firm has made a careful inventory of the major new products and processes it has developed each year and forecasted the discounted profits from each such technological development.[3] Moreover, in each subsequent year, it has revised these forecasts in the light of new information. For example, after making its initial estimate in 1965 of the discounted profits from each process or product developed in 1964, revised estimates of this sort were made in 1966, 1967, 1968, and so on. Because these estimates have been systematically and carefully updated, they provide a relatively unique opportunity to study how quickly forecasts of this sort converge on their true value.

Based on this firm's experience, there frequently are rather significant revisions of the profit forecasts during the first 5 years after a new product or process is developed, but, as one would expect, these revisions become more minor as time goes on (and more and more of the uncertainties are resolved). By 9 years after the development process ends, it appears, in this firm at least, that a reasonably definitive estimate can be made of the discounted profits from the new technology. In very few cases are any significant revisions made in this profit estimate in the tenth to thirteenth year after termination of development. Thus, we can safely use the estimate of a new product's or new process's discounted profits made 9 years after its development as an adequate approximation to its actual discounted profits.

To see how rapidly the forecasting errors diminish as time goes on (after the development of a new product or process), we divide the forecast made 1 year later, 2 years later, and so on, for each product or process by its actual discounted profits (i.e., the forecast 9 years after development). Then, as a simple measure of the size of the forecasting errors, we calculate the proportion of cases where this ratio was greater than or equal to 2.0 or less than or equal to 0.5. Figure 1 shows the decrease that occurs in this measure of forecasting error as one revision after another is made in the forecasts.[4] The initial forecasts— those made 1 year after development—were generally quite poor, the proportion in figure 1 being 0.50 for processes and 0.62 for products. During the first 4 years after the initial forecast, the size of the forecasting error, as measured by this proportion, decreased at a relatively constant rate. By 5 years after development, this proportion was 0.06 for processes and 0.15 for products.

In this firm, there seemed to be a tendency during this period for these profitability estimates to be revised downward during the first

3. Only developments where the forecasted discounted profits exceed $200,000 are included; others are considered by the firm to be too important to be included.

4. For 2 and 3 years after development, forecasts for some of the processes and products were unavailable, but there is no reason to believe that this results in any bias. Also, the measure in fig. 1 is only one of many possible measures of forecasting error. As an alternative, we calculated the mean square deviation between the logarithms of the forecasted and actual discounted profits; the results are essentially the same as in fig. 1.

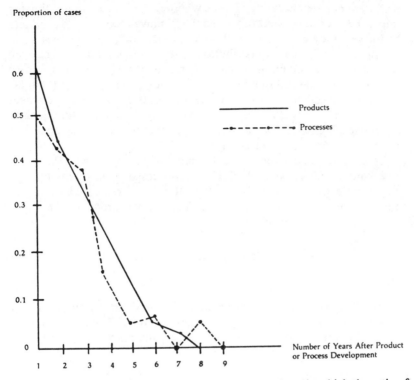

Fɪɢ. 1.—Proportion of new processes or new products in which the ratio of forecasted discounted profits to actual discounted profits was greater than (or equal to) 2.0 or less than (or equal to) 0.5, 57 new products and processes, 1–9 years after product or process development.

few years after the development of the new product or process. By about 4 or 5 years after its development, its discounted profits generally were underestimated, and the remaining revisions in these estimates tended to be upward. Whether or not this pattern is idiosyncratic to this firm is hard to say. But it would not be surprising if, in many firms, a few years of experience tended on balance to lessen profit expectations and if this tendency toward more pessimistic expectations were pushed too far. According to some observers, a tendency of this sort has existed in other kinds of innovative activity, such as the development and introduction of new weapons systems.[5]

Accuracy of Initial Forecasts

Figure 1 provides dramatic evidence that the initial profitability estimates for individual product and process innovations developed by this

5. See Klein 1965.

firm were not very accurate. To see whether the firm's initial estimates improved over time, we categorized the 57 new processes and products by the year they were developed—1960, 1961, 1962, 1963, or 1964—and calculated the frequency distribution of the ratio of initially forecasted to actual discounted profits in each such category.[6] The results, shown in table 1, indicate that there was no tendency (at least during 1960–64) for the initial estimates to improve over time. If the proportion of cases where the ratio is greater than (or equal to) 2.0 or less than (or equal to) 0.5 is used once more as a measure of forecasting error, this error was greater in 1964 than in earlier years.

To see how closely correlated the initial forecasts are with the actual discounted profits from each of the new processes or new products and to estimate the relationship between them, we regressed the initial forecasts on the actual discounted profits. For new products, the resulting least-squares regression is

$$F_i = 0.71 + 0.24 \ A_i \qquad (\bar{R}^2 = .14), \qquad (1)$$
$$(3.78) \ \ (2.41)$$

where F_i is the initially forecasted discounted profits and A_i is the actual discounted profits for the ith new product. The t-statistics are shown in parentheses. For new processes, the resulting regression is

$$F_i = 1.38 + 0.46 \ A_i \qquad (\bar{R}^2 = .87). \qquad (2)$$
$$(2.08) \ \ (10.44)$$

For both products and processes, F_i and A_i are measured in millions of dollars.

Equations (1) and (2) indicate several things. First, in the case of new products, there is a surprisingly low correlation between the initial forecasts and the actual discounted profits, $\bar{R}^2$ being only .14. However, the correlation, while low, is significantly different from zero. Second, in the case of new processes, the correlation is much higher, $\bar{R}^2$ being about .87. Thus, the initial forecasts for processes tended to relate more closely to the actual outcomes than those for products. Third, both for processes and products, the initial forecasts tend to be relatively optimistic in cases where actual profits were small and relatively pessimistic in cases where actual profits were large. Specifically, the forecasts underestimated the profitability of new processes that had discounted profits exceeding about $3 million and of new products

---

6. Recall that the initial forecast was made about 1 year after the development of the new product or process and that the "actual" discounted profits are the discounted profits estimated 9 years after development.

TABLE 1   **Ratio of Initially Forecasted to Actual Discounted Profits, 57 New Products and Processes, by Year of Development**

Forecasted Discounted Profits / Actual Discounted Profits	Year of Development					Total
	1960	1961	1962	1963	1964	
	New Products					
Less than 0.3	2	0	1	2	1	6
0.3–0.59	1	0	1	1	2	5
0.6–0.89	0	1	1	1	1	4
0.9–1.09	0	0	1	3	0	4
1.1–1.49	0	0	1	1	1	3
1.5–1.99	2	1	1	0	1	5
2.0–2.99	2	0	1	0	0	3
3.0–3.99	0	0	0	1	0	1
Greater than 4.0	1	2	0	0	5	8
	New Processes					
Less than 0.3	0	0	0	0	0	0
0.3–0.59	3	2	0	1	1	7
0.6–0.89	0	1	0	1	1	3
0.9–1.09	0	1	0	1	0	2
1.1–1.49	1	1	0	0	0	2
1.5–1.99	0	1	0	0	0	1
2.0–2.99	0	0	0	0	0	0
3.0–3.99	1	0	0	0	0	1
Greater than 4.0	0	0	0	1	1	2

where they exceeded about $1 million, and overestimated the profitability of less profitable new products and processes.[7]

Accuracy of Forecasted Total Profits from All New Processes and Products Developed Annually

Besides investigating the accuracy of the initial forecasts for individual new processes or new products, we also must look at the accuracy of the initially forecasted total discounted profit from all of them developed in a given year. This firm (and others) is interested in comparing the total discounted profit from new products and new processes with the firm's total investment in such new technology. Even if the initial forecasts for individual new processes or new products are relatively poor, the sum of these forecasts may be reasonably accurate because the error for one process or product may tend to cancel the error for another process or product. To see whether this is the case, we took all the new products or new processes introduced in a particular year and summed up their initially forecasted discounted profits;

7. This finding is quite consistent with the results of Tull's study (1967) concerning new products.

then we divided this sum by the sum of their actual discounted profits. The results, shown in table 2, indicate that the errors in the forecasts for individual processes or products by no means cancel out. In only 1 year (1961) was the initially forecasted total discounted profits for new products within 25% of its actual value, and in none of the years was the initially forecasted total discounted profits for new processes within 25% of its actual value.

Two other points regarding table 2 are also worth noting. First, unlike forecasts of development cost and time, which tend to be highly optimistic, initial profit forecasts show no such bias. On the contrary, this firm consistently underestimated (generally by a wide margin) the profitability of its new products and processes. This is quite consistent with Tull's finding that, for new products, there was no persistent upward bias in profit forecasts.[8] Second, this downward bias was even stronger for new processes than for new products. On the average, the initial forecast of total discounted profits from processes tended to be about 40% below the actual figure.

Implications and Conclusions

These results have a number of implications. First, they indicate that the initial forecasts of the profitability of a new product or a new

TABLE 2   **Ratio of Initially Forecasted Total Discounted Profits from New Products or New Processes Developed in Given Year to Total Actual Discounted Profits from These New Products or New Processes, 1960–64**

Year and Type of New Technology	Ratio
1960:	
Products	.72
Processes	.45
Products and processes	.50
1961:	
Products	.95
Processes	.52
Products and processes	.78
1962:	
Products	.62
Processes	. . .
Products and processes	.62
1963:	
Products	.46
Processes	.65
Products and processes	.62
1964:	
Products	1.30
Processes	.75
Products and processes	.92

8. See ibid.

process are no more reliable than forecasts of development cost and time.[9] (And they are less reliable than forecasts by users of the estimated profitability of using a new technique which has already been used for several years by other firms.)[10] This is not because of inadequate forecasting or analytical work on the part of the firm studied here. Based on all available indications, this firm is among the more competent in this regard in the country. Instead, these results reflect the inherent uncertainty involved in estimating the profitability of an innovation. Given these enormous uncertainties, it seems clear that the many quantitative techniques to allocate R & D (and related) resources, which rely on such forecasts, must be rather frail reeds on which to base decisions concerning investments in new products and processes.[11]

Second, our results indicate that it takes 4 or 5 years after the development of a new product or process before this firm can estimate reasonably well the discounted profits from the innovation. Undoubtedly, this length of time varies from firm to firm, and we cannot be sure that this firm is typical in this regard. But to the extent that it is typical, potential innovators must reckon on relatively long periods of time when they will be unable to tell with much accuracy whether it was wise or foolish to have developed a particular new process or product. Obviously, this makes life difficult for a potential innovator, who would like to buy information concerning success or failure quickly and cheaply.

Third, in this firm at least, there seem to be large forecasting errors both for new processes and new products, and how long it takes after the new technology is developed to estimate the discounted profits reasonably well does not seem to vary much between new products and new processes. This may seem surprising, since one might think that the firm could estimate its own savings from a new process far better than it could its sales of a new product to other firms and the

9. Mansfield et al. (1971) present data regarding the accuracy of forecasts of development cost and time in two drug firms. For the ethical drug firm, in about 40% of the cases the ratio of actual to forecasted development cost exceeded 2.0 or fell below 0.5, and in about 20% of the cases the ratio of actual to forecasted development time exceeded 2.0 or fell below 0.5. This is better than the results in table 1. However, the proprietary drug firm did no better than table 1. Of course, we are not concerned here with military projects.

10. Romeo (1975) presents data concerning the accuracy of forecasts of the profitability of using numerically controlled machine tools. These data seem to indicate that these forecasts are much more highly correlated with the actual profitability and that the ratio of forecasted to actual profitability tends to be closer to one than in the case of the forecasts studied here.

11. For a discussion of some of these techniques, see Mansfield et al. (1971, 1977). Note that, for those techniques that attempt to help allocate R & D resources, the estimates of profitability of innovations must be made *before*, not *after*, the development of the new process or product, so the forecasting errors are likely to be even bigger than those considered here.

public. But it must be recognized that the firm finds it difficult to forecast future input prices, royalty receipts, and a variety of other factors influencing the profitability of a new process.

Fourth, and perhaps most interesting from the point of view of public policy, there seems to be a tendency for this firm (and others as well)[12] to underestimate the profitability of very profitable innovations and to overestimate the profitability of relatively unprofitable innovations. In part, this seems to stem from the belief by the forecasters that the penalties for being conservative in their estimates are less than those for being too far out on a limb (particularly in an upward direction). In general, but perhaps not in the case of this firm, this reduction in the forecasted increment between the discounted profits from the expected "big winners" and the more run-of-the-mill innovations may result in a distorted allocation of resources. Because the extra profits to be obtained from the expected big winners are underestimated, many of them may not be carried out on as big a scale or as quickly as would seem justified if the forecasts were unbiased in this regard.[13]

Fifth, and related to the previous point, there is no evidence that this firm has overestimated the profitability of new products and processes. On the contrary, it seems on the average to have underestimated their profitability. Again, it is difficult to know how typical this sort of conservatism is. But to the extent that it is typical, it could, of course, result in some underinvestment in new processes and products, and it could help to explain why estimated private rates of return from innovative activity during this time period are relatively high, according to some recent studies.[14]

Finally, the limitations of this paper should be noted. Since the results pertain entirely to a single firm, we must be very careful to emphasize that this firm may be atypical in various respects. Also, the results pertain only to products and processes that emerged from development during 1960–64. (However, it is worth noting that the partial data that are available concerning the new products and new processes developed by this firm during 1965–70 bear out our conclusions.) Nonetheless, since the firm is one of the biggest in the world, and since data of this sort concerning the accuracy of forecasts of the profitability of new products and processes are extremely hard to come by, we believe that the results should be of widespread interest.

12. See Tull 1967.
13. All that we can do here is cite the possibility of such an effect on the allocation of R & D resources. In any specific firm, it may not exist. In particular, the relevant officials of this firm deny its existence. Until we learn more about the magnitude and frequency of this effect in the economy as a whole, there is no way to estimate how important (or unimportant) it may be.
14. For some relevant discussion, see Griliches (1975), Mansfield (1976), and Mansfield et al. (1977).

References

Griliches, Z. 1975. Returns to research and development expenditure in the private sector. Paper presented at the Conference on Research in Income and Wealth, Williamsburg, Va.,

Klein, B. 1965. Policy issues involved in the conduct of military development programs. In Richard A. Tybout (ed.), *Economics of Research and Development*. Columbus: Ohio State University Press.

Mansfield, E. 1976. Federal support of R & D activities in the private sector. In Joint Economic Committee of Congress, *Priorities and Efficiency in Federal Research and Development*. Washington, D. C.: Government Printing Office.

Mansfield, E.; Rapoport, J.; Romeo, A.; Villani, E.; Wagner, S.; and Husic, F. 1977. *The Production and Application of New Industrial Technology*. New York: Norton.

Mansfield, E.; Rapoport, J.; Romeo, A.; Wagner, S.; and Beardsley, G. 1977. Social and private rates of return from industrial innovations. *Quarterly Journal of Economics* 91, no. 2 (May): 221–404.

Mansfield, E.; Rapoport, J.; Schnee, J.; Wagner, S.; and Hamburger, M. 1971. *Research and Innovation in the Modern Corporation*. New York: Norton.

Marschak, T.; Glennan, T.; and Summers, R. 1967. *Strategy for R & D*. New York: Springer-Verlag.

Meadows, D. 1968. Estimate accuracy and project selection models in industrial research. *Industrial Management Review* 9, no. 3 (Spring): 105–19.

Romeo, A. 1975. Errors in estimating the profitability of an innovation. *R & D Management* 6 (October): 45–47.

Tull, D. 1967. The relationship of actual and predicted sales and profits in new-product introductions. *Journal of Business* 40 (July): 233–50.

15

I

Introduction

In recent years, cost and time overruns in military development have made the front pages of newspapers. Long before these overruns made the headlines, economists were interested in them. For example, studies carried out by the RAND Corporation in the late fifties showed that there were substantial errors in the estimates (made prior to development) of the costs of producing various types of military hardware. When adjusted for unanticipated changes in factor prices and production lot-sizes, the average ratio of the actual to estimated cost was 1.7 (fighters), 3.0 (bombers), 1.2 (cargo and tanker aircraft) and 4.9 (missiles). The extent to which costs were understated was directly related to the extent of the technological advance. In cases where a "large" technological advance was required, the average ratio was 4.2; in cases where a "small" technological advance was required, the average ratio was 1.3.[1]

Turning to development costs, Peck and Scherer reported an average ratio of actual to expected costs of 3.2 for 12 plane and missile development projects.[2] Both the RAND study and the study by Peck and

---

1. A. Marshall and W. Meckling, "Predictability of the Costs, Time, and Success of Development," The Rate and Direction of Inventive Activity (Princeton, N.J.: Princeton University Press, 1962).
2. M. Peck and F. Scherer, The Weapons Acquisition Process, (Cambridge, Mass: Harvard University Press, 1962).

1

Scherer also presented data on the average ratio of actual to estimated project length. The RAND study estimated that schedule slippage on ten programs ranged from two to five years, with an average ratio of actual to estimated length of 1.5.[3] The corresponding ratio for the 12 programs examined by Peck and Scherer was 1.36.[4]

There also has been interest in the accuracy of various firms' estimates of a project's probability of technical success. Estimates of this sort are used to help enable decision-makers to make rational project-selection decisions. Recent evidence indicates that the bulk of the larger industrial laboratories in such important industries as chemicals, petroleum, and electronics use these estimates to help select their R&D portfolios.[5]

This paper is divided into six sections. In the next section, we analyze the accuracy of estimates of development cost and development time in a large ethical drug firm. How accurate are these cost and time estimates, and to what extent (and in what direction) are they biased? What factors seem to be associated with the size of the overrun for an individual project? How does the size of the overruns in this industry compare with the size of those in military procurement? Also, we study the size of the errors in sales estimates made by the firm before a new product is marketed. In Section III, we describe the accuracy of the estimates of the probability of technical success made

---

3. Marshall and Meckling, op. cit.

4. Peck and Scherer, op. cit.

5. See E. Mansfield, J. Rapoport, J. Schnee, S. Wagner and M. Hamburger, Research and Innovation in the Modern Corporation (New York: W. W. Norton, forthcoming).

in the central laboratory of a large electrical equipment firm.   In
Section IV, we describe and analyze the accuracy of the estimates of
the probability of technical completion, development cost, and development time made by a proprietary drug laboratory.   Finally, in Section V,
we describe the results of a study of the attitudes of laboratory administrators in four industries toward estimates of this sort, and in Section VI
we summarize our findings.

3

II

Estimates of Cost, Time, and Sales for an Ethical Drug Firm

A. DATA FOR THE ETHICAL DRUG FIRM

Exceptionally detailed data were obtained from one of the nation's major ethical drug firms. (Ethical drugs are those sold only on a doctor's prescription.) Using the development blueprint for a project, cost estimates were obtained for 49 projects and time estimates for 50 projects. Estimated and actual sales were obtained for 59 new products during their first 12 months on the market.[6] The sales estimates were obtained from the marketing plan prepared by the appropriate product manager in the marketing division of the firm. In order to assess the accuracy of the estimates, the ratio of actual to estimate was computed to obtain a cost factor, time factor, and sales factor:

$$\text{Cost Factor} = \frac{\text{Actual Development Cost}}{\text{Estimated Development Cost}}$$

$$\text{Time Factor} = \frac{\text{Actual Development Time}}{\text{Estimated Development Time}}$$

$$\text{Sales Factor} = \frac{\text{Actual First Year Sales}}{\text{Estimated First Year Sales}}$$

---

6. The 59 new products resulted from 57 development projects. Normally, each development project yielded one new product. Even in those cases where more than one dosage form was developed, one (cont'd.)

The frequency distribution for each factor is shown in Table 1. Data on the mean, standard deviation, and root-mean-square-deviation-from-one for the three types of factors are contained in Table 2.

Table 1

DISTRIBUTIONS OF RATIOS OF ACTUAL TO ESTIMATED COST,
TIME, AND SALES, ETHICAL DRUG FIRM

Ratio	Cost	Time	Sales
	Number of Projects		
00-.50	1	0	12
.51-1.00	5	16	21
1.01-1.50	18	17	12
1.51-2.00	6	9	8
2.01-2.50	6	2	2
2.51-3.00	10	3	1
3.01-3.50	3	1	1
3.51-10.00	0	2	2
Total	49	50	59

estimate was prepared in the marketing plan if all dosage forms were marketed at the same time. There were two projects which resulted in two products because the two dosage forms developed during the project were marketed at different times.

6

Table 2

PARAMETERS OF DISTRIBUTIONS OF RATIOS OF ACTUAL
TO ESTIMATED COST, TIME, AND SALES,
ETHICAL DRUG FIRM

	Cost	Time	Sales
New Chemical Entities			
Mean	2.25	1.89	1.75
Standard deviation	.72	.97	2.24
Root mean square deviation from 1	1.38	1.32	2.36
Percentage of cases where ratio exceeds 1	100	93	46
Number of projects	13	14	13
Compounded Products			
Mean	1.70	1.60	1.11
Standard deviation	.72	1.4	.71
Root mean square deviation from 1	1.00	1.52	.72
Percentage of cases where ratio exceeds 1	83	74	50
Number of projects	23	23	24
Alternate Dosage Forms			
Mean	1.51	1.33	1.20
Standard deviation	.71	.44	1.54
Root mean square deviation from 1	.88	.57	1.55
Percentage of cases where ratio exceeds 1	84	84	36
Number of projects	13	13	22
Total			
Mean	1.78	1.61	1.29
Standard deviation	.74	1.15	1.38
Root mean square deviation from 1	1.09	1.34	1.58
Percentage of cases where ratio exceeds 1	88	82	49
Number of projects	49	50	59

7

Several interesting characteristics of the estimates emerge from the two tables. First, the data indicate the extent of the bias and variability of the three types of estimates. If the estimates had been substantially correct, the cost, time, and sales factors would have been close to unity. The fact that the mean of all three distributions is above 1 (average cost factor = 1.78, average time factor = 1.61, and average sales factor = 1.29) would seem to indicate that the actual value is generally greater than the estimate in the three categories.[7] We might have expected substantial differences in the size and direction of errors for the three types of estimates. A number of studies have shown that the optimistic bias that exists in sales estimates frequently causes forecasted sales to be greater than actual sales.[8] On the other hand, the hazards involved in predicting the cost of complex, uncertain activities, such as the construction of a railroad or the development of a new fighter plane, usually results in actual costs exceeding original expectations.[9] Table 2 indicates that the estimates of cost and time

---

7. Of course, a mean factor above 1 does not necessarily mean that most of the values are greater than 1. See Tables 1 and 2.

8. See for example, R. Ferber, "Measuring the Accuracy and Structure of Businessmen's Expectations," Journal of the American Statistical Association, XLI, No. 263 (September 1953), pp. 385-413; M. Hastay, "The Dun and Bradstreet Surveys of Businessmen's Expectations," Proceedings of the Business and Economics Statistics Section of the American Statistical Association (September 1954), pp. 93-123; H. Theil, Economic Forecasts and Policy (Amsterdam: North Holland Publishing Company, 1961), Chapters III and IV; D. Tull, "The Relationship of Actual Sales to Predicted Sales for New Products," Journal of Business (July 1967), pp. 233-250.

9. See the discussion of military cost estimating errors in T. Marschak, T. Glennan, and R. Summers, Strategy for R and D (New York: Springer-Verlag, 1967).

conform to these expectations, the average ratio of actual to estimated values being well above 1. But the average ratio of actual to estimated sales exceeds 1. (Note, however, that the ratio of actual to estimated sales is less than 1 in most cases.)

Second, there are differences in the average cost, time, and sales factors for new chemical entities, compounded products, and alternate dosage forms. However, the only statistically significant differences occur among the cost factors, the average cost factor for new chemical entities being significantly higher than the average cost factor for the other two categories at the 5 percent level. The higher average cost and time factors for new chemical entities probably reflect the fact that such projects are marked by the greatest uncertainty. Sales forecast errors are also highest for the most innovative products (new chemical entities), but the difference does not appear to be statistically significant.

Third, if we compare the extent of the time overruns in this ethical drug firm with the extent of the time overruns in weapons system development, we find that the time overruns tend to be somewhat larger in drug development. The average ratio of actual to estimated development time in this firm is 1.61, whereas the average ratio reported by RAND is 1.5 (for ten weapons systems) and the average ratio reported by Peck and Scherer is 1.36 (for 12 plane and missile development projects).[10] The average time overrun in this firm is also higher

---

10. Marshall and Meckling, op. cit., and M. Peck and F. Scherer, op. cit.

than the average estimated time overrun reported by Mansfield and Brandenburg in their study of a large equipment and appliance manufacturer.[11]

Fourth, we can also compare the cost overruns in this firm with those in weapons development. As noted above, Peck and Scherer reported an average ratio of actual to estimated development cost of 3.2 for 12 weapons system projects. Thus, since the average ratio in this firm is 1.78, the cost overruns in this ethical drug firm are not as large as among the weapons systems. But among the more innovative products--new chemical entities--the average cost overrun (2.25) is closer to that among weapons systems, the average overrun being about 60 percent of that found by Peck and Scherer. This result is interesting since it suggests that, when commercial activity is devoted to distinctly new products, it begins to approximate weapons system development in the extent of overruns. More will be said about this topic subsequently.[12]

Fifth, the sales forecast errors for the 59 new drug products are somewhat higher than those reported in Tull's study of 63 new products introduced by 16 companies. Using the absolute relative error (defined

---

11. The Mansfield and Brandenburg data are not exactly comparable to our data. First, they measure an average "slippage factor" which is the revised estimated time to project completion divided by the original estimated time to completion. The drug development time factors are ratios of actual time to estimated time. Second, they measure average slippage only for those projects that are delayed while we compare actual time to estimated time for all completed projects. Our average time factor would be higher if all projects completed on time were excluded. See E. Mansfield, Industrial Research and Technological Innovation (New York: W. W. Norton, 1968).

12. See Peck and Scherer, op. cit., pp. 44-45.

as ARE $= \left| \dfrac{F-A}{A} \right| \cdot 100$ where F is the forecast and A is the actual value)

as a measure of forecast accuracy, Tull found that the mean and median

absolute relative errors for the 63 new products were 65 percent and 26

percent, respectively. The mean and median ARE for the 59 new drug

products were 76 percent and 45 percent, respectively. In terms of fore-

casting accuracy, the new drug products are more like the industrial

products (mean ARE = 85 percent) in Tull's sample than the consumer

products (mean ARE = 49 percent). There are also differences in the

direction of the error between the Tull and new drug product samples,

the sales forecasts for the 63 new products in the Tull sample being

more optimistic than the estimates for the new drug products.[13] This

may be partly caused by the very rapid growth of the drug market during

this period.

B. ANALYSIS OF COST OVERRUNS

What factors are associated with the size of the cost overrun for a

particular project? To help answer this question, we construct a simple

model in which the logarithm of the ratio of actual to estimated develop-

ment cost is the dependent variable, and various project characteristics

are the independent variables.[14] The first project characteristic used

as an independent variable is the degree of technological advance

attempted by a project.[15] The magnitude of the technological advance

---

13. Tull, op. cit.

14. Interviews with research executives within the firm indicate
that they generally agreed with this approach of pooling all projects in
a single regression.

15. See E. Mansfield, J. Rapoport, J. Schnee, S. Wagner, and
M. Hamburger, op. cit., for details of how the technological advance
score was computed. Essentially, the respondents were asked to rate
the state-of-the-art advance represented by each development project on (cont'd.)

sought in the development project will, in part, determine the degree
of initial uncertainty and the frequency with which the original development plan is changed. Since these revised development plans generally
result in actual costs and times that are above the estimates in the
development blueprint, the overruns in cost and time should be relatively
large when the attempted technological advance is great.

Turning to the next independent variable, a project that attempts
to develop a product with a broad spectrum of activity (i. e. , a multiple-
market product) is more likely to encounter unanticipated problems than
is a project that attempts to develop a product with a narrow spectrum
of activity (i . e. , a single-market product). Consequently, one might
expect the cost overruns to be larger for products with a broad spectrum
of activity. Thus, the second variable included in the regression is a
dummy variable denoting the product's spectrum of activity. [16]

The third independent variable is the year the estimate was made.
Calendar year proved to be a significant variable in explaining the
magnitude of development cost, and we might expect it to be important
here as well, for two reasons. The data include estimates made as early
as 1950 and as late as 1962. Since skills improved significantly in
virtually all technical fields during that period, we might expect an

---

a five-point scale whose end points were "very much" (rating = 5. 0) and
"not at all" (rating = 1. 0). The technological advance score for each
project was obtained by averaging all respondent ratings for the project.
This is the same sort of procedure as that used by Peck and Scherer,
op. cit. , and Marschak, Glennan, and Summers, op. cit. Its crudeness
need not be belabored.

16. See ibid. for a discussion of the significance and meaning of a
product's spectrum of activity.

improvement in estimating techniques as well. On the other hand, the effects of more complex development procedures and inflation probably increased inaccuracies in cost and time estimates over time. The impact of these changes may well have outweighed any improvements in forecasting proficiency within the firm.

The fourth independent variable is the actual duration of the development project. The longer a project goes on, the more likely it is that changes will be made in the nature of the product being developed and that overrun will grow. This variable has proved useful in studies of military cost overruns.

The fifth independent variable is the estimated cost of carrying out the development project. The percentage overrun in development costs is likely to be smaller, all other things equal, for a big, expensive project than a smaller one. Why? Because the absolute size, as well as the percentage size, of the overrun is of importance. A small overrun is more likely to be tolerated than a large one, even if in percentage terms they are the same: As an overrun becomes larger in absolute terms, it becomes more and more likely that it will result in trouble for the relevant people in the firm.[17]

---

17. Of course, it should be noted that we are regressing the logarithm of a ratio on, among other variables, the logarithm of the denominator. It may be objected that this results in some spurious correlation. But the results change relatively little if $\ln C_F^i$ is omitted from the regression. This is true as well in the other cases in this paper. Note, too, that R_c^i can be greater or less than 1, the consequence being that under some circumstances, a "bigger overrun" is really a smaller "underrun."

The specific form of the multiple regression model is:

$$\ln R_c^i = \alpha_0 + \alpha_1 \ln A_i + \alpha_2 s_i + \alpha_3 \ln t_i + \alpha_4 \ln C_E^i + \alpha_5 \ln L_i, \qquad (1)$$

where $\ln R_c^i$ is the logarithm of the ratio of the ith project's actual to estimated development cost, α_0 is the constant, $\ln C_E^i$ is the logarithm of the ith project's estimated development cost, $\ln A_i$ is the logarithm of its technological advance score, s_i is a dummy variable that equals 1 if the ith project is meant for more than a single market and 0 otherwise, $\ln t_i$ is the logarithm of the year the estimate was made (less 1949), and L_i is the actual duration of the ith project. The resulting regression equation is:

$$\ln R_c^i = -.01 + .51 \ln A_i + .32 s_i + .39 \ln t_i - .38 \ln C_E^i$$
$$\qquad (.17) \qquad (.16) \qquad (.12) \qquad (.09)$$
$$+ .40 \ln L_i, \qquad\qquad\qquad\qquad (2)$$
$$(.12)$$

R^2--corrected for degrees for freedom--being .34.

Equation 2 provides a considerable amount of information concerning the hypotheses presented in previous paragraphs. It appears that all five of the variables discussed above have statistically significant effects on the size of a project's cost overrun. In line with our hypotheses, the regression coefficients of the logarithm of the technological-advance score, the spectrum-of-activity dummy variable, the logarithm of the project's duration and the logarithm of calendar time are positive,[18] while the regression coefficient of the logarithm of estimated cost is negative. According to Eq. 2, cost overruns tend to be greater for projects attempting considerable advances in the state of the art than

---

18. Our hypotheses said nothing about the sign of the coefficient of $\ln t_i$, however.

for less ambitious projects. Specifically, a 1 percent increase in
the technological-advance score is associated with a .51 percent
increase in the size of the cost overrun.[19] Moreover, cost overruns
tend to be greater for products with a broad spectrum of activity than
for single-market products. The effect of this variable is quantitatively
important, the average size of the cost overrun being about 38 percent
greater for projects with a broad spectrum of activity than for single-
market products.

In addition, cost overruns seem to have increased over time, a
1 percent increase in t_i being associated with a .39 percent increase
in the cost overrun. Thus, the effects of changing development procedures and inflation seem to have offset any improvements in forecasting
accuracy. Cost overruns also seem to be smaller (in percentage terms)
for bigger projects, a 1 percent increase in estimated costs being
associated with a .38 percent decrease in the average cost overrun.
And cost overruns tend to be bigger for longer projects, a 1 percent
increase in a project's duration being associated with a .40 percent
increase in the average cost overrun. Finally, although these variables
have a significant effect on the size of a project's cost overrun, they
cannot explain more than about one-third of the variation among projects
in cost overruns. This is not surprising, partly for reasons discussed
in the final paragraphs of this subsection.[20]

---

19. These results concerning the effects of technological advance
are similar to those reported in the RAND study of production costs.
See Marschak, Glennan, and Summers, op. cit. The cost factors for
the 22 weapons systems were directly related to the extent of the technological advance.

20. There are many other factors affecting the size of overruns,
among them deliberate underestimation of costs and time.

Based on these results one can explain why cost overruns for new chemical entities tend to be larger than for compounded products and alternate dosage forms (Table 2): The highest proportion of projects with a broad spectrum of activity are in the new-chemical-entity category, and the average technological-advance score is highest for new chemical entitites (Table 2). However, although the larger overruns among new chemical entities can be explained in this way, we can also obtain equally good results by simply using the project category--new chemical entity, compounded product, or alternate dosage form--as a surrogate for the extent of the technological advance and the risks involved. Specifically, if we modify Eq. 2 by eliminating $\ell n\, A_i$, the logarithm of the technological-advance score, and s_i, the spectrum-of-activity dummy variable, and by substituting two dummy variables, n_{1i} and n_{2i}, which equal 1 for new chemical entities and compounded products respectively (and 0 otherwise), the results are:

$$\ell n\, R_c^i = -.23 + .66\, n_{1i} + .27\, n_{2i} + .39\, \ell n\, t_i - .32\, \ell n\, C_E^i$$
$$ (.16) \qquad (.13) \qquad (.17) \qquad (.06)$$

$$+.43\, \ell n\, L_i, \qquad\qquad\qquad\qquad\qquad\qquad (3)$$
$$(.12)$$

R^2 being .36. Both of the new variables, n_{1i} and n_{2i}, are statistically significant, and the regression coefficients of both new variables have the expected signs. The logarithm of estimated development cost, the logarithm of duration, and the logarithm of calendar time, all of which were significant in Eq. 2, retain their significance in Eq. 3. While Eq. 3 seems to provide a slightly better fit to the data than Eq. 2, the results are not sufficiently different to permit a choice between the equations on the basis of goodness-of-fit.

Finally, we should note that the variation in the size of overruns is not due entirely to the uncertainty associated with certain project characteristics. Development costs and times may be deliberately underestimated in a project's development blueprint. Because of the intrafirm competition for resources, there may be incentives to use low estimates as a means of marshalling support for particular development projects. If all estimates were uniformly adjusted downward by, for example, 10 or 20 percent, R^2 would be unaffected. It appears more likely, however, that some estimates may be cut by 25 percent, others by 10 percent, and some not at all. This variability would limit our ability to explain the observed variation in cost and time factors. This deliberate downward adjustment of estimates is not, of course, a phenomenon unique to this firm. Many observers have noted that industrial scientists sometimes pursue scientific and professional goals that may not be consistent with the strictly commercial objectives of the firm.[21] While the observed variation in the accuracy of estimates is probably a composite of uncertainty and deliberate underestimating, there is no effective way to separate out the effects of deliberate underestimating.

C. ANALYSIS OF TIME OVERRUNS

What factors seem to be associated with the size of the time overrun for a particular project? To help answer this question, we construct a model similar to that discussed in the previous subsection. The same

---

21. For a discussion of this conflict see S. Marcson, The Scientist in American Industry (New York: Harper, 1960), and W. Kornhauser, Scientists in Industry: Conflict and Accommodation (Berkeley: University of California Press, 1962).

17

set of project characteristics make up the independent variables. However, the logarithm of the ratio of the actual to estimated project length is substituted, of course, for the logarithm of the ratio of the actual to estimated project cost as the dependent variable; and the logarithm of the estimated project length replaces the logarithm of the estimated cost among the independent variables. The resulting regression is:

$$\ln R_L^i = .81 + .21 \ln A_i + .46 s_i - .01 \ln t_i - .29 \ln L_E^i, \qquad (4)$$
$$\quad\;\; (.14) \qquad\quad (.16) \qquad\; (.12) \qquad\quad (.16)$$

where $\ln R_L^i$ is the logarithm of the ith project's ratio of actual to expected length, and $\ln L_E^i$ is the logarithm of the ith project's estimated length. The fit for the time overruns is slightly poorer than for the cost overruns, R^2 being .23.

As in the case of the cost overruns, the effects of s_i and $\ln L_E^i$ are statistically significant. Time overruns tend to be larger for products with a broad spectrum of activity than for single-market products, the overrun being about 60 percent greater among broad-spectrum products. As expected, time overruns tend to be smaller (in percentage terms) for projects expected to take a long period of time than for those expected to be completed quickly. On the average, a 1 percent increase in estimated time is associated with a .29 percent decrease in the time overrun. Also, there is some tendency for time estimates (like cost estimates) to be less accurate for projects with high technological-advance scores, but (in contrast to cost estimates) this tendency is not statistically significant. Unlike the case of the cost estimates, there is no evidence that time overruns have tended to increase over time. However, neither is there any evidence that time overruns have tended to decrease over time.

18

As in the case of cost overruns, we can also compute the regression where dummy variables representing project category are substituted for spectrum of activity and technological-advance score. When $\ln A_i$, the technological-advance score, and s_i, the spectrum-of-activity dummy variable, are replaced by n_{1i}, the new-chemical-entity dummy variable, and n_{2i}, the compounded-products dummy variable, the results become:

$$\ln R_L^i = 1.07 + .32 \, n_{1i} - .01 \, n_{2i} + .06 \, \ln t_i - .36 \, \ln L_E^i . \quad (5)$$
$$ (.17) \phantom{n_{1i} -} (.12) \phantom{n_{2i} +} (.09) (.19)$$

The effect of n_{1i} is significant, but that of n_{2i} is not. Equation 5 does not fit as well as Eq. 4, R^2 being only .06.

D. ANALYSIS OF ERRORS IN SALES ESTIMATES

What factors seem to be associated with the extent of the overrun in the sales forecast for a particular project? A model similar to those employed in subsections B and C is used to analyze the overruns in the sales estimates. Four independent variables are used in this analysis: (1) the innovativeness of the new product, (2) the calendar year of the estimate (less 1949), (3) the identity of the forecaster, and (4) the product's estimated sales. With regard to the first variable, it is often hypothesized that the degree of innovativeness of a product affects the accuracy of the sales forecast.[22] Since new chemical entities are more

---

22. Tull hypothesized that a product's degree of innovativeness would affect forecast accuracy. He grouped the products in his sample into three categories: (a) innovative products--products that are new to the economy; (b) emulative products--products that the company has never marketed before although they are marketed in essentially the same form by other companies; (c) adaptive products--products that result when the (cont'd.)

innovative than compounded products or alternate dosage forms, the two dummy variables, n_{1i} and n_{2i}, were used as independent variables.

Turning to the second variable, we might expect the accuracy of sales forecasts to improve over time. During 1950 through 1967, considerable progress was made in developing and refining techniques for new product sales forecasting. In addition, increased knowledge and experience in specific therapeutic markets should have improved forecasting accuracy over time. Turning to the third variable, we might expect knowledge of the source of a sales estimate to be helpful in judging its accuracy. Five product managers were responsible for the 59 sales forecasts; consequently, four dummy variables were introduced into the regression to account for the identity of the forecaster. Finally, the accuracy of a sales forecast may be related to the extent of the product's estimated sales.

The following model is used:

$$\ell n \, R_s^i = k + \gamma_1 \, \ell n \, S_e^i + \gamma_2 \, \ell n \, t_i + \gamma_3 \, I_{1i} + \gamma_4 I_{2i} + \gamma_5 I_{3i}$$
$$+ \gamma_6 I_{4i} + \gamma_7 n_{1i} + \gamma_8 n_{2i} \tag{6}$$

where $\ell n \, R_s^i$ is the logarithm of the ratio of the ith product's actual to estimated sales; k is a constant; $\ell n \, S_e^i$ is the logarithm of the ith product's estimated sales; $\ell n \, t_i$ is the logarithm of its calendar year (less 1949); I_{1i}, I_{2i}, I_{3i}, and I_{4i} are dummy variables indicating the identity of the

---

company makes a significant differentiation in an existing product that it now markets. The innovative and emulative products were combined and the mean absolute relative error of this class was compared to the mean absolute relative error of adaptive products. No significant difference was found. See Tull, op. cit., p. 245.

20

forecaster; and n_{1i} and n_{2i} are dummy variables denoting new chemical

entities and compounded products, respectively.

The results are:

$$\ell n\, R^i_s = .94 - \underset{(.13)}{.18}\, \ell n\, S^i_e - \underset{(.67)}{.18}\, \ell n\, t_i + \underset{(.31)}{.33}\, I_1 - \underset{(.29)}{.02}\, I_2$$

$$+ \underset{(.39)}{.31}\, I_3 + \underset{(0.48)}{1.01}\, I_4 + \underset{(.28)}{.19}\, n_{1i} + \underset{(.24)}{.16}\, n_{2i}. \tag{7}$$

The value of R^2--.08--is lower than that achieved with the models

concerning development cost and development time. Although new

product sales forecasting is generally more accurate in this firm than

the forecasting of development time and cost, we are unable to explain

the variation in sales overruns (on the basis of the variables considered

here) as well as we could explain the variation in cost and time overruns.

Moreover, our results, like Tull's,[23] provide no evidence of differences

between more innovative and less innovative products in the size of the

sales forecast errors.

The only statistically significant variable in Eq. 7 is a dummy

variable identifying one of the forecasters. However, this does not

mean that the observed differences among the forecasters are due to

differences in personal characteristics alone. The product managers

who prepared the sales forecasts differed considerably in the number

and diversity of the product lines they managed. The least accurate

forecasts were generated by a product manager who had responsibility

for the firm's entire product line in the early fifties. As the firm grew,

the product management and accompanying new product sales forecasting

---

23. Ibid.

21

responsibility were divided among three individuals. Under this arrange-
ment each product manager prepared sales forecasts for products in one
or two product categories. Hence, the allocation of greater resources to
new product sales forecasting and the increased market specialization
that resulted may have contributed to the improved forecast accuracy
among the other forecasters. The moral here is simple, but important
and frequently overlooked: It is that the accuracy of a forecast is
dependent on the amount of resources devoted to making it. Unfortunately, despite the obvious relevance of this variable , it is seldom
included in studies of this sort.

III

Accuracy of Estimated Probabilities
of Technical Success in an Electrical Equipment Firm

Let's turn from the ethical drug firm to one of the nation's biggest electrical equipment manufacturers. When R&D projects are proposed in its central laboratory, estimates must be made of each project's probability of technical success. How accurate are these estimates? This is an important question because the techniques recommended by economists and operations researchers for selecting R&D projects depend on the use of such estimates. If it is impossible to make reasonably accurate estimates, techniques that are relatively sensitive to errors in the estimates should be avoided even if they have other features that seem desirable.[24]

To find out how accurate the estimates (that is, P*) were, we construct a statistical discriminant function to predict whether a project was successful on the basis of its value of P*. This function is optimal in the sense that, under specified conditions,[25] it minimizes the proportion of incorrect predictions. To estimate this discriminant function,

---

24. Unfortunately, the discussions of selection techniques seldom, if ever, contain any treatment of the sensitivity of the results to errors of this kind.

25. This assumes that the a priori probability of a success is 0.5. See T. Anderson, An Introduction to Multivariate Statistical Analysis (New York: John Wiley and Sons, 1958). These conditions are only approximately fulfilled, but if better approximations were used, the results would be about the same. See note 27.

we define a variable, U_i, where

$$U_i = \begin{cases} -n_1/(n_1 + n_2) & \text{if the } i^{th} \text{ project is not a success} \\ n_2/(n_1 + n_2) & \text{if the } i^{th} \text{ project is a success,} \end{cases}$$

and n_1 is the number of successes, and n_2 is the number of failures. Then we regress U_i on P_i^*, the result being

$$U_i = -0.6655 + 0.84 \ P_i^*. \tag{8}$$
$$(0.44)$$

Projects that were not carried out as planned are obviously not relevant here. The results are based on a sample of 25 projects.[26]

If a project's value of U_i calculated from Eq. 8 exceeds 0, one should predict success; if not, one should predict failure. This rule makes optimal use of the data on P_i^*, in the sense that it minimizes the probability of an incorrect prediction. How accurate is it? The fact that the regression coefficient of P_i^* in Eq. 8 is statistically significant indicates that P_i^* is of some use in predicting success or failure. However, it does not seem to be of great use, since it predicts incorrectly in about one-third of the cases on which Eq. 8 is based.[27]

---

26. We include "partial successes" with "successes" here. It would make more sense to include them with "failures," but there are so few that it makes little difference which way they are treated. See note 27.

27. Of course, good or bad performance is relative; what is good enough for one purpose is not good enough for another. One can obtain a probability of misclassification equal to 1 - P' (where P' is the a priori probability of technical success) merely by predicting that all projects will be successes, regardless of their estimated probability of technical success. The probability of misclassification based on this naive prediction (which makes no use of the estimated probabilities of technical success) can be employed as a standard against which to judge the probabilities of (cont'd.)

Of course, P_i^* may be more useful as a predictor if various other factors are held constant. To find out how much improvement there is, we included the age and experience of the department manager and the type of project (cost reduction, product improvement, consulting) as additional explanatory variables. Unfortunately, there was no evidence that their inclusion made any difference, since none of these variables turned out to be statistically significant factors in the discriminant function.

To sum up, although there is a direct relationship between the estimated probability of success and the outcome of a project, it is not strong enough to permit very accurate predictions. Using a statistical discriminant function, the probability of error is about one-third.

---

misclassification based on the discriminant function. The results depend on the a priori probability of technical success, but they do not vary greatly in the relevant range ($0.5 \leq P' \leq 0.75$). In this range, if "partial successes" are treated as failures, the probability of misclassification based on the discriminant function is only 10 to 30 percent lower than the probability of misclassification based on the naive prediction.

The probability of error cited in the text (about one-third) is an average of the probability of error based on (1) the classification of "partial successes" as successes and (2) the classification of "partial successes" as failures. If a similar average is used for alternative values of P' in the relevant range, the probability of misclassification based on the discriminant function is about 30 percent lower than the probability of misclassification based on the naive prediction. Thus, the probability of error generally is greater when "partial successes" are classified as failures rather than successes. Also, the results based on this average do not depend much on P' (at least in the relevant range).

25

IV

Accuracy of Estimates of Probability of Technical Completion, Development Cost, and Development Time in a Proprietary Drug Firm

A. PROBABILITY OF TECHNICAL COMPLETION

Next, let's look at the experience of a proprietary drug firm. (Proprietary drugs are those sold over-the-counter, and promotion of these products is directed at the consumer.)   In this firm, records of many completed projects include an estimate of the probability of achieving the technical objectives, as stated in the project proposal.[28] This estimate is made at the time of formal project proposal.   How accurate are these estimates ? Are such estimates generally optimistic, perhaps to sell the project to management ? What project characteristics are associated with the size of the error in the estimate ? Since labora- tory management uses these estimates in project selection, these questions are of practical importance as well as being of scholarly interest.

Data for 79 completed projects are used to help answer these questions. Each of the projects has records containing an estimated

---

28. Note that project completion means that the original technical objectives are achieved but not necessarily within the estimated time and cost. Presumably, these probabilities are based on the supposition that only certain cost and time overruns will be allowed, but no explicit maximum ratio of actual to expected cost or time is specified. Note too that attempts are sometimes made to adjust a project's objectives so as to make them conform with its results. For this reason, the original objectives are the relevant ones here.

probability of successful completion, and each either succeeded or failed technically. For obvious reasons, projects that were not completed for nontechnical reasons are excluded.[29] As Table 3 shows, the estimated probability of technical completion is, <u>on the average</u>, a good indicator of actual outcome, the average estimated probability of technical completion (.81) being very close to the actual proportion of projects that were completed (.76). However, the fact that the <u>average</u> estimated probability of technical completion is close to the actual proportion of projects that were completed does not mean that the estimates are useful in predicting <u>which</u> projects are more likely to be completed. How useful are the estimates in predicting whether a particular project will be completed? Table 3 indicates that they are of some use, the average estimate being higher for projects that were completed than for projects that were not completed.

To get a better idea of the usefulness of these estimates in predicting which projects will be completed, we construct a discriminant function. Defining U_i, the dependent variable, as 1 if the ith project is completed and 0 if it is not completed, and regressing U_i on the estimated probability of technical completion, P_i, yields the following equation:

$$U_i = .0001 + .94\ P_i.$$
$$\quad\ (.216)\quad (.26) \tag{9}$$

---

29. The estimates are based on the supposition that the projects are carried out. If some projects are not carried out because their objectives no longer seem commercially worthwhile, it is not fair to expect the estimates to anticipate this eventuality.

28

Table 3

RELATIONSHIP BETWEEN ESTIMATED PROBABILITY
OF TECHNICAL COMPLETION AND PROJECT OUTCOME,
PROPRIETARY DRUG LABORATORY

Estimated Probability of Technical Completion	Technical Outcome of Projects		
	Not Completed	Completed	Total
	(Proportion of Projects)		
Below .70	.42	.08	.16
.70-.79	.16	.17	.16
.80-.89	.11	.17	.15
.90-1.00	.32	.58	.52
Total[a]	1.00	1.00	1.00
Average Estimated Probability of Technical Completion			.81
Proportion of Projects Technically Completed			.76

a. Note: Because of rounding, sums of individual items may
   not equal totals.

If the right-hand side of this equation is greater than .76, we should
predict that the project will be completed; if not, we should predict
that it will not be completed. According to well-known statistical
theory, this procedure should, under particular circumstances, minimize
the probability of an incorrect prediction. (It is really the same as the
procedure in the preceding section, although U is defined differently.)
How well does this discriminant function "predict" the data? It
correctly predicts 70 percent of the outcomes and is wrong 30 percent
of the time.

29

Thus, the estimated probabilities of technical completion are of some use in predicting which projects will be completed and which ones will not. But they are not of much use. Even if they are used in such a way that the probability of an incorrect prediction is minimized, they predict incorrectly in about 30 percent of the cases. (As shown elsewhere, one would expect to make incorrect predictions in only 36 percent of the cases by chance.) This result is very close to that obtained in Section III.[30]

Table 4 compares the actual proportion of projects that are technically completed with the average estimated probability of technical completion for projects attempting small, medium, and large technical advances. For those attempting small technical advances, the estimated probability of completion, on the average, overstates the risk of failure. On the other hand, for those attempting medium or large technical advances, the estimated probability of completion, on the average, understates the risk of failure. These biases can be used to extend the discriminant functions. Let L_i be a dummy variable that is 1 if the ith project attempts a large technical advance and 0 otherwise, and M_i be a dummy variable that is 1 if the ith project attempts a medium technical advance and 0 otherwise. Using L_i and M_i as additional independent variables,

$$U_i = .43 - .71\ L_i - .37\ M_i + .57\ P_i. \quad (10)$$
$$(.20)\ (.14)\quad (.10)\quad (.23)$$

This discriminant function predicts correctly in 80 percent of the cases.

---

30. Also see E. Mansfield, op. cit., Chapter 3.

Table 4

ACTUAL PROPORTION OF PROJECTS TECHNICALLY COMPLETED
AND AVERAGE ESTIMATED PROBABILITY OF TECHNICAL COMPLETION
FOR SMALL, MEDIUM, AND LARGE TECHNICAL ADVANCES,
PROPRIETARY DRUG LABORATORY

| | Size of Technical Advance Sought | | | |
	Small	Medium	Large	Total
Average Estimated Probability of Technical Completion	.84	.71	.74	.81
Actual Proportion of Projects Technically Completed	.91	.47	.14	.76

Thus, it appears that the usefulness of the estimates may be increased by combining them with the information concerning the size of the technical advance sought by the projects. However, further work must be carried out before this result can be accepted fully. It is possible that the people who rated the size of the technical advance attempted by a project were influenced by whether it was completed. (The ratings were made after the projects were terminated.) If there was a tendency to rate projects that were not completed as more ambitious than those that were completed, the results in Eq. 10 are spurious. One way to get around this difficulty in future work is to obtain the ratings of the size of the attempted technical advance at the beginning of the project.

B.   COST OVERRUNS IN THE PROPRIETARY DRUG FIRM

In the proprietary drug firm, how accurate are the estimates of development cost made at the time of project proposal? Is there a

31

persistent overoptimism in forecasting costs, resulting in overruns of actual above estimated expenditures? Is the size of the overrun associated with the characteristics of the project described in Section IIB? To help answer these questions, data regarding 69 projects at this firm are analyzed. (For obvious reasons, only projects that were technically completed could be included.)[31] Table 5 shows the frequency distribution of projects by the ratio of actual to estimated costs. The distribution is quite skewed, the median ratio being .80 but the mean ratio being 2.11. Thus, most projects did not experience a cost overrun. But on the average, there is a large cost overrun, actual costs being 211 percent of estimated costs.

Table 5

DISTRIBUTION OF RATIO OF ACTUAL TO ESTIMATED COST,
FOR 69 PROJECTS, PROPRIETARY DRUG LABORATORY

Ratio of Actual to Estimated Cost	Percentage of Projects
0.39 and less	22
0.40–0.79	28
0.80–1.19	9
1.20–1.59	6
1.60–1.99	7
2.00–2.99	10
3.00 and above	19
Total	100

31. It would make no sense to compare the estimated cost of doing something with the actual cost of not doing it.

32

We have sufficient data to classify projects according to relative technical ambition and project type. This allows us to extend the findings in Sections II, A and B, as well as those of Klein, Summers, and Peck and Scherer.[32] We would expect the average ratio of actual to estimated cost to be higher, and the standard deviation of this ratio also to be higher, for new product developments than for product improvements and for large and medium technical advances than for small technical advances. Table 6 shows that these expectations are fulfilled. For example, the average ratio of actual to estimated cost is 2.75 for new products and 1.41 for product improvements; it is 3.66 for large and medium technical advances and 1.82 for small technical advances.[33]

How does the size of these cost overruns compare with that described in Section I for weapons systems? For those projects that aimed at new products, the average overrun--175 percent--was about four-fifths of the average overrun for the weapons systems. For those projects that aimed at medium or large technical advances, the average overrun in the proprietary drug firm was larger than the average overrun found by Peck and Scherer for airplane and missile development

32. B. Klein, "The Decision Making Problem in Development," The Rate and Direction of Inventive Activity (New York: National Bureau of Economic Research, 1962); Marschak, Glennan, and Summers, op. cit.; and M. Peck and F. Scherer, op. cit.

33. These differences may not be statistically significant, but Eq. 11 shows that the extent of a project's technical ambition is significantly related to the size of the cost overrun. As in the case of the ethical drug firm, the firm's executives rated all projects with regard to technical ambition; but in this firm they were asked to classify them into three groups: large, medium, and small technological advances. The crudeness of this procedure need not be belabored.

33

Table 6

AVERAGE AND STANDARD DEVIATION OF RATIO
OF ACTUAL TO ESTIMATED COST, BY PROJECT TYPE
AND RELATIVE SIZE OF TECHNICAL ADVANCE
FOR 69 TECHNICALLY COMPLETED PROJECTS,
PROPRIETARY DRUG LABORATORY

Project Type	Size of Technical Advance		
	Small	Large and Medium	Total
	(Ratio of Actual to Estimated Cost)		
Product Improvement			
Average	1.39	1.49	1.41
Standard deviation	1.39	1.64	1.41
Number of projects	28	5	33
New Products			
Average	2.21	5.46	2.75
Standard deviation	3.56	5.86	4.11
Number of projects	30	6	36
Total			
Average	1.82	3.66	2.11
Standard deviation	2.74	4.73	3.18
Number of projects	58	11	69

34

projects. This finding adds further weight to the conclusion in Section IIA that the cost overruns for civilian projects begin to approximate those for military projects when entirely new types of products are attempted.

Finally, we computed a regression similar to those in Section IIB, the dependent variable being $\ln R_c^i$, the logarithm of the ith project's ratio of actual to estimated cost, and the independent variables being $\ln C_E^i$, the logarithm of the ith project's estimated cost; W_i, a dummy variable that equals 1 if the ith project represented a medium or large technical advance and 0 otherwise; V_i, a dummy variable that equals 1 if the ith project is a new product and 0 if it is a product improvement; $\ln L_i$, the logarithm of the ith project's duration; and $\ln t_i$, where t_i is the year (less 1960) when the ith project was started. The result is

$$\ln R_c^i = -.29 - \underset{(.12)}{.10} V_i + \underset{(.17)}{.36} W_i + \underset{(1.12)}{1.76} \ln t_i - \underset{(.15)}{.56} \ln C_E^i$$

$$+ \underset{(.29)}{1.30} \ln L_i, \tag{11}$$

R^2 being .31. The effects of W_i, $\ln L_i$, and $\ln C_E^i$ are statistically significant. Their effects are in the expected direction and are quantitatively important. On the average, a project attempting a large or medium technical advance had a 43 percent larger cost overrun than a project attempting a small technical advance. A 1 percent increase in estimated cost was associated with a .56 percent decrease in the cost overrun, and a 1 percent increase in the duration of a project was associated with a 1.3 percent increase in the cost overrun.

C. TIME OVERRUNS IN THE PROPRIETARY DRUG FIRM

How great are the time overruns in the proprietary drug firm ?
Using data regarding the same 69 projects discussed in the previous
subsection, we attempt to answer this question. As in the previous subsection, the estimates were made at the time of project proposal.
Table 7 shows the frequency distribution of projects by the ratio of
actual to estimated time. Apparently, project durations almost always
overrun the estimates in the laboratory, the ratio of actual to estimated
time exceeding 1 in 88 percent of the cases. On the average, the ratio
of actual to estimated time was 2.95. For the same reasons as in the
preceding subsection, we might expect the average ratio of actual to
estimated time to be higher, and the standard deviation of this ratio also
to be higher, for new products than for product improvements, and for
large and medium technical advances than for small technical advances.
Table 8 shows that there is some tendency for the average and standard
deviation of this ratio to be higher for new products than for product
improvements (although the differences are not statistically significant).
Also, the standard deviation of this ratio may be somewhat greater--
but the average is not--for medium or large technical advances than for
small technical advances.

Comparing the size of these time overruns with that of the weapons
systems described in Section I, we find that the average overrun in this
proprietary drug firm is considerably greater than in weapons system
development. The average ratio of actual to estimated time was 1.5 in
the RAND study and 1.36 in the study by Peck and Scherer, as contrasted
with 2.95 in this firm (and 1.61 in the ethical drug firm discussed in

36

Section II). This result seems quite reasonable, since the pressure for meeting time schedules was almost certainly greater in weapons development than in proprietary (or ethical) drugs.

Table 7

DISTRIBUTION OF RATIO OF ACTUAL TO ESTIMATED TIME, FOR 69 PROJECTS, PROPRIETARY DRUG LABORATORY

Ratio of Actual to Estimated Time	Percentage of Projects
0.79 and less	3
0.80-1.19	12
1.20-1.59	3
1.60-1.99	7
2.00-2.99	30
3.00-3.99	22
4.00 and more	23
Total	100

Finally, we regressed the logarithm of the ith project's ratio of actual to estimated time ($\ell n\ R_t^i$) on the logarithm of the ith project's estimated time ($\ell n\ L_E^i$), a dummy variable indicating whether the ith project was a small or a medium-to-large technical advance (W_i), a dummy variable indicating whether the ith project was a new product or a product improvement (V_i), and the logarithm of its calendar year less 1960 ($\ell n\ t_i$). The results are:

$$\ell n\ R_t^i = 1.89 + .074\ V_i + .078\ W_i - 1.62\ \ell n\ t_i - .65\ \ell n\ L_E^i,$$
$$(.048)\qquad(.070)\qquad(0.41)\qquad(.11)$$

(12)

37

Table 8

AVERAGE AND STANDARD DEVIATION OF RATIO
OF ACTUAL TO ESTIMATED TIME, BY PROJECT TYPE
AND RELATIVE SIZE OF TECHNICAL ADVANCE,
FOR 69 TECHNICALLY COMPLETED PROJECTS,
PROPRIETARY DRUG LABORATORY

Project Type	Size of Technical Advance		
	Small	Large and Medium	Total
	(Ratio of Actual to Estimated Time)		
Product Improvement			
Average	2.80	1.74	2.64
Standard deviation	1.28	0.84	1.27
Number of projects	28	5	33
New Products			
Average	3.14	3.70	3.24
Standard deviation	1.74	2.19	1.80
Number of projects	30	6	36
Total			
Average	2.98	2.80	2.95
Standard deviation	1.53	1.93	1.58
Number of projects	58	11	69

38

R^2 being .37. All of the regression coefficients have the expected signs.[34] The effects of calendar year and the estimated length of the project are statistically significant and quantitatively important. Unlike the ethical drug firm discussed in Section IIC, there is definite evidence that this firm has witnessed smaller time overruns as time has gone on. The effects of the dummy variables representing project type and extent of technical advance are not significant, but the difference between new products and product improvements is nearly significant.

---

34. Actually, the sign of the coefficient of $\ln t_i$ is not specified by our hypotheses.

V

Use of Estimates and Attitudes Toward Their Accuracy

In previous sections we have presented and analyzed data concerning the accuracy of estimates of development cost, development time, and project outcome in a major ethical drug firm, a major electrical equipment firm, and a major proprietary drug firm. In addition, we have compared the size of the errors in these estimates with the size of the errors in the corresponding estimates in weapons development. At this point, we turn to two further questions concerning estimates of this sort: First, how widely are such estimates used? Second, how reliable are these estimates considered by laboratory managers?

Table 9 shows the percentage of 19 laboratories we interviewed that made and used various kinds of estimates concerning research projects and development projects in 1966. Several things are apparent from these data. First, laboratories more commonly make such estimates for <u>development</u> projects than for <u>research</u> projects. In view of the fact that development is more predictable than research, this is what we would expect. Second, practically all of the laboratories make formal estimates of a project's manpower requirements, its cost, and its duration. Third, a somewhat smaller percentage--about 80 percent-- estimate the probability of technical success, the probability of market

41

success, the size of market, and capital facility requirements for
<u>development</u> projects.[35]   Fourth, a still smaller percentage--about
50 or 60 percent--estimate the probability of technical success, the
probability of market success, the size of market, and capital facility
requirements for <u>research</u> projects.

Table 9

USE OF SELECTED ESTIMATES, 19 LABORATORIES, 1966[a]

Type of Estimate	Percent of Laboratories Making and Using Estimates	
	Research Projects	Development Projects
	(Percent)	
Project Cost	90	95
Manpower Requirements	100	100
Project Duration	84	100
Size of Market	63	74
Probability of Technical Success	63	84
Probability of Market Success	58	79
Capital Facility Requirements	42	74

a. Source: See Section IVC.

---

35. For a description of the way in which these estimates are made
and used, see E. Mansfield, <u>op.</u> <u>cit.</u> ; N. Baker and W. Pound, "R and D
Project Selection: Where We Stand," IEEE Transactions in Engineering
Management (June 1964); and works cited there.

Thus, the bulk of these laboratories say that they make and use estimates of this sort in evaluating and selecting development projects. How reliable do the administrators of these laboratories feel these estimates are? The director of each of the 19 laboratories was asked to rate the accuracy of each of the 12 estimates in Table 10 as totally unreliable, poor, fair, good, or excellent.[36]   Table 10 shows the percentage of administrators that rated each type of estimate as good or excellent and the percentage that rated each type of estimate as poor or totally unreliable. Also included are the findings of a similar survey by Seiler,[37] these findings being reasonably similar to our own.

About one-half or more of the laboratory directors in our sample-- and about one-third or more in Seiler's sample--feel that estimates of a project's manpower requirements, its development cost, its capital requirements, its research cost, its probability of technical success, and its development time are good or excellent. Only about 10 to 20 percent of the laboratory directors in our sample--and about 5 to 20 percent in Seiler's sample--regard these estimates as poor or totally untrustworthy. Given the data provided in previous sections concerning the errors in estimates of development cost, time, and outcome, it appears that laboratory directors may be unduly optimistic about the

---

36. Similar questions are asked in a much larger sample of firms by R. Seiler, Improving the Effectiveness of Research and Development (New York: McGraw-Hill Company, 1965).
    37. Ibid.

Table 10

PERCEIVED ACCURACY OF RESEARCH AND DEVELOPMENT
PROJECT ESTIMATES, FOR SAMPLE LABORATORIES
AND SEILER STUDY

Type of Estimate	Judgment of Estimate Accuracy			
	Good or Excellent		Poor or Totally Unreliable	
	Sample Laboratories	Seiler Study	Sample Laboratories	Seiler Study
	(Percentage of Laboratory Administrators)			
Manpower	79	37	11	10
Cost of Development	69	41	16	12
Capital Facilities Required	63	n.a.	21	n.a.
Cost of Research	53	31	16	17
Probability of Technical Success	53	55	16	6
Duration of Development	47	36	21	22
Cost Reduction	42	68	16	18
Duration of Research	42	30	26	30
Probability of Market Success	32	37	37	25
Net Profit	26	n.a.	37	n.a.
Market Revenue	21	41	37	30
Market Life	16	33	63	38

n.a. = not available

44

accuracy of these estimates, unless, of course, they are able to make much better estimates than our two drug firms and the electrical equipment firm.[38]

Also, judging from both Seiler's and our findings, a larger percentage of the laboratory administrators regards the estimates of market factors--probability of market success, revenue, profit, and market life--to be poor or totally unreliable than regards the estimates of development cost, development time, and the probability of technical success to be poor or totally unreliable. If their judgment is correct-- and we have no reason to question it--and if their estimates of development cost, development time, and the probability of technical success are as poor as those made by the firms considered here, the errors in the estimates of these market factors must be very large indeed, since they must be even larger than the errors (described in previous sections) in the estimates of development cost, development time, and the probability of technical success.

---

38. There is a small amount of data for other firms that suggests that our firms are not unrepresentative. Dennis Meadows provides some data for two chemical firms. One of these firms (Laboratory B) has cost overruns that seem to be larger, on the average, than the ones in our two drug firms, while the other (Laboratory A) has smaller cost overruns than our drug firms. Meadows also compares the estimated probability of success in a chemical laboratory with actual results. Dennis Meadows, "Estimate Accuracy and Project Selection Models in Industrial Research," Industrial Management Review (Spring 1968). Also, see E. Mansfield, op. cit.

VI

Summary

The principal conclusions of this paper are as follows: First, based on very detailed data for a major ethical drug firm and a major proprietary drug firm, there are sizable errors in the cost and time estimates made at the beginning of drug development projects. For over 80 percent of the projects in the ethical drug firm, the actual cost and time exceeded the estimated values. The average ratio of actual to estimated cost was 1.78; the average ratio of actual to estimated time was 1.61. Cost and time estimates were less reliable for new chemical entities than for compounded products and alternate dosage forms. In the proprietary drug firm, the average ratio of actual to estimated cost was 2.11, and the average ratio of actual to estimated time was 2.95. Again, the overruns were greater for more ambitious projects.

Second, when we compare the overruns in these two drug firms with those in weapons development, we find that the cost overruns are less than those in weapons development and that the time overruns are greater than in weapons development. However, this ignores the fact that the weapon systems are aimed at greater technical advances. When we look only at the more innovative drug projects, the results indicate that, when commercial activity is devoted to distinctly new

47

products, it begins to approximate weapons system development in the extent of cost overruns. For example, the average ratio of actual to expected cost is 2.3 for new chemical entities in the ethical drug firms, and 2.8 for new products in the proprietary drug firm, as compared with 3.2 for a sample of airplane and missile projects.

Third, in the ethical drug firm, we tested various hypotheses concerning the effects of certain factors on the size of a project's cost overrun. In accord with these hypotheses, it turns out that technically more ambitious projects tend to have greater cost overruns than technically less ambitious projects. Also, products with wider spectra of activity tend to have larger cost overruns than single-market products, and projects with small estimated costs or of longer duration tend to have larger cost overruns than projects with large estimated costs or of shorter duration. In the proprietary drug firm, there is also a significant tendency for technically more ambitious projects and projects with smaller estimated costs and longer duration to have larger cost overruns. In the ethical drug firm, and perhaps in the proprietary drug firm, cost overruns seem to have increased over time.

Fourth, when the same kind of model is used to analyze development time, the results are rather similar to those for development cost. In the ethical drug firm, there is a significant tendency for products with wider spectra of activity and projects with smaller estimated lengths to have greater time overruns. In the proprietary drug firm, there is also a significant tendency for projects with small estimated lengths to have greater time overruns; moreover, new products tend to have larger time overruns than product improvements, (but the difference

48

is not quite significant. In the proprietary drug firm, time overruns seem to have decreased significantly over time.

Fifth, in the ethical drug firm, the ratio of actual to estimated sales of new products was 1.75. There is some tendency for this ratio to be higher for entirely new chemical entities than for compounded products or alternate dosage forms, but the difference is not statistically significant. The forecasts made by this firm seem to be somewhat less accurate than the average reported by Tull. An important reason why some of the firm's forecasts are more accurate than others is that some forecasters had more resources at their disposal than others. As would be expected, the accuracy of a forecast seems to be related to the amount of resources devoted to the preparation of the forecast.

Sixth, in the proprietary drug firm and the electrical equipment firm, we studied the accuracy of the estimated probabilities of project completion. The average probability of technical completion turned out to be very close to the actual proportion of projects that were success-fully completed. Moreover, the estimated probabilities of technical completion are of some use in predicting which projects will be completed and which will not. But they are not of much use, since even if they are used to minimize the probability of an incorrect prediction, they lead to an incorrect prediction in about 30 percent of the cases. There is some reason to believe that their accuracy may be increased if the extent of the technical advance is taken into account, but more work needs to be done before we can be at all sure of this.

Seventh, based on our sample of laboratories in four industries, practically all laboratories make formal estimates of a project's

49

manpower requirements, cost, and duration; and most of them also make formal estimates of the probability of technical success, the probability of market success, and other such variables. Judging from their estimates of the reliability of the estimates of cost, time, and the probability of technical success, it appears that they may be unduly optimistic concerning the accuracy of these estimates. Furthermore, if their judgment is correct, the errors in the estimates of various market factors may be very large indeed, since they regard these estimates as even less accurate than those regarding development cost, time, and the probability of technical success.

16

MANAGEMENT SCIENCE
Vol. 28, No. 2, February 1982
Printed in U.S.A.

FIRMS' FORECASTS OF ENGINEERING EMPLOYMENT*

PETER BRACHT† AND EDWIN MANSFIELD†

In this paper we present data concerning the accuracy of firms' forecasts of engineering employment and suggest a simple model that may be of use in improving their accuracy. The results, which pertain to 54 firms in the aerospace, electronics, chemical, and oil industries, should be of use to managers, because the formulation of proper manpower policies clearly depends on the precision of such forecasts. Our approach also may be applicable to personnel other than engineers: better forecasts may result from the application of this simple model.
(RESEARCH AND DEVELOPMENT; FORECASTING—TIME SERIES; ENGINEERING—APPLICATIONS)

1. Introduction

Policy makers in government, universities, and business must make decisions that depend, explicitly or implicitly, on forecasts of the number of engineers employed in various sectors of the economy at various points in time. For example, in evaluating the adequacy of existing engineering manpower, public policy makers must try to forecast how many engineers will be employed in the private sector. Many groups, including the National Science Foundation and the Bureau of Labor Statistics, have made forecasts of this sort for decades.[1] Although such forecasts sometimes are based on a collection of forecasts made by firms of their own engineering employment, very little is known concerning the accuracy of firms' forecasts of this kind.

In this paper, we present data concerning the accuracy of such forecasts and suggest a simple model that may be of use in improving their accuracy. The results should be of use to managers because the formulation of proper manpower policies clearly depends on the precision of such forecasts. Very detailed data were obtained from a well-known engineering association which has collected such forecasts from firms for many years. For 54 firms in the aerospace, electronics, chemical, and petroleum industries, comparisons were made of each firm's forecasted engineering employment with its actual engineering employment during 1957 to 1976. Since data were obtained concerning a number of forecasts of each firm, the accuracy of 218 such forecasts could be evaluated.[2]

The results indicate that the forecasting errors for individual firms in the aerospace industry have been large, as can be seen in Table 1. For example, even when firms

---

* Accepted by Burton V. Dean; received November 4, 1980. This paper has been with the authors 1 month for 1 revision.

† University of Pennsylvania.

[1] For example, see National Science Foundation [10], [11] and Folk [4].

[2] These four industries were chosen because they employ almost 60 percent of all engineers in manufacturing. The firms that were included tend to be among the largest in these industries. All firms are included for which usable data were obtained by the engineering association. Each firm forecasted what its engineering employment would be at the end of about 6 months, 2 years, 5 years, and 10 years. Subsequently, each such forecast was compared with the firm's actual engineering employment then. (In some cases, the firm provided a high and low forecast, in which case the mean was used.) Both the forecast and the actual figure were reported to the engineering association from which we received the data.

In a relatively few cases, the actual figure had to be approximated by interpolation between figures given for somewhat different dates. Also, in a relatively few cases, because the firm did not include nongraduate engineers in its figures, it was necessary to assume that the ratio of nongraduate to graduate engineers equaled what it was in an earlier period. These adjustments have no effect at all on the results pertaining to the 6-month forecasts, since none of the observations were adjusted. They almost always have very little effect on the results pertaining to the 2-year or 5-year forecasts. But for the 10-year forecasts, the errors for

156

0025-1909/82/2802/0156$01.25

TABLE I

*Mean Percentage Error in a Firm's Forecast of Its Engineering
Employment, 54 Firms, 1957–76*

Industry	Forecasting Interval[a] (Years)			
	0.5	2	5	10
	(percentages)			
Aerospace	10.3	15.9	41.2	88.7
Electronics	4.6	12.4	15.4	26.5
Chemicals	3.2	5.7	17.3	22.0
Petroleum	2.8	5.5	13.1	9.4

[a]The forecasting interval is the length of time between the
data when the forecast is made and the date to which is
applies.

have forecasted only six months ahead, the mean percentage error was about 10 percent. In the electronics, chemical, and petroleum industries, the forecasting errors for individual firms have been much less, although the mean percentage error for 2-year forecasts in the electronics industry was about 12 percent. The relatively large forecasting errors in the aerospace industry (and to a lesser extent, the electronics industry) seem to be due to its heavy dependence on government defense and space programs which were volatile and hard to predict.

As might be expected if there is no major bias in the forecasts, although the forecasting errors for individual firms are substantial, they tend to be smaller when we consider the total engineering employment for all firms in the sample. On the average, the 6-month forecasts were in error by about 2 percent, the 2-year forecasts were in error by about 1 percent, and the 5-year forecasts were in error by about 3 percent.[3] The fact that there was so little bias in the forecasts is encouraging since, for many purposes, the principal aim is to forecast total engineering employment in some sector of the economy, not the engineering employment of a particular firm.

Studies of forecast errors often indicate that, when the actual quantity is relatively high, the forecast is too low, and that, when the actual quantity is relatively low, the forecast is too high (as illustrated by line AB in Figure 1). This was found to be true by Tull [9] in his study of the accuracy of the forecasts of new product sales, and by Beardsley and Mansfield [1] in their study of the accuracy of forecasts of the profitability of new products and processes. However, our data indicate that this is not the case for engineering employment. On the contrary, holding constant the length of the forecasting interval, the average relationship between forecasted and actual employment by firms can be approximated by a straight line through the origin, as represented by line $0C$ in Figure 1. Based on regression analysis, we found no statistically significant indication that the intercept of the actual vs. forecasted line is nonzero.[4]

---

the unadjusted observations tended to be smaller than for all observations. Thus, our results may overstate the forecast errors for the 10-year forecasts.

An engineer is defined here as someone who has attained engineering status through company training or work experience as well as through a degree in engineering. Such nongraduates comprise a small percentage of total engineering employment. For a good discussion of various definitions of an engineer, see Cain, Freeman, and Hansen [3].

[3]The 10-year forecasts showed an average upward bias of about 27 percent, due no doubt in part to the extrapolation of the relatively high rates of growth in engineering employment during the late 1950s and early 1960s to later periods. Also see footnote 2.

[4]Holding industry and forecasting interval constant, when a firm's forecasted employment is regressed on its actual employment, the intercept of the regression (in 12 out of 13 cases) does not differ significantly from zero (at the 0.05 level).

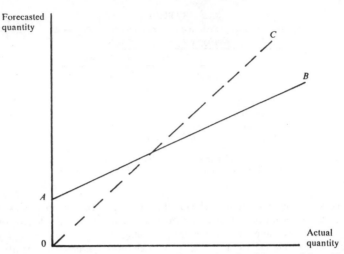

FIGURE 1.   Alternative Possible Relationships between Actual and Forecasted Quantities.

Economists sometimes construct models in which it is hypothesized that firms at each point in time have a desired employment level for a particular kind of labor, and that they set their actual employment level for this kind of labor so as to move part way toward this desired employment level. Thus, in the case of engineers, firms are continually adjusting their employment toward the level that they would regard as optimal if changes in employment levels could be made instantaneously and if the inefficiencies involved in too rapid a change in engineering employment could be avoided. If $E_i(t)$ is the ith firm's engineering employment at time t, and if $\tilde{E}_i(t + 1)$ is its optimal or desired employment one year hence, then $E_i(t + 1)$ can be represented as

$$E_i(t + 1) = E_i(t) + \theta_i(t)\big[\, \tilde{E}_i(t + 1) - E_i(t)\,\big]. \tag{1}$$

In other words, $\theta_i(t)$ is the proportion of the way that the ith firm's engineering employment moves toward the desired level between time t and time $t + 1$.

If one can estimate $\theta_i(t)$, equation (1) can be used to forecast $E_i(t + 1)$, since data can be obtained at time t regarding $E_i(t)$ and $\tilde{E}_i(t + 1)$. The engineering association collected data concerning $\tilde{E}_i(t + 1)$ for various times between 1957 and 1968, so we were able to obtain direct estimates of $\theta_i(t)$ for 7 major chemical firms and 6 major petroleum firms during this period. These were all of the firms for which appropriate data were available.[5] The mean value of $\theta_i(t)$ is very similar for the two industries: it is 0.73 in chemicals and 0.72 in petroleum. These results are quite similar to those of Freeman [4], although his estimates of the rate of adjustment are based on quite different kinds of data.

To explain differences among time periods and firms in the value of $\theta_i(t)$, it seems reasonable to assume that

$$\theta_i(t) = \phi_0 + \phi_1 D_i(t) + \phi_2 I_i(t) + u_i(t), \tag{2}$$

---

[5] The engineering association, cited above, obtained data during this period regarding each firm's desired and actual levels of engineering employment. Such data were not obtained for previous or subsequent years. The definition of the desired level was not exactly the same as that given above, but it was regarded by officials of the association as being reasonably close. It called for the number of engineers desired to meet the firm's goals and commitments. All firms in these industries were included where $\tilde{E}_i(t + 1) > E_i(t)$. See footnote 6.

where $D_i(t)$ is the desired percentage increase in engineering employment between time t and time $t + 1$, $I_i(t)$ is the percentage change in the ith firm's profits during this period, and $u_i(t)$ is a random error term.[6] A priori, we would expect ϕ_1 to be negative since, if attaining its desired employment level means that the firm must increase its employment by a relatively large percentage, this firm will move a relatively small proportion of the way toward this desired level because of the costs of rapid change in employment levels. Similarly, we would expect ϕ_2 to be positive because relatively large increases in profits will influence firms' expectations and make them bolder in moving toward desired employment levels.

To see how well the hypothesized model in (2) fits the data, we obtained least-squares estimates of ϕ_0, ϕ_1, and ϕ_2, as shown in Table 2. The results show that each of the regression coefficients has the expected sign and is statistically significant. This model explains over three-quarters of the variation in $\theta_i(t)$ in chemicals and about one-half of such variation in petroleum.[7] Using the least-squares estimates of ϕ_0, ϕ_1, and ϕ_2, one can estimate $\theta_i(t)$ for each firm on the basis of its values of $D_i(t)$ and $I_i(t)$. Inserting this estimate of $\theta_i(t)$ into equation (1), one can forecast $E_i(t + 1)$. Based on the data for these firms, the resulting forecasts are appreciably better than those of the firms themselves.[8]

In conclusion, in view of the importance of technical manpower in promoting technological change in both civilian and military fields, both government agencies and private organizations must continually assess, as best they can, the future state of the labor market for many kinds of professional and technical personnel. Our results pertain entirely to engineers, but the approach adopted above may be applicable to other types of personnel as well. Better forecasts may result from the application of this simple sort of model. At the same time, our findings are tentative in many respects, even for engineers.[9] This seems to be one of the first reasonably comprehen-

TABLE 2

Estimated Regression Coefficients,[a] *Equation (2)*

Industry	Independent Variables			
	ϕ_0	$D_i(t)$	$I_i(t)$	$\bar{R}^2$
Chemical	0.32	− 4.61	0.74	0.78
	(0.95)	(5.8)	(2.15)	
Petroleum	− 1.21	− 6.55	2.33	0.51
	(1.2)	(3.1)	(2.35)	

[a]The t-statistic is shown in parentheses below each regression coefficient.

[6]This model assumes that $\bar{E}_i(t + 1) > E_i(t)$, which was the typical case during 1957–68. The data regarding $I_i(t)$ come from *Moody's*. For the chemical firms, $I_i(t)$ is the ith firm's net income in year $t + 1$ divided by its net income in year t; for the petroleum firms, it is the firm's net income in year t divided by its net income in year $t − 1$.

[7]Mansfield [6] found that a similar model worked quite well for R and D expenditures in these industries. Also, see Mansfield et al. [7], [9], as well as Braunstein, Baumol and Mansfield [2] and Mansfield [8].

[8]The mean percentage error for the chemical firms is about 0.25 percentage points and for the petroleum firms is about 1.25 percentage points, which is considerably less than in Table 1. Since the estimates of the ϕ's are based on the same data, these results are essentially a measure of goodness of fit. The next step might be to try out a model of this sort over a reasonably long period of time, and see how well it works and how it can be improved. Obviously, the present results are only a first step.

[9]Although we are fortunate to have such a large sample in Table 1 (over 200 forecasts), the sample is by no means ideal. For example, many of the forecasts relate to a considerable number of years ago. It would be desirable to have more information on changes over time in the accuracy of firms' forecasts, but the data obtained from the engineering association cannot support an adequate study of this matter because a number of relevant variables cannot be held constant and for other reasons. For additional limitations of this study, see notes 2, 5, 6, and 8.

sive studies of firms' forecasts of engineering employment. Much more needs to be done.[10]

[10]The work on which this paper is based was supported by a grant to Mansfield from the National Science Foundation, which, of course, is not responsible for the views expressed here. We are grateful for this support, as well as for the cooperation of the engineering association that provided us with data. The calculations and data collection involved in this paper were carried out by Brach. Some of the results of this paper were included in Mansfield's Andersen Lectures at the University of Brussels in 1981.

References

1. BEARDSLEY, G. AND MANSFIELD, E., "A Note on the Accuracy of Industrial Forecasts of the Profitability of New Processes and Products," *J. Business* (January 1978), pp. 127–135.
2. BRAUNSTEIN, Y., BAUMOL, W. AND MANSFIELD, E., "The Economics of R and D," in B. Dean and J. Goldhar (eds.), *Management of Research and Innovation*, TIMS Studies in the Management Sciences, Vol. 15, North-Holland, Amsterdam, 1980, pp. 19–32.
3. CAIN, G., FREEMAN, R. AND HANSEN, W. L., *Labor Markets Analysis of Engineers and Technical Workers*, Johns Hopkins, Baltimore, Md., 1973.
4. FOLK, H., *The Shortage of Scientists and Engineers*, Heath Lexington, Lexington, Mass., 1970.
5. FREEMAN, R., "Scientists and Engineers in the Industrial Economy," unpublished National Science Foundation report, 1971.
6. MANSFIELD, E., *Industrial Research and Technological Innovation*, W. W. Norton, New York, for the Cowles Foundation for Research in Economics at Yale University, 1968.
7. ———, RAPOPORT, J., ROMEO, A., VILLANI, E., WAGNER, S. AND HUSIC, F., *The Production and Application of New Industrial Technology*, Norton, New York, 1977.
8. ———, "Technological Innovation: Recent Economic Results Relevant to Managers," *Harvard Business Rev.* (to appear).
9. ———, ROMEO, A., SCHWARTZ, M., TEECE, D., WAGNER, S. AND BRACH, P., *Technology Transfer, Productivity, and Economic Policy*, Norton, New York (to appear).
10. NATIONAL SCIENCE FOUNDATION, *Science Indicators, 1978*, Government Printing Office, Washington, D.C., 1979a.
11. ———, *Projections of Science and Engineering Doctorate Supply and Utilization, 1982 and 1987*, Government Printing Office, Washington, D.C., 1979b.
12. TULL, D., "The Relationship of Actual and Predicted Sales and Profits in New Product Introductions," *J. Business* (July 1967).

Erratum

The top three lines on page 159 (251) should read: 'where $D_i(t)$ is the desired proportional increase in engineering employment between time t and time $t+1$ (that is, $D_i(t) = [\tilde{E}_i(t+1) - E_i(t)] \div E_i(t))$, $I_i(t)$ is the ratio of the ith firm's profits in time t to those in time $t-1$, and $u_i(t)$ is a random error term. A priori, we would expect ϕ_1 to be negative'.

PART IV

TECHNOLOGICAL CHANGE, ECONOMIC GROWTH AND INFLATION

17

Contribution of R & D to Economic Growth in the United States

The author, now at the Center for Advanced Study in the Behavioral Sciences at Stanford, California, is professor of economics at the Wharton School of the University of Pennsylvania. This article was commissioned by the National Science Foundation, and was presented at the NSF symposium on Research and Development and Economic Growth and Productivity Increase which was held in Washington, DC, on 24 April 1971.

Technological change is clearly an important factor in economic growth, both in the United States and in other countries, both now and in the past. In recent years – after neglecting the study of technological change for a long time – economists have shown a considerable interest in examining the relationship between research and development (R & D), on the one hand, and the rate of economic growth and productivity increase, on the other. In addition, there have been a number of discussions of whether we, as a nation, are underinvesting in certain kinds of R & D. In this article I describe briefly what we know – or think we know – about the relationship between R & D and economic growth and productivity increase. Also, some attention is devoted to the question of whether there may be an underinvestment in R & D. Finally, I try to indicate the trustworthiness and accuracy of existing findings, and suggest areas in which more research is needed.

At the outset, two important points should be noted. First, by focusing attention on the economic effects of R & D, I am not implying that only these effects of R & D are important. On the contrary, increased knowledge is clearly of great importance above and beyond its strictly economic benefits. Second, by looking at our nation's rate of economic growth and productivity increase, I am not assuming explicitly or implicitly that economic growth is, in some simple sense, what public policy should attempt to maximize. Clearly, the desirability of a particular growth rate depends on the way it is achieved, how the extra production is distributed, how growth is measured, and many other things.

R & D and economic growth

The pioneering studies of the relationship between technological change and economic growth – by Solow[1], Abramowitz[2], and Fabricant[3] – occurred in the mid-1950s. In many respects, Solow's paper was most influential. Assuming that there were constant returns to scale, that capital and labour were paid their marginal products, and that technological change was neutral, Solow attempted to estimate the rate of technological change for the nonfarm American economy during the period from 1909 to 1949. His findings suggested that, for the period as a whole, the average rate of technological

255

change was about 1.5 per cent per year. More precisely, the output that could be derived from a fixed amount of inputs increased at about 1.5 per cent per year.

. Based on these findings, he concluded that about 90 per cent of the increase in output per capita during this period was attributable to technological change, whereas only a minor proportion of the increase was due to increases in the amount of capital employed per worker. This conclusion received a great deal of attention – and caused some consternation among economists who had focused much more attention on the factors underlying the amount of capital employed per worker than on those underlying the rate of technological change. A flurry of papers followed Solow's, each modifying his techniques slightly or using a somewhat different database.

After the first wave of papers in the mid-1950s, investigators began to feel increasingly uneasy about the basic methodology used in these studies. In essence, this methodology was the following. Economists, who view the total output of the economy as being due to various inputs of productive services into the productive process, began by specifying these inputs as labour and capital and by attempting to estimate the contribution of these inputs to the measured growth of output. Then, whatever portion of the measured growth of output that could not be explained by these inputs was attributed to technological change. The crudeness of this procedure is obvious. Since the effect of technological change is equated with whatever increase in output is unexplained by other inputs, the resulting measure of the effect of technological change does not isolate the effects of technological change alone. It also contains the effects of whatever inputs are excluded – which, depending on the study, may be economies of scale, improved allocation of resources, changes in product mix, increases in education, or improved health and nutrition of workers.

To remedy some of these limitations, a number of additional studies were carried out in the early 1960s, the most comprehensive and influential one being by Denison.[4] Denison attempted to include many inputs – particularly changes in labour quality associated with increases in schooling – that had been omitted, largely or completely, in earlier studies. Since it was relatively comprehensive, his study resulted in a relatively low residual increase in output unexplained by the inputs included. Specifically, Denison concluded that the 'advance of knowledge' – his term for the residual – was responsible for about 40 per cent of the total increase in national income per person employed during 1929-1957.

Of course, technological change can stem from sources other than organized R & D, as evidenced by the findings of Jewkes *et al.*[5] concerning the importance of independent investors as a source of major inventions, and the findings by Hollander[6] and others concerning the importance of technological changes that depend in no significant way on formal R & D. Denison estimates that about one-fifth of the contribution to economic growth of 'advance of knowledge' in 1929-1957 can be attributed to organized R & D. But this is the roughest kind of guess, and Denison himself would be the first to admit that this estimate is based largely on conjecture.

Fundamental problems of measurement
How firmly based is the current state of the art in this area? In other words, how reliable are the estimates of the contribution of R & D to economic growth in the United States? I have already indicated some of the difficulties present in these estimates. Unfortunately,

there are a number of additional problems of a fundamental nature that must be understood as well. First, the measured rates of growth of output on which these estimates are based suffer from a very important defect, particularly for present purposes, because, to a large extent, they fail to give proper credit and weight to improvements in the quality of goods and services produced, and these improvements are an important result of R & D. For example, the growth rate would have been the same whether antibiotics were developed or not, or whether we devoted the resources used to reach the moon to public works. In general, only those changes in technology that reduce the costs of end products already in existence have an effect on measured economic growth. Unfortunately, the measured growth of national income fails to register or indicate the effects on consumer welfare of the increased spectrum of choice arising from the introduction of new products.

Second, the models on which these estimates are based may not take into account the full complexity of the relationships among the various inputs. In particular, as Nelson, Peck, and Kalachek[7] have pointed out, if the returns to some input are dependent on the rate of technological change, and if this is not recognized explicitly, some of technology's contribution to economic growth will be attributed incorrectly to other inputs. This may be the case with education, since the returns to education would probably have been less if technological change had occurred at a slower pace. It may also be the case with 'the reallocation of resources,' a factor sometimes used to explain part of the residual increase in output.

Third, it is not clear how one can get from an estimate of the contribution to economic growth of technological change (or advance of knowledge, in Denison's terms) to an estimate of the contribution to economic growth of R & D. Clearly, there is no reason that these two estimates should be the same; on the contrary, one would expect the latter estimate to be smaller than the former. But the estimate that results from the models discussed above is the former estimate, not the latter – which is the one we want. As pointed out, Denison does make an attempt to derive the latter estimate from the former, and to do so, he is forced to make extremely rough assumptions. To a certain extent, numbers must simply be pulled out of the air.

Fourth, there are difficulties in measuring inputs, the measurement of aggregate capital being a particularly nettlesome problem. Since errors in the measurement of inputs will result in errors in the estimated contribution of these inputs to economic growth, these errors will also be transmitted to, and will affect, the residual unexplained increase in output, which is used to measure the contribution of technological change to economic growth. Also, it is difficult to adjust for quality changes in inputs, and there are problems in constructing proper price deflators. According to Jorgensen and Griliches[8], there are important errors of measurement and aggregation in the measures that are ordinarily used, and these errors inflate the residual.

Fifth, difficulties are caused by the fact that much of the nation's R & D is devoted to defence and space purposes. For example, some observers note the tremendous increase in expenditures on R & D in the postwar period and conclude that, because productivity has not risen much faster in this period than it did before the war, the effect of R & D on economic growth must be very small. What these observers forget is that the bulk of the nation's expenditures on R & D has been devoted to defence and space objectives and that the contribution of such expenditures to economic growth may have been limited. Moreover, they fail to realize that improvements in defence and space capability per dollar spent will not show up in measures of output because government output is valued at cost. (Also, they fail to recognize the fact that product improvements and new products often fail to register in output measures and that the effects of R & D often occur with a considerable lag.)

Based on this catalogue of problems and limitations, it is clear that the current state of the art in this area is not strong enough to permit very accurate estimates of the contribution of R & D to the economic growth of the United States. At best, the available estimates are rough guidelines. In no sense is this a criticism of the economics profession or of the people working in this area. On the contrary, a great deal of progress has been made since the pioneering ventures into this area a little over a decade ago. Given the small number of people working in this area and the inherent difficulty of the problem, it is hard to see how much more could have been achieved.

R & D and productivity increase in individual industries

During the late 1950s, important work concerning the rate of productivity increase in various industries was going on at the National Bureau of Economic Research; this project culminated in Kendrick's book.[9] As part of this work, Terleckyj[10] carried out a study of the relationship between an industry's rate of increase of total factor productivity during the period from 1919 to 1953 and various industry characteristics. According to his results, an industry's rate of growth of total factor productivity was related in a statistically significant way to its ratio of R & D expenditures to sales, its rate of change of output level, and the amplitude of its cyclical fluctuations. Specifically, the rate of growth of total factor productivity increased by about 0.5 per cent for each tenfold increase in the ratio of R & D expenditures to sales and by about 1 per cent for every 3 per cent increase in the industry's growth rate.

Subsequently, two other papers appeared on this topic, one pertaining to agriculture, one pertaining to manufacturing. The agricultural study, by Griliches[11], investigated the relationship in various years between output per farm in a given state and the amounts of land, labour, fertilizer, and machinery per farm, as well as average education and expenditures on research and extension in a given state. The results indicate that, holding other inputs constant, output was related in a statistically significant way to the amount spent on research and extension. Moreover, the regression coefficient of this variable remains remarkably stable when cross-sections are deleted or added and when the specification of the model is changed somewhat.

The manufacturing study, by Mansfield[12, 13], was based on data regarding ten large chemical and petroleum firms and ten manufacturing industries in the postwar period. Both for firms and for industries, the measured rate of productivity change was related in a statistically significant way to the rate of growth of cumulated R & D expenditures made by the firm or industry. The specific form of the relationship depends somewhat on whether technological change is assumed to be disembodied (better methods and organization that improve the efficiency of both old capital and new) or capital embodied (innovations that must be embodied in new equipment if they are to be utilized). When technological change was disembodied, the average effect of a 1 per cent increase in the rate of growth of cumulated R & D expenditures was a 0.1 per cent increase in the rate of productivity increase. When technological change was capital embodied, it was a 0.7 per cent increase in the rate of productivity increase.

In addition, Minasian[14] studied the relationship between value added, and labour, capital, and cumulated R & D expenditures in 17 firms in the chemical industry from 1948 to 1957.[15] In all but one of the specifications of the model tried by Minasian, a firm's cumulated R & D expenditures are related in a statistically significant way to the firm's value added, holding its labour and capital inputs constant. Moreover, his estimate of the regression coefficient for cumulated R & D expenditures is strikingly close to the result obtained by Mansfield. Thus, the findings of the two studies tend to reinforce one another.

Finally, Brown and Conrad[16] carried out a study of the relationship between R & D expenditures (as well as education and other variables) and productivity increase in a number of US manufacturing industries in the postwar period. Their results, published in 1967, indicated that R & D expenditures had a statistically significant effect on the rate of productivity increase. Also, in their judgment, their findings indicate that a given percentage increase in R & D expenditures in durable goods industries produces a substantially larger percentage increase in productivity than does the same percentage increase in R & D expenditures in nondurable goods industries.

Evaluation of productivity studies

How reliable are these estimates of the relationship between R & D and productivity increase in individual industries? Clearly, one advantage of these studies is that the effect of R & D is not derived indirectly as a residual. Instead, an industry's – or a firm's or area's – R & D expenditures are introduced as an explicit input in the productive process. Thus, it is possible to obtain explicit relationships between R & D and productivity increase; it is no longer necessary to attribute to technology or R & D whatever cannot be explained by other factors. This is a real advantage.

But a number of important problems remain. First, too little is known about the characteristics of the activities that firms call 'research and development'. This lack of information has been a hindrance to progress in this area, since, without a reasonable amount of information on this score, it is difficult to interpret or evaluate models relating R & D expenditures to other economic variables. Clearly, if the figures on 'research and development' contain routine technical services and other such activities, the estimates based on these figures will be affected. It is difficult to tell how important this problem is, but, for some purposes, I would guess it to be a serious problem.

Second, even if one were sure that R & D figures were reliable, there would still be the possibility of spurious correlation. Firms and industries that spend relatively large amounts on R & D may tend to have managements that are relatively progressive and forward looking. To what extent is the observed relationship between R & D and productivity increase due to this factor rather than to R & D? Obviously, this is difficult to answer because the quality of management is very difficult to measure. Nonetheless, most investigators seem to feel that only a small part of the observed relationship is due to spurious correlation of this sort.

Third, a large percentage of the R & D carried out by many industries is directed at productivity increase in *other* industries. Consequently, relationships between R & D in an industry or firm and productivity increase in the *same* industry or firm catch only part of the effects of R & D. Unfortunately, too little effort has been directed at introducing interindustry or interfirm flows of technology into the sorts of models that underlie these relationships. Also, the estimates that are obtained depend on the extent of the lag between the time that R & D is carried out and the time that the effects of R & D show up in productivity indexes. Clearly, this lag is often substantial. Unfortunately, the models on which these estimates are based often make very crude assumptions concerning the length of the lag.

Fourth, there is a host of technical problems. To what extent is technological change disembodied, and to what extent is it capital embodied? If R & D is treated as investment in new knowledge – as it is in most of these studies – what depreciation rate should be used? Also, there is the perennial problem of how R & D expenditures should be deflated, as well as the problem of the form of the production function that should be used in particular cases. The answer one gives to these questions can have a significant effect on the estimates one obtains.[17] However, none of these problems is entirely resolved, although some work has been devoted to the deflation problem and to the form of the production function.

Fifth, studies of the relationship between R & D and productivity increase in individual industries suffer, of course, from a number of the same problems that beset studies of the contribution of R & D to economic growth. Some of these problems are inadequacies of the output measures used, poor specification of the relationship among inputs, and difficulties in measuring inputs.

Based on this discussion of the problems in the existing estimates of the relationship between R & D and productivity increase in individual industries, it is clear that the current state of the art in this area is not strong enough to permit definitive estimation of these relationships. Nonetheless, although the results are subject to considerable error, they establish certain broad conclusions. In particular, existing econometric studies do provide reasonably persuasive evidence that R & D has a significant effect on the rate of productivity increase in the industries and time periods that have been studied.

Externalities, riskiness, and investment in R & D

At this point, I turn to the question of whether or not, from a purely economic point of view, the United States is underinvesting in R & D. Certain propositions bearing on this question are widely accepted by economists and should be set forth at the beginning of this discussion. The first proposition is that, because the results of research are often of little direct value to the sponsoring firm but of great value to other firms, there is good reason to believe that, left to its own devices, the market would allocate too few resources to R & D – and that the shortfall would be particularly great at the more basic end of the R & D spectrum. The reason for this is fairly obvious: the market operates on the principle that the benefits go to the person bearing the costs, and vice versa. If a firm or individual takes an action that contributes to society's welfare, but it cannot appropriate the full gain, then it obviously is less likely to take this action than would be socially desirable.

The second proposition is that, because R & D is risky for the individual firm, there is good reason to believe that the market, left to its own devices, would allocate too few resources to R & D. Of course, the risk to the individual investor in R & D is greater than the risk to society, since the results of the R & D may be useful to someone else, not to himself, and he may be unable to obtain from the user the full value of the information. Because the economic system has limited and imperfect ways of shifting risks, there would be an underinvestment in R & D. For this reason, too, one would expect the underinvestment to be greatest at the more basic end of the R & D spectrum.[18]

These defects of the market mechanism in allocating resources to R & D have long been recognized. For example, Pigou set some of them forth quite clearly in the 1920s.[19] Moreover, they have been recognized in the realm of practical affairs and of social organization, as well as in the realm of social science. Our society, taking account of these defects of the market mechanism, does not depend exclusively on the market for an investment in R & D. On the contrary, a very large proportion of the nation's expenditures on R & D stems from government agencies, private foundations, and universities, all of which supplement the R & D supported through the market mechanism. Thus, the relevant question is not whether the market mechanism requires supplementing, but whether the type and extent of supplementary support provided at present is too large or too small, and whether it is allocated properly.

Salient characteristics of the nation's investment in R & D

Before discussing the above question, several important characteristics of the nation's investment in R & D must be noted. First, as is well-known, the nation's investment in R & D is focused very strongly on defence and space technology. During the early 1960s, over 55 per cent of the nation's R & D expenditures were for these purposes. With the passage of time, this percentage has decreased, but even in 1970, about 43 per cent of the nation's investment in R & D was for these purposes.[20] The relevance to economic growth of much of this huge investment in defence and space R & D has been questioned by many economists.

Numerous groups within the government – an early example being the White House Panel on Civilian Technology – have been interested in the extent of the benefits to civilian technology – the 'spillover' or 'fallout' – from military and space R & D. Obviously, the extent of this spillover has implications regarding the extent to which the investment in defence and space R & D has relevance for economic growth. It is perfectly clear that the value of the spillover that has occurred in the past has been substantial – the computer, numerical control, integrated circuits, atomic energy, and many other significant advances having stemmed at least partly from military R & D. However, it is also clear that the contribution of a dollar of military and space R & D to economic growth is considerably less than the contribution of a dollar of civilian R & D. Moreover, in the opinion of some observers, the spillover per dollar of military-space R & D is unlikely to be as great as it was in the past, because the capabilities that are being developed and the environment that is being explored are less closely connected with civilian pursuits than they were in the past.

Second, just as the government's expenditures on R & D are concentrated largely in a few agencies (the Department of Defense, the National Aeronautics and Space Administration, and the Atomic Energy Commission) with defence and space missions, so industry's expenditures on R & D are concentrated in a few industries. In 1969, 82 per cent of all industrial R & D expenditures took place in only five industries –

aerospace, electrical equipment and communication, chemicals (including drugs), machinery, and motor vehicles. Of course, this concentration is due in part to the fact that these industries perform a great deal of R & D for the federal government. But if one looks only at company-financed R & D, the concentration is nearly the same, with these five industries accounting in 1969 for 75 per cent of all company-financed R & D expenditures. Moreover, this concentration seems to be increasing.[21]

Industry's R & D expenditures are also concentrated largely on products, not processes. For example, according to a survey of business firms carried out in the early 1960s, about 47 per cent of the firms reported that their main purpose was to develop new products, and about 40 per cent reported that it was to improve existing products: only 13 per cent reported that it was to develop new processes.[22] However, lest there be any misunderstanding, it should be recognized that one industry's products may be part of another industry's processes. Thus, when a machinery producer improves its products or when a chemical producer improves its products, the result may be an improvement in the processes of industries that buy and use the machinery or chemicals.

Third, this nation's investment in R & D is focused very strongly on development, not research. The distinction between research and development, although hazy and indistinct in some cases, is important. Research is aimed primarily at the search for new knowledge, whereas development is aimed at the reduction of research findings to practice. In 1970, according to estimates made by the National Science Foundation, about two-thirds of the nation's investment in R & D went for development, only about one-third for research (p. 7).[20] Much of the development work carried out by industry and government is aimed at very specific objectives and involves large expenditures on prototypes and pilot plants. It is important to avoid the (unfortunately common) mistake of confusing this activity with research.

Moreover, it is important to recognize that much of the R & D carried out by industry is aimed at fairly modest advances in the state of the art. Studies carried out by Hamberg[23], Jewkes *et al.*[5], and others seem to indicate that the really major inventions seldom stem from industrial laboratories of major firms, which are primarily contributors of minor 'improvement' inventions. Also, surveys indicate that firms emphasize relatively short payout periods for R & D, this emphasis being another indication that most R & D carried out by the responding firms is aimed at improvements or minor changes in existing products.[22] In addition, detailed studies of the characteristics of the R & D portfolio of a number of industrial laboratories by Mansfield,[13, 24] Meadows[25] and others provide direct evidence that the bulk of the work involves rather small technical risks.

Recent judgments on the adequacy of the nation's investment in R & D

Is the type and extent of R & D support that society presently uses to supplement the market mechanism adequate from an economic point of view, and is this support allocated properly? In recent years, there have been several discussions of this question, each carried out by people who have devoted considerable time and energy to this task. I will summarize their views and then discuss the evidence underlying their conclusions.

In 1963, the Organisation for Economic Co-operation and Development (OECD) published a report by Freeman, Poignant, and Svennilson which concluded, 'It seems therefore inherently improbable that the scale on which governments supplement civil R & D in sectors other than atomic energy is anything like sufficient to attain the optimum'.[26] In their view, 'in spite of all the factors which concur to increase the level of R & D activity, there are serious reasons for believing that this level is in many cases inadequate for sustained and rapid economic growth' (p. 35).[26] In 1964, the US Council for Economic Advisors sounded a similar note when they stated that 'in a number of industries the amount of organized private research undertaken is insignificant, and the technology of many of these low-research industries has notably failed to keep pace with advances elsewhere in the economy'.[27]

In 1966, the President's Commission on Technology, Automation, and Economic Progress concluded that too little was being spent by the government on R & D in the fields of urban transportation, pollution control, and housing. For example, on housing the commission stated: 'As it has in agriculture, the Federal Government should actively stimulate research in housing and community development through research grants and through its own building activities. It should also support basic research to establish performance criteria (e.g., moisture resistance, insulation, lighting, etc.) for housing and housing components'.[28]

In 1967, Nelson, Peck, and Kalachek, summarizing a two-year study of this question, concluded that there were several important areas where there existed a significant degree of market failure which was not remedied adequately by government programmes. They suggested that a national institute of technology be established to provide grants for R & D aimed at placing the technology of various industries on a stronger scientific base and to test the feasibility and desirability of advanced designs. In their view, work of this sort, which falls between basic research and product development, is in need of additional support. In cases where a broad-scale systems view is needed but is prevented by the smallness of firms and fragmentation of markets, the institute would support work through the middle and later stages of development (p. 177).[7]

At about the same time, Capron, formerly assistant director of the Bureau of the Budget, stated: 'My own view on this is that we can say nothing with much confidence on theoretical grounds about the social adequacy of our total R & D effort – though my hunch is that as a nation we are underinvesting in R & D over all. However, I think we can say with assurance that the existence of noncompetitive elements and sectors of the economy produces a misallocation of resources within the R & D total'.[29] Specifically, it is Capron's view that too large a fraction of the total R & D effort is spent in oligopolistic industries and on relatively modest improvements, too little being spent in more competitive industries and on more far-reaching work.

Nature of the evidence
I have summarized briefly the conclusions of a number of economists who have been concerned with the question of whether or not the R & D support that society presently gives to supplement the market mechanism is adequate in total and allocated properly. They generally seem to be of the opinion that the nation's investment in R & D may be too small, but this opinion is often characterized as little more than a hunch. They

are much more confident, it appears, that, whether or not the total investment in R & D is too small, the investment is not properly allocated, there being too little R & D devoted to (i) more ambitious attempts to place the technology of various industries on a stronger scientific base (Nelson, Peck, and Kalachek), (ii) urban transportation, pollution control, and housing (Automation Commission), and (iii) more competitive and fragmented industries (Capron). Or, more precisely, this is what they believed at the time they expressed their views in print.

What sorts of evidence are these conclusions based on? First, some of these studies rely largely on judgment combined with economic theory. For example, Nelson, Peck, and Kalachek, who lean heavily on this kind of support, believe that[7] (pp. 172–3):

> While the present state of knowledge is not strong enough to permit derivation of quantitative rates of return, or optimal allocations of resources, it is strong enough to suggest that for certain kinds of activities there are serious market imperfections ... When there are significant external economies, unsupplemented private initiative is unlikely to support work to the extent that is socially optimal. Where government policies already exist which provide added incentive or reduce private costs, or which supplement effort directly, it is difficult to say whether the latent tendency toward underallocation of private effort has been compensated. However, where policies do not exist, where incentive modifications appear minor relative to the gap between private and social returns, or where direct supplements appear small relative to the scope of socially desirable work (clearly a matter of judgment), a presumption exists that further allocation of resources would yield a higher than average rate of return, and that government policies to achieve such an expansion are in the public interest.

Second, these studies rely on the results of several econometric investigations which indicate that, for the industries and fields under investigation, the marginal rate of return from an investment in R & D has been very high. One of the first studies of this kind was Griliches' study of the returns from agricultural R & D.[30] He found that the rate of return from the investment in agricultural research between 1937 and 1951 in the United States was between 35 and 170 per cent. For two very successful projects – hybrid corn and hybrid sorghum – the rate of return on the investment was several hundred per cent (but these two projects are obviously far from representative). Subsequently Griliches[11] estimated that the gross social rate of return to research (and extension) expenditures was about 300 per cent – a figure that he regarded as being quite consistent with his estimate of 35 to 170 per cent net social rate of return to agricultural research, based on different data and a different approach.[31]

For manufacturing, Mansfield[12] and Minasian[14] estimated the marginal rate of return from R & D in the chemical and petroleum industries. Mansfield's results indicated that the marginal rate of return was about 40 per cent or more in the petroleum industry, and about 30 per cent in the chemical industry, if technological change were capital embodied (but much less if it were disembodied). Minasian's results indicated about a 50 per cent marginal rate of return on investment in R & D in the chemical industry. In addition, Mansfield provided some evidence that the marginal rate of return seemed relatively high (15 per cent or more) in the food, apparel, and furniture industries.

Finally, based on computations for the economy as a whole, Denison[4] concluded that the rate of return from R & D was about the same as the rate of return from investment in capital goods. His estimate of the returns from R & D was lower than the estimates of other investigators, perhaps because he assumed no lag between R & D expenditures and their contribution to economic growth. The calculated rate of return on R & D could be much higher if R & D's contribution occurred only with a lag.[32] In his 1969 presidential address to the American Economic Association, Fellner[33] estimated the average social rate of return from technological progress activities and concluded that it is 'substantially in excess' of 13 or 18 per cent, depending on the cost base, and that this is much higher than the marginal rate of return from physical investment at a more or less given level of knowledge.

Evaluation of the evidence

How conclusive is the evidence described above? First, consider the judgmental approach adopted by Nelson, Peck, and Kalachek, among others. Clearly, this approach, although sensible and frequently used in all fields, is limited by the large subjective component that inevitably must enter the calculations. It is very difficult to estimate the extent of the external economies arising from particular types of R & D, or to determine whether incentive modifications are small relative to the gap between private and social returns, or to tell whether supplementary R & D provided by government and nonprofit institutions is small relative to the scope of socially desirable work. The weight one places on this evidence must depend on the confidence one puts in the judgment and objectivity of the investigators.[34]

Second, consider the econometric approach adopted by Griliches, Mansfield, and others. This approach is more objective in many respects. Certainly the assumptions underlying the estimates are specified clearly, and one can see how sensitive the results are to changes in these assumptions. But this does not mean that the results can be accepted uncritically. On the contrary, since most of these estimates depend on, and are derived from, the studies of R & D and productivity growth in individual industries, they are subject to many of the limitations of these studies. The seriousness of these limitations has been stressed earlier, and should be stressed again.[35] In addition, practically all of these econometric studies were carried out several years ago, and the estimates generally pertain to the late 1950s or early 1960s. It is by no means clear that the results would be different today, but, of course, one cannot rule out that possibility. In addition, some of these studies try to measure the social returns from R & D, while others measure only the private returns to R & D (and perhaps part of the social returns not included in the private returns).

Yet, having taken pains to point out the limitations of the individual bits of evidence that have been amassed, we must not lose sight of an impressive fact: no matter which of the available studies one looks at [other than Denison's[36]], the conclusions seem to point in the same direction. In the case of those using the judgmental approach, there is considerable agreement that we may be underinvesting in particular types of R & D in the civilian sector of the economy. In the case of the econometric studies, every study of which I am aware indicates that the rate of return from additional R & D in the civilian sector is very high.

Needed research concerning R & D

I have indicated that, although considerable progress has been made in the last decade in furthering understanding of the relations between R & D and economic growth and productivity increase, existing knowledge is too weak to permit very confident or definitive statements concerning these relations. Although existing knowledge may be of some use in formulating public policy in this area, it is limited by many serious problems and can only be regarded as tentative. Given that this is the case, what steps might be taken to further knowledge in this area? In addressing myself to this question, I will first describe the needed research concerning R & D, then the needed research concerning the process of technological change, and finally the needed research concerning economic growth and productivity increase. Needless to say, I shall have to be selective, and my choice of topics will probably be influenced by my own biases.

With regard to R & D, there are at least six important areas that are in need of considerable additional research.

1. Much more information is needed concerning exactly what is included as R & D in various industries. It is perfectly clear that without such information it will be impossible to interpret relations – or lack of relations – between measured R & D and other economic variables with any real confidence. What proportion of R & D, as measured by the customary figures, is routine service work? What proportion is aimed at fairly certain, and modest, design improvements? My co-workers and I have made detailed studies of the characteristics of the R & D portfolios of a sample of firms in the chemical, petroleum, and electrical equipment industries.[37] But this work is only a beginning. Work is also needed to provide better price indexes for R & D in particular industries, so that it will be possible to compare more accurately expenditure data at various times. Some work has been done on this score too,[38] but much more needs to be done. In addition, attempts should be made to develop measures of inventive effort that include the work of independent inventors and that are comparable for both large and small firms.

2. Given more detailed breakdowns of R & D in various industries, it is important to disaggregate R & D in the models used to relate R & D to economic growth and productivity increase. On the basis of existing work, it is perfectly clear that R & D expenditures include outlays on activities of quite different sorts, which would be expected to have quite different effects on productivity. Although it was reasonable to use total R & D expenditures in earlier studies, an attempt should now be made to go beyond this crude beginning. After all, some of the most interesting questions in this area relate to the returns from various kinds of R & D – R & D directed at small product improvements, R & D directed at more major inventions, and so on. Unless we disaggregate R & D, such questions cannot be answered.

3. We need more information about the expected profitability and risk attached to the R & D portfolios of particular laboratories and firms, as well as more data concerning the decision-making process with regard to project selection and the allocation of R & D funds in various laboratories and firms. Such information would allow a determination of the extent to which firms are risk-averters and a study of the social implications of the decision rules employed, explicitly or implicitly, by the firms. My co-workers and I have made a number of such studies,[37, 39] but they pertain to only a small sample of laboratories. Since studies of this sort must utilize detailed data that can only be derived from intensive work with individual firms, progress in this area depends on researchers being willing to immerse themselves in the operation of individual laboratories.

4. We need more information concerning economies of scale in particular types of R & D. There are numerous reasons for thinking that there are economies of scale in R & D up to some point – 'lumpiness' of capital equipment used in R & D, advantages from specialization of labour, reduction of risks due to the law of large numbers, and so forth. However, we know very little – industry by industry – about the extent of these economies of scale for particular kinds of work or about the size of R & D establishment beyond which further increases in size bring little or nothing in the way of further efficiency for the type of work in question. Freeman[40] has shed some light on this subject in the electronics industry, but it is still largely unexplored. This is very unfortunate, since the returns derived from a certain expenditure on R & D – and the socially optimal organization of R & D – will depend on these economies of scale.

5. We need more information concerning the conditions and mechanisms leading to the application of basic science and its translation into new products and processes. According to recent studies,[41] the United States has been more adept than Western Europe at the application and translation of the findings of basic science into economically significant innovations. What are the reasons for this superiority, if indeed it exists? What is the mechanism in various areas leading to the translation of new basic science into technology? These are important questions, and ones about which little is known – although the TRACES study[42] provides some relevant and significant information. To appreciate the importance of these questions, it should be noted that the country that does the basic scientific work in a particular area may not be the one that reaps the greatest economic benefits from the technological innovations in that particular area. The extent of the economic benefits from fundamental research depends on the facility and efficiency with which the results of fundamental research are applied. Fortunately, according to the OECD studies, the United States seems to have been relatively adept at the application of fundamental research, the consequence being that the economic returns from basic research have probably been relatively high in the United States. But why has this been the case, and can we be sure it will continue to be the case in the future?

6. We need more information concerning the coupling of industrial R & D with marketing and production. Industrial R & D can have little economic impact unless it is applied. And the difficulties in bridging the gap between R & D, on the one hand, and marketing and production, on the other hand, are greater than is usually recognized. Systematic, in-depth studies of the problems in this area – and the ways in which industry has attempted to solve these problems – would be of considerable use. It is high time to begin to build this aspect of the R & D process into models relating R & D expenditures to productivity increase and economic growth. Also, it should be recognized that a large part of the riskiness of industrial R & D is due to commercial, not technical, uncertainty. For example, recent studies indicate that the probability of a firm's solving the technical problems involved in the typical R & D project is much greater than its turning out to be economically justified in having gone to the trouble and expense of solving them.[37, 43] If this is indeed the case, it raises questions concerning the extent to which there is proper coordination between the R & D people, on the one hand, and the marketing and production people, on the other. Detailed and intensive studies should be carried out to shed light on this question, which has received limited – and often superficial – treatment in the past.

Needed research concerning the process of technological change
In addition, considerable research is needed to promote fuller understanding of the
process of technological change.

1. We need to know much more concerning the role of R & D in the entire process
of technological innovation. Until a few years ago, there was a tendency to equate R
& D with innovation, the consequence being that the non-R & D activities associated
with innovation were neglected. It now seems that the non-R & D aspects of innovation
– tooling and construction of plant, manufacturing start-up, marketing start-up, and
so on – frequently account for as large a proportion of the total costs of a successful
product innovation as does R & D.[37, 44] We must recognize the importance of these
non-R & D prerequisites to innovation in models of technological change. Also, it is
important to learn more about the areas in which – and conditions under which – little
or no formal R & D is required for innovation. Studies by Myers and Marquis,[45] as
well as others, show quite clearly that many innovations require little in the way of
formal R & D. We need to know more about the origin, type, significance, and
frequency of such innovations in a variety of industries.

2. Studies are needed of the conditions that promote or thwart the rapid conversion
of an invention into an innovation, given that market and technical factors make such
a conversion socially desirable. According to recent OECD studies,[46] American firms
are much more adept at achieving such a conversion than are Western European firms.
In the United States, there is some evidence,[47] albeit crude, that firms are achieving
such a conversion more rapidly than they did in the past. But existing information
tells us far too little. To what extent does an industry's market structure determine
the average rate of conversion? To what extent do problems of interindustry and interfirm
coordination lessen the average rate of conversion? Does the use of various management
techniques that are currently in vogue have a perceptible or demonstrable effect? What
are the characteristics of the managers and managements that seem to perform best
in this regard?

3. We need to know much more about the sources of invention and innovation in
various industries. With regard to invention, what has been the relative importance
of independent inventors, small firms, large firms, universities, and so on, as sources
of significant inventions in particular industries? The studies by Jewkes, Sawers, and
Stillerman,[5] Hamberg,[23] Enos,[48] and others are valuable, but there is a need for much
more empirical work of this sort. Moreover, with regard to innovation. what has been
the relative importance of firms of various kinds – large, small, conglomerate, single
product, and so on – in particular industries? My co-workers and I have tried to provide
data[13, 37] for a handful of industries – petroleum, steel, coal, ethical drugs. Attempts
should be made to identify the firms that pioneered in the introduction of important
new processes and products in other industries. Such information is needed if we are
to obtain a better understanding of the factors and conditions conducive to invention
and innovation and the relative efficiency and creativity of various kinds of organizations.

4. Studies are needed of the effects of market structure on an industry's rate of technological change. What is the effect of market structure on the amount spent by an
industry on R & D and other innovative activities, the sort of R & D and other

innovative activities carried out, the productivity of the industry's R & D, the quickness of the firms to innovate, and the rate of acceptance of new techniques and products (both those arising within and those arising outside the industry)? To what extent are giant firms in various industries required to ensure a rapid rate of technological change? These are extremely important questions. For some time, I – and a number of other economists – have been trying to gain a better understanding of them, but we are far from having trustworthy answers to these questions.[49]

5. We need to know much more about the factors influencing the rate of diffusion of innovations. Mansfield and Griliches have formulated models of the diffusion process and obtained detailed data concerning the diffusion of a number of important innovations in manufacturing and agriculture.[13, 50] These models have been used by Mansfield [51] and others for technological forecasting. However, existing data pertain to only a handful of industries, and much more work of theoretical and econometric sorts is needed. We also need to know much more about the mechanism and costs of transferring technology from organization to organization and from country to country. Although a 1966 conference[52] sponsored jointly by NSF and the National Planning Association helped to clarify some aspects of this topic, a great deal of work remains to be done. Theoretical work – such as that done by Arrow[53] – and detailed empirical work – such as Hall and Johnson's study[54] of the transfer of the production of the F-104 to Japan – is needed.

6. It seems to me that much more information and work are needed to measure more accurately the 'spillover' to civilian technology from military and space R & D. I realize that an enormous amount of verbiage and papers of dubious distinction have been produced on this topic, but, as far as I know, the amount of penetrating, quantitative, objective analysis has been surprisingly limited.[55] In view of the great importance of this question, more should be done. In addition, attempts should be made to study and evaluate various approaches designed to increase such 'spillover'. For example, NASA has adopted a number of approaches in its work with Midwest Research Institute, the Aerospace Research Applications Center at Indiana University, the University of Maryland, and other places. It would be extremely valuable to find out what the experience of these groups can teach us about the relative cost and effectiveness of various approaches.

Needed research on economic growth and productivity increase
Considerable research is needed to promote a fuller understanding of the process of economic growth and productivity increase.

1. We need to improve the measures of output on which the productivity statistics depend. As noted previously, existing measures of output do not record the effects of the introduction of new or improved products. This is a very important limitation. Some very competent observers, for example, the Price Statistics Review Committee, have recommended that the government experiment with price series that allow, even roughly, for product improvement. More might be done along this line. Also, measures such as gross national product do not recognize the social costs – pollution, accidents, and so on – arising from technological changes. To the extent that these costs are borne by government, not industry, they are counted as end products of a

positive sort. Economists are becoming increasingly aware of this problem, but more should be done.

2. Better information of other kinds is needed as input to studies of the rate of productivity increase and technological change. For one thing, the price indexes used to deflate construction expenditures are questionable; indeed, they seem to be cost, not price, indexes.[56] There are problems in adjusting capital inputs for the extent of capacity utilization (and better estimates of the elasticity of substitution are needed). Obviously, errors from these sources can result in errors in the estimated rates of growth of capital and labour, which in turn can result in errors in productivity estimates. Turning to a different, but related topic, we need studies of the rate of technological change in various sectors of the economy that make greater use of engineering data and experience. For various reasons, economists, with some notable exceptions, have tended to avoid using engineering estimates. Here is a place where interdisciplinary work is badly needed. Also, it is extremely important that we develop better measures of the rate of productivity increase – and of the determinants of the rate of productivity increase – in the service sector of the economy.

3. We need a better understanding of the complex interrelationships among R & D, education, management, and capital formation in the process of economic growth. For example, consider the relationship between R & D and education. In most economic models, the contribution of education is perfectly straightforward: more educated workers are able to produce more than are less educated workers. As far as it goes, no one can take issue with this hypothesis. Nonetheless, the hypothesis may result in a misspecification of these models because it oversimplifies the relationship between education and economic growth.[7] In part, the effect of education on economic growth depends on the rate of technological change, since an important effect of more education is to make managers and workers more adaptable to change and quicker to adopt innovations. Moreover, an investment in education of certain kinds is likely to increase the rate of technological change. For these and other reasons, the relations among these variables are richer and more complex than they are pictured in most contemporary economic models. We must learn more about the nature of these relationships and formulate models accordingly.

4. Continuing the last paragraph's discussion, we should learn more about the extent to which technological change in various industries has been capital embodied or disembodied. That is, attempts should be made to estimate the extent to which new techniques and products in various industries in recent years have required new plant and equipment, the extent to which they could be 'grafted' onto old plant and equipment and the cost of doing so, and the extent to which they can be accommodated or used without altering existing plant and equipment.[57] Also, much more should be known about the process of 'learning by doing'.[58] These questions are important because the effects of capital formation on economic growth – and the extent to which utilization of new technology requires capital formation – depend on them.

5. In models designed to relate R & D to productivity increase in particular sectors of the economy, a better account should be taken of interindustry – and in some cases, interfirm – flows of technology. Specifically, we must take more realistic account of the fact that R & D in one firm or industrial sector often increases productivity in another firm or industrial sector. Some progress has been made in incorporating this fact into

economic models, the study by Brown and Conrad[16] being a beginning. But much more must be done. Unless we learn how to do this more effectively, our estimates of the effects of R & D cannot help but be very crude.

6. We need to extend many kinds of studies of productivity increase to a larger number of countries. In many areas, we lack reliable data for countries other than the United States. For example, according to a recent OECD study,[46] the rate of economic growth in the member countries is closely correlated with their performance in the diffusion of technological innovations. Yet very little is known about the diffusion process in countries other than the United States. A study is now under way to compare the rate of diffusion of selected innovations in various countries, but this study is only a beginning.[59] Although there are many pitfalls in international comparisons, they obviously can be helpful, if carried out carefully, in disclosing the factors influencing diffusion rates.

In passing, it may be worthwhile to mention a few of the common pitfalls in international comparisons. For present purposes, perhaps the most important thing to note is that one cannot conclude that the returns from R & D in the United States are small because some countries that have invested a fair amount in R & D have relatively low growth rates, and some countries that have invested little in R & D have relatively high growth rates. Many factors other than R & D affect economic growth and should be taken into account in any such comparisons.[60] Moreover, the fact that some countries spend much more than others on defence and space R & D should be taken into account – together with the fact that many important effects of R & D on true economic growth are not reflected in measured growth rates. Further, some countries that have not invested heavily in R & D have nonetheless achieved high rates of technological change by importing technology and by imitating and catching up with the technological leaders. Obviously, the technological leaders cannot achieve high rates of technological change in this way. Furthermore, some countries that have invested relatively large amounts in R & D have not been as efficient in converting the results of their R & D into innovation as the United States has. Thus, the returns from R & D in these countries may be a poor guide to returns in the United States.

Conclusions

Technological change has certainly contributed in a very important way to economic growth in the United States. Although existing studies have not been able to estimate this contribution with great accuracy, they have certainly indicated that this contribution has been large. Moreover, although econometric studies of the relationship between R & D and productivity increase have been subject to many limitations, they provide reasonably persuasive evidence that R & D has an important effect on productivity increase in the industries and time periods that have been studied. Turning to the adequacy of the nation's investment in R & D, there is too little evidence to support a very confident judgment as to whether or not we are underinvesting in certain types of R & D. However, practically all of the studies addressed to this question seem to conclude, with varying degrees of confidence, that we may be underinvesting in particular types of R & D in the civilian sector of the economy, and the estimated marginal rates of return from certain types of civilian R & D seem very high. Additional research is badly needed to determine more adequately the relationship of R & D to economic growth. I have indicated a number of specific areas where work is needed.

References and Notes

1. R. Solow, *Rev. Econ. Statist.*, **39**, 312, August 1957.
2. M. Abramowitz, *Amer. Econ. Rev.*, **46**, 5, May 1956.
3. S. Fabricant, *Economic Progress and Economic Change* (34th annual report of the National Bureau of Economic Research, Princeton N.J.: Princeton Univ. Press, 1954.
4. E. F. Denison, *The Sources of Economic Growth in the United States* (Committee for Economic Development, New York, 1962).
5. J. Jewkes, D. Sawers, R. Stillerman, *The Sources of Invention* (Norton, New York, 1970).
6. S. Hollander, *The Sources of Increased Efficiency* (MIT Press, Cambridge, 1965).
7. R. R. Nelson, M. J. Peck, E. D. Kalachek, *Technology, Economic Growth, and Public Policy* (Brookings Institution, Washington, D.C., 1967).
8. D. W. Jorgensen and Z. Griliches, *Rev. Econ. Stud.*, **34**, 249 (July 1967). It is important to note that quality change in inputs often is a consequence of technological change.
9. J. Kendrick, *Productivity Trends in the United States* (National Bureau of Economic Research, Princeton Univ. Press, Princeton N.J., 1961).
10. N. Terleckyj, thesis, Columbia University (1959).
11. Z. Griliches, *Amer. Econ. Rev.*, **54**, 961 (December 1964).
12. E. Mansfield, *ibid.* **55**, 310 (May 1965). This material also appears, with some modifications, in (13). When I speak of productivity increase, I really refer to rates of movement of the production function based on labour and capital alone.
13. E. Mansfield, *Industrial Research and Technological Innovation* (Norton, New York, 1968).
14. J. Minasian, *Amer. Econ. Rev.*, **59**, 80 (May 1969).
15. J. Minasian, in *The Rate and Direction of Inventive Activity*, R. Nelson (ed.) (National Bureau of Economic Research, Princeton Univ. Press, Princeton, N.J., 1962), pp. 88–105.
16. M. Brown and A. Conrad, in *The Theory and Empirical Analysis of Production*, M. Brown, (ed.) (Columbia Univ. Press, New York, 1967), pp. 341–71.
17. E. Mansfield, *ibid.*, pp. 122–5.
18. K.J. Arrow, in *The Rate and Direction of Inventive Activity* (National Bureau of Economic Research, Princeton Univ. Press, Princeton, N.J., 1962), pp. 210–15; R. R. Nelson, *J. Polit. Econ.*, **67**, 297 (June 1959).
19. A. C. Pigou, *The Economics of Welfare* (Macmillan, London, 1928), ed. 3.
20. National Science Foundation, *National Patterns of R & D Resources 1953–70* (Government Printing Office, Washington, D.C., 1969), p. 36.
21. National Science Foundation, *Research and Development in Industry 1968* (Government Printing Office, Washington, D.C., 1970), p. 9.
22. McGraw-Hill, *Business Plans for Expenditures on Plant and Equipment* (McGraw-Hill, New York, published annually).
23. D. Hamberg, *J. Polit. Econ.* **71**, 95 (April 1963).
24. E. Mansfield, *Amer. Econ. Rev.*, **59**, 65 (May 1969) .
25. F. Meadows, *Ind. Manage. Rev.* (spring 1968), p. 105.
26. C. Freeman, M. R. Poignant, I. Svennilson, *Science, Economic Growth, and Government Policy* (Organisation for Economic Co-operation and Development, Paris, 1963), p. 43.
27. Council of Economic Advisers, *Annual Report* [transmitted to Congress, January 1964 (Government Printing Office, Washington, D.C., 1964), p. 105].
28. National Commission on Technology, Automation, and Economic Progress, *Technology and the American Economy* (Government Printing Office, Washington, D.C., 1966), p. 87.
29. W. Capron, *Amer. Econ. Rev.*, **56**, 508 (May 1966).
30. Z. Griliches, *J. Polit. Econ.*, **66**, 419 (October 1958).
31. W. L. Peterson estimated that the rate of return to poultry research has been about 20 to 30 per cent [*J. Farm Econ.*, **49**, 656 (August 1967)].
32. M. Abramowitz, *Amer. Econ. Rev.*, **52**, 762 (September 1962).
33. W. Fellner, *ibid.* **60**, 1 (March 1970).
34. Also, some of the studies were made several years ago and the authors may feel that some of the problems existing then have been ameliorated considerably since their studies were made. However, this is certainly not the case for Nelson, Peck, and Kalachek (7), and Capron (29), and it is very doubtful for the others.

35. For a discussion of these limitations, see E. Mansfield, *The Economics of Technological Change* (Norton, New York, 1968).
36. Also, Jorgensen and Griliches suggest that the social rate of return from R & D is 'comparable' to that on other forms of investment; but the authors are careful to point out that they 'have made no attempt to isolate the effects of expenditures on research and development from expenditures on other types of current inputs or investment goods ... (8, p. 274).
37. E. Mansfield, J. Rapoport, J. Schnee, S. Wagner, M. Hamburger, *Research and Innovation in the Modern Corporation* (Norton, New York, 1971).
38. H. Milton, *Oper. Res.*, **14**, 977 (November 1966). Also, work in this area has gone on at the Rand Corporation and at the National Science Foundation.
39. E. Mansfield and R. G. Brandenburg, *J. Bus.*, **39**, 447 (October 1966).
40. C. Freeman, *Nat. Inst. Econ. Rev.*, **34**, 40 (November 1965).
41. J. Ben David, *Fundamental Research and the Universities* (Organisation for Economic Co-operation and Development, Paris, 1968).
42. Illinois Institute of Technology Research Institute, *Technology in Retrospect and Critical Events in Science* (prepared for the National Science Foundation, Chicago, 1968). Other recent studies are the Defense Department's Project Hindsight, which, of course, has been the subject of considerable controversy, and National Academy of Sciences Materials Advisory Board, *Report on Principles of Research Engineering Interaction* (National Academy of Sciences, Washington D.C., 1966).
43. For some discussion of the importance of this topic, see National Academy of Sciences, *Applied Science and Technological Progress* (National Academy of Sciences, Washington, D.C., 1967).
44. See U.S. Department of Commerce, *Technological Innovation: Its Environment and Management* (Government Printing Office, Washington, D.C., 1967).
45. S. Myers and D. Marquis, *Successful Industrial Innovations* (Government Printing Office, Washington, D.C., 1969).
46. Organisation for Economic Co-operation and Development, *Gaps in Technology: General Report* (Organisation for Economic Co-operation and Development, Paris, 1968).
47. F. Lynn, in *The Employment Impact of Technological Change*, appendix to vol. 2, *Technology and the American Economy* (report of the National Commission on Technology, Automation, and Economic Progress, Government Printing Office, Washington D.C., 1966).
48. J. Enos, *Petroleum Progress and Profits* (MIT Press, Cambridge, 1962).
49. For a summary of my findings, see (35) and E. Mansfield, 'Determinants of the speed of application of new technology' (paper presented at the 1971 meeting of the International Economic Association, San Anton, Austria, 31 August 1971).
50. E. Mansfield, *Econometrica*, **29**, 741 (October 1961): Z. Griliches, *ibid.*, **25**, 501 (October 1957).
51. E. Mansfield, *Numerical Control: Diffusion and Impact in the Tool and Die Industry* (Small Business Administration, Washington, D.C., 1968).
52. National Science Foundation, *Proceedings of a Conference on Technology Transfer and Innovation* (Government Printing Office, Washington, D.C., 1967).
53. K. J. Arrow, *Amer. Econ. Rev.*, **59**, 29 (May 1969).
54. G. R. Hall and R. E. Johnson, in *The Technology Factor in International Trade*, R. Vernon (ed.) (Columbia Univ. Press, New York, 1970), p. 304.
55. For an interesting study, see Denver Research Institute, *The Commercial Application of Missile-Space Technology* (Denver Research Institute, Denver, Colo., 1963).
56. Z. Griliches, in *The Theory and Empirical Analysis of Production*, M. Brown (ed.) (Columbia Univ. Press, New York, 1967)
57. Denison believes that the importance of this question has been exaggerated. See E. F. Denison [*Amer. Econ. Rev.*, **54**, 721 (March 1964)].
58. K. J. Arrow, *Rev. Econ. Stud.*, **9**, 155 (June 1962).
59. G. Ray, *Nat. Inst. Econ. Rev.*, **48**, 40 (May 1969).
60. For some estimates of residual growth rates – after the effects of labour, capital, education, and other non-R & D factors have been taken into account – in various European countries, see E. F. Denison, *Why Growth Rates Differ* (Brookings Institution, Washington D.C., 1967).

18

LONG WAVES IN ECONOMIC ACTIVITY

Long Waves and Technological Innovation

By EDWIN MANSFIELD*

In recent years, there has been a renewed interest in long waves, a subject that received considerable attention from economists like Kondratiev and Schumpeter. The slowdown in economic growth during the 1970's and 1980's prompted this renewed interest, since some economists believe that, after the expansion of the 1950's and 1960's, we are now experiencing the recessionary phase of the Kondratiev cycle. The existence of long waves is, of course, controversial. Some, like Christopher Freeman and Jay Forrester, believe in their existence; others, like Paul Samuelson, regard them as "science fiction."

At least since the days of Schumpeter, long waves have been associated with innovation. Although the past twenty-five years have seen a very significant increase in the amount of empirical research carried out by economists on various aspects of technological change, only a small amount of this research has been devoted to the timing of innovations. My assignment in this paper is to describe and review (and in a few cases, try to extend) what little we know about three interrelated questions: (1) Are there long waves in innovation? (2) Has the innovation rate declined in the 1970s and 1980s? (3) Do depressions tend to trigger innovations?

I. Are There Long Waves in Innovation?

Because of the enormous difficulties in defining, dating, and weighting inventions and innovations, there is very little information concerning the extent to which they cluster together and whether these clusters (if they exist) occur about forty to sixty years

apart. The best known work is that of Gerhard Mensch (1979) who has assembled data concerning the number of "basic" innovations introduced during each decade from 1740 to 1960. Mensch regards basic innovations as those that "are the source from which new products and services spring and in turn create new markets and new industrial branches to supply them" (p. 122). Mensch's data seem to indicate some clustering around 1770, 1825, 1885, and 1935. According to George Ray (1980), each cluster of innovations seemed to occur about ten to twenty years before the trough of a Kondratiev long wave.

However, as Mensch probably would be the first to point out, these data should be viewed with the utmost caution. What he is trying to do is to date the beginning of new industries, which is a very difficult job. To illustrate how hard it sometimes is to date a basic innovation, consider the case of the diesel locomotive. Whereas Mensch dates it at 1934, one could argue that an equally plausible date is 1913, two decades before the General Motors locomotive appeared. In addition, it is not clear how basic innovations should be (or are) distinguished from other innovations. For example, Mensch does not include the electronic computer or the birth control pill as basic innovations, but does include the zipper. Moreover, the reasons for excluding the many important, but not basic, innovations are not obvious, at least to me. Further, one wonders whether some attempt should not be made to weight basic innovations since they undoubtedly were of quite unequal importance.

For these and other reasons, there has been considerable criticism of these data. John Clark, Christopher Freeman, and Luc Soete (1981) emphasize that Mensch's data rely heavily on the sample of inventions in

*University of Pennsylvania. My research was supported by a grant from the National Science Foundation.

141

TABLE 1—PATENTS GRANTED IN THE UNITED STATES BY NATIONALITY OF INVENTOR, 1966–77

Year	Total	Granted to Nationals	Granted to All Foreigners	Foreign Patents Granted to U.S.
1966	68,406	54,634	13,772	49,098
1967	65,652	51,274	14,378	47,982
1968	59,102	45,782	13,320	48,229
1969	67,557	50,395	17,162	50,852
1970	64,427	47,073	17,354	48,807
1971	78,136	55,988	22,328	49,849
1972	74,818	51,515	23,293	49,628
1973	74,139	51,501	22,638	43,326
1974	76,275	50,643	25,632	39,990
1975	71,994	46,603	23,391	39,300
1976	70,236	44,162	26,074	38,028
1977	65,269	41,383	23,886	39,477

Source: National Science Foundation (1981).

John Jewkes et al. (1958), which was not claimed to be a statistically reliable sample. They point out that, because the book was done in the mid-1950's, it could not have done justice to the innovations in the 1950's or 1960's. Also, since Jewkes et al. were concerned with inventions, not innovations, there may well be a tendency to underestimate the number of innovations at the beginning of this century (see Peter Senge, 1982). Further, it is not clear why Mensch excludes about a dozen of the Jewkes et al. cases (such as bakelite and stainless steel), apparently because they had a relatively short lag between invention and innovation.

Given the many criticisms of these data, I think that it is fair to conclude that, although they are interesting, they must be supplemented with a great deal of additional work before any reasonably firm conclusions can be drawn from them. Until such work is carried out, it is difficult to take other than a rather agnostic stance concerning the existence of Mensch's long waves.

II. Has there been a Decline in the Rate of Innovation?

Some proponents of long waves in economic activity believe that the rate of technological innovation has been falling in recent decades. To what extent is such a belief supported by the available evidence? Without question, the sharp reduction in the rate of productivity growth in the United States (and many other countries) during recent years is consistent with such a view. But a variety of factors (including declines in the rate of increase of the capital-labor ratio, the huge increases in oil prices, and the impact of various kinds of regulations) could have been partly responsible. Certainly the fact that there has been a productivity slowdown does not prove by itself that there has been a slowdown in the rate of innovation.

The patent rate in the United States fell after 1971 (Table 1). In practically all of the 52 product fields for which data are available, the number of patents granted annually (by year of application) to U.S. inventors declined during the 1970's. Further, a decline in the patent rate seems to have occurred too in many other countries, such as Germany, France, the United Kingdom, and Canada (but not Japan). However, the crudeness of patent statistics as a measure of the rate of innovation should be emphasized. The average importance of the patents granted at one time and place may differ from those granted at another time and place, and the proportion of total inventions that are patented may vary significantly. Also, patents are generally used to measure the rate of invention, not the rate of innovation. (See my article with M. Schwartz and S. Wagner, 1981.)

In the industries where one can measure the number of major innovations that are carried out per unit of time, there seems to be direct evidence of a fall in the rate of innovation. For example, in the pharmaceutical industry, the number of new chemical entities introduced per year in the United States has declined relative to the 1950's and early 1960's. In the pesticide industry, too, there was a decline during the 1970's in the number of new products marketed per year. These measures suffer from the fact that it is difficult to find suitable weights for different innovations. Also, these measures overlook the small innovations that sometimes have a bigger cumulative effect than some of the more spectacular innovations. But nonetheless the results are of interest.

Thus, many of the available bits and scraps of data point to a slackening of the rate of innovation in the United States. But the data are so crude and incomplete that it would be foolish to put much weight on them. Also, it is important to distinguish between various sectors of the economy. In pharmaceuticals and agricultural chemicals, there may very well have been a decrease in the rate of innovation, due partly to increases in regulatory requirements. But in other parts of the economy, such as electronics and telecommunications, the rate of innovation seems to be very impressive. For example, recent advances in microprocessors and microcomputers are of great importance. Without denying that a slackening of the rate of innovation may have occurred in some industries, it seems to me that there is little evidence of such a decrease in other important industries. Overall, there may have been a slackening, but I know of no serious attempt in the United States to measure its size with reasonable precision.[1]

III. Do Major Depressions Trigger Innovations?

Many proponents of long waves seem to believe that the innovation rate was relatively high during the Great Depression of the 1930's. Some, such as Mensch, believe that major depressions tend to trigger and accelerate innovations. This is not a new idea. For example, William Brown (1957) and Ruth Mack (1941) have argued that new designs tend to be postponed during good times and that ideas that accumulate are tried out, and new ones explored, during depressions. In recent years, Mensch's statement and defense of this thesis have provoked considerable controversy.

In particular, Clark, Freeman, and Soete, while acknowledging that there may have been a clustering of major innovations during the 1930's, deny that it was due to the depression. Instead, they attribute it to quite different causes. In the case of synthetic materials, they point to the advances in basic science due to the work of Staudinger on the structure of long chain molecules and the pressure on the demand side due to German rearmament (especially in connection with synthetic rubbers). Further, they point out that, because of technical links, one innovation often leads to others.

With respect to some industries, like iron and steel, petroleum refining, and bituminous coal, what little data we have do not indicate that the innovation rate was relatively high when capacity utilization rates were very low. Based on data regarding 175 innovations in these industries during 1919–58, I estimated the relationship in each industry between the number of innovations in a particular year and the industry's capacity utilization rate in that year. Up to some point (about 70 percent of capacity in each of these industries), increases in the rate of utilization of capacity seemed to be associated with increases in the rate of occurrence of process innovations; beyond that point they were associated with decreases in their rate of occurrence.[2]

---

[1] It is important to point out that there were a number of reasons why, based on existing econometric models of R&D, innovation, and productivity, one would have expected some decrease in the rate of innovation in the 1970s and 1980s. See Mansfield et al. (1982).

[2] These results were based on a quadratic equation. All of the regression coefficients were significant at the 0.10 level, and most were significant at the .05 level. For a description of the data, see my 1968 study. Needless to say, this analysis and these data are very rough. For one thing, as pointed out earlier, it sometimes is difficult to date innovations, although the problems of this sort for these innovations seem much less severe than for some of the basic innovations discussed there.

According to executives in these industries, new processes are unlikely to be introduced when an industry is operating at low levels of capacity utilization, because the risks involved seem particularly great under those circumstances, profits being slim and the future seeming particularly uncertain. On the other hand, when an industry is operating at very high levels of capacity utilization, there is some reluctance to innovate because it will interfere with production schedules: there is little unutilized capacity that can easily and cheaply be used for "experimental" purposes.

Turning to product innovations, there was no statistically significant evidence that the rate of innovation in these industries varied appreciably over the business cycle. However, this may have been due in part to "noise" in the basic data, which are probably not as accurate as those for process innovations. Also, it should be recognized that most of both these process and product innovations are of less importance than those studied by Mensch, who focused on innovations that resulted in the formation of new industries and the revolutionizing of old ones.

Although these and other available data are far from adequate, I share the skepticism of Clark, Freeman, and Soete concerning the proposition that severe depressions trigger and accelerate innovations. One could argue that neither severe depression nor rapid inflation is conducive to major innovations. When sales are depressed and the future looks grim, the climate for innovation is hardly bright. And when double digit inflation occurs, this reduces the efficiency of the price system as a mechanism for coordinating economic activity and discourages investments in innovation and long-term $R \& D$ (see my 1980 article). But although this view is consistent with the above results concerning process innovations in the steel, oil, and coal industries, the limitations and tentativeness of these results should be stressed.

IV. Conclusion

My review of the published evidence does not persuade me that the the number of major technological innovations conforms to long waves of the sort indicated by Mensch's data. Although it is likely that some clustering occurs in the number of innovations, the evidence supporting the view that well-defined clusters occur every forty to sixty years seems limited and open to serious criticism. Much more work of both empirical and theoretical sorts is needed if we are to understand whether there are long waves in innovation or invention, and if so, why they occur. At present, very little work of this sort is going on (particularly in the United States). In part, this is due to the very severe measurement problems that are encountered in this specific area, as well as questions concerning the existence and explanations of long waves in economic activity in general.

The hypothesis that severe depressions trigger and accelerate innovations is also questionable. To obtain further information on this score, more attention should be devoted to the timing of innovations and the effects of macroeconomic conditions and policies on innovation and technological change (as well as the reverse effects). Many models totally ignore the links between the macroeconomic climate, on the one hand, and the rate of innovation and productivity change, on the other. Despite all of the evidence to the contrary amassed in the past twenty-five years, there is still a tendency in some quarters to view innovation and technological change as exogenous to the economic system (or linked to it in an oversimplified fashion). This is very unfortunate, both from the point of view of economic analysis and policy formulation.

REFERENCES

Brown, William H., "Innovation in the Machine Tool Industry," *Quarterly Journal of Economics*, August 1957, *17*, 406–25.

Clark, John, Freeman, Christopher and Soete, Luc, "Long Waves, Inventions, and Innovations," *Futures*, August 1981, *4*, 308–22.

Jewkes, John, Sawers, David and Stillerman, Richard, *The Sources of Invention*, London: Macmillan, 1958.

Mack, Ruth, *The Flow of Business Funds and Consumer Purchasing Power*, New York: Columbia, 1941.

Mansfield, Edwin, *Industrial Research and Technological Innovation*, New York: W. W. Norton, 1968.

_____, "Research and Development, Productivity, and Inflation," *Science*, September 5, 1980, *209*, 1091–93.

_____, **Schwartz, M. and Wagner, S.,** "Imitation Costs and Patents: An Empirical Study," *Economic Journal*, December 1981, *91*, 907–18.

_____ **et al.,** *Technology Transfer, Productivity, and Economic Policy*, New York: W. W. Norton, 1982.

Mensch, Gerhard, *Stalemate in Technology*, Cambridge: Ballinger, 1979.

Ray, George, "Innovation in the Long Cycle," *Lloyds Bank Review*, January 1980, 14–28.

Senge, Peter, "The Economic Long Wave: A Survey of Evidence," unpublished paper, Massachusetts Institute of Technology, April 1982.

National Science Foundation, *Science Indicators 1980*, Washington: Government Printing Office, 1981.

[19]

Research and development, productivity, and inflation

The author is professor of economics at the University of Pennsylvania, Philadelphia 19104. This article
is adapted from the lecture he delivered at the AAAS Colloquium on R & D policy on 19 June 1980 in
Washington, D.C.

Summary

R & D, through its effects on the rate of productivity increase, can significantly
restrain the rate of inflation in the medium and long run. High rates of inflation
damage the workings of the price system and impair the efficiency of practically all
economic activities, including R & D. Findings suggest that the percentage increase
between 1969 and 1979, in total real R & D expenditures, has been exaggerated due
to the inadequacy of the gross national product deflator as applied to R & D.

Earlier this year, the inflation rate hit 18 per cent, and even now, as we seem to be
sliding into a substantial recession, the inflation rate has not fallen below 10 per cent.
Clearly, inflation is one of the central problems in the American economy, but why
should it be of central importance in discussions of public and private policy toward
R & D? I think that there are two reasons: (i) R & D influences the rate of inflation
and (ii) the rate of inflation influences R & D. This article summarizes what I think
we know about these relations between R & D and inflation and presents findings of
an ongoing study of the rate of inflation in R & D.

Effects of R & D on productivity increase

It is essential to recognize that R & D has an important effect on the rate of productivity increase. Economists have used econometric techniques to estimate the
relationship between output, on the one hand, and labour, capital, and R & D on the
other. Studies[1] in the 1960s provided reasonably persuasive evidence that R & D had
a significant effect on the rate of productivity increase in the industries that were investigated. A variety of both agricultural and manufacturing industries were included in
these early investigations. Without exception, it was found that an industry's or firm's
rate of productivity increase was directly related to the amount spent on R & D.[1]

More recently, Zvi Griliches[2] conducted a study for which he used data from
almost 900 manufacturing firms. His results, like those of the earlier studies, indicate
that a firm's rate of productivity increase is directly related to the amount it has spent
on R & D. Nestor Terleckyj,[3] using data for entire industries, found that an industry's
rate of productivity increase is directly related to both the amount of its own R & D
and the amount of R & D carried out by industries that supply it with inputs. This is
reasonable since one industry's R & D often results in improved machines and inputs
for other industries.

279

There is also some evidence that the composition of an industry's or firm's R & D expenditures, as well as their size, influences the rate of productivity increase. I found that there is a direct relation between the amount of basic research carried out by an industry or firm and its rate of productivity increase when its expenditures on applied R & D are held constant. Whether the relevant distinction is between basic and applied research is by no means clear; basic research may be acting to some extent as a proxy for long-term R & D. Holding constant the amount spent on applied R & D and basic research, an industry's rate of productivity increase between 1948 and 1966 seemed to be directly related to the extent to which its R & D was long term.[4]

Effects of productivity increase on inflation

The rate of productivity increase has an important impact on the rate of inflation. Total cost per unit of output equals total cost per hour of labour divided by output per hour of labour. Thus, the rate of increase of total cost per unit of output equals the rate of increase of total cost per hour of labour minus the rate of increase of labour productivity (defined as output per hour of labour). If the rate of increase of labour productivity is high, the rate of increase of total cost per unit of output will be much lower than the rate of increase of total cost per hour of labour. If the rate of increase of labour productivity is low, the rate of increase of total cost per unit of output will be almost as great as the rate of increase of total cost per hour of labour.

As an illustration, suppose that total cost per hour of labour is increasing at 13 per cent per year. If labour productivity is increasing at 3 per cent per year, total cost per unit of output will increase at 10 per cent per year. On the other hand, if labour productivity is not increasing at all, total cost per unit of output will increase at 13 per cent per year. Thus, if prices increase at about the same rate as unit costs, the inflation rate will be 3 percentage points lower if labour productivity is increasing at 3 per cent per year than if it is not increasing at all.

This point is widely recognized. Many economists, including the President's Council of Economic Advisers,[5] have pointed out that, in addition to its adverse effects on our rate of economic growth and on the competitiveness of some of our goods in international markets, the slowing of our rate of productivity growth in recent years has exacerbated the problem of quelling inflation. Of course, factors other than the slowing of our rate of productivity growth have been major culprits responsible for the excessive recent rates of inflation in the United States. This factor, nonetheless, has been an important one.

Considering that R & D affects the rate of productivity increase and that the rate of productivity increase affects the rate of inflation, it follows that R & D, by increasing productivity, exerts a restraining influence on inflation. Petroleum refining provides an example. According to John Enos,[6] the cost of making enough gasoline for 100 ton-miles of transportation would have been $1.47 in 1955 if the Burton process had still been used. Instead, because of a number of major cracking innovations, the actual cost was only 26 cents. In the case of ammonia production, the advent of large-scale ammonia plants in the mid-1960s reduced the cost of ammonia by more than 20 per cent, according to SRI International. In any R & D-intensive industry, it is relatively easy to find such illustrations.

Effects of inflation on productivity increase

The effects of R & D and productivity increase on the rate of inflation are only part of the story. The rate of inflation affects both productivity increase and R & D in important ways. Inflation that is high on the average tends to be very variable in its rate and, as Milton Friedman[7] pointed out in his Nobel lecture, this reduces the efficiency of the price system as a mechanism for coordinating economic activity. A major function of a price system is to transmit the information that economic agents and organizations need in order to decide what to make and how to make it, or how to use owned resources. The relevant information concerns relative prices – the price of one product relative to another, of the services of one input relative to another, of products relative to inputs, or of current prices relative to prices in the future. In practice, the information is transmitted in the form of absolute prices – prices in dollars and cents. As Friedman states:

> If the price level is on the average stable or changing at a steady rate, it is relatively easy to extract the signal about relative prices from the observed absolute prices. The more volatile the rate of general inflation, the harder it becomes to extract the signal about relative prices from the absolute prices: the broadcast about relative prices is, as it were, being jammed by the noise coming from the inflation broadcast ... At the extreme, the system of absolute prices becomes nearly useless, and economic agents resort either to an alternative currency or to barter, with disastrous effects on productivity ...[7]

In particular, economists, both liberal and conservative, worry about the effects of high rates of inflation on investment. Thus, Robert Nathan[8] recently stated:

> There are many serious consequences of an economic, social, and political nature flowing from high rates of inflation. Perhaps its most clearly identifiable negative impact has to do with investment. High interest rates, difficulties in floating equity securities, the tendency of government policies to fight inflation with recessions, the drop in the value of the dollar, all relate to inflation and all serve to discourage new investment.

Clearly, inflation means that depreciation allowances frequently tend to be too small. As the late Arthur Okun[9] put it, 'the gap [created by inflation] between actual, historical costs of old plant and equipment and current or predicted costs of new facilities creates agonies in capital budgeting and weakens investment'.

Investment tends to increase productivity because it provides workers with more and better tools. In the United States, investment is a relatively small percentage of total output. In manufacturing, whereas Germany has devoted about 16 per cent of its output to capital investment and Japan has devoted about 29 per cent, we have devoted only about 9 per cent of our output to capital investment.[10] This is one of the reasons for our sluggish rate of productivity increase. Very high rates of inflation are unlikely to be conducive to the increase in investment rates that so many observers regard as desirable.

Effects of inflation on R & D

Besides affecting the rate of productivity increase, high rates of inflation, through their effects on investment and through other channels, also affect R & D. Alone, R & D frequently is of little value to a firm. Only when combined with plant and equipment and with manufacturing, marketing, and financial capabilities does R & D result in a commercially meaningful new product or process.[11] To the extent that inflation reduces investment rates it tends to discourage R & D that requires new plant and equipment for its use. To the extent that inflation makes long-run prediction of prices and circumstances increasingly hazardous, it tends to discourage R & D that is long term and relatively ambitious. Indeed, many of the reasons why inflation adversely affects investment in plant and equipment hold equally well for investment in relatively ambitious R & D projects. This does not mean that firms necessarily cut back on R & D expenditures in inflationary times. For example, according to National Science Foundation (NSF) data, firms increased R & D expenditures by more than 10 per cent between 1978 and 1979. But it does suggest that firms often are less inclined to fund relatively ambitious R & D projects than would be the case under a regime of relative price stability. In the words of a General Electric executive, 'the additional discounting now required to compensate for inflation is leading to even more emphasis on shorter term programs where an adequate return can be projected'.[12]

In addition to affecting industry-financed R & D, inflation can have a negative impact on government-financed R & D. Faced with excessive inflation, governments may feel compelled to trim R & D budgets as part of an anti-inflationary fiscal policy. To the extent that R & D would promote more rapid productivity increase in the long run, this may have the unintended effect of lowering productivity growth and perhaps worsening inflation.

Inflation also has a pernicious influence on R & D decision-making in both the public and private sectors because of the great difficulties in measuring the rate of inflation in R & D. In view of the inherent difficulties and the strong assumptions underlying the few alternative measures that have been proposed, the official government R & D statistics use the GNP (gross national product) deflator to deflate R & D expenditures. The relevant government agencies are well aware that the GNP deflator is only a rough approximation. For example, the Comptroller General's 1979 report on science indicators[13] suggested the use of alternative price indexes for R & D. Little is known, however, about the extent to which price indexes for R & D inputs, if they were constructed in various industries, would differ from the GNP deflator.

The preliminary results of a small-scale NSF-funded study that my students and I are conducting may shed some new light on the extent to which the use of the GNP deflator is misleading. Our basic data were obtained from more than 30 firms in the chemical, electrical equipment, oil, primary metals, fabricated metal products, rubber, textiles, and stone, clay and glass industries. These industries account for a large share of the privately financed R & D carried out by US industry. The firms in our sample account for about one-ninth of all company-financed R & D in the United States. For each firm and industry, a price index for R & D inputs (including scientists and engineers, support personnel, materials and supplies, the services of R & D plant and equipment, and other inputs) was estimated. This was basically a Laspeyres index with 1969 as the base year and 1979 as the given year. According to the Organization for Economic Cooperation and Development,[14] this type of index has been preferred in experimental work in other countries.

In practically all the industries, the rate of increase of the price index for R & D inputs exceeded the rate of increase of the GNP deflator between 1969 and 1979. Only in the electrical equipment industry was the former less than the latter. Thus, for these industries as a whole, the official statistics concerning deflated R & D expenditures seem to overestimate the increase during this period in R & D performance, if these R & D price indexes are reasonably accurate. Taking all of these industries together, deflated R & D expenditures increased by about 5 per cent, based on the GNP deflator, but only by 1 per cent on the basis of our price indexes for R & D inputs. Taken at face value, this seems to indicate that the bulk of the apparent increase in real R & D in these industries was due to the inadequacies of the GNP deflator. Of course, this result should be viewed with considerable caution for a variety of reasons.[15] But it does illustrate how inflation can distort the basic statistics on which major policy-makers depend.

Conclusion

In summary, I have tried to make five points: (i) R & D, through its effects on the rate of productivity increase, can have a significant restraining effect on the rate of inflation in the medium and long run. (ii) High rates of inflation damage the workings of the price system and impair the efficiency of practically all economic activities, including R & D. (iii) Serious inflation tends to discourage investment, including investment in certain kinds of R & D, because it increases uncertainties concerning relative prices in the future. (iv) Serious inflation can have a significant effect on government-financed R & D if it stimulates an anti-inflationary fiscal policy that affects the size and type of government R & D programmes. (v) Inflation can distort the basic R & D statistics on which policy-makers depend. In particular, if price indexes for R & D inputs based on the preliminary and tentative findings of a study of more than 30 major firms are correct, the percentage increase in total, real R & D expenditures during the last decade in the chemical, electrical equipment, oil, primary metals, fabricated metal products, rubber, textiles, and stone. clay and glass industries has been exaggerated due to the inadequacy of the GNP deflator for this purpose.

References and Notes

1. E. Mansfield, *Science*, **175**, 477 (1972).
2. Z. Griliches, in *New Developments in Productivity Measurement and Analysis*, J. Kendrick and B. Vaccara (eds.) (National Bureau of Economic Research, Chicago, 1980), pp. 419–54.
3. N. Terleckyj; *Effects of R and D on the Productivity Growth of Industries: An Exploratory Study* (National Planning Association, Washington, DC, 1974).
4. E. Mansfield, *Am. Econ. Rev.* in press.
5. Council of Economic Advisers, *Annual Report* (Government Printing Office, Washington, DC, 1979), pp. 67-72.
6. J. Enos, *Petroleum Progress and Profits* (MIT Press, Cambridge, Mass., 1962).
7. M. Friedman, *J. Political Econ.*, **85**, 466 (1977).
8. R. R. Nathan, in *Stimulating Technological Progress* (Committee for Economic Development, Washington, DC, 1980), p. 68.
9. A. Okun, address to the Economics Club of Chicago, 6 October 1977.
10. R. R. Nathan, in *Stimulating Technological Progress* (Committee for Economic Development, Washington, DC, 1980), p. 3.
11. E. Mansfield, J. Rapoport, A. Romeo, E. Villani, S. Wagner, F. Husic, *The Production and Application of New Industrial Technology* (Norton, New York, 1977).
12. L. Steele, testimony before the House Subcommittee on Science, Research, and Technology (U.S. Congress, House Subcommittee on Science, Research and Technology, *Productivity and Technical Innovation*, 96th Cong., 1st sess., 23 July 1979, vol. 7, pp. 12-13). In my study (4), the firms in the sample that cut back on relatively basic, long-term, and risky R & D during 1967-1977 were asked

why this occurred. One of the most frequently mentioned reasons was inflation (which, of course, was less severe than now). It was cited by about 40 per cent of them. During 1967-1977, there was a general tendency for firms to cut the proportion of R & D expenditures devoted to relatively basic, risky, and ambitious projects. But there was no apparent decrease in the average proportion devoted to relatively long-term projects. According to a number of firms, this was due largely to regulatory and related factors. If we omit the industries (for example, the drug industry) where firms stated that regulatory change resulted in a significant lengthening of projects, there was about a 4 per cent decline in the average proportion of R & D expenditures devoted to relatively long-term projects.

13. General Accounting Office, *Report by the Comptroller General on Science Indicators* (Government Printing Office, Washington, DC, 1979), pp. 46–7.

14. *Trends in Industrial R and D in Selected OECD Member Countries, 1967–75* (Organization for Economic Cooperation and Development, Paris, 1979).

15. I should emphasize that this project is still under way, and the estimates are preliminary. The data will be refined and, if possible, alternative price indexes will be developed since Laspeyres indexes, although generally preferred for work, have well-known limitations. Because they ignores substitution effects, they may exaggerate price increases. Furthermore, NSF has not yet published data on R & D expenditures in these industries for 1979. To obtain rough estimates, we multiplied 1978 NSF figures by 1.12 since NSF stated that on the average, firms planned a 12 per cent increase in R & D expenditures in 1979 [National Science Foundation, *Science Resources Studies Highlights* (Government Printing Office, Washington, DC, 1980)]. This is a crude procedure, but it seems unlikely that the general results will be affected.

20

MANAGEMENT SCIENCE
Vol. 33, No. 1, January 1987
Printed in U.S.A.

PRICE INDEXES FOR R AND D INPUTS, 1969–1983*

EDWIN MANSFIELD

*Center for Economics and Technology, University of Pennsylvania,
Philadelphia, Pennsylvania, 19104*

This paper presents the first R and D price indexes based largely on actual prices and expenditures reported by firms. The results, based on a carefully designed sample of about 100 firms, show that the GNP deflator, which is used in the official government R and D statistics, has tended to underestimate the rate of inflation in R and D. For managerial and economic purposes, such as R and D budgeting and productivity studies, these indexes should be of widespread use.
(RESEARCH AND DEVELOPMENT; DEFLATORS; PRICE INDEXES)

1. Introduction

Management scientists, government officials, managers, and others concerned with R and D policy have urged that price indexes be constructed for industrial R and D inputs, based on data obtained from firms regarding actual prices and expenditures.[1] Government agencies, in making the basic estimates of real R and D expenditures in the United States, use the GNP deflator to deflate R and D expenditures. Many observers have questioned this procedure and have emphasized that inaccurate price indexes can result in substantial analytical and policy errors. The purpose of this paper is to report the findings of a detailed study, based heavily on a carefully-designed survey of about 100 firms, which provides R and D price indexes, by industry, for 1969–83. The results seem to be the most comprehensive and direct measures of the rate of inflation in industrial R and D available to date.

2. Laspeyres R and D Price Indexes

To estimate the extent to which American firms have had to pay more for R and D inputs during recent years, we surveyed a carefully-designed sample of all firms spending over $1 million (or 1 percent of sales, if sales were at least $35 million) on R and D in 1981.[2] This population of firms accounts for over 90 percent of all industrial R and D. A random sample of 100 firms was chosen from this population. Data were obtained from 93 of them, which account for about 15 percent of all R and D expenditures in the population. In aircraft, electrical equipment (including communications), and chemicals, three of the top R and D-performing industries, about a third of the R and D expenditures in the population are included in the sample. This survey, together with the other data described in the Appendix, provides the basis for this study.

All R and D inputs are classified into five types: (1) engineers and scientists, (2) support personnel, (3) materials, (4) plant and equipment, and (5) other inputs. Based on the methods described in the Appendix, an annual price index for each type of input was estimated for each industry. Then we calculated a Laspeyres price index for all R

---

* Accepted by Burton V. Dean; received July 11, 1985. This paper has been with the author 1 month for 1 revision.

[1] For discussions of the importance of developing better price indexes of this sort, see General Accounting Office (1979) and Office of Technology Assessment (1980). Early work on this score was carried out by Johnson and Milton (1961) and Milton (1966). For subsequent developments, see Mansfield (1985). The present study is the first attempt to construct annual Laspeyres price indexes of this sort, based on data obtained from firms regarding actual prices and expenditures.

[2] For the relevant frame, see *Business Week*, July 5, 1982.

124

and D inputs combined. For a particular industry, the Laspeyres price index is defined as:

$$\frac{\sum_{j=1}^{5} Q_{0j}P_{1j}}{\sum_{j=1}^{5} Q_{0j}P_{0j}} = \sum_{j=1}^{5} W_j\left(\frac{P_{1j}}{P_{0j}}\right) \tag{1}$$

where P_{0j} and P_{1j} are the price indexes for the jth type of input in the base and given years, Q_{0j} and Q_{1j} are the quantities used of the jth type of input in the base and given years, and $W_j = Q_{0j}P_{0j} \div \sum_{j=1}^{5} Q_{0j}P_{0j}$. As indicated above, based on the methods described in the Appendix, we have P_{1j}/P_{0j} for each year from 1969 to 1983 for each of the five types of R and D inputs in each industry. To estimate W_j for each type of input in each industry, we used two sources: the National Science Foundation (1972, 1981a) and Goldberg (1978). Both provide data concerning the proportion of R and D costs in each industry devoted to each of these inputs, but the concept of the cost of R and D plant and equipment is different.[3] Because the results are very similar, we present in Table 1 the findings based only on the NSF data.[4]

TABLE 1

Laspeyres Price Index for R and D Inputs (1979=100), by Industry, 1969–83.

Industry	1969	1970	1971	1972	1973	1974	1975	1976	1977	1978	1979	1980	1981	1982	1983
Chemicals and oil	46.5	49.3	52.7	55.2	59.2	65.3	73.6	78.6	83.7	91.2	100.0	111.6	122.7	129.6	135.5
Electrical equipment	52.6	55.3	58.0	60.2	63.6	69.4	76.2	80.4	85.1	91.8	100.0	111.9	123.4	131.6	138.2
Primary metals	49.1	51.9	54.6	57.0	61.0	67.7	73.7	78.6	83.7	91.0	100.0	119.9	124.2	128.7	134.9
Fabricated metal products	47.1	50.1	53.4	56.2	60.2	66.0	73.5	78.4	83.8	91.4	100.0	110.7	121.3	131.5	138.7
Rubber	48.9	51.5	54.6	57.0	61.1	67.2	74.9	79.4	84.4	91.3	100.0	111.6	121.5	130.4	139.3
Stone, clay, glass	54.6	57.2	60.2	62.4	65.8	70.5	76.8	81.3	86.0	92.7	100.0	112.0	123.7	131.7	137.7
Automobiles	50.3	52.8	56.2	59.1	62.7	67.8	74.9	79.8	85.3	92.5	100.0	112.6	127.9	133.7	137.1
Aircraft	50.8	53.5	56.6	59.2	63.0	68.4	75.8	80.2	85.1	92.2	100.0	113.2	125.7	134.0	140.2
Food	50.5	53.3	56.4	59.1	65.0	69.9	76.1	79.9	84.5	92.0	100.0	111.4	120.9	127.6	133.4
Machinery	52.9	55.5	58.6	61.1	64.7	69.4	76.1	80.6	85.3	92.4	100.0	111.1	122.4	128.5	132.6
Instruments	52.0	54.8	57.8	59.9	63.5	68.5	75.4	80.2	84.9	92.0	100.0	113.0	127.2	132.9	137.8
Other	45.7	48.8	52.0	54.7	59.2	65.3	72.3	76.9	82.3	90.1	100.0	112.1	125.5	129.1	135.8
Total[a]	50.6	53.3	56.3	58.8	62.6	68.1	75.3	79.8	84.8	91.9	100.0	112.4	124.6	131.9	137.7

Source: see 2.

[a] Weighted average of indexes for individual industries, where industry R and D expenditures are the weights.

[3] Goldberg's data are based on cash expenditures, whereas the NSF data include depreciation allowances for R and D plant and equipment, not cash expenditures. Nonetheless, the resulting price indexes are extremely similar. For the NSF data, see National Science Foundation (1972, 1981a). Since the NSF data lump together plant and equipment and "other" costs, we use the mean index of these two inputs for the combined input category. Goldberg's estimates of W_j pertain to 1967; for the NSF data, the 1969 values of W_j are used for 1969–78, and the 1979 values are used for 1979–83. Because the 1979 data lump together engineers and scientists and support personnel, we assume that the ratio of the value of W_j for engineers and scientists to the sum of W_j for them and support personnel was the same in 1979 as in 1969. There seems to have been very little change over time in the value of W_j in a particular industry, so the results do not seem to be very sensitive to the exact year to which the value of W_j pertains.

[4] To check the resulting price indexes, we obtained overall price indexes for R and D inputs for each firm, and calculated the weighted average in each industry of these indexes. (The weight used was each firm's R and D expenditure.) The results are very close to the results in Table 1.

Based on Table 1, it appears that the rate of price increase for R and D inputs was higher in some industries than in others. Although these interindustry differences are not (and would not be expected to be) very large, the average rate of price increase sometimes differs among industries by more than 1 percentage point per year, which is not insignificant. In particular, the rate of inflation seems to have been highest in fabricated metal products, chemicals, oil, and "other industries," and lowest in machinery, stone, clay and glass, and electrical equipment. These interindustry differences are entirely consistent with our earlier paper, where we showed that they were statistically significant. See Mansfield, Romeo, and Switzer (1983).

3. Comparisons with the GNP Deflator

The official government statistics in the United States use the GNP deflator to deflate R and D expenditures. The relevant government agencies are well aware that the GNP deflator is only a rough approximation, but little is known about the extent to which the results would change if price indexes for R and D inputs were used instead of the GNP deflator. A comparison of the price indexes in Table 1 with the GNP deflator indicates that, if one is interested in making short-term comparisons of total national R and D spending, the GNP deflator is reasonably accurate. For example, in comparisons of successive years, the percent change in real R and D expenditures based on the GNP deflator is generally within a percentage point of that based on our R and D price index in Table 1.

However, for longer-term comparisons of national R and D expenditure, the use of the GNP deflator can result in substantial errors. As shown in Table 2, whereas real R and D expenditure went up by 38 percent during 1969–83, based on the GNP deflator, it really went up by only 26 percent, according to our price index. Thus, about one-third of the increase in real R and D indicated by the official statistics appears to have been due to the inadequacies of the GNP deflator. This problem is especially severe in particular industries, like chemicals. Based on the GNP deflator, real R and D expenditure in the chemical industry grew by about 77 percent during 1969–83, but based on the R and D price index, it grew by only about 51 percent during this period.

The reason why the GNP deflator performs worse in the long run than in the short run is that, for the vast majority of the years for which we have data, it has tended to underestimate the rate of inflation in R and D. To see why this has been true, it is important to recognize that the GNP deflator is an output deflator, not an input deflator. It reflects both the rate of increase of input prices in the economy as a whole and the rate of productivity increase. Because of productivity increase, it tends to increase less rapidly than input prices.

TABLE 2

*Percentage Increase in Real Industrial R and D
Expenditure, Based on GNP Deflator and R and
D Price Index, Total and for
Selected Industries, 1969–83.*

	Percentage Increase in Real R and D Expenditure	
Industry	GNP Deflator	R and D Price Index
Total[a]	38	26
Chemicals	77	51
Electrical equipment	26	19
Automobiles	38	25
Aircraft	−5	−14
Machinery	119	117

[a] Total for all industries, not only for those listed below.
Source: The 1983 R and D expenditure data (in current dollars) come from *Science Resources Studies Highlights,* National Science Foundation, May 31, 1985. The 1969 R and D expenditure data (in current dollars) come from *Research and Development in Industry,* 1979 (National Science Foundation, 1981).

4. Indexes Based on the Cobb-Douglas Production Function

According to the Organization for Economic Cooperation and Development (1979), the Laspeyres index has been preferred in work of this kind. Nonetheless, the Laspeyres index has well-known limitations. Because it ignores substitution effects, it may exaggerate price increases. If we assume that the production function for R and D in each industry is Cobb-Douglas (with constant returns to scale), we can calculate an exact R and D price index for each industry. Even though there is little or no information concerning the nature of the production function for R and D, it is interesting to compare the resulting indexes with the Laspeyres indexes. If the production function is Cobb-Douglas, the ratio of minimum cost of producing a particular amount of R and D in the given year to the minimum cost of producing the same amount in the base year is

$$I = \prod_{j=1}^{5} \left(\frac{P_{1j}}{P_{0j}}\right)^{\alpha_j}, \tag{2}$$

where α_j is the jth input's exponent in the Cobb-Douglas function.[5]

Given the price indexes for individual R and D inputs (obtained in the ways described in the Appendix), we used equation (2) to calculate a price index for all R and D inputs in each industry.[6] The results are remarkably close to those in Table 1. For example, in chemicals and oil, the two indexes were precisely the same in 12 out of 15 years, and differed by less than $\frac{1}{2}$ of a percent in the other 3 years. Apparently, our results in Table 1 are very robust, in the sense that it makes essentially no difference whether we use a Laspeyres index or a price index based on the Cobb-Douglas production function. Although Laspeyres indexes may exaggerate price increases because they ignore substitution effects, there is no indication that this was of importance in Table 1.[7]

5. Conclusions

In conclusion, it is important to stress the need for better price indexes for R and D inputs. The Controller General's report on science indicators has emphasized the needs in this regard of federal agencies. The Organization for Economic Cooperation and Development has stressed the needs of other industrialized countries. Business firms have been handicapped too. For the lack of anything better, they frequently have used indexes that, from a statistical point of view, have well-known theoretical flaws.[8]

The price indexes presented here seem to be the most comprehensive and direct measures available to date. However, they have obvious limitations. For one thing, they contain sampling errors. However, in 1983, for the major R and D performing indus-

---

[5] If the production function is Cobb-Douglas, $Y = A\prod_{j=1}^{5} X_j^{\alpha_j}$, where Y is the output from R and D, X_j is the quantity of the jth input used, and A and α_j are constants that differ from industry to industry. For a derivation of equation (2), see Mansfield, Romeo, and Switzer (1983).

[6] Goldberg (1978) calculated the proportion of R and D costs in each industry devoted to each of these inputs. Using his proportions as estimates of the α_j values, we can use our data to calculate a price index for each year. Alternatively, we can use NSF data (regarding the proportion of R and D costs devoted to each input) to estimate the α_j values in each industry. (See note 3.) Regardless of which set of α_j values is used, the results are almost precisely the same.

[7] We also obtained data concerning the rate of increase of input prices for stages of the innovation process other than R and D (plant and equipment, manufacturing startup, marketing startup). The results indicate that the rate of inflation in the innovation process during 1969–83 did not differ much from that in R and D.

[8] See U.S. General Accounting Office (1979) and Organization for Economic Cooperation and Development (1979). Some firms use an index of R and D cost per scientist and engineer. As has frequently been pointed out, such an index does not hold constant the quantity of other inputs purchased or the characteristics of the scientists and engineers.

tries, the standard error generally was only about 1 percent, and for the index for total industrial R and D, the standard error was only about $\frac{1}{2}$ of 1 percent.[9]

Another limitation is that these indexes end in 1983. One way to update them is to use published data concerning proxies for input prices. We have carried out some experiments along this line, and have found the results to be encouraging.[10] However, since the results seem to be much more accurate in some industries than in others, it probably will be necessary to get survey data every five or ten years for benchmark purposes. Given the fundamental importance for both analysis and policy of reasonably accurate R and D statistics, it is clear that continuing work in this area should be encouraged.[11]

Appendix

The purpose of this appendix is to describe how an annual price index was estimated for each type of input in each industry. The survey cited in §2 provided data concerning the changes during 1979–81 and 1981–83 in the average price paid by each firm for each of the five types of R and D inputs. Using each firm's R and D expenditure as a weight, we took a weighted average of the firm data to calculate price indexes (1979 = 100) for each type of input in each industry for 1981 and 1983.[12] Mansfield, Romeo, and Switzer (1983) obtained data from a sample of firms concerning the price increase for each of these types of R and D inputs from 1969 to 1979. Using each firm's R and D expenditures as a weight, we took a weighted average of the firm data to obtain a price index (1979 = 100) for each type of input in each industry for 1969.[13]

[9] These estimates of the standard errors are rough. The assumptions on which they are based are discussed in Mansfield (1985).

[10] The proxies described in the Appendix (published by the Bureau of Labor Statistics, the Bureau of Economic Analysis, and the Bureau of the Census) can be used to approximate the percentage increase in the price of each of the five types of inputs. If D_j^i is the ratio of the proxy for the price of the jth type of input in the ith industry in year t to that in 1983, we can update our R and D price indexes to year t by calculating:

$$100 \sum_{j=1}^{5} W_j^i \pi_j^i D_j^i \tag{3}$$

where π_j^i equals the ratio of the price of the jth input in the ith industry in 1983 to its price in the base period, and W_j^i equals the proportion of R and D costs in the ith industry spent on the jth input in the base period.

To get some idea of how accurate this updating procedure may be, we used it to update the 1979 indexes to 1980, 1981, 1982, and 1983 for the six major R and D-performing industries: chemicals, electrical equipment, automobiles, aircraft, machinery, and instruments. In other words, we acted as if we had indexes only up to 1979, and needed to update them to 1980–83. In the chemical, automobile, machinery, and instruments industries, the procedure based on proxies performed reasonably well, but in aircraft and electrical equipment, this procedure resulted in an underestimate of the rate of price increase. For example, in aircraft, the proxies indicate a 31 percent increase during 1979–83, whereas it actually was 40 percent.

Another updating procedure can be based on Jaffe (1972). Our results indicate that this is less accurate for 1980–83 than the above procedure. See Mansfield (1985). Also, see Griliches (1984) and Schankerman (1979).

[11] The research on which this paper is based was supported by a grant from the Division of Science Resource Studies of the National Science Foundation. Of course, the Foundation is not responsible for the views expressed here. Thanks go to John Chirichiello of the National Science Foundation for his comments and suggestions. I also want to thank the 93 firms that provided us with the basic data. Without their cooperation, this study could not have been carried out. Anthony Romeo was responsible for gathering part of the basic data, but was not able to participate in the subsequent stages of the project.

[12] The number of firms included in the survey (by industry) is: chemicals and oil, 21; machinery, 20; electrical equipment, 12; instruments, 10; food, 5; automobiles, 4; primary metals, 4; fabricated metal products, 3; rubber, 3; stone, clay and glass, 2; aircraft, 2; and other, 7. Our results indicated that R and D input prices in the chemical and oil industries behaved quite similarly during 1969–79. Thus, it seemed reasonable to lump them together in this study. Note that the chemical industry includes drugs. Each firm was classified by industry on the basis of its SIC code; thus, the industrial classification of some firms differs from that in the publication cited in note 2. For further description of this sample, see Mansfield (1985).

[13] Six of the twelve industrial categories were included in the earlier study. For the machinery, instruments, and "other" industries, data were obtained from firms in our sample concerning price changes in these industries from 1969 to 1979. For the auto, aircraft, and food industries, we assumed that the percentage increase in price from 1969 to 1979 for each input was equal to the weighted mean percentage increase for this input in the other industries in the sample. Judging from 1979–1983, for which we have data for all industries, this assumption is a reasonable approximation. During this period, the mean percentage price increase for the

Proxies were used to interpolate between the years (1969, 1979, 1981, and 1983) for which we have survey data.[14] The Bureau of Labor Statistics' mean pay of Engineers V and VI was used as a proxy for the price of engineers and scientists. The average hourly earnings of production workers was used as a proxy for the price of support personnel. The Bureau of Economic Analysis's Index of Cost of Materials was used as a proxy for R and D materials prices. A weighted average of BEA's price index for private purchase of producer durable equipment and its price index for industrial nonresidential structures was used as a proxy for R and D plant and equipment costs.[15] The Census Bureau's median weekly salary of managers and administrators was used as a proxy for the price of "other R and D inputs."

Note that, for each type of input, we did not assume that the price index was proportional to the relevant proxy. Instead, we assumed that the relationship was linear, which is reasonable (particularly since this relationship is allowed to vary from input to input, from industry to industry and from time period to time period). To illustrate how these proxies were used, consider the case of engineers and scientists. Our price index for R and D engineers and scientists for 1970–78 was calculated as:

$$E_t^i = E_{1969}^i + \left(\frac{B_t - B_{1969}}{B_{1979} - B_{1969}}\right)(E_{1979}^i - E_{1969}^i),$$

where E_t^i equals our price index for engineers and scientists for the ith industry in year t, B_t equals the mean pay of Engineers V and VI in year t, and t runs from 1970 to 1978. Our survey data provided E_{1969}^i and E_{1979}^i. Similar procedures were used to calculate E_{1980}^i and E_{1982}^i on the basis of our survey data concerning E_{1979}^i, E_{1981}^i, and E_{1983}^i, as well as the BLS series concerning the mean pay of Engineers V and VI. For further details, see Mansfield (1985).

---

five types of inputs in all other industries in the sample was equal to the mean percentage price increase for the five types of inputs in these three industries. Nonetheless, this assumption, forced by lack of complete data from the responding firms, is only an approximation.

[14] In choosing proxies, we compared their behavior with our survey results. See Mansfield (1985).

[15] According to Goldberg (1978), about two-thirds of R and D plant and equipment expenditures go for equipment and about one-third go for plant. Thus, the weights we used were two-thirds for the former and one-third for the latter. According to Goldberg, the "other R and D inputs" are composed largely of administrative and overhead items. The median salary of managers and administrators is published in the *Statistical Abstract of the United States*. However, since the latest available data were for 1981, the 1982 and 1983 figures were estimated from a regression of the median weekly salary of managers and administrators on the average weekly earnings in private nonagricultural industries during 1969–81.

References

GOLDBERG, L., "Federal Policies Affecting Industrial Research and Development," presented at the meetings of the Southern Economic Association, November 9, 1978.

GRILICHES, Z., "Comment," in Z. Griliches (Ed.), *R and D, Patents, and Productivity*, National Bureau of Economic Research, Chicago, 1984.

JAFFE, S., "A Price Index for Deflation of Academic R and D Expenditures," National Science Foundation NSF 72-310, 1972.

JOHNSON, E. AND H. MILTON, "A Proposed Cost-of-Research Index," *IRE Trans. Engineering Management*, (December 1961).

MANSFIELD, E., "Contribution of R and D to Economic Growth in the United States," *Science*, (February 4, 1972).

———, A. ROMEO AND L. SWITZER, "R and D Price Indexes and Real R and D Expenditures in the United States," *Research Policy*, (April 1983), 105–12.

———, ET AL., *The Production and Application of New Industrial Technology*, W. W. Norton, New York, 1977.

———, ET AL., *Technology Transfer, Productivity, and Economic Policy*, W. W. Norton, New York, 1982.

———, "Price Indexes for R and D Inputs," report to the National Science Foundation, 1985.

MILTON, H., "Cost of Research Index, 1920–1970," *Oper. Res.*, 20 (1972), 1–18.

NATIONAL SCIENCE FOUNDATION, *R and D in Industry*, Government Printing Office, Washington, 1972, 1981a, 1982.

———, *Science Indicators*, Government Printing Office, Washington, 1979, 1981b, 1983.

ORGANIZATION FOR ECONOMIC COOPERATION AND DEVELOPMENT, *Trends in Industrial R and D in Selected OECD Member Countries, 1967–75*, OECD, Paris, 1979.

SCHANKERMAN, M., "Essays in the Economics of Technical Change," unpublished Ph.D. thesis, Harvard University, 1979.

U.S. GENERAL ACCOUNTING OFFICE, *Report by the Comptroller General on Science Indicators*, Government Printing Office, Washington, 1979.

U.S. OFFICE OF TECHNOLOGY ASSESSMENT, *Impact of Inflation on the Federal R and D Investment*, Staff Paper Prepared by the National R and D Policies and Priority Program, June 1980.

PART V

MARKET STRUCTURE, SIZE OF FIRM AND TECHNOLOGICAL CHANGE

21

SIZE OF FIRM, MARKET STRUCTURE, AND INNOVATION[1]

EDWIN MANSFIELD

University of Pennsylvania and Harvard University

I. INTRODUCTION

WHAT are the effects of an industry's market structure on its rate of technical progress? In recent years economists have become interested once again in this classic problem, and have discussed at length the relative merits of various market structures—and the role of corporate giants—in promoting technical change.[2] Unfortunately, little agreement has been reached, and the question remains. To shed further light on this problem, the present paper does five things. First, it investigates the extent to which the largest firms in several industries have been the innovators.[3] Second, it outlines

---

[1] The work on which this report is based was supported by a contract with the Office of Economic and Statistical Studies of the National Science Foundation, by a Ford Foundation Faculty Research Fellowship, and by the Cowles Foundation for Research in Economics at Yale University. It is part of a broader study of research, innovation, and economic growth that I am conducting. The paper, which was written largely when I was at Carnegie Institute of Technology and Yale University, will be reprinted as a Cowles Foundation Paper. My thanks go to A. Meltzer and J. Muth for helpful comments, to G. Haines and C. Phillips for their assistance, and to many people in industry who provided data and granted interviews. A version of this paper was presented at the December, 1960, meeting of the Econometric Society.

[2] For example, see J. Schumpeter, *Business Cycles* (New York: McGraw-Hill Book Co., 1939); J. Galbraith, *American Capitalism* (Boston: Houghton-Mifflin Co., 1952); A. Kaplan, *Big Enterprise in a Competitive System* (Washington: Brookings Institution, 1954); D. Lilienthal, *Big Business: A New Era* (New York: Harper & Bros., 1953); W. MacLaurin, "Technological Progress in Some American Industries," *Quarterly Journal of Economics*, February, 1953; H. Villard, "Competition, Oligopoly, and Research," *Journal of Political Economy*, December, 1958; E. Mason, "Schumpeter on Monopoly and the Large Firm," *Review of Economics and Statistics*, May, 1951; W. Mueller, "A Case Study of Product Discovery and Innovation Costs," *Southern Economic Journal*, July, 1957; G. W. Nutter, "Monopoly, Bigness, and Progress," *Journal of Political Economy*, December, 1956; G. Stigler, "Industrial Organization and Economic Progress," *The State of the Social Sciences* (Chicago: University of Chicago Press, 1956); J. Bain, *Pricing, Distribution, and Employment* (New York: Henry Holt & Co., 1953);

Y. Brozen, "Invention, Innovation, and Imitation," *American Economic Review*, May, 1951; J. Robinson, *The Rate of Interest* (New York: Macmillan Co., 1952); G. Stocking, *Testimony before Subcommittee on Study of Monopoly Power* (Judiciary Committee, House of Representatives, 1950); J. Jewkes, D. Sawers, and R. Stillerman, *The Sources of Invention* (New York: St Martin's Press, 1958); I. Stelzer, "Technical Progress and Market Structure," *Southern Economic Journal*, July, 1956; J. Schmookler, "Bigness, Fewness, and Research," *Journal of Political Economy*, December, 1959; T. Scitovsky, "Economic Theory and the Measurement of Concentration," *Business Concentration and Price Policy* (Princeton, N.J.: Princeton University Press, 1955); and W. Fellner, "The Influence of Market Structure on Technological Progress," *A.E.A. Readings in Industrial Organization and Public Policy* (Homewood, Ill.: Richard D. Irwin, Inc., 1958).

[3] The customary distinction is made between the inventor and the innovator, the latter being the firm that first introduced a new process or product commercially in this country. Being concerned entirely with innovation, this paper provides a necessary link between my findings regarding the effects of a firm's size on the extent and effectiveness of its research activities (see my "The Expenditures of the Firm on Research and Development," Cowles Foundation Discussion Paper, No. 136) and my findings regarding the effects of a firm's size and an industry's market structure on the rate of diffusion (see my "Technical Change and the Rate of Diffusion," *Econometrica*, October, 1961; "The Speed of Response of Firms to New Techniques," *Quarterly Journal of Economics*, May, 1963; and "Intrafirm Rates of Diffusion of an Innovation," *Review of Economics and Statistics*, November, 1963). Other relevant findings are contained in my "Entry, Gibrat's Law, Innovation, and the Growth of Firms," *American Economic Review*, December, 1962, and "Innovation and Technical Change in the Railroad Industry," in *Universities–NBER Conference on Transportation Economics* (Princeton, N.J.: Princeton University Press, forthcoming).

a simple model that seems to be useful in explaining why these giants accounted for a disproportionately large share of the innovations in some industries, but not in others. Third, it tries to estimate whether fewer innovations would have been introduced if the largest firms had been broken up.

Fourth, it tries to determine whether the smaller firms do less innovating, relative to the larger firms, than in the past. Fifth, it shows how, under certain circumstances, historical data identifying the innovators can be used to determine the effect of a change in market structure on how rapidly inventions made outside the industry where they are applicable will be applied. Of course, the results are are by no means free of difficulties, since the basic models are often convenient first approximations, and the data are often rough. Nonetheless, they should be useful to those interested in the process of technical change and the effects of industrial organization on economic progress.

II. INNOVATION AND SIZE OF FIRM

Several decades ago Schumpeter challenged the then prevailing view and asserted that in recent times innovations have been carried out primarily by very large firms. More recently, Galbraith, Kaplan, Lilienthal, and Villard have taken much the same position, resting their case in considerable part on the following three arguments. First, the costs of innovating are so great that only large firms can now become involved. Second, projects must now be carried out on a large enough scale so that successes and failures can in some sense balance out. Third, for innovation to be worthwhile, a firm must have sufficient control over the market to reap the rewards.[4]

This position has been questioned by Mason and others, on the ground that there is no evidence that a disproportionately large share of the significant innovations has been carried out by very large firms. However, neither Mason and his followers nor Schumpeter, Galbraith, *et al.* have carried out the empirical studies that are needed to settle the question. Thus, the argument continues.[5]

This section presents empirical findings regarding three basic industries— iron and steel, petroleum refining, and bituminous coal. Because of the difficulties involved in obtaining fairly complete data, it was impossible to include a larger number of industries. The findings are very rough, both because these industries may not be entirely representative and because of the obvious difficulties any study of this sort must face. Nonetheless, they should help to fill an important gap.

To obtain the data, trade associations and trade journals in each industry were asked to list the important processes and products first introduced in the industry since 1918.[6] They were also asked to rank

[4] Some of these writers were concerned primarily with invention, not innovation; but if the largest firms are likely to carry out a disproportionately large share of the inventions, they are even more likely to carry out a disproportionately large share of the innovations, since innovation is generally more risky and costly than invention.

[5] Empirical studies of this sort have been recommended by Mason, *op. cit.*, P. Hennipman, "Monopoly: Impediment or Stimulus to Economic Progress," *Monopoly and Competition and Their Regulation* (New York: Macmillan Co., 1954), and Scitovsky, *op. cit.*; but very little has been done in this area. Of course, there are considerable—and obvious—difficulties in defining a particular innovation, in singling out the innovators, and in gauging the relative importance of various innovations. In view of these difficulties, any empirical study must be arbitrary in some respects and the results can only be a rough approximation.

[6] The distinction between a process and a product innovation may sometimes be blurred because a new technique that reduces the cost of some product may also alter it somewhat. In such cases, we asked the respondent to make a judgment as to whether the alteration was great enough for it to be considered a new product.

them by importance. Having obtained these lists, I consulted technical journals and corresponded with various firms inside and outside the industry to determine which firm first introduced each innovation commercially and when this took place. This information could be obtained for about 80 per cent of the in-

novations. The results are contained in Tables 1A–1C.[7]

[7] For further comments on the source of Table 1 see the Appendix. Note that the first installation of a new process, or the first introduction of a new product, may not be the most important in many technical and financial respects. Also a number of firms sometimes are among the first, and it is difficult to decide which one had priority. In such cases, the

TABLE 1A

INNOVATIONS AND INNOVATORS, IRON AND STEEL INDUSTRY, 1919–38 AND 1939–58

1919–38		1938–58	
Innovation	Innovator	Innovation	Innovator
Austempering............	U.S. Steel	Stretch process for hot re-	
Continuous wide strip mill.	Armco	ducing tubes...........	U.S. Steel
Continuous pickling.......	Wheeling	All-basic open-hearth fur-	
Continuous galvanizing...	Armco	nace..................	U.S. Steel
Mechanical scarfing......	U.S. Steel	Ultrasonic testing........	Republic
Multiple block wire drawing	U.S. Steel	High top pressure blast fur-	
Automatic operation of		nace..................	Republic
open hearth............	Laclede	Jet tapper..............	Republic
Electronic inspection of tin		Differential coating of tin	
plate...................	Jones and Laughlin	plate..................	National
Electrically welded pipe...	Republic	Electric eye for Bessemer	
Dolomite gun............	Donner	turndown..............	Jones and Laughlin
Coreless induction electric		Vacuum melting.........	Allegheny Ludlum;
furnace.................	Heppenstall		Crucible
Electrolytic tin plate......	U.S. Steel	Continuous casting.......	Allegheny Ludlum;
High-strength alloy steels..	U.S. Steel		Crucible
Low-tungsten high-speed		Vacuum degassing (pour-	
tool steel..............	Universal and Cyclops	ing)...................	Bethlehem; U.S. Steel
Grain-oriented electric		L-D oxygen process.......	McLouth
steel..................	Allegheny	Oxygen lancing of open	
Non-aging steel..........	Armco	hearth................	Bethlehem; National;
18-8 stainless steel........	Allegheny		Jones and Laughlin;
Nitriding steels..........	Ludlum		Republic; U.S. Steel
Boron-treated steels......	U.S. Steel	Automatic programming of	
Valve steels.............	Ludlum	mills..................	Allegheny Ludlum
5 per cent chrome hot-work		Killed bessemer steel......	U.S. Steel
tool steels.............	Braeburn	Precipitation-hardening	
Continuous annealing*....	Crown Cork and Seal	stainless steel.........	Armco
Continuous butt-weld pipe*	Fretz-Moon	Manganese stainless steel..	Allegheny; Republic
High-temperature alloys*..	Timken Roller Bearing	Aluminum-clad sheets....	Armco
Nickel-bearing electrical		Titanium-treated enamel-	
steel*.................	Western Electric	ing steels.............	Inland
		Columbium-treated high-	
		strength steel.........	National
		Extra low carbon stainless	
		steel..................	U.S. Steel; Armco; Al-
			legheny Ludlum;
			Crucible; Republic
		Closed television circuits*..	Babcock and Wilcox
		Carbon lining for blast fur-	
		nace*.................	Interlake Iron
		Hot extrusion*..........	Babcock and Wilcox
		Sendzimir cold mill*......	Signode Steel Strap

* Innovations excluded from Tables 2–5 because innovator had no ingot capacity or because it was engaged primarily in another business.
Source: See Appendix.

Next, I obtained data regarding the size of each firm in each of the industries —the ingot capacity of each iron and steel firm in 1926 and 1945, the daily crude capacity of each petroleum firm in 1927 and 1947, and the production of each coal firm in 1933 and 1953. These data were collected primarily from gov-

credit is split equally among the firms. In a few cases where there was more than one innovator, firms that were not primarily steel firms or ingot producers were among the innovators, but for the reasons discussed in the Appendix, they are not listed in Table 1. For example, Babcock and Wilcox is excluded in

the case of continuous casting. Also, there is occasionally a question about whether a particular installation was commercial or experimental. For example, it can be argued that the installations of continuous casting by Allegheny Ludlum, Babcock and Wilcox, and Republic were experimental. If so, it would not change our results in any important way.

TABLE 1B

INNOVATIONS AND INNOVATORS, PETROLEUM REFINING INDUSTRY, 1919–38 AND 1939–58

1919–38		1939–58	
Innovation	Innovator	Innovation	Innovator
Burton-Clark cracking........	Standard (N.J.)	Moving-bed catalytic cracking..	Socony
Dubbs cracking..............	Shell	Fluid-bed catalytic cracking....	Standard (N.J.)
Fixed-bed catalytic cracking...	Sun	Catalytic reforming..........	Standard (Ind.)
Propane deasphalting of lubes..	Union	Platforming..................	Old Dutch
Solvent dewaxing of lubes.....	Indian	Hydrogen treating............	Standard (N.J.)
Solvent extraction of lubes.....	Associated	Unifining....................	Union; Sohio
Catalytic polymerization.......	Shell	Solvent extraction of aromatics.	Standard (N.J.)
Thermal polymerization.......	Phillips	Udex process................	Eastern States
Alkylation (H$_2$SO$_4$)...........	Standard (N.J.)	Propane decarbonizing........	Cities Service
Desalting of crude............	Ashland	Alkylation (H Fl)............	Phillips
Hydrogenation...............	Standard (N.J.)	Butane isomerization.........	Shell
Pipe stills and multidraw towers	Atlantic	Pentane and hexane isomeriza-	
Delayed coking..............	Standard (Ind.)	tion.....................	Standard (Ind.)
Clay treatment of gasoline.....	Barnsdall	Molecular sieve separation.....	Texaco
Ammonia....................	Shell	Fluid coking.................	Standard (N.J.)
Ethylene....................	Standard (Ind.)	Sulfur......................	Standard (Ind.)
Propylene...................	Standard (N.J.)	Cyclohexane.................	Phillips
Butylene....................	Standard (N.J.)	Heptene.....................	Standard (N.J.)
Methanol....................	Cities Service	Trimer......................	Atlantic
Isopropanol..................	Standard (N.J.)	Tetramer....................	Atlantic
Butanol.....................	Standard (N.J.)	Aromatics...................	Standard (N.J.)
Aldehydes...................	Cities Service	Paraxylene	Standard (Calif.)
Napthenic acids..............	Standard (Calif.)	Ethanol.....................	Standard (N.J.)
Cresylic acids................	Standard (Calif.)	Butadiene...................	Standard (N.J.);
Ketones.....................	Shell		Shell
Detergents..................	Atlantic	Styrene.....................	Shell
Odorants....................	Standard (Calif.)	Cumene.....................	Standard (Calif.)
Ethyl chloride...............	Standard (N.J.)	Oxo alcohols................	Standard (N.J.)
Tetraethyl lead as antiknock		Dibasic acids................	Standard (Calif.)
agent[a].....................	Refiners	Carbon black (oil furnace).....	Phillips
Octane numbers scale[a]........	Ethyl	Glycerine....................	Shell
		Synthetic rubber.............	Standard (N.J.)
		Ethylene dichloride...........	Standard (N.J.)
		Diallyl phthalate polymers....	Shell
		Epoxy resins.................	Shell
		Polystyrene..................	Cosden
		Resinous high-styrene copoly-	
		mers.....................	Shell
		Polyethylene.................	Phillips

[a] Innovations excluded from Tables 2–5 because innovator had no crude capacity or because it was engaged primarily in another business.

Source: See Appendix.

ernment documents and trade directories, but in a few cases they had to be obtained directly from the firms. Next, I determined how many of these innovations were first introduced by the largest four firms in each industry. Since the recent situation probably differed from

of their resources as smaller firms both to inventive activity and to the testing and development of other people's ideas, if they could obtain applicable results as easily, and if they were as efficient and as quick to apply the results, one would expect their share of the innovations to

TABLE 1C

INNOVATIONS AND INNOVATORS, BITUMINOUS COAL PREPARATION, 1919–38 AND 1939–58

1919–38		1939–58	
Innovation	Innovator	Innovation	Innovator
Simon-Carves washer..	Jones and Laughlin; Central Indiana	Raymond flash dryer..	Enos
		CMI drying unit......	Hanna
Stump air-flow cleaner.	Barnes	Link-belt separator....	Pittsburgh
Chance cleaner........	Rock Hill	Bird centrifugal filter..	Consolidation
"Roto Louvre" dryer..	Hanna	Baughman "Verti-	
Vissac (McNally) dryer.	Northwestern Improvement	Vane" dryer........	Central Indiana
		Vissac Pulso updraft	
Ruggles-Cole kiln dryer	Cottonwood	dryer.............	Northwestern Improvement
Rheolaveur...........	American Smelting		
Menzies cone separator.	Franklin County	Link Belt multi-louvre	
Deister table..........	U.S. Steel	dryer.............	Diamond; Elkhorn; Bethlehem; Eastern Gas and Fuel
Carpenter dryer.......	Colorado Fuel and Iron		
Froth flotation........	Pittsburgh		
		Eimco filter..........	United Electric
		Dorrco fluosolids machine.............	Lynnville
		Parry entrainment dryer.................	Freeman
		Heyl and Patterson fluid bed dryer..........	Jewell Ridge
		Feldspar type jig......	Northwestern Improvement
		Bird-Humboldt centrifugal dryer..........	Clinchfield
		Wemco Fagergren flotation unit	Hanna; Sevatora; Diamond
		Continuous horizontal filter..............	Island Creek
		Cyclones as thickeners[a].	Dutch State Mines

[a] Omitted from Tables 2–5 because innovator was not a domestic firm.
Source: See Appendix.

that in the prewar era, innovations that occurred during 1939–58 were separated from those that occurred during 1919–38.

Do the results indicate that the largest firms introduced a disproportionately large share of the innovations? Of course, this depends on what one means by a disproportionately large share. But if the largest firms devoted the same proportion

equal their share of the market.[8] According to the rather crude measurements in Table 2, the largest four coal and petro-

[8] It could also be that they devote more of their resources to inventive activity and less to testing and trying out inventions made by outsiders, and that fewer innovations are produced per dollar of expenditure on the former activity. This is difficult to check. But there is no evidence that it was the case in the steel industry—the only case where their share of the innovations was less than their share of the market.

leum firms carried out a larger number of innovations than this, but the largest four steel producers carried out fewer. Thus, if the Schumpeterian hypothesis is taken to mean that the largest firms accounted for a larger share of the innovations than of the market, it seemed

III. A SIMPLE MODEL

Why did the largest four firms introduce a relatively large share of the innovations in some cases, but not in others? Consider the innovations of a particular type (that is, process or product) that were introduced during a given period

TABLE 2

Per Cent of Innovations and Capacity (or Output) Accounted for
by Largest Four Firms, Steel, Petroleum Refining, and
Bituminous Coal Industries, 1919–38 and 1939–58[a]

Item	Per Cent of Industry Total					
	Steel[b]		Petroleum[c]		Coal[d]	
	Weighted	Un-weighted	Weighted	Un-weighted	Weighted	Un-weighted
1919–38:						
Process innovations.....	39	41	34	36	27	18
Product innovations....	20	20	60	71	....	....
All innovations[e]........	30	32	47	54	27	18
Capacity (or output)....	62	62	33	33	11	11
1939–58:						
Process innovations.....	58	64	58	57	30	27
Product innovations....	27	27	40	34	....	....
All innovations[e]........	43	51	49	43	30	27
Capacity (or output)....	63	63	39	39	13	13

[a] In the columns headed "weighted," each innovation is weighted in proportion to its average rank by "importance" in the lists obtained. For processes I suggested that total savings be used to judge relative importance; for new products I suggested that sales volume be used.

[b] Ingot capacity is used to measure each firm's size. The industry is defined to be those firms with ingot capacity, but firms with such capacity that are engaged primarily in some other business were excluded. For the earlier period, a firm's size refers to 1926; for the later period it refers to 1945.

[c] Crude capacity is used to measure each firm's size. The industry is defined to be those firms with crude capacity. For 1919–38, a firm's size refers to 1927; for 1939–58, the figures refer to 1947. The product innovations included here are petrochemicals; in each case the innovator is the first petroleum company that produced it.

[d] Annual production is used to measure each firm's size. The industry is defined to include all who produced bituminous coal. For 1919–38 a firm's size refers to 1933; for 1939–58 these figures refer to 1953. The innovations included here are all new devices for preparing coal. This was the only kind of data I could obtain.

[e] For the weighted data this is just the unweighted average of the figures for process and product innovations.
Source: Tables 1A–1C and Appendix.

generally to hold in petroleum and coal, but not in steel.[9]

[9] For some similar data regarding the size of the innovators in the railroad industry see my "Innovation and Technical Change in the Railroad Industry," *op. cit.* Unfortunately, the railroad data, gathered since this present article was finished, pertain to only a small number of innovations.

The unweighted data in Table 2 suffer from lack of a clear-cut way to define an innovation and gauge its importance. Conceivably, some of these innovations could be regarded as a set of separate innovations—not one. If they were, the results using unweighted data would depend on how many elements

of time in a particular industry. More particularly, consider those which required, for their introduction, a minimum

were recognized in each case. The weighted data should eliminate this problem, but the weights are obviously very crude. In addition, the lesser—and some important—innovations are excluded altogether; and hence sampling errors and perhaps biases (despite the opinions quoted in the Appendix) are present.

Finally, note that in Table 2 there is much less variation in the share of innovations accounted for by the four largest firms than in their share of capacity or output.

investment of i. Letting $\pi_j(i)$ be the proportion of these innovations introduced by the jth firm in this industry, we assume that

$$\pi_j(i) = 0 \qquad \text{if } S_j' < M \tag{1}$$

$$\pi_j(i) = B_1(i) + \beta_2(i)S_j' + E_j(i) \text{ if } S_j' \geq M$$

where S_j' is the size (measured in terms of assets) of the jth firm. Of course, $B_1(i)$, $\beta_2(i)$, and M vary among industries, time periods, and types of innovations, $\beta_2(i)$ is presumed to be always positive, and $E_j(i)$ is a random error term.

Firms below a certain size (M) introduce none of the innovations because they lack the volume of production required to use the innovations profitably. For simplicity, I assume that the minimum size of firm required to use an innovation is approximately the same for innovations of the same type that occur in a particular time interval in a given industry. For firms larger than M, I suppose that the proportion of these innovations introduced by a firm is a direct, linear function of its size, for the reasons discussed in Section II.[10]

Next, I assume that a firm's size has more effect on $\pi_j(i)$ if the innovations require relatively large investments than if they can be introduced cheaply. If the

innovations require very large investments, one would expect that larger firms would be required to finance these projects and to take the risks.[11] More specifically, I assume that

$$\beta_2(i) = a_1 + a_2 i/S_M + z, \tag{2}$$

where S_M is the average assets of the firms with assets greater than or equal to M, a_2 is presumed to be positive, and z is a random error term. The ratio of i to S_M (rather than i alone) is used because in the present context the size of the investment must be related to the average size of the relevant firms. Measures other than S_M (for example, M) could have been used instead, but the results would have been much the same as those presented below.[12]

If these assumptions hold, it follows that the proportion of all of the innovations—of a particular type that were introduced in a given period of time in a particular industry—carried out by the four largest firms is

$$\pi = 4/N(M) + 4a_1[S_4 - S_M] + 4a_2 I[S_4 - S_M]/S_M + z', \tag{3}$$

where $N(M)$ is the number of firms with assets greater than or equal to M, S_4 is the average assets of the four largest firms, I is the average minimum investment required to introduce these innova-

---

[10] A linear function is only a convenient simplification. Up to some point, increases in size may bring progressively greater increases in $\pi_j(i)$ because a certain minimum size must be attained before a research laboratory can be maintained, assuming that this size exceeds M (see Sec. II). Beyond some point, increases in size may result in less than proportionate increases in the number of innovations, because little further advantage is gained from the viewpoint of the pooling of risks or the ease with which innovations can be financed, and, as is often alleged, the motivation to innovate may become weaker and administrative difficulties may multiply (see Stocking, *op. cit.*). Also, one might use a firm's per cent of the industry's assets rather than its assets in eq. (1). See n. 15.

[11] The results in my "The Speed of Response of Firms . . . ," *op. cit.*, seem to be consistent with this.

[12] Had i/M rather than i/S_M been used in eq. (2), the results in eq. (4) would have been

$$\pi - \frac{4}{N(M)} = \underset{(.00009)}{.00013} [S_4 - S_M]$$

$$+ \underset{(.0010)}{.00032} I \left[\frac{S_4 - S_M}{M} \right],$$

and the estimate of a_2 would still be positive and statistically significant.

tions, and z' is a random error term.[13] Thus, $N(M)$, $(S_4 - S_M)$, and I/S_M determine whether or not the four largest firms introduce a disproportionately large share of the innovations.

According to this model, the characteristics (particularly I and M) of the innovations that can profitably be introduced in a particular industry during a given time interval are exogenous variables determined by the largely unpredictable nature of the technical breakthroughs made previously by members of the industry, equipment manufacturers, and independent research organizations. If, on the contrary, these characteristics are influenced by the extent to which the largest firms are the innovators, an identification problem arises in equation (3).

For example, if smaller (larger) firms in the industry, when confronted with various research and innovative opportunities, favor those with small (large) values of i and M, π may be directly related to I and M although the line of causation is the reverse of that underlying equation (3). Though an identifica-

tion problem of this sort may turn out to be troublesome in some industries, interviews indicate that it is probably of little significance in the industries used here.[14] Lacking other evidence, I proceed on this assumption.

To see how well this model can explain the observed difference in π, I obtained rough estimates of I, M, $N(M)$, S_4, and S_M for the innovations of each type in steel and petroleum during each period. Unfortunately, suitable data of this sort could not be obtained for coal. The results are shown in Table 3. Using these data, I derived least-squares estimates of a_1 and a_2. Inserting them into equation (3), I obtained

$$\pi - 4/N(M) = .00014\,[S_4 - S_M]$$
$$(.00007)$$
$$+ .0289\,I\,[S_4 - S_M]/S_M\,,$$
$$(.0063)$$

(4)

where the figures in parentheses are standard errors and z' is omitted. As the model predicts, the estimate of a_2 is positive and statistically significant.[15]

---

[13] Since the sum of $\pi_j(i)$ is one, it follows that, if $f(S_j')$ is the number of firms of size S_j' and if the sum of the $E_j(i)$ is zero,

$$1 = \Sigma\,[B_1(i) + B_2(i)\,S_j']\,f(S_j')\,,$$
$$S_j' > M$$
$$= B_1(i)\,N(M) + B_2(i)\,N(M)\,S_M\,.$$

Thus,

$$B_1(i) = [N(M)]^{-1} - B_2(i)\,S_M\,.$$

Substituting this expression for $B_1(i)$ (and the expression for $B_2(i)$ in eq. [2]) into eq. (1), weighting $\pi_j(i)$ by the proportion of all innovations that require a minimum investment of i and summing over i to obtain the proportion of all innovations introduced by the jth firm, and summing the results for the four largest firms, we have eq. (3). Of course, $z' = 4z[S_4 - S_M]$ plus the sum for the four largest firms of the average value of $E_j(i)$; and $B_2(i)$ must be greater than $N(M)[S_M - M]^{-1}$. Using the estimates of $B_2(i)$, the latter inequality almost always seems to hold for $i = I$.

[14] According to interviews with executives of engineering associations and research directors of firms, the line of causation has predominantly run in the direction presumed by the model. But such evidence is hardly conclusive, and the problem may be more serious than they indicate.

[15] Note three things. (1) Because the error term would be more nearly homoscedastic, it might be argued that both sides of eq. (3) should be divided by $(S_4 - S_M)$ and that least-squares estimates should then be made of a_1 and a_2. The resulting estimates, and their standard errors, turn out to be almost precisely the same as those in eq. (4). (2) The model can be extended without too much difficulty to take account of differences among innovations in M. (3) If, as is suggested in n. 10, $\pi_j(i)$ is assumed to be a linear function of

$$S_j'/\Sigma S_j'\qquad S_j' > M$$

rather than S_j', it turns out that

$$\pi - \frac{4}{N(M)}$$

should equal

Figure 1 shows that this equation can represent the data in Table 2 quite well, the coefficient of correlation (adjusted for degrees of freedom) being 0.88.[16] Moreover, the results are rather insensitive to changes in I and M, the values of

the sign being randomly chosen, the results remained essentially the same (in all half-dozen trials) as in equation (4).

There is also some evidence that the model can represent the situation in industries other than steel and petroleum.

TABLE 3

VALUES OF M, $N(M)$, I, S_i, AND S_M, STEEL AND PETROLEUM REFINING INDUSTRIES, PROCESS AND PRODUCT INNOVATIONS, 1919–38 AND 1939–58

INDUSTRY AND TYPE OF INNOVATION	PARAMETER[a]				
	M	$N(M)$	I	S_i	S_M
	1919–38				
Steel:					
Process...........	46.0	19	0.60	858.5	245.2
Product...........	47.0	18	0.10	858.5	256.2
Petroleum:					
Process...........	10.0	81	1.75	554.4	72.6
Product...........	18.2	50	3.30	554.4	109.2
	1939–58				
Steel:					
Process...........	26.3	29	1.30	1238.0	256.3
Product...........	23.5	30	0.50	1238.0	248.6
Petroleum:					
Process...........	13.3	82	1.77	1243.0	144.0
Product...........	36.4	34	2.08	1243.0	314.7

[a] Symbols: M, the average minimum size (assets) of firm required to use the innovations; $N(M)$, the number of firms exceeding this size; S_M, the average size (assets) of the firms exceeding this size; S_i, the average size (assets) of the four largest firms; and I, the average minimum investment required to install the innovations. All but $N(M)$ are expressed in millions of dollars.
Source: See Appendix.

which (in Table 3) are probably subject to error. When each of these estimates was varied by plus or minus 20 per cent,

$$V_1 \frac{S_i - S_M}{N(M)S_M} + V_2 \frac{I}{S_M} \frac{S_i - S_M}{N(M)S_M}.$$

An equation of this sort fits about as well as eq. (4), the least-squares estimate of V_1 being 1.12 and that of V_2 being 183 (and statistically significant). It is difficult at this point to choose between these two forms of the model.

[16] Note two things. (1) There is no tendency for the residuals from eq. (4) to be positive in one industry or time period and negative in another. They seem quite random in this regard. (2) Even if we include only firms larger than M, the largest four

I show elsewhere that equation (4) is of some use in predicting the value of π in the railroad industry during 1920–50. In summary, the highly simplified model can explain most of the observed difference in π, and is useful in predicting π in at least one other industry.

petroleum firms seem to account for a disproportionately large share of the product innovations in 1919–38 and the process innovations in 1939–58. For process innovations in 1919–38 and product innovations in 1939–58, they account for about the "expected" share. Of course, including only firms larger than M, the largest four steel firms fare even worse than in Table 2.

SIZE OF FIRM, MARKET STRUCTURE, AND INNOVATION   565

IV. DISSOLUTION OF CORPORATE GIANTS

Thus far, we have considered whether or not the largest firms accounted for a disproportionately large share of the innovations. More basically, one would like to know whether fewer innovations would have been introduced during each period if these giants had been broken up. If one is willing to ignore the effects of *all* factors other than a firm's size on

the number of innovations it carried out, some very rough answers can be obtained, but these results should obviously be treated with the utmost caution.

We assume that

$$n_j = a_0 + a_1 \ln S_j + a_2 (\ln S_j)^2 \\ + a_3 (\ln S_j)^3 + z'', \qquad (5)$$

where n_j is the number of innovations carried out by the jth firm, S_j is the firm's

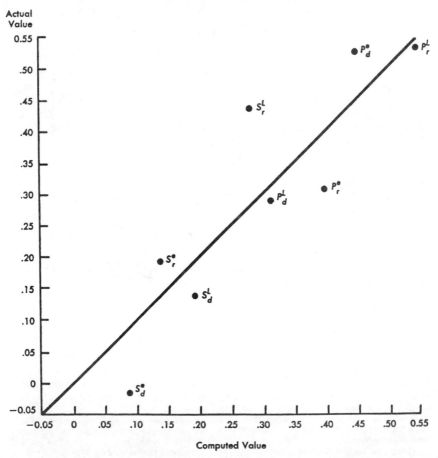

FIG. 1.—Plot of actual value of $\pi - 4/N(M)$ against that computed from equation (4), process and product innovations, steel and petroleum refining industries, 1919–58. Source: Table 3. The line is a 45° line through the origin. S = steel, P = petroleum, superscript e = earlier period, superscript L = later period, subscript r = process innovations, and subscript d = product innovations.

size measured in terms of physical capacity or output, and z'' is a random error term. This model is more useful and convenient than equation (1) for present purposes. Needless to say, the use of equation (5) rather than equation (1) involves no more than a substitution of one sort of approximation for another.[17] The logarithm of S_j is used, rather than S_j, because its distribution is less skewed.

Let the computed regression in equation (5) be $N(S_j)$ and ignore the sampling errors in it. Then if $N(S_j)/S_j$ is a maximum at or very near the size of the largest firm, it would appear on the basis of these assumptions that the dissolution of the largest firms would have resulted in fewer innovations being carried out. On the other hand, if $N(S_j)/S_j$ reaches a maximum far below the size of the largest firm, their dissolution would presumably have had a positive effect.[18]

Such an analysis is extremely crude, but what do the results suggest? Table 4 contains the estimates of the a's, the great majority of which are highly significant in a statistical sense and (taking account of differences in the total number of innovations) reasonably stable over time. In the petroleum and coal industries, the regressions indicate that $N(S_j)/S_j$ reaches a maximum at about the size of the sixth largest firm. Thus, they suggest that fewer innovations would have been introduced if firms other than the top few had been broken up. In view of the sampling errors in the regressions,

the true maximum value of $N(S_j)/S_j$ may occur at an even larger value of S_j and the dissolution of the largest few firms might also have had deleterious effects.[19]

On the other hand, the results in the steel industry are in complete conflict with the Schumpeterian view, the maximum value of $N(S_j)/S_j$ always being found among very small firms. These findings lend support to Stocking's assertion that the largest steel producers have not tended to be the technical leaders. Judging by our results, it would be difficult to justify the existence of these firms on the basis of their past performance as innovators.[20]

Finally, several points should be noted regarding Table 4. First, a firm's residual from a process-innovation regression is positively, but weakly, correlated in each case with its residual from the corresponding product-innovation regression, the correlation coefficient being about 0.3. Thus, holding size of firm constant, a firm that did considerable innovating with regard to processes also tended to do considerable innovating with regard to products. Second, if S_j is used rather than

---

[17] As we pointed out in n. 10, eq. (1) ignored the fact that n_j might be a curvilinear function of S_j'; on the other hand, eq. (5) ignores the fact that n_j may be zero below some value of S_j. Equation (5) is more convenient here because ordinary regression techniques can be used to estimate the a's, and its disadvantages are avoided in large part by excluding the very smallest firms.

[18] See the Appendix for some of the difficulties in these estimates of the optimal size of firm.

[19] If $N(S_j)/S_j$ is plotted as a function of S_j, one finds that its maximum occurs at about 200,000 barrels of crude capacity (1919–38), 300,000 barrels of crude capacity (1939–58), 3,600,000 tons of coal (1919–38), and 7,800,000 tons of coal (1939–58). In the steel industry, the maximum occurs in every case at less than 1,000,000 tons of ingot capacity.

[20] Note two points. First, the future situation in steel may be quite different. In the interviews described in the Appendix, several executives claimed that U.S. Steel was becoming much more of an innovator than in the past. Second, although U.S. Steel has frequently been criticized on this score, its performance seems to be much better than the second-largest firm—Bethlehem.

For discussions of the situation in petroleum see J. Bain, *The Economics of the Pacific Coast Petroleum Industry* (Berkeley: University of California Press 1944), Vol. III. For both steel and petroleum see D. Hamberg, *Testimony on Employment, Growth, and Price Levels before the Joint Economic Committee of Congress* (Washington: 1959).

SIZE OF FIRM, MARKET STRUCTURE, AND INNOVATION   567

ln S_j in equation (5), the results are generally like those described above. The maximum value of $N(S_j)/S_j$ is found among the very largest firms in the petroleum and coal industries and among very small firms in the steel industry.[21]

[21] To what extent were the significant innovations in these industries introduced by new firms? According to some authors, society frequently must rely on such firms to be the innovators. For example, see E. Domar, "Investment, Losses, and Monopoly," *Income, Employment, and Public Policy* (New York: W. W. Norton, 1948). In young industries where barriers to entry are relatively weak and the technology is changing rapidly, this may often be true. But in industries like steel and petroleum, where entry was difficult, this seems less likely. As it turns out, not one of the innovations for which we have data was introduced by a new firm.

In the coal industry, the results are the same—but the data may be biased somewhat. The innovations in the coal industry are new techniques for preparing coal; and according to interviews with the Bureau of Mines personnel, such techniques were probably less likely to be introduced by new firms and small firms than many other types. However,

TABLE 4

LEAST-SQUARES ESTIMATES OF a_0, a_1, a_2, AND a_3, STEEL, PETROLEUM REFINING, AND BITUMINOUS COAL INDUSTRIES, PROCESS AND PRODUCT INNOVATIONS 1919–38 AND 1939–58[a]

INDUSTRY AND TYPE OF INNOVATION	ESTIMATES				CORRELATION COEFFICIENT	NO. OF FIRMS
	a_0	a_1	a_2	a_3		
1919–38						
Steel: Process.........	−1.12	.901* (.323)	−.221* (.063)	.017* (.004)	0.73	101
Product........	−0.62	.583 (.324)	−.144* (.063)	.011* (.004)	0.43	101
Petroleum: Process........	−0.02	.135* (.052)	−.103* (.027)	.021* (.004)	0.64	269
Product........	−0.04	.305* (.060)	−.245* (.031)	.045* (.004)	0.78	269
Coal: Process.........	0.04	.031* (.011)	.024* (.007)	.009* (.004)	0.28	639
1939–58						
Steel: Process.........	−0.82	.624 (.662)	−.153 (.117)	.012* (.006)	0.72	68
Product........	0.59	.331 (.434)	.048 (.077)	−.001 (.004)	0.58	68
Petroleum: Process.........	−0.05	.235* (.040)	−.155* (.018)	.025* (.002)	0.83	269
Product........	−0.07	.300* (.010)	−.208* (.043)	.035* (.005)	0.70	269
Coal: Process.........	0.02	.038* (.014)	.046* (.004)	.015* (.003)	0.51	582

• The smallest firms were omitted. See n. 21.
* Significant at 0.05 probability level.
Source: Tables 1A–1C.

EDWIN MANSFIELD

Third, it is possible of course that the average delay in utilizing inventions, not the number utilized, would be affected if the largest firms were broken up. Section VI investigates this possibility in the case where the inventor is not a member of the industry. Fourth, judging by the correlation coefficients in Table 4, equation (5) fits the data only moderately well. For the innovations in coal and the product innovations in steel, the fit is particularly unimpressive.

Fifth, the regressions indicate that in all cases n_j is an increasing function of S_j throughout all, or almost all, of the relevant range—which is what one would expect. Sixth, the data on which the regressions are based are quite consistent with the estimates of M in Table 2. Firms smaller than M seldom, if ever, introduced an innovation in these industries.[22]

V. THE CHANGING ROLE OF LARGE AND SMALL FIRMS

It is frequently asserted that a small firm does less innovating now, relative to a large firm, than it did in the past.[23] Because of rising development costs and the greater complexity of technology,

this hypothesis seems plausible for a wide range of industries. Does it hold in steel, petroleum, and coal? To help answer this question, I use the regressions in equation (5) to compute the ratio, for each value of S_j, of the average value of n_j in 1939–58 to its average value in 1919–38. That is, taking a particular industry and a particular type of innovation and letting $a_0 \ldots a_3$ stand for the 1939–58 estimates of the a's and $a_0' \ldots a_3'$ stand for the 1919–38 estimates of the a's, we compute

$$[a_0 + a_1 \ln S_j + a_2 (\ln S_j)^2 + a_3 (\ln S_j)^3]/$$

$$[a_0' + a_1' \ln S_j + a_2' (\ln S_j)^2 + a_3' (\ln S_j)^3]$$

for each value of S_j. If this ratio increases as S_j increases, it suggests that the small firms have become less important, on the average, as a source of innovations, relative to large firms.

The results indicate that in all three industries and for both types of innovations, the ratio was higher among the largest firms than among the smallest ones (see Table 5 for the ratio at selected values of S_j). Thus, the smallest firms have in each case become less important in this respect.[24] The estimates in Table 3 shed some additional light on the factors causing this decline in the relative importance of the smallest firms. In steel it may have been due to an increase in the capital requirements for innovating, but not to an increase in the minimum size of firm that could profitably use the innovations. In petroleum it may have been due to an increase in the minimum size of firm that could profitably use the innovations, but not to an increase in capital requirements. Unfortunately, es-

this bias is unlikely to be great enough to reverse the results in this section: had it been possible to include other types of innovations as well, the largest firms would probably have continued to account for a disproportionately large share, but the difference might not have been so large. Note that the equipment producers had a very important hand in developing most of these innovations.

[22] Of course, the fact that a few firms below our estimate of M are innovators does not mean that our estimates are incorrect. We assume in Sec. III that M is the same for all innovations, but this really is not the case and our estimates are really of the average value of M. Thus the size of some innovators may fall below them. Note too that a variant of the Tobin-Rosett technique for handling limited dependent variables might have been used to estimate M.

[23] For example, see Hamberg, *op. cit.*, for some discussion on this.

[24] These results are very rough. For one thing, they assume that the 1919–38 relationship between n_j and S_j can be extrapolated somewhat, since the largest firms in 1939–58 were larger than those in 1919–38.

timates of M and I are not available for the bituminous coal industry.

Finally, one additional point should be noted. Whereas the ratio of the average value of n_j during 1939–58 to its average value in 1919–38 rises monotonically with S_j in the petroleum and coal industries, it rises and then falls in steel. Thus, relative to a very large firm, a medium-sized steel firm introduced, on the average, a larger number of innovations during 1939–58 than during 1919–38.[25] The reasons for this are by no means clear, but it may have been that the medium-sized firms increased their research and development activities by a greater proportion than did the large firms. This would be consistent with a hypothesis recently put forth by Schmookler.[26]

VI. MARKET STRUCTURE AND THE RATE OF INTRODUCTION OF INVENTIONS

Suppose that an individual or firm invents a device that could be used profitably in a particular industry, but suppose also that the inventor is not a member of this industry and that consequently he must induce some firm in the industry to introduce it or enter the industry himself. For this type of invention, an important question is: What effect would a change in market structure have on the length of time that elapses before someone in-

[25] The range of firm sizes in Table 5 was chosen so that it just about covers the range in which the innovators lie. Thus, very small steel firms must be included (because they have done a good deal of the innovating).

[26] He asserts that "given the progressive improvement in the quality of management . . . given the growing recognition . . . of the value of research, and given the increasing supply of engineers and scientists, a rise in the relative importance of organized research and development among small and medium-sized firms is perhaps to be expected" (Schmookler, *op. cit.*, p. 631). Our results could be due in part to such a movement in the past, since it would be expected that the medium-sized firms would react before the small ones.

troduces the invention? This question has received considerable attention—both recently and in the past. On the one hand, there are some—like Bain, Brozen, Joan Robinson, and Stocking—who believe that inventions would be applied most rapidly under purely competitive conditions. They argue that if many firms exist, there is more protection against an invention's being blocked by the faulty judgment of only a few men. Moreover, they allege that the existence of many competitors will force a firm to seek out and apply new ideas, whereas a live-and-let-live policy may develop otherwise.

TABLE 5

AVERAGE NUMBER OF INNOVATIONS CARRIED OUT BY FIRMS OF GIVEN SIZE IN 1939–58 DIVIDED BY AVERAGE NUMBER CARRIED OUT BY FIRMS OF THE SAME SIZE IN 1919–38, STEEL, PETROLEUM REFINING, AND BITUMINOUS COAL INDUSTRIES

SIZE OF FIRM	RATIO OF AVERAGE No. OF INNOVATIONS IN 1939–58 TO AVERAGE No. IN 1919–38	
	Process	Product
Steel (ingot capacity, tons):		
100,000	0.22	0.00[a]
1,000,000	0.93	6.50
5,000,000	0.84	1.25
10,000,000	0.80	0.90
25,000,000	0.78	0.65
Petroleum (crude capacity, barrels):		
30,000	0.00[a]	[b]
60,000	0.00[a]	0.45
120,000	0.47	0.60
240,000	0.66	0.65
480,000	0.77	0.68
Coal (production, tons):		
600,000	0.44	....
1,200,000	0.68	....
2,400,000	1.14	....
4,800,000	1.43	....
9,600,000	1.59	....

[a] According to the regression in eq. (5), the average number of innovations in 1939–58 was negative. It seems reasonable in this context to substitute zero for such negative numbers.

[b] According to the regressions in eq. (5), both the average number of innovations in 1919–38 and that in 1939–58 were negative. Thus, the ratio would have no meaning.

Source: Table 4.

On the other hand, there are others— like Villard—who think that new ideas would be applied most rapidly if industries contained relatively few large firms. They point out that such firms are better able to finance the introduction of inventions and to take the necessary risks. In addition, they claim that large firms will have better managers who will be more inclined to innovate. Although each group has some convincing points to make, there is no evidence that one group's arguments are universally more valid than the other's, and in a particular case we are unable to tell how these factors should be quantified and weighted so that a conclusion can be reached. This section contains some exploratory attempts to devise operational techniques to handle this problem.

Suppose that an industry is composed of $n - 1$ firms. If at time t a particular invention of this sort has not yet been introduced, suppose that the probability that the ith firm will introduce it between time t and time $t + \Delta$ is $\lambda_i \Delta$. Suppose that the probability that the inventor or some other new entrant into the industry will introduce it then is $\lambda_n \Delta$. Assume too that there is no collusion among the firms to prevent the application of the technique. That is, assume that the probability that the ith firm will introduce it between time t and time $t + \Delta$ does not depend on whether some other firm decides to do so.[27]

Under these conditions, one can easily obtain expressions for L, the expected length of time that will elapse before the invention is applied, and P_j, the probability that the jth firm will be the innovator. Letting Δ become very small so that we approach a continuous measurement of time, it can easily be seen that

$$L = \lim_{\Delta \to 0} \Delta \sum_{r=1}^{\infty} r p(r),$$

where $p(r)$ is the probability that it will take r periods of length Δ before the invention is applied. Letting Θ be the probability that no existing or new firm introduces it during a period of length Δ, and $(1 - \Theta)$ be the probability that one or more existing or new firms introduces it during such a period, it follows that

$$L = \lim_{\Delta \to 0} \Delta \sum_{r=1}^{\infty} r (1 - \Theta) \Theta^{r-1},$$

$$= \lim_{\Delta \to 0} \Delta (1 - \Theta) \sum_{r=1}^{\infty} r \Theta^{r-1},$$

$$= \lim_{\Delta \to 0} \Delta (1 - \Theta) \left(\frac{d}{d\Theta} \sum_{r=0}^{\infty} \Theta^r \right)$$

$$= \lim_{\Delta \to 0} \Delta (1 - \Theta) \left(\frac{d}{d\Theta} \frac{1}{1 - \Theta} \right)$$

$$= \lim_{\Delta \to 0} \Delta / (1 - \Theta) .$$

Since

$$\Theta = \prod_{j=1}^{n} (1 - \lambda_j \Delta) ,$$

$$L = \lim_{\Delta \to 0} \frac{\Delta}{1 - \prod_{j=1}^{n} (1 - \lambda_j \Delta)} ,$$

$$= \lim_{\Delta \to 0} \frac{\Delta}{1 - 1 + \sum_{j=1}^{n} \lambda_j \Delta + o(\Delta)} ,$$

[27] All this is assumed to hold only for small Δ. In the analysis below, Δ tends to zero and terms of higher order in Δ would vanish.

We assume that the development work has already been done by the inventor or that it will take about the same length of time regardless of which firm does it. Of course, this may not be the case. Attention is focused strictly on the mean delay, but for some purposes higher moments might also be relevant.

Finally, the arguments presented at the beginning of this section are only a few of those that have been used.

where $o(\Delta)$ stands for terms which tend to zero when, after dividing by Δ, we let Δ tend to zero. Consequently,

$$L = \lim_{\Delta \to 0} \frac{1}{\sum_{j=1}^{n} \lambda_j + o(\Delta)/\Delta}$$

$$= \left(\sum_{j=1}^{n} \lambda_j \right)^{-1}. \qquad (6)$$

Similarly, it is apparent that

$$P_i = \lim_{\Delta \to 0} \sum_{r=1}^{\infty} G_i(r),$$

where $G_i(r)$ is the probability that the ith firm will introduce the invention in the rth period and that it will be the first firm to do so. Letting ρ_i be the probability that only the ith firm will introduce it during the rth period,

$$P_i = \lim_{\Delta \to 0} \sum_{r=1}^{\infty} \rho_i \theta^{r-1}$$

$$= \lim_{\Delta \to 0} \rho_i \sum_{r=1}^{\infty} \theta^{r-1}$$

$$= \lim_{\Delta \to 0} \rho_i / (1 - \theta).$$

Since

$$\rho_i = \lambda_i \Delta \prod_{\substack{j=1 \\ \neq i}}^{n} (1 - \lambda_j \Delta),$$

$$P_i = \lim_{\Delta \to 0} \left[\frac{\lambda_i \Delta \prod_{\substack{j=1 \\ \neq i}}^{n} (1 - \lambda_j \Delta)}{1 - \prod_{j=1}^{n} (1 - \lambda_j \Delta)} \right]$$

$$= \lim_{\Delta \to 0} \frac{\lambda_i \Delta [1 + u(\Delta)]}{1 - 1 + \sum_{j=1}^{n} \lambda_j \Delta + o(\Delta)}$$

$$= \lim_{\Delta \to 0} \frac{\lambda_i [1 + u(\Delta)]}{\sum_{j=1}^{n} \lambda_j + \dfrac{o(\Delta)}{\Delta}},$$

where $u(\Delta)$ stands for terms that vanish as Δ tends to zero. Thus,

$$P_i = \frac{\lambda_i}{\sum_{j=1}^{n} \lambda_j} = \lambda_i L. \qquad (7)$$

Suppose that a change is being contemplated in the size distribution of firms in a given industry. Assume that each firm's size and its value of λ have been relatively constant in the recent past, and that, once this reorganization is either carried out or dropped, each firm's size and its value of λ will again remain relatively constant for some time.[28] Suppose that, if the proposed reorganization occurs, the frequency distribution of firms by size will be $n(S)$; if it does not occur, it will be $m(S)$. Ignore differences among inventions in a firm's value of λ and the possibility that the inventor will enter the industry. Although they complicate things, these matters can be introduced without altering the essentials of the argument.[29]

[28] This simplification can be relaxed. All that we need to assume is that the future can be divided into epochs within which each firm's size and value of λ is relatively constant, that these epochs are very long relative to L, and that forecasts are available of the size distribution of firms (given that the reorganization does or does not occur) in each epoch. Then one can estimate the effects in each epoch.

[29] These factors can be introduced in the following way. The relationship between a firm's size and its value of λ is likely to differ, depending on the characteristics of the innovation. Thus, one should classify innovations by their capital requirement and other characteristics causing differences in the shape of this relationship. Factors (like the over-all profitability of the invention) that cause all the λ's to increase or decrease in proportion may be ignored. (If all λ_i's vary in proportion, the P_i will remain constant, and $f(S)$ and the result in eq. [9] will be unaffected. Inventions with proportional λ_i can be lumped into one class so long as the composition of the class with regard to profitability, etc., is unlikely to change much over time.) Classes should be established so as to maximize differences—ignoring proportional variations in all λ_i—in the shape of the relationships. Then $f(S)$ can be estimated in each

What effect will the proposed reorganization have on *L?* It seems reasonable to believe that a firm's value of λ is a function of its size. Suppose that, whether or not the proposed change in market structure occurs, the average value of λ for firms of given size will be proportional to the average value in the recent past (the coefficient of proportionality being Φ). Of course, whether or not this is true depends on the particular change in market structure and on the characteristics of the industry.[30]

If this assumption holds and if λ *(S)* is the average value of λ for firms of

size *S* in the recent past, the expected delay, given that the reorganization occurs, is

$$L_0 = \left[\Phi \sum_s \lambda(S) n(S) \right]^{-1}, \quad (8)$$

and if f(S) is the regression in the recent past of the proportion of the innovations of this type that a firm carried out on its size, an estimate of the percentage change in average delay resulting from the proposed change in the size distribution of firms is

$$C = 100 \left[\frac{\sum_s m(S) f(S)}{\sum_s n(S) f(S)} - 1 \right]. \quad (9)$$

Since *n(S)* and *m(S)* are given and f(S) can be estimated from past data, the expression in equation (9) can be evaluated.[31]

As an illustration, consider process innovations in steel. In 1926 suppose that we wanted to estimate the effect of splitting U.S. Steel into four smaller firms of equal size and keeping the rest of the steel producers at their 1926 size, the alternative being that all firms (including U.S. Steel) would maintain their 1926 size. Assuming that λ_i did not vary much from invention to invention and that the relation between the proportion of the innovations of the relevant kind that a firm carried out in the period immediately before 1926 and its 1926 size was like that between the proportion of all process innovations it carried out during 1919–38 and its 1926 size,

$$f(S) = -.09 + .075 \ln S - .018 (\ln S)^2 \\ + .001 (\ln S)^3 \quad (10)$$

To derive equation (10), merely divide equation (5)—after inserting the esti-

class, the goodness of fit being some indication of how homogeneous the class is. In each class, eq. (9) can be used to estimate the percentage reduction in delay. To obtain an over-all estimate of the effect on all innovations, one must forecast the proportion of the innovations in the period ahead that will be in each class and estimate the average delay in each class in the previous period. These data—and the classes—must often be rough, but it is difficult to see how any technique could be devised that would not require them.

If λ_n in the period ahead remains in the same proportion to the average value of λ in each size class (whether or not the reorganization occurs) one can easily handle the possibility of new entrants being the innovators. The proportion of the innovations carried out by new entrants is an estimate of P_n in the past—which equals $\Phi\lambda_M'$, where λ_M' is the value of λ_n in the future. Hence, this proportion can merely be added to both the numerator and denominator of the first term in parentheses on the right-hand side of eq. (9). Essentially, this assumes that the reorganization will not seriously impede or promote entry into the industry. Whether or not this is true depends on the particular reorganization.

[30] Can the facts in Sec. IV be brought to bear on this assumption? Suppose that all the innovations included there were of the type considered here and that λ_i did not vary much from invention to invention. According to eq. (7), λ_i is proportional to P_i, and the proportion of innovations carried out by the *i*th firm is an estimate of P_i. Take firms that resulted from important mergers in 1925–38 and compare their proportion of the innovations in 1939–58 with those of other firms of their (new) size. If a firm's value of λ_i adjusts relatively quickly to a change in its size, as we assume, their proportion should not differ significantly from the others. In fact, this turns out to be the case. This is an interesting, but crude, test of this assumption.

[31] Note that this regression should only include data for innovations invented outside the industry.

mates of the a's in Table 4 into it—by the number of process innovations during 1919–38, 12.

Since $S = 22,628$ for U.S. Steel, it follows from equations (9) and (10) that the average delay, according to these crude estimates, would have been reduced by about 15 per cent if U.S. Steel had been broken up in this way. To derive this figure, note that

$$\sum_i m(S)\mathfrak{f}(S)$$

is necessarily one because the residuals from a least-squares regression sum to zero. Moreover,

$$\sum_i n(S)\mathfrak{f}(S) = 1 - \mathfrak{f}(22,628) + 4\mathfrak{f}(5,657),$$

since all firms other than U.S. Steel will maintain their size, even if the reorganization occurs. Since equation (10) shows that $\mathfrak{f}(22,628) = 0.26$ and $\mathfrak{f}(5,657) = 0.11$, it follows that $C = -15$. In absolute terms, a 15 per cent reduction in delay is likely to be a reduction of at least one year.

Needless to say, these results can only be suggestive, since a change of this magnitude in an industry's structure might alter the relationship between the average value of λ and firm size.[32] This technique is likely to be more useful when the changes in market structure are less drastic.

VII. SUMMARY AND CONCLUSION

This paper studies the effects of an industry's market structure on its rate

[32] In addition, the assumptions underlying eq. (10) are obviously very rough. For example, a firm's growth rate and other characteristics may affect its value of λ. We assume that these effects can be represented by the usual sort of random error term. Although this may not be too bad an approximation, attempts should be made in future research to include additional independent variables in eqs. (10) and (5).

of technical progress. Its principal findings are as follows: First, although it is often alleged that the largest firms introduce a disproportionately large share of the innovations, this is not always the case. In petroleum refining and bituminous coal, the largest four firms accounted for a larger share of the innovations than they did of the market. But in steel they accounted for less.

Second, the largest four firms seemed to account for a relatively large share of the innovating in cases where (1) the investment required to innovate was large relative to the size of the potential users, (2) the minimum size of firm required to use the innovations profitably was relatively large, and (3) the average size of the largest four firms was much greater than the average size of all potential users of the innovations. A simple model that focused particular attention on these factors could explain most of the observed interindustry and temporal differences.

Third, some very rough estimates suggest that, during 1919–58, the sixth largest firms in the petroleum and coal industries were of about optimal size from the point of view of maximizing the rate of innovation. In the steel industry much smaller firms seem to have been optimal in this respect. These estimates are crude and should be treated with considerable caution.

Fourth, there is evidence that the smallest steel, oil, and coal firms did less innovating—relative to large and medium-sized firms—in recent years than in the period before World War II. In steel, this may have been due to an increase in the average investment required to innovate; in petroleum, it may have been due to an increase in the minimum size of firm that could use the innovations profitably.

Fifth, under certain circumstances, one can estimate the effect of a proposed change in market structure on the average time interval that elapses before an invention made outside the industry is applied. If a simple model of the innovation process holds, historical data identifying the innovators can be used to estimate these effects. This technique can be used only under certain circumstances, but it should be a useful step toward the general solution of this problem.

These findings should be of interest to economists interested in industrial organization and the micro-economic aspects of technical change. For the first time, data of more than a fragmentary nature have been collected regarding the identity and characteristics of the innovators in several important industries, and models have been devised to help relate these empirical findings to questions bearing on public policy.

Further efforts should be made to obtain the theoretical and empirical results so badly needed in the area. Although an industry's market structure is but one of many factors influencing the rate of technical progress, it is important in formulating public policy that we learn more about the direction and magnitude of its effects.

APPENDIX

DATA AND METHODS

Source of Table 1.—The lists of innovations were obtained from trade associations and trade journals. To make sure that the lists were reasonably complete, they were checked with members of the Carnegie Institute of Technology engineering faculty and the Bureau of Mines. A few innovations were added to the lists (or dropped) on their recommendation. I could determine the identity of the innovator in about 90 per cent of the cases in petroleum refining, 50 per cent of the cases in steel, and practically all of the cases in coal. Although the data on the identity of the innovators are generally reliable, there are a few cases in each industry where the data, based on the recollection of suppliers, etc., may possibly be wrong. Various trade journals and members of the Carnegie Institute of Technology engineering faculty were asked whether, in their judgment, the results seemed to be biased in favor of large or small firms. For example, if the lesser innovations omitted from Tables 1A–1C were introduced primarily by small firms, the results would obviously be biased in favor of the large ones. No such bias could be detected, but this test is obviously rough.

In the case of petroleum refining, the product innovations are petrochemicals. We used a classification of important petrochemicals developed by a major oil company for its internal use, and sales in 1958 (from the Tariff Commission) were used to rank them by importance. Some of the classes are very broad. The innovator is defined to be the first petroleum company that produced the product commercially from a petroleum base. In a considerable number of these cases the product had been previously produced by chemical companies, but the petroleum company generally used a different process. Of course, the innovations might have been considered as process innovations, but this would have made little difference to the final results.

In steel, innovations in iron ore preparation, handling, etc., are excluded. In the coal industry, the innovations are all new techniques for the preparation of coal. This was the only type of innovation for which data could be obtained at all readily, and it may not be representative of all process innovations in bituminous coal. Most of the results in Table 1C were computed from data and information appearing in *Coal Age*, a McGraw-Hill publication.

With regard to the rankings by importance, no sales data could be obtained to rank the product innovations in steel. In the other cases (besides product innovations in petroleum), ranks were obtained both from respondents and Carnegie (or Bureau of Mines) personnel; and the average of these ranks was used. These data are obviously very rough, but it is noteworthy that in each case the independent rankings were very highly correlated, indicating a considerable amount of agreement.

Source of Table 2.—The daily crude capacity of each petroleum refiner (other than the top twenty companies) in 1927 was obtained from the *Petroleum Register.* For 1947 it was obtained from Bureau of Mines, *Petroleum Refineries, including Cracking Plants in the United States.* The daily crude capacity (domestic and overseas) of the top twenty companies was obtained directly from the firms. The ingot capacity of each firm in 1926 and in 1945 was obtained from the *Directory of the American Iron and Steel Institute.*

For the coal industry, size distributions of firms in the "base states" are provided by H. Risser (*The Economics of the Coal Industry* [Lawrence: University of Kansas, 1958]), for 1933 and 1953. We multiplied the number in each size class (under one million tons of production annually) by the ratio of the total production in the country to that in the "base states." A complete count of firms with over one million tons produced in 1933 and 1953 was obtained from the *Keystone Coal Buyer's Guide.* The production of the innovators was also obtained from this source. Risser's data exclude firms producing less than one thousand tons annually.

In the steel industry, innovations introduced by firms without any ingot capacity or by firms engaged primarily in some other business had to be omitted. To include them on the basis of their ingot capacity would have been to misstate their true size, and no measure of size other than ingot capacity (or pig iron capacity) is readily available for most of the firms in the steel industry. Such innovations are marked with an asterisk in Table 1A. In the petroleum industry, a few innovations had to be omitted for much the same sort of reason. In the coal industry, innovations introduced by firms engaged

primarily in some other business were not omitted. Such firms account for a large proportion of the industry's output, and the results would not have been altered much in any event if they had been omitted.

We follow the convention (adopted in most studies of industrial concentration) of using the largest four firms as a basis for concentration measures. In steel, the largest firms' share of the market is their share of the industry's ingot capacity; in petroleum, it is their share of the industry's daily crude capacity; in bituminous coal, it is their share of the industry's (tonnage) production. Other measures—for example, per cent of value added or per cent of employment—might have been used instead. But Census data for petroleum in 1935 and 1947 and for steel in 1947 indicate that the results would change only slightly. For 1919–38, the largest petroleum firms' share of the innovations would have exceeded their share of value added or employment, but the difference would have been somewhat smaller than in Table 2. For 1939–58, the results in petroleum would have been about the same as in Table 2. For 1939–58, the largest steel firms' share of the innovations would have been less than their share of the assets or employment, but larger than their share of value added.

In 1919–38 the difference between the largest firms' share of the innovations and their share of the market was almost always statistically significant in steel and petroleum. In 1939–58, the share of the innovations introduced by the largest firms was closer to their share of the market than in 1919–38, and often the differences may not have been statistically significant in steel and petroleum. In bituminous coal, there was a relatively small probability that the differences in Table 2 were due to chance in either period.

Source of Table 3.—The data regarding M and I were obtained primarily from interviews with officials of engineering associations and firms, although some came from published sources. Estimates of M and i were obtained for as many of the innovations in Tables 1A and 1B as possible and the average values of M and i were used in Table 3. To some extent, the estimate of i for each innovation was also an average, since i would vary depending on a firm's existing plant. Of course, there was some variation among innovations in the value of M, the assumption in the text being only a convenient simplification.

Using the data described above, we determined $N(M)$. Since M was quoted in ingot capacity or crude capacity, we used the ratio of the largest firm's assets to its capacity in the mid-fifties to estimate M, S_M, and S_4 in terms of dollars (rather than capacity). This obviously is a very rough procedure. (For one thing, the capacities and assets sometimes pertained to somewhat different points in time. But if this is corrected, the results turn out to be almost exactly the same as those in equation [4].) The estimates of I are in (approximately) 1950 dollars. The weighted data regarding π are used.

Estimates of the optimal size of firm.— There are several obvious difficulties in the sort of analysis carried out in Section IV.

1. Although a firm's size influences the number of innovations it carries out, this is not the only factor. The preferences of its management with respect to risk, its profitability and rate of growth, and the size of its competitors may also be important. Thus, if the largest firms had been broken up, the behavior of their smaller successors might not have been like that of other smaller firms.

2. If the largest firms had been broken up, the innovations that were introduced might have been of a different type. Only the largest firms may have been able to carry out some kinds of innovations. We assume that such innovations were no more important than those that their smaller successors would have introduced. There is no evidence in these industries that an innovation introduced by a larger firm tended to be any more—or less—important than one introduced by a smaller firm, but the data are very rough.

3. If the largest firms had been broken up, changes might have occurred outside the industry. For example, if the largest firms had carried out a relatively large amount of research, there might have been some transfer of research activities to independent laboratories. The amount of inventive activity might not have been greatly affected, but the reorganization of the industry might have affected how many of the research results were applied—and how quickly.

4. As the literature on cost and production functions clearly shows, there are many difficulties in interpreting least-squares relationships between a firm's size and other variables. Some of these difficulties are present here; for example, there is an identification problem. For some reason, certain firms may be innovators, and as a consequence they may grow more rapidly than others. If so, they may eventually become relatively large and the largest may account for a disproportionately large share of the innovations—even though size per se brings no particular advantages. The problem may not be too important, but this is difficult to check.

The following points should be noted regarding the regressions. In steel, firms with less than 5,000 tons of ingot capacity were omitted in 1919–38, firms with less than 10,000 tons were omitted in 1939–58, and S_j was measured in units of 1,000 tons. In petroleum, firms with less than 500 barrels of capacity were omitted, and S_j was measured in units of 1,000 barrels. In coal, firms producing less than 100,000 tons annually were omitted, approximate size data were used for the 100,000–1,000,000 ton ranges, and S_j was measured in units of 1,000,000 tons.

Finally, note three other points. First, all of this pertains only to the existing ranges of firm size. There is no way to tell how firms bigger than the largest existing firm would have behaved. Second, since the size data are only approximate for coal firms producing less than 1,000,000 tons, we confined ourselves to the range above 1,000,000 tons when we looked for the maximum value of $N(S_j)/S_j$. Third, there are substantial sampling errors in the estimates of the a's and consequently in the estimates of the values of S_j where $N(S_j)/S_j$ is a maximum.

22

Reprinted from
THE REVIEW OF ECONOMICS AND STATISTICS
Published for Harvard University
by the North-Holland Publishing Company
Copyright, 1981, by the President and Fellows of Harvard College
Vol. LXIII, No. 4, November, 1981

COMPOSITION OF R AND D EXPENDITURES: RELATIONSHIP TO SIZE OF FIRM, CONCENTRATION, AND INNOVATIVE OUTPUT

Edwin Mansfield*

I. Introduction

One of the most obvious and important characteristics of an industry's or firm's R and D expenditures is their heterogeneity. Yet practically all economic studies of the relationship between size of firm and industrial concentration, on the one hand, and research and development, on the other, have focused exclusively on the total amount spent on R and D. No attempt has been made to determine the relationship between these variables and the composition of R and D expenditures. Nor has an attempt been made to study the effects of the composition (as well as size) of a firm's R and D expenditures on its innovative output.[1] The purpose of this paper is to help fill these important gaps.

II. Size of Firm and the Composition of R and D Expenditures

No data are published regarding the composition of the R and D expenditures of individual firms. With the exception of the National Science Foundation's data concerning the percentage of various industries' R and D expenditures going for basic research, applied research and development, little or no data of this kind are published for entire industries.[2] To help fill this void, we obtained information from 108 firms concerning the composition of their company-financed R and D expenditures in 1977. The firms included in our sample, all of which spent over $10 million on R and D in 1976, accounted for about one-half of all industrial R and D expenditures in the United States in 1976. Although this sample has its shortcomings, it is by far the

most comprehensive currently available. (See Mansfield (1980).)

As would be expected, there are very substantial interindustry differences in the composition of R and D expenditures (table 1). Also, there is an impressive amount of variation in this regard among firms in the same industry. (The coefficients of variation in table 1 average about 1.) To what extent are these intraindustry differences associated with differences in size of firm? Previous studies have indicated that, in most industries, increases in size of firm are not associated (at the upper end of the size range) with more than proportional increases in total R and D expenditures.[3] However, these findings ignore the possibility that the largest firms may be doing a somewhat different kind of R and D than their smaller competitors. This section provides the first reasonably comprehensive investigation of this topic.

Among the firms in our sample, to what extent are increases in size of firm associated with more than proportional increases in expenditures on basic research and on relatively long-term, ambitious, and risky R and D projects? To find out, we assume in each industry that

$$\ln b_i = \phi_1 + \nu_1 \ln S_i + z_{1i}$$

$$\ln l_i = \phi_2 + \nu_2 \ln S_i + z_{2i}$$

$$\ln n_i = \phi_3 + \nu_3 \ln S_i + z_{3i}$$

$$\ln p_i = \phi_4 + \nu_4 \ln S_i + z_{4i}$$

where b_i is the amount spent on basic research[4] by the

Received for publication November 17, 1980. Revision accepted for publication March 3, 1981.

* University of Pennsylvania.

The research on which this paper is based was supported by the National Science Foundation which, of course, is not responsible for the views expressed here. I am grateful to the Foundation, as well as to the 108 firms that provided data, for making this work possible. Some of the material presented here was included in the Andersen Lectures I gave at the University of Brussels in 1981 and in a lecture at Middlebury College.

[1] Surveys of this literature are found in Scherer (1980) and Kamien and Schwartz (1975). For a study of the relationship between the size of a firm's R and D expenditures and its innovative output, see Mansfield (1968).

[2] See note 5.

[3] See note 1.

[4] These data are based on the National Science Foundation (1959) definition of basic research, which is "original investigation for the advancement of scientific knowledge . . . which do[es] not have immediate commercial objectives." For four industries, we can compare our percentage of R and D expenditure going for basic research with the National Science Foundation (1976) percentage for 1974. Our percentages are positively correlated with NSF's, but they do not always agree. This is not surprising, since our definition of each of these industries differs from NSF's, NSF's coverage is different from ours, and our figures pertain to 1977, not 1974.

Some firms estimated that 0% of their R and D expenditures went for basic research in 1977. Inquiries indicated that this was a rounded figure and that about $10,000 had been spent on it. Thus, we used $10,000 in our calculations. In a few cases, the same sort of procedure was used for the other characteristics. Our results would not have been altered in

NOTES

TABLE 1.—PERCENTAGE OF COMPANY-FINANCED R AND D EXPENDITURE GOING FOR BASIC, LONG-TERM, AMBITIOUS, AND RISKY R AND D, 108 FIRMS, 1977

Industry	Basic Research		Projects Lasting Five or more Years		Projects Aimed at Entirely New Products and Processes		Projects with Less than a 50–50 Estimated Chance of Success	
	Percentage	Coefficient of Variation	Percentage	Coefficient of Variation	Percentage	Coefficient of Variation	Percentage	Coefficient of Variation
Metals	2.4	1.00	22	0.57	18	0.57	11	0.63
Chemicals	5.9	1.30	39	0.77	33	0.62	30	0.96
Aerospace	1.7	1.58	24	1.00	26	0.76	27	1.03
Automobiles	0.2	1.75	20	1.18	16	1.13	45	1.83
Petroleum	8.1	0.87	27	0.74	25	0.44	23	0.67
Drugs	16.4	1.16	66	0.45	68	0.37	40	0.73
Food	4.1	0.79	16	1.00	22	0.60	18	0.72
Instruments	3.3	1.50	40	1.23	22	0.96	9	1.07
Soap and cosmetics	3.9	1.14	30	1.00	48	0.45	55	1.18
Machinery	3.6	1.58	31	0.97	18	0.89	5	0.89
Electronics and electrical equipment	4.6	1.07	14	0.86	45	0.46	5	0.91
Office equipment and computers	1.8	1.67	55	1.33	60	1.04	9	0.96
Mean	4.7	1.28	32	0.92	33	0.69	23	0.97

Source: See section II.

i^{th} firm in the industry, S_i is its 1976 sales, l_i is the amount it spent on R and D projects lasting 5 or more years, n_i is the amount it spent on R and D projects aimed at entirely new products and processes,[5] and p_i is the amount it spent on R and D projects with less than a 50-50 estimated chance of success.[6] (All are

---

any important way if a somewhat different procedure had been used.

[5] The distinction between an entirely new product or process and an improved or modified product or process is often arbitrary (although it frequently is used). Thus, comparisons in this regard of one industry with another should be treated with caution since the definitions used in one industry may be quite different from those used in another industry. However, since the definitions used by various firms in the same industry are likely to be similar, there should be much less difficulty with comparisons of this sort among firms in the same industry. Fortunately, the comparisons made here are of the latter kind. (Note that model changes in the auto industry are not regarded as entirely new products.)

In its annual *Business Plans for Research and Development Expenditures,* McGraw Hill presents data by industry concerning the percentage of R and D aimed at new products, improving existing products, and new processes. Their data are not comparable with ours because they include government-financed R and D, their "new processes" include process improvements whereas we distinguish between them, the industry definitions and the definition of a new product are different, and the sample of firms is different.

[6] Success was defined to include both technical and commercial success, since both are relevant. For earlier results concerning such probabilities (and other measures used here), see Mansfield et al. (1971, 1977, forthcoming) and Mansfield (1981).

---

expressed in millions of dollars.) The ϕ's and ν's are parameters that vary from industry to industry and the z's are random error terms. Least-squares estimates were made of these parameters.

In most industries, increases in size of firm are associated with more than proportional increases in the amount spent on basic research (table 2). On the average, a 1% increase in a firm's sales is associated with about a 1.65% increase in basic research expenditure. (The estimate of 1.65 differs significantly from 1.)[7] In most industries, increases in size of firm are associated with more than proportional increases in the amount spent on R and D projects lasting 5 or more years, but this tendency is not statistically significant. In most industries, increases in size of firm are associated with less than proportional increases in the amount spent on R and D projects aimed at entirely new products and processes. On the average, a 1% increase in a firm's sales seems to be associated with about a 0.78% increase in the amount spent on such projects. (The estimate of 0.78 differs significantly from 1.)[8] Based on

---

[7] Since this sample of industries includes a large proportion of all manufacturing industries, the finite population correction factor must be applied in estimating the standard error of the mean value of $\hat{\nu}_1$. Since the observed mean value of $\hat{\nu}_1$ differs from 1 by more than 2 of its standard errors, the difference seems significant at the 0.05 level if a one-tailed test is used.

[8] For the reason given in note 7, the finite population correction factor must be applied. Since the observed mean value of $\hat{\nu}_3$ differs from 1 by more than 2.6 of its standard

table 2, there is little consistent tendency for increases in size of firm to be associated with more or less than proportional increases in the amount spent on R and D projects with less than a 50-50 estimated chance of success.

Thus, whereas the largest firms seem to carry out a disproportionately large share of the basic research (and perhaps the long-term R and D) in most industries, there is no consistent tendency for them to carry out a disproportionately large share of the relatively risky R and D or of the R and D aimed at entirely new products and processes. On the contrary, they generally seem to carry out a disproportionately small share of the R and D aimed at entirely new products and processes. These results are not contradictory. Basic research is by no means the same thing as R and D aimed at entirely new products and processes. Also, since both basic research and applied R and D can be relatively risky, the riskiness of a firm's R and D need not be closely correlated with the percentage of its R and D devoted to basic research.[9]

III.   Industrial Concentration and the Composition of R and D Expenditures

Some economists, like John Kenneth Galbraith (1952, p. 91) believe that an "industry of a few large

---

errors, the difference seems significant at the 0.05 level if a two-tailed test is used.

[9] Holding their 1976 sales and industry constant, firms that devoted a relatively large percentage of sales to R and D appeared to devote a relatively large share of their R and D to entirely new products and processes, and a relatively small share to basic research in 1977. Holding these factors constant, there appears to be no relationship between a firm's 1976 profit (as a percentage of stockholder equity) and the characteristics of its R and D portfolio considered here.

firms [is] an almost perfect instrument for inducing technical change." One reason why a relatively high level of industrial concentration might promote technological change is that it might lead to relatively large amounts of R and D spending. In fact, however, the relationship between an industry's concentration level and its R and D spending is rather weak. Another reason why a relatively high level of industrial concentration might promote technological change is that it might lead to a larger share of R and D spending going for relatively basic, long-term, ambitious, and risky projects. At present, nothing is known about whether or not this is true.

To help fill this important gap, we correlated an industry's four-firm concentration level with four characteristics of its R and D portfolio: (1) the percentage of its R and D expenditures going for basic research, (2) the percentage of its R and D projects lasting 5 or more years, (3) the percentage of its R and D expenditures aimed at entirely new products and processes, and (4) the percentage of its R and D expenditures going for projects with less than a 50-50 estimated chance of success. The results provide little or no indication that very concentrated industries tend to devote a relatively large percentage of R and D to basic research and to long-term, ambitious, and risky projects.

On the contrary, more concentrated industries devote a smaller, not larger, percentage of R and D expenditures to basic research. For example, whereas industries with a 75% concentration ratio devote about 0.5%, on the average, of their R and D expenditures to basic research, industries with a 40% concentration ratio devote about 6%, on the average, to basic research.[10] This relationship is statistically significant,

[10] The data concerning the concentration level in each in-

TABLE 2.—ESTIMATED PARAMETERS OF RELATIONSHIP BETWEEN SIZE OF FIRM AND EXPENDITURES ON BASIC, LONG-TERM, AMBITIOUS, AND RISKY R AND D, 108 FIRMS, 1977

Industry	Basic Research			Projects Lasting 5 or more Years			Projects Aimed at Entirely new Products and Processes			Projects with Less than 50–50 Estimated Chance of Success		
	$\hat{\phi}_1$	$\hat{v}_1$	r^2	$\hat{\phi}_2$	$\hat{v}_2$	r^2	$\hat{\phi}_3$	$\hat{v}_3$	r^2	$\hat{\phi}_4$	$\hat{v}_4$	r^2
Metals	−22.01	2.60	0.85	−3.41	0.66	0.41	−0.61	0.28	0.13	−2.34	0.34	0.01
Chemicals	−13.05	1.69	0.34	−8.66	1.44	0.55	−5.91	1.11	0.54	−9.41	1.51	0.49
Aerospace	−16.82	1.97	0.34	−3.73	0.78	0.27	−0.21	0.37	0.13	−21.71	3.04	0.75
Automobile	3.85	−0.86	0.29	−9.10	1.35	0.41	−10.12	1.42	0.41	−10.58	1.22	0.20
Petroleum	−16.52	1.87	0.77	−8.52	1.17	0.48	−7.70	1.08	0.62	−9.40	1.26	0.41
Drugs	−8.79	1.54	0.66	−4.76	1.18	0.49	−2.62	0.89	0.45	−3.62	0.93	0.30
Food	−32.49	3.84	0.34	7.08	−0.76	0.04	−4.16	0.68	0.11	17.41	−2.00	0.41
Instruments	−24.99	3.65	0.53	−20.17	3.18	0.21	−1.69	0.60	0.34	−9.34	1.41	0.07
Soap and cosmetics	4.64	−0.85	0.12	−6.21	1.02	0.56	−0.79	0.47	0.34	−4.32	0.81	0.29
Machinery	−4.87	0.43	0.01	−7.31	1.22	0.18	−1.16	0.34	0.02	−1.03	0.07	0.00
Electronics and electrical equipment	−14.49	1.79	0.61	−8.84	1.29	0.46	−2.50	0.71	0.63	7.30	−0.95	0.34
Office equipment and computers	−18.06	2.09	0.42	−21.39	2.98	0.75	−6.90	1.37	0.94	−18.18	2.43	0.69
Mean	−13.63	1.65	0.44	−7.92	1.29	0.40	−3.70	0.78	0.39	−6.21	1.17	0.33

Source: See section II.

but not very strong ($r^2 = 0.46$). Relatively concentrated industries also tend to devote a relatively small, not large, proportion of their R and D expenditures to long-term projects and to projects aimed at entirely new products and processes, but the correlation (in each case, r^2 is about 0.09) is far from statistically significant. While there is a positive correlation ($r^2 = 0.15$) between an industry's concentration level and the proportion of its R and D expenditures going for relatively risky projects, this correlation too is far from significant.

With regard to each of these four characteristics of the R and D portfolio, more concentrated industries tend to have more interfirm variation than less concentrated industries. The coefficient of variation (among firms) of each of these characteristics is positively (and significantly) correlated with an industry's concentration level.[11] This is interesting because it suggests that, when there is competition among the very few, they tend to adopt quite different policies concerning the composition of their R and D portfolio. Apparently, they do not converge on the same sort of R and D strategy; instead, they tend to vary more in this regard than firms in less concentrated industries.

IV. The Composition of R and D Expenditures and Innovative Output

Very little is known about the effect of the composition of an industry's or a firm's R and D expenditures on its innovative output. The only published evidence indicates that, holding constant the amount that an industry spent on both basic research and applied R and D, its rate of increase of total factor productivity during 1948–66 was directly and significantly related to the extent to which its R and D was long term

---

dustry pertain to 1972, and come from the 1979 *Statistical Abstract* and from Shepherd (1979). Where an industry contains more than a single four-digit SIC code, a weighted average of the four-firm concentration ratios of the four-digit industries is used. See Shepherd (1979). If one uses the NSF data described in note 4, rather than ours, the results are quite consistent with those described in the text. For the seven industries for which NSF provides data, there is an inverse relationship between an industry's concentration level and its percentage of R and D expenditure devoted to basic research; and the relationship is quite similar to that described in the text. Of course, despite the fact that they are commonly used, concentration ratios of this sort have well-known weaknesses, which should be recognized.

[11] When an industry's coefficient of variation (among firms) of the percentage of R and D expenditure devoted to projects with less than a 50-50 estimated chance of success is correlated with the industry's concentration ratio, r^2 equals 0.83. When an industry's coefficient of variation (among firms) of the percentage devoted to basic research—or to entirely new products and processes, or to projects lasting 5 or more years—is correlated with the industry's concentration ratio, r^2 equals about 0.4.

(Mansfield, 1980). To explore this topic further, we obtained data for 23 chemical and petroleum firms concerning their total R and D expenditures and percentage of total R and D expenditures devoted to basic research in the early 1960s. Data have been published by Mansfield et al. (1977) and Teece and Armour (1977) concerning the number of major innovations carried out by each of these firms (during 1951–71 in the case of the chemical firms and during 1959–76 in the case of the petroleum firms). Using these data, we tried to determine whether, when a firm's total R and D expenditures were held constant, its innovative output seemed to be related to the percentage of its R and D expenditures devoted to basic research.[12]

In each of these industries, we assume that

$$I_i = \alpha_0 + \alpha_1 R_i + \alpha_2 B_i + u_i. \tag{1}$$

For chemical firms, I_i is the number of innovations during 1951–71 that were developed by the ith firm, R_i is the ith firm's R and D expenditures (in millions of dollars) in 1960, and B_i is the ith firm's percentage of R and D expenditures devoted to basic research in 1960.[13] For petroleum firms, I_i is the number of process and product innovations carried out by the ith firm during 1959–76, R_i is the firm's R and D expenditures (in millions of dollars) in 1965, and B_i is the ith firm's percentage of R and D expenditures devoted to basic research in 1965. For each industry, the α's are parameters, and u_i is a random error term. Since the least-squares estimates of α_1 and α_2 do not differ significantly between the two industries, we pool all of the observations, the resulting equation being

$$I_i = 1.10 + 0.091\,R_i + 0.312B_i - 3.75D_i,$$
$$(2.76)\quad\ (2.11)\qquad (3.39)$$

$$(\bar{R}^2 = 0.70) \tag{2}$$

where D_i is a dummy variable that equals 1 if the ith firm is a chemical firm and zero if the ith firm is a petroleum firm. (The figures in parentheses are t-ratios.)

Holding a firm's R and D expenditures constant, its innovative output seems to be directly (and significantly) related to the percentage of its R and D expenditures going for basic research. In view of the roughness of both the data and the analysis, these findings should be viewed as preliminary and tenta-

---

[12] We would like to include other variables (besides B_i) pertaining to the composition of a firm's R and D expenditures in equations (1) and (2), but the necessary data are lacking.

[13] In general, there is a high correlation between a firm's value of B_i in one year and its value in another year, and a high correlation between a firm's value of R_i in one year and its value in another year. Thus, in chemicals the 1960 values of B_i and R_i (and in petroleum the 1965 values of B_i and R_i) should be quite representative of earlier years as well.

tive.[14] Nonetheless, they constitute some of the first evidence concerning the effects of the composition of a firm's R and D expenditures on its innovative output.

V. Correlation among Characteristics of an R and D Portfolio

To what extent are various characteristics of an industry's or firm's R and D portfolio intercorrelated? For example, do firms that devote a large percentage of their R and D funds to basic research tend to devote a relatively large percentage to long-term, ambitious, and risky projects as well? At the industry level, there seems to be a significant correlation ($r^2 = 0.38$) between an industry's percentage of R and D expenditure devoted to basic research and its percentage devoted to projects lasting 5 or more years. There is also a significant correlation ($r^2 = 0.31$) between an industry's percentage devoted to basic research and its percentage devoted to projects aimed at entirely new products and processes, as well as a significant correlation ($r^2 = 0.39$) between an industry's percentage devoted to projects lasting 5 or more years and its percentage devoted to projects aimed at entirely new products and processes. But there is essentially no correlation between an industry's percentage devoted to projects with less than a 50-50 estimated chance of success and its percentage devoted to basic research, long-term projects, or ambitious projects. This may reflect the fact that many projects may be very risky without being basic, long-term, or technically ambitious because much of the risk is commercial, not technical.

When we turn from a comparison of industries to a comparison of firms within industries, the results are quite different. There is generally a very low correlation between any pair of these characteristics of a firm's R and D portfolio.[15] This finding has at least two implications. First, the percentage of R and D expenditure devoted to basic research may act (to some extent) as a surrogate for the percentage of R and D expenditure devoted to long-term and ambitious proj-

ects in interindustry analyses, such as in Mansfield (1980). But in intraindustry analyses based on data concerning individual firms, as in equation (2), the percentage devoted to basic research is not a surrogate for these other variables. Thus, while it is hard to say whether basic research is the relevant variable in equation (2) or whether it is a proxy for something else, we can be sure that it is not a proxy for the other variables included here. Second, in interpreting the National Science Foundation's data concerning basic research, it is sometimes assumed that basic research can be used as a proxy for long-term or ambitious or risky R and D. While this is true to some extent in interindustry comparisons, our results show how misleading this assumption can be in comparisons among firms in the same industry.

VI. Conclusion

Based on data for over 100 firms in a dozen industries, for the first time an investigation has been carried out of the relationship between size of firm and industrial concentration, on the one hand, and the composition of R and D expenditures, as well as the relationship between the composition of R and D expenditures and innovative output. While we believe that important new light has been thrown on these topics, it is evident that much more needs to be done. Additional data of many kinds are needed. Also, more comprehensive and detailed models should be constructed to explain the variation among firms and over time in the composition of R and D expenditures. Economists must recognize that, for many purposes, the composition of R and D expenditures may be as important as their total size.

---

[14] The limitations of the data and the analysis are obvious, and need not be belabored. For one thing, it would be desirable if the innovations could be weighted, but we lack the data to do this. (Note that, if taken at face value, equation (2) seems to suggest that appropriability problems attached to basic research in industry may not be as severe as is commonly assumed.)

[15] Of course, the value of r^2 depends on which pair of characteristics is correlated and on which industry is considered. But for each of the 6 pairs of characteristics, the mean value of r^2 in the 12 industries included here is always less than 0.19. Since there are 6 pairs of characteristics and 12 industries, there are 6×12, or 72 values of r^2. In only 7 of these 72 cases is the observed value of r^2 significantly different from zero at the 0.05 level. This, of course, is only slightly more than would be expected due to chance.

REFERENCES

Galbraith, John Kenneth, *American Capitalism* (Boston: Houghton Mifflin, 1952).

Kamien, Morton, and Nancy Schwartz, "Market Structure and Innovation: A Survey," *Journal of Economic Literature* 13 (Mar. 1975), 1–37.

Mansfield, Edwin, *Industrial Research and Technological Innovation* (New York: W. W. Norton for the Cowles Foundation for Research in Economics at Yale University, 1968).

———, "Basic Research and Productivity Increase in Manufacturing," *American Economic Review* 70 (Dec. 1980), 863–873.

———, "How Economists See R and D," *Harvard Business Review* 59 (Nov. 1981).

Mansfield, Edwin, John Rapoport, Jerome Schnee, Samuel Wagner, and Michael Hamburger, *Research and Innovation in the Modern Corporation* (New York: W. W. Norton, 1971).

Mansfield, Edwin, John Rapoport, Anthony Romeo, Edmond

Villani, Samuel Wagner, and Frank Husic, *The Production and Application of New Industrial Technology* (New York: W. W. Norton, 1977).

Mansfield, Edwin, Anthony Romeo, Mark Schwartz, David Teece, Samuel Wagner, and Peter Brach, *Technology Transfer, Productivity, and Economic Policy* (New York: W. W. Norton, forthcoming).

National Science Foundation, *Methodology of Statistics on Research and Development* (Washington, D.C.: Government Printing Office, 1959).

———, *Research and Development in Industry, 1974* (Washington, D.C.: Government Printing Office, 1976).

Scherer, F. M., *Industrial Market Structure and Economic Performance,* 2nd ed. (Chicago: Rand McNally, 1980).

Shepherd, William, *The Economics of Industrial Organization* (Englewood Cliffs: Prentice-Hall, 1979).

Teece, David, and Henry Armour, "Innovation and Divestiture in the U.S. Oil Industry," in D. Teece (ed.), *R and D in Energy* (Stanford: Stanford University, 1977).

23

R&D AND PRODUCTIVITY INCREASES

Technological Change and Market Structure:
An Empirical Study

By EDWIN MANSFIELD*

It has long been recognized that technological change is one of the major forces influencing an industry's market structure. Karl Marx stressed this fact over a century ago. Like Marx, many economists, including Arthur Burns (1936) and John Kenneth Galbraith (1967), have been convinced that technological change tends to increase plant sizes and the level of industrial concentration. Others, like John Blair (1972), have argued that, although such a trend existed in the past, it has been reversed since World War II because of a fundamental change in the nature of technological advance whereby centralizing technologies have been displaced and superceded by decentralizing technologies.

In recent years, there has been a revival of interest in the effects of technological change on market structure. Richard Nelson and Sidney Winter (1978) have formulated a computer model and Richard Levin (1980) has estimated an econometric model, both aimed at representing these effects. In general, these models seem to suggest that a relatively rapid rate of technological change in a particular industry is likely to result in a relatively high level of concentration. However, these authors are careful to point out that their results are preliminary and tentative.

*University of Pennsylvania. My research was supported by a grant from the National Science Foundation. I am grateful to the Foundation, as well as to the 34 firms that provided essential information used here. Preliminary versions of parts of this paper were presented at the Conference on *R* and *D*, Patents, and Productivity held by the National Bureau of Economic Research in 1981, and in invited lectures at the International Institute of Management in Berlin and the University of Louvain in 1982. A more complete version of this paper is available on request from the author.

Although the effects of technological change on market structure are of fundamental importance to both economic analysis and public policy, it is surprising how little systematic study has been devoted to them. We know little or nothing about the effects of the various process and product innovations that have occurred in recent years in various industries. And we have very little information concerning the relationship between the rate of technological change in a particular industry and the changes in the industry's market structure. My purpose in this paper is to try to begin filling these notable gaps.

I. Effects of Major Process Innovations on Minimum Efficient Scale of Plant

As a first step toward testing Blair's hypothesis that, since World War II, fewer innovations have tended to increase the minimum efficient scale of plant than in the past, I obtained data regarding the proportion of major process innovations in the chemical, petroleum, and steel industries that have resulted in increases in minimum efficient scale of plant. To obtain these data, a sample of innovations was drawn at random from published lists of the major new processes in each of these industries since about 1920. (See my 1968 book, my 1977 book with others, and Ralph Landau, 1980.) Nine chemical firms, 12 petroleum firms, and 4 steel firms agreed to indicate the effect of each innovation on the minimum efficient scale of plant. For 35 of the innovations, the firms (or more accurately, their highest-level engineers) were unanimous (or virtually so) in their evaluation of the direction of the innovation's effect. Also, where possible, this

TABLE 1—PERCENTAGE DISTRIBUTION OF MAJOR NEW PROCESSES BY EFFECT ON MINIMUM EFFICIENT SCALE OF PLANT,
AND OF MAJOR NEW PRODUCTS BY EFFECT ON FOUR-FIRM CONCENTRATION RATIO

Effect of Process or Product	Chemicals (1929–76)	Drugs (1947–78)	Petroleum (1919–76)	Steel (1919–60)
Percentage Distribution of Major New Processes, by Effect on Minimum Efficient Scale of Plant				
Increase	92	–[a]	75	43
No effect	8	–[a]	25	43
Decrease	0	–[a]	0	14
Total	100	–	100	100
Percentage Distribution of Major New Products, by Effect on Four-Firm Concentration Ratio				
Increase	43	17	60	43
No effect	29	8	40	57
Decrease	29	75	0	0
Total	100[b]	100	100	100

[a] Process innovations in the drug industry are excluded. The emphasis of pharamaceutical R & D is on new products, and lists of new processes in drugs have not been published.
[b] Because of rounding errors, figures do not sum to total.

evaluation was checked against published studies.

In the chemical and petroleum industries, the bulk of these process innovations resulted in increases in minimum efficient scale of plant (Table 1). In steel, only about half of these process innovations resulted in such increases, but most of the rest had little or no effect on minimum efficient scale. Thus, in all three industries, scale-increasing innovations far outnumbered scale-decreasing innovations. And if the innovations were weighted by a measure of their importance, the results would be the same. Moreover, it is very unlikely that the preponderance of scale-increasing innovations is due merely to sampling errors. Based on the usual statistical procedures, the probability is more than 0.95 that scale-increasing innovations outnumber scale-decreasing innovations by at least 3 to 1 in these industries. These results are in accord with the observed changes in minimum efficient scale of plant. There appear to have been considerable increases in minimum efficient scale of plant in all of these industries during the relevant period.

In what ways do the characteristics of the scale-increasing process innovations differ from the others? Perhaps because they may be more likely than other process innovations to entail the construction of a new plant or the major overhaul of an old plant, scale-increasing process innovations seem to require larger investments by users than other process innovations, and (partly for this reason) they seem to be more likely than other process innovations to be introduced initially by one of the industry's four largest firms. Further, they are much more likely than other innovations to be invented by the innovator, which is explained partly by the fact that their innovators are relatively likely to be among the largest firms. (For example, in the chemical industry, relatively small firms seem to be less likely than the largest firms to invent their own innovations; they rely more heavily on engineering firms and foreign sources of technology. See my 1977 study with others.) But with regard to their profitability to users and their rates of diffusion, scale-increasing process innovations do not seem to differ significantly from other process innovations.

To test Blair's hypothesis, I compared the proportion of innovations introduced after 1950 that resulted in an increase in minimum efficient scale of plant with the proportion introduced before or during 1950 that did so.

VOL. 73 NO. 2   R&D AND PRODUCTIVITY INCREASES   207

Contrary to Blair's hypothesis, the proportion was higher, not lower, in the later period. Of course, these results pertain only to three industries, and the situation may be different elsewhere. But in these industries at least, the data do not seem to support Blair's contention.

II. Effects of Major Product Innovations on the Four-Firm Concentration Ratio

The bulk of firms' research and development is directed at new products, not new processes. To learn about the effects of new products on concentration, I obtained data regarding the proportion of major product innovations in the chemical, drug, petroleum, and steel industries that have resulted in increases in the four-firm concentration ratio. To obtain these data, a sample of innovations was drawn at random from published lists of the major new products in each of these industries. (See my 1968 book, my studies with others, 1971; 1977, and David Schwartzman, 1976.)

When a major new product is introduced, it generally competes with existing products. Depending on how the relevant market is defined, the new product may increase or decrease concentration. The definition of the relevant market (and in some cases, the choice of which market is most important or typical) is a thorny task requiring an intimate and detailed knowledge of the new product's characteristics and its relationships to existing products. To carry out this task, I turned for help to the firms in each industry. Nine chemical firms, 9 drug firms, 12 petroleum firms, and 4 steel firms agreed to define the relevant market and to indicate the effect of each innovation on the four-firm concentration ratio in that market. For 31 of the innovations, the firms (or more accurately, their market research and economics staffs) were unanimous (or virtually so) in their evaluation of the direction of the innovation's effect. Also, where possible, this evaluation was checked against published studies.

In the petroleum and steel industries, the concentration-increasing product innovations greatly outnumbered the concentration-decreasing product innovations. But in the chemical industry, there were almost as many concentration-decreasing innovations as concentration-increasing innovations; and in the drug industry, the concentration-decreasing innovations outnumbered the concentration-increasing innovations. Based on the available data, there is no evidence in these industries that concentration-increasing innovations were more important, on the average, than concentration-decreasing innovations. Moreover, sampling errors are very unlikely to have been responsible for concentration-decreasing innovations being a substantial percentage of the total in the drug and chemical industries combined. If concentration-decreasing innovations were much fewer than concentration-increasing innovations in these industries combined, the probability that my results would have occurred is less than 0.04.

These results are noteworthy, given the common tendency among economists to view technological change as a concentration-increasing force. In some major industries, it appears that concentration-decreasing innovations are a very substantial proportion of the total. To see how consistent my data are with observed changes in concentration in these industries, I regressed the change in the four-firm concentration ratio in each industry in 1947–58 and 1958–67 on the percentage of the industry's product innovations (during the relevant period) that increased the four-firm concentration ratio.[1] As might be expected, they seem to be directly related (although the correlation coefficient is significant only at the 0.10 level). The correlation is only moderate ($r = .51$), but this reflects the fact that many factors other than product innovation affect concentration ratios (and that my data are crude and contain sampling errors).

To get a better idea of why the percentage of concentration-increasing product innovations in the drug industry was relatively low,

---

[1] Of course, a simple count of innovations does not give an unambiguous signal of their net effect on concentration. Even if more innovations are concentration-decreasing than concentration-increasing, the net effect of all of them may be to increase concentration, if the concentration-increasing innovations are more important in the relevant industry and time period.

I looked in some detail at the sources of the drug innovations in our sample. In over half of the cases, the innovators were established firms entering markets that were new to them. In another one-sixth of the cases, the innovator was in the relevant market, but not among the top four firms in that market. The large proportion of cases where the innovator was a new entrant to the relevant market or a relatively small seller in that market is, of course, one reason for the drug industry's relatively low proportion of product innovations that increased the four-firm concentration ratio.

III. The Rate of Technological Change, the Character of Process and Product Innovation, and Changes in Concentration

According to some economic models, concentration levels are more likely to increase in industries and time periods characterized by relatively rapid technological advance than in those characterized by relatively slow advance. If this is true, one might expect that the proportion of product innovations that are concentration-increasing (and perhaps the proportion of process innovations that are scale-increasing) would be higher in industries and time periods where technological change is rapid than in those where it is slow. To find out whether this was the case in the industries considered here, I took various periods (each about 10–15 years long) in each industry for which data are available concerning the rate of increase of total factor productivity. Then it was determined whether the rate of productivity increase in a period is related to the percent of new products that were concentration-increasing during this period. (Also, I determined whether it is related to the percent of new processes that were scale-increasing during this period.) If the rate of productivity increase is a reasonable measure of the rate of technological change in these industries, this analysis should provide some of the first direct evidence on this score. However, in view of the small number of industries included, the results should obviously be treated with the utmost caution.

It turns out that there is essentially no correlation in these industries between the rate of productivity growth, on the one hand, and the percent of product innovations that were concentration increasing (or the percent of process innovations that were scale increasing). Since the rate of productivity increase may not be a very good measure of the rate of technological change, I used the ratio of $R\&D$ expenditures to sales instead. The results are much the same. There is no significant relationship between this ratio and the percent of product innovations that are concentration increasing (or the percent of process innovations that are scale increasing). Indeed, there is a negative (but statistically nonsignificant) relationship between the ratio of $R\&D$ expenditures to sales and the percentage of product innovations that were concentration-increasing. Moreover, if the time periods used in the analysis are lengthened to about twenty years, the results are essentially the same.

Turning to all 2-digit manufacturing industries, is there in fact a close relationship between an industry's rate of technological change (as measured by its rate of productivity increase and its ratio of $R\&D$ expenditures to value-added) and the change in its average four-firm concentration ratio? To find out, I considered various periods for which data are available concerning the average annual rate of increase of total factor productivity. The coefficient of correlation between an industry's rate of increase of productivity and the change in its average four-firm concentration ratio turns out to be generally negative and never positive. If an industry's ratio of $R\&D$ expenditures to value-added is used (in place of the rate of productivity increase) as a measure of the rate of technological change, the results are the same. The coefficient of correlation between this ratio and the change in an industry's average four-firm concentration ratio is negative and far from statistically significant. Whether these results would change appreciably (and if so, how) if the effects of other variables were held constant is an open question (and an important one) that lies outside the scope of this paper.

To prevent misunderstanding, it is important to recognize that these results do not deny that an increased rate of technological change is often associated with increased concentration. Without question, such an association often exists. But whether it exists depends on the nature and sources of the new technology. Unless we know something about these and other variables, prediction of the effects of technological change on concentration is likely to be hazardous. One reason why existing models predict that innovation tends to increase concentration is that they often assume that no entry exists in the market under consideration. (Unfortunately, they assume too that no real product innovation occurs.) As Nelson and Winter point out, "things would clearly be different if entrants came in at large scale, as technological leaders, and motivated by subtle long-run strategic considerations" (p. 543). This, in fact, is what has happened frequently in the drug and chemical industries (as shown in Section II). Moreover, this sort of "innovation by invasion" occurs in many other industries too. In situations of this sort, innovation may (as we have seen) reduce existing concentration levels, not increase them. Difficult though it may be, the interesting models that have been constructed in recent years should be extended to take these important factors into account.

In conclusion, the empirical results presented in this paper should be regarded as tentative first steps; much more should be done. However, I doubt very much that future work will alter the principal point of this discussion, which is that, unless we know the nature and sources of new technology, the prediction of the effects of technological change on concentration is hazardous indeed.

REFERENCES

Blair, John, *Economic Concentration: Structure, Behavior, and Public Policy*, New York: Harcourt Brace Jovanovich, 1972.

Burns, Arthur, *The Decline of Competition*, New York: McGraw-Hill, 1936.

Galbraith, John Kenneth, *The New Industrial State*, Boston: Houghton Mifflin, 1967.

Landau, Ralph, "Chemical Industry Research and Development," in W. N. Smith and C. Larson, eds., *Innovation and U.S. Research*, Washington: American Chemical Society, 1980.

Levin, Richard, "Toward an Empirical Model of Schumpeterian Competition," Yale University, March 1980.

Mansfield, Edwin, *Industrial Research and Technological Innovation*, New York: W. W. Norton, 1968.

_____ et al., *Research and Innovation in the Modern Corporation*, New York: W. W. Norton, 1971.

_____ et al., *The Production and Application of New Industrial Technology*, New York: W. W. Norton, 1977.

_____ et al., *Technology Transfer, Productivity, and Economic Policy*, New York, W. W. Norton, 1982.

Nelson, Richard and Winter, Sidney, "Forces Generating and Limiting Concentration under Schumpeterean Competition," *Bell Journal of Economics*, Autumn 1978, 9, 524–48.

Schwartzman, David, *Innovation in the Pharmaceutical Industry*, Baltimore: Johns Hopkins, 1976.

Name index

Abegglen, J. 70
Abramowitz, M. 272
Adelman, I. 50
Adelman, M. 50
American Iron and Steel Institute 50
Anderson, T. 146, 223
Andrews, S. 70
Aoki, M. 173
Armour, H. 319
Aron, P. 80
Arrow, K. 18, 108, 272, 273
Ayres, R. 80, 95, 177

Bain, J. 50, 293, 303
Baker, N. 146, 152, 186, 240
Baranson, J. 70, 80
Bass, L. 108
Baumol, W. 251
Bean, A. 70
Beardsley, G. 22, 96, 201
Becker, H. 179
Ben David, J. 273
Bessant, J. 96
Blackman, A. 184
Blair, J. 324
Bonini, C. 51
Brach, P. 319
Brandenburg, R. 122, 146, 273
Braunstein, Y. 251
Bright, J. 177
Bronfenbrenner, J. 50
Brooks, H. 70
Brown, M. 272
Brown, W. 277
Brozen, Y. 293
Bureau of Mines 50
Burger, R. 173
Burns, A. 324
Business Higher Education Forum 80

Cain, G. 249
Capron, W. 272
Carter, A. 181
Carter, C. 96, 146, 147, 152
Caves, R. 70
Cetron, M. 177, 178, 179, 185
Churchill, B. 50
Clark, C. 147

Clark, J. 277
Clark, K. 70, 96
Clark, R. 70
Collins, N. 50
Conrad, A. 272
Cooper, A. 56
Council of Economic Advisers 272, 283
Currie, J. 6

Dalkey, N. 179
Davidson, W. 70
De Chazeau, M. 50
Dean, B. 147
Denison, E. 182, 272, 273
Denver Research Institute 273
Domar, E. 304
Dory, J. 192

Economic Commission for Europe 96
Enos, J. 147, 273, 283
Epstein, R. 50
Ewell, R. 121

Fabricant, S. 272
Feigenbaum, E. 70
Fellner, W. 272, 293
Ferber, R. 208
Ferguson, C. 50
Freeman, C. 158, 189, 272, 273, 277
Freeman, R. 147, 185, 249
Friedman, M. 283

Galbraith, J. 293, 318, 324
General Accounting Office 284, 290
Gerwin, D. 96
Gilbrat, R. 50
Glennan, T. 126, 187, 201, 208
Goldberg, L. 290
Goldhar, J. 152, 179
Gordon, T. 179
Greenwood, N. 96
Griliches, Z. 16, 108, 121, 122, 147,
    173, 182, 183, 201, 272, 273, 283,
    290
Guerard, J. 70

Hall, G. 273
Hamberg, D. 124, 147, 272, 303

Economists of the Twentieth Century

Monetarism and Macroeconomic Policy
Thomas Mayer

Studies in Fiscal Federalism
Wallace E. Oates

The World Economy in Perspective
Essays in International Trade and European Integration
Herbert Giersch

Towards a New Economics
Critical Essays on Ecology, Distribution and Other Themes
Kenneth E. Boulding

Studies in Positive and Normative Economics
Martin J. Bailey

The Collected Essays of Richard E. Quandt (2 volumes)
Richard E. Quandt

International Trade Theory and Policy
Selected Essays of W. Max Corden
W. Max Corden

Organization and Technology in Capitalist Development
William Lazonick

Studies in Human Capital
Collected Essays of Jacob Mincer, Volume 1
Jacob Mincer

Studies in Labor Supply
Collected Essays of Jacob Mincer, Volume 2
Jacob Mincer

Macroeconomics and Economic Policy
The Selected Essays of Assar Lindbeck, Volume I
Assar Lindbeck

The Welfare State
The Selected Essays of Assar Lindbeck, Volume II
Assar Lindbeck

Classical Economics, Public Expenditure and Growth
Walter Eltis

Money, Interest Rates and Inflation
Frederic S. Mishkin

The Public Choice Approach to Politics
Dennis C. Mueller

The Liberal Economic Order
Volume I   Essays on International Economics
Volume II Money, Cycles and Related Themes
Gottfried Haberler
Edited by Anthony Y.C. Koo

Economic Growth and Business Cycles
Prices and the Process of Cyclical Development
Paolo Sylos Labini

International Adjustment, Money and Trade
Theory and Measurement for Economic Policy, Volume I
Herbert G. Grubel

International Capital and Service Flows
Theory and Measurement for Economic Policy, Volume II
Herbert G. Grubel

Unintended Effects of Government Policies
Theory and Measurement for Economic Policy, Volume III
Herbert G. Grubel

The Economics of Competitive Enterprise
Selected Essays of P.W.S. Andrews
Edited by Frederic S. Lee and Peter E. Earl

The Repressed Economy
Causes, Consequences, Reform
Deepak Lal

Economic Theory and Market Socialism
Selected Essays of Oskar Lange
Edited by Tadeusz Kowalik

Trade, Development and Political Economy
Selected Essays of Ronald Findlay
Ronald Findlay

General Equilibrium Theory
The Collected Essays of Takashi Negishi, Volume I
Takashi Negishi

The History of Economics
The Collected Essays of Takashi Negishi, Volume II
Takashi Negishi

Studies in Econometric Theory
The Collected Essays of Takeshi Amemiya
Takeshi Amemiya

Exchange Rates and the Monetary System
Selected Essays of Peter B. Kenen
Peter B. Kenen

Econometric Methods and Applications (2 volumes)
G.S. Maddala

National Accounting and Economic Theory
The Collected Papers of Dan Usher, Volume I
Dan Usher

Welfare Economics and Public Finance
The Collected Papers of Dan Usher, Volume II
Dan Usher

Economic Theory and Capitalist Society
The Selected Essays of Shigeto Tsuru, Volume I
Shigeto Tsuru

Methodology, Money and the Firm
The Collected Essays of D.P. O'Brien (2 volumes)
D.P. O'Brien

Economic Theory and Financial Policy
The Selected Essays of Jacques J. Polak (2 volumes)
Jacques J. Polak

Sturdy Econometrics
Edward E. Leamer

The Emergence of Economic Ideas
Essays in the History of Economics
Nathan Rosenberg

Productivity Change, Public Goods and Transaction Costs
Essays at the Boundaries of Microeconomics
Yoram Barzel

Reflections on Economic Development
The Selected Essays of Michael P. Todaro
Michael P. Todaro

The Economic Development of Modern Japan
The Selected Essays of Shigeto Tsuru, Volume II
Shigeto Tsuru

Money, Credit and Policy
Allan H. Meltzer

Macroeconomics and Monetary Theory
The Selected Essays of Meghnad Desai, Volume I
Meghnad Desai

Poverty, Famine and Economic Development
The Selected Essays of Meghnad Desai, Volume II
Meghnad Desai

Explaining the Economic Performance of Nations
Essays in Time and Space
Angus Maddison

Economic Doctrine and Method
Selected Papers of R.W. Clower
Robert W. Clower

Economic Theory and Reality
Selected Essays on their Disparity and Reconciliation
Tibor Scitovsky

Doing Economic Research
Essays on the Applied Methodology of Economics
Thomas Mayer

Institutions and Development Strategies
The Selected Essays of Irma Adelman, Volume I
Irma Adelman

Dynamics and Income Distribution
The Selected Essays of Irma Adelman, Volume II
Irma Adelman

The Economics of Growth and Development
Selected Essays of A.P. Thirlwall
A.P. Thirlwall

Theoretical and Applied Econometrics
The Selected Papers of Phoebus J. Dhrymes
Phoebus J. Dhrymes

Innovation, Technology and the Economy
The Selected Essays of Edwin Mansfield (2 volumes)
Edwin Mansfield

Economic Theory and Policy in Context
The Selected Essays of R.D. Collison Black
R.D. Collison Black

Capitalism, Socialism and Post-Keynesianism
Selected Essays of G.C. Harcourt
G.C. Harcourt

Time Series Analysis and Macroeconometric Modelling
The Collected Papers of Kenneth F. Wallis
Kenneth F. Wallis

Foundations of Modern Econometrics
The Selected Essays of Ragnar Frisch (2 volumes)
Olav Bjerkholt

Growth, the Environment and the Distribution of Incomes
Essays by a Sceptical Optimist
Wilfred Beckerman